AF842119

~~£30~~

£85

J92129

Japanese Government Loan Issues on the London Capital Market 1870–1913

Japanese Government Loan Issues on the London Capital Market 1870-1913

Toshio Suzuki

THE ATHLONE PRESS
London and Atlantic Highlands, NJ

First published 1994 by
THE ATHLONE PRESS
1 Park Drive, London NW11 7SG
and 165 First Avenue,
Atlantic Highlands, NJ 07716

© *T Suzuki, 1994*

British Library Cataloguing in Publication Data
A catalogue record for this book is available from the British Library

ISBN 0 485 11446 1

Library of Congress Cataloging in Publication Data
Suzuki, Toshio, 1948 July 29-
Japanese government loan issues on the London Capital market, 1870–1913 / Toshio Suzuki.
p. cm.
Thesis (Ph.D.)--University of London, 1991
Includes bibliographical references and index.
ISBN 0-485-11446-1 : $90.00
1. Government securities--Japan--History. 2. Capital market--England--London--History. 3. Loans, British--Japan--History.
I. Title.
HG4715.S89 1994 94-2695
332.63'232'0952--dc20 CIP

All rights reserved. No part of this publication may be reproduced, stored in a retrieval system, or transmitted in any form or by any means, electronic, mechanical, photocopying or otherwise, without prior permission in writing from the publisher.

Typeset by
Bibloset, Chester

Printed and bound in Great Britain by
Bookcraft Ltd, Bath, England

Contents

Tables and Charts

Abbreviations

ARCHIVES

AGA	Antony Gibbs Archives (Guildhall Library)
AJAA	American Jewish Association Archives (Cincinnati, Ohio)
AMAE	Archives du Ministère des Affaires Etrangères (Paris)
AMF	Archives du Ministère des Finances (Paris)
AN	Archives Nationales (Paris)
ASABA	Anglo-South American Bank Archives (DMS Watson Library, University College)
BBA	Baring Brothers & Co. Archives
BCA	R. Benson & Co. Archives
BEA	Bank of England Archives
BJA	Bank of Japan Archives (Tokyo)
BLPESA	British Library of Political & Economic Science Archives
BTAA	Bank of Tarapacá & Argentina Archives (DMS Watson Library, University College)
BTLA	Bank of Tarapacá & London Archives (DMS Watson Library, University College)
CBA	Chartered Bank of India, Australia & China Archives
CIBA	City Bank Archives
CCBA	Capital & Counties Bank Archives
HA	C.J. Hambro & Son Archives (Guildhall Library)
HSBA	Hongkong & Shanghai Banking Corporation Archives (Hongkong)
IBPA	Imperial Bank of Persia Archives
JMFA	Japanese Ministry of Finance Archives (Tokyo)
JMFAA	Japanese Ministry of Foreign Affairs Archives (Tokyo)

JNDL	Japanese National Diet Library (Tokyo)
KA	Kleinwort & Sons Co. Archives (Guildhall Library)
LBA	Lazard Brothers Co. Archives
LBBA	London & Brazilian Bank Archives (DMS Watson Library, University College)
LJSBA	London Joint Stock Bank Archives
LCMBA	London City & Midland Bank Archives
LSEA	London Stock Exchange Archives (Guildhall Library)
LSWBA	London & South Western Bank Archives
MA	Mitsui Archives (Tokyo)
MBA	Midland Bank Archives
MGA	Morgan Grenfell & Co. Archives (to 1910 J.S. Morgan & Co. Archives) (Guildhall Library)
MTBA	Mitsui Bank Archives (Tokyo)
PAAA	Politische Archiv des Auswärtigen Amts (Bonn)
PBA	Parr's Bank Archives
PRO	Public Record Office
RAL	N.M. Rothschild & Sons Co. Archives
SA	J. Henry Schröder & Co. Archives
SOASA	School of Oriental & African Studies Archives (University of London)
UBLA	Union Bank of London Archives
ULSBA	Union of London & Smiths Bank Archives
WBA	Westminster Bank Archives

OTHERS

Add. MS	Additional Manuscripts (British Library)
C	Chancery (Public Record Office)
FO	Foreign Office (Public Record Office)
Ms.	Manuscripts (Guildhall Library)
T	Treasury (Public Record Office)

COMPANIES AND BANKS

Banque de Paris	Banque de Paris et des Pays-Bas
Banque Française	Banque Française pour le Commerce et l'Industrie
Baring Brothers	Baring Brothers & Co.
Benson	R. Benson & Co.
Brown Shipley	Brown, Shipley & Co.

Chartered Bank	Chartered Bank of India, Australia & China
Comptoir d'Escompte	Comptoir National d'Escompte
Crédit Industriel et Commercial	Société Générale de Crédit Industriel et Commercial
Erlanger	E. Erlanger & Co
Gibbs	Antony Gibbs & Sons
Glyn, Mills & Co.	Glyn Mills, Currie & Co. (from 1864)
Hambros	C.J. Hambro & Son
Hongkong Bank	Hongkong & Shanghai Banking Corporation
Huth	Frederick Huth & Co.
Industrial Bank	Industrial Bank of Japan
Kleinworts	Kleinwort, Sons & Co.
Lazard Brothers	Lazard Brothers & Co.
Oriental Bank	Oriental Bank Corporation
Panmure Gordon & Co.	Panmure Gordon, Hills & Co. (1885–1902)
Schröder	J.Henry Schröder & Co.
Standard Bank	Standard Bank of South Africa
The London Rothschilds	N.M. Rothschild & Sons
The Paris Rothschilds	M.M. de Rothschild Frères
Warburg	M.M. Warburg & Co.

BOOKS AND JOURNALS

BPP	British Parliamentary Papers
CSS	*Chūgai Shōgyō Shinpō (Domestic and Foreign Commercial News)*
DDF	*Documents diplomatiques français*
GKS	*Gaisai Kankei Shiryō (Papers related to Foreign Loans)*
GTR	*Ginkō Tsūshin Roku (Japanese Bankers' Magazine)*
IMM	*Investor's Monthly Manual*
JIB	*Journal of the Institute of Bankers*
JRSS	*Journal of the Royal Statistical Society*
MHSKT	*Meiji-ikō Honpō Shuyō Keizai Tōkei (Hundred-Year Statistics of the Japanese Economy)*
MTZ	*Meiji Taishō Zaiseishi (History of Japanese Finance in the Meiji and Taishō Eras)*
MZ	*Meiji Zaiseishi (History of Japanese Finance in the*

	Meiji Era)
MZKSS	*Meiji-zenki Zaisei Keizai Shiryō Shūsei (Collected Papers on the Financial and Economic Histories in the Early Period of the Meiji Era)*
NGHS	*Nippon Ginkō Hyakunenshi (One Hundredth Anniversary History of the Bank of Japan)*
NGB	*Nippon Gaikō Bunsho (Japanese Diplomatic Records)*
NKGGS	*Nippon Kōgyō Ginkō Gojūnenshi (Fiftieth Anniversary History of the Industrial Bank of Japan)*
SEOI	*Stock Exchange Official Intelligence*
SID	*Segai Inouekō Den (Biography of Inoue Kaoru)*
TKJ	*Takahashi Korekiyo Jiden (Autobiography of Takahashi Korekiyo)*
TKZ	*Tokyo Keizai Zasshi (Tokyo Economic Journal)*
YSGZS	*Yokohama Shōkin Ginkō Zenshi (Complete History of the Yokohama Specie Bank)*

Rates of Exchange (1913)

(£1 sterling=20 shillings=240 pence)

Nation	*Currency*	*Shillings*	*Pence*
France	franc		9½
Germany	mark		11⅘
Japan	yen	2	½
USA	dollar	4	1½
Hongkong	Hongkong dollar	4	6

Source: *SEOI*, for 1913, p 1691;
F.H.H. King, *The Hongkong Bank in the Period of Imperial China, 1864–1902*, vol 1 (Cambridge, 1987), p xxxviii.

Definition

In this book the term 'foreign' refers to countries outside the British Empire.

Preface and Acknowledgments

This book is based upon my doctoral dissertation submitted to the University of London in 1991. It describes the Japanese government's financial activities mainly in London during the years 1870 to 1913. Japan's trade surplus recently hit record levels but only a century ago Japan was suffering serious trade deficits. These deficits inevitably caused Japan to undertake heavy foreign borrowings. Indeed, during the 1910s it was a rather notorious fact throughout European financial circles that Japan, as well as Tsarist Russia, was in near crisis due to the burdens of debt service. Nevertheless, Japan eventually improved its awkward financial position on the international capital markets. Although a historian has the satisfaction of simply telling his story to readers, the history of how the Japanese government was able to raise necessary money abroad is, I believe, worthwhile when we ponder the present day debt problems of underdeveloped countries.

The topic of loans to foreign governments belonged to a neglected area of scholarship in British financial history. Because of the banking communities responsibility to safeguard their customers, banks concerned with loan issues, especially merchant banks, imposed strict limitations upon access to their confidential business records. Without consulting documents, it is almost impossible to analyse loan issues on the market. In the 1980s, however, such restriction was lifted and several commissioned histories of merchant banks strong enough to endure academic criticism were published. I had the good fortune to begin my research efforts under these more favourable circumstances and have been able to bring them to completion via the help and co-operation of various warm-hearted City people.

Above all, I would like to thank Professor T.C. Barker and Dr W.P. Kennedy, of the London School of Economics, who were so patiently willing to supervise a foreign student and invariably encouraged me to complete the study. I am greatly indebted to Professor G. Jones, of the University of Reading, for his generous supervision while he was at the London School of Economics. I also wish to acknowledge my special gratitude to Professor M. Daunton, of University College London, and Dr C.W. Munn, formerly of the University of Glasgow and now with the Chartered Institute of Bankers in Scotland, who kindly and judiciously commented on my present work as an examiner. Concerning errors of fact and interpretation, however, I alone must be held responsible.

While many archivists and librarians have contributed greatly to the completion of this study, I owe a special debt of gratitude to Mr E. Green (Midland Bank) and Dr M.J. Orbel (Baring Brothers & Co.) for their outstanding help and support. I am afraid that a strange non-native English speaking researcher must have greatly interrupted their usual archival work activities. Other archivists, librarians and institutions who kindly assisted my research are: Dr J. Booker (Lloyds Bank), Madame I. Brot (Archives nationales), Mr D.G. Corble (Hill Samuel & Co.), Mr C. Cove-Smith (National Westminster Bank), Mr H. Gillet (Bank of England), Mr G. Knight (N.M. Rothschild & Sons), Mrs M. Lee (Hong Kong Bank), Ms S. Mace (N.M. Rothschilds & Sons), Mr B. McGónigle (Lazard Brothers & Co.), Mr G.F. Miles (Barclays Bank), Mr M. Purton (Kleinwort Benson), Mr R.M. Reed (National Westminster Bank), American Jewish Association Archives, Archives du Minisètre des Affaires Etrangères, Archives économiques et financières, Bank of Japan Archives, British Library of Political & Economic Science, Auswärtiges Amt, Broadland Archives Trust, Européenne de Banque, Guildhall Library, Hambros Bank Ltd., Institute of Historical Research (University of London), Japanese Ministry of Finance Archives, Japanese Ministry of Foreign Affairs Archives, Mitsui Archives, Morgan Grenfell Group, National Diet Library (*Kensei Shiryōshitsu*), School of Oriental and African Studies Library (University of London), Standard Chartered Bank Archives and Sakura Bank Archives.

I am under great obligation to a wide variety of people whose professional and personal generosity has been immense. Some of those who have furthered my study in various ways are: Dr K. Burk, Dr S.J. Diaper, Ms L. Doole, Professor Shin-ichi Gotō, Professor Shin Gotō, Professor H. Ichihara, Professor T. Kanegae, Professor F.H.H. King, Dr D. Kynaston, Mr C. Monk, Professor K. Nakamura, Professor I.H. Nish, Professor T. Nakajima, Dr R.W.

Roberts, Professor N. Tamaki, Dr P. Thane, Professor S. Yonekawa and Professor M. Yoneyama.

I would also like to express my thanks to Mr Brian Southam, of The Athlone Press, who has guided me and kindly accepted such a financially unrewarding publication. Finally the greatest thanks I mention last are to my wife Kieko and son Tetsu. This study would not have been possible without their enduring assistance in many things over a long period.

Toshio Suzuki

Introduction

This study aims to analyse the character of foreign government loan issues on the London capital market before the First World War. It addresses the following basic questions: firstly, how foreign governments were able to raise funds on the London capital market and, secondly, what the role of financial institutions involved in these operations was? These questions are answered in relation to the history of Japanese government loan issues on the London capital market in the period from 1870 to 1913.

Consideration centres on the London capital market, but the significance of other markets, especially the Paris capital market,[1] is also taken into consideration. Previous research has established that borrowers seeking to improve the terms of loan issues would sound out other main capital markets when London's conditions seemed unfavourable. International market linkages in simultaneous loan issues, the integration of capital markets, is looked into more seriously,[2] although London became the centre for the Japanese government foreign loan issues. This also raises the question of a borrower's efficient access to foreign capital markets.

Some scholars have neglected the role of Japan's foreign borrowings at the early stage of its industrialisation,[3] but the importance of Japan's large capital imports after the turn of the century, which resulted mainly from increased military outlay, is generally admitted,[4] comprising over 20 per cent of the total foreign government loan issues in London in the period from 1900 to 1913. The scale of the Japanese government loan issues reached its apogee during the Russo-Japanese War period (1904–1905), and these financial operations on the international capital markets, especially London, New York, Berlin and Paris, attracted a great deal of attention from financiers and public investors.[5]

The activities of Japanese banks in the London capital market before the First World War are another subject of interest. Japan had been a mysterious and unknown country to Western investors in the 1870s, but by about the turn of the century its creditworthiness on the London capital market had improved remarkably. Japanese-owned banks, supported by the Japanese government, played a significant role in enhancing Japan's borrowing position abroad. The banks, in collaboration with foreign financiers, arranged many Japanese government foreign loan issues on favourable terms.

Hitherto, very little has been said about Japan's financial activities on foreign capital markets before 1914. There has been no serious study of Japanese government foreign loan issues. In fact, Feis, the author of the famous book *Europe the World's Banker, 1870–1914*, published in 1930, devoted only 8 out of his 469 pages to Japanese loans.[6] M. Takahashi, one of the leading Japanese financial historians, declared that the study of the activities of foreign financiers involved in Japanese government loan issues was impossible because of the unavailability of the relevant historical records.[7] Allen mentioned Japan's success in raising loans abroad after the Russo-Japanese War, but did not further elaborate on the reason for this success, or the means by which it was achieved.[8]

The neglected area of Japanese government foreign loan issues also forms a part of the wider neglected area of the loan issue mechanism on the London capital market, although, exceptionally, Hall[9] and Gilbert[10] have scrutinized the Australian governments loan issues. This neglect is curious in view of the long debate about British foreign investment.[11]

The 'backwardness' of research on the mechanism of loan issues can be ascribed mainly to the problem of sources. Restrictions on access to loan issue banks' papers made the research almost impossible in the past. In addition, the transitory character of loan issue organizations complicated the study.[12] Loan issue terms published in a prospectus or journal told nothing of the negotiations, which can only be revealed by the loan issue banks' records.

Jacob Viner observed in 1929 that

> no documented and detailed study of this phase of European diplomacy has ever been published by any historian or economist. It has been necessary, therefore, to piece together the miscellaneous bits of information which could be gathered from contemporaneous literature and from the flood of diplomatic

> documents and memoirs published since 1914. But the secrecy which ordinarily surrounds transactions such as are here dealt with when they occur, the reticence of diplomats even in their memoirs, and the rarity of informative memoirs or biographies of the financiers who participated in the transactions, make it impossible to hope for anything like a complete account, even if all published sources of information had been found and used, of the relations between *haute finance* and *haute politique*.[13]

Recently in Britain, the 'secrecy' of the foreign loan issues before the First World War has lifted partially because loan issue banks have permitted access to most of their records. This study is based primarily on the research at the archives of Baring Brothers, the London Rothschilds, the Paris Rothschilds, Parr's Bank and the Hongkong Bank, which were involved most deeply in Japanese government loan issues in the period from 1897 to 1910. However, the situation in Japan is different. The banks concerned with the foreign loan issues are still unwilling to admit access to their archives.[14] Nevertheless, this research has been based on several Japanese banks' archives.[15]

The official histories of the Japanese Ministry of Finance are another major problem. These histories are important and useful sources for the study of Japanese government foreign loan issues, but have referred to them without any footnotes or references.[16] Therefore, this study is founded on records at the Ministry of Finance Archives, the Ministry of Foreign Affairs Archives and the National Diet Library. So far no one has studied Japanese government foreign loan issues using both Japanese government's (borrower's) and loan issue banks' (lenders') records.

This study is firmly based on business history methodology. As mentioned, published loan issue terms told nothing of loan issue negotiations, and only archival research in surviving records at loan issue banks can reveal the details of loan issue negotiations. Each of the Japanese government loan issues is examined as a case study. Such a close study of the development of these loan issues on the market can provide the basis for generalizations about the whole loan issue process. It is hoped that this study will make a substantial contribution to the knowledge about Japanese government foreign loan issues in the period from 1870 to 1913, and also provide new insights into the loan issue mechanism on the London capital market before the First World War.

PART I

Foreign Government Loan Issues on the London Capital Market

1

Foreign Government Loan Issues in London 1870–1913

It is not too much to say that the modern foreign policy of Great Britain has been primarily a struggle for profitable markets of investment. To a larger extent every year Great Britain has been becoming a nation living upon tribute from abroad, and the classes who enjoy this tribute have had an ever-increasing incentive to employ the public policy, the public purse, and the public force to extend the field of their private investments, and to safeguard and improve their existing investments. This is, perhaps, the most important fact in modern politics, and the obscurity in which it is wrapped has constituted the gravest danger to our State.

J.A. Hobson, Imperialism: A Study

From the early nineteenth century the London capital market was deeply involved in many foreign governments' financial operations. In fact, the financial activities of Baring Brothers, the oldest London merchant bank, were regarded almost as one of the 'Six Powers in Europe'.[1] This clearly shows the magnitude of the contemporary London capital market in foreign government loan business. Chapter 1 presents a general overview of foreign government loan issues on the London capital market in the period from 1870 to 1913, giving consideration to trends, geographical distribution, yields, commissions and market linkages.

TRENDS

Although during the era of 'railway mania' between the 1830s and the 1850s domestic railway securities attracted British investors, Consols remained the primary object for investment for many throughout the nineteenth century because of their safety. However, Consols' large share in transactions diminished rapidly after 1863,[2] and more investors sought a prudent way to invest money abroad and to return a higher rate of interest than at home. There was now a search for higher anticipated returns from overseas lending. The number of foreign government loan issues in London increased in the 1860s and 1870s, and foreign government bonds became the centre of the market. The British economy had by this time entered into the high age of capital exports. After the Franco–Prussian War (1870–1871), Paris lost its foremost position and, conversely, London became established in its place as the world's centre for foreign lending.[3] 'Now London has a manifest monopoly of every new issue of any importance,' *The Economist* observed, 'the names of other foreign markets are mentioned in the prospectuses, but they obviously play a second part.'[4]

It was also during the 1860s and 1870s that London merchant banks briskly expanded their loan issue business. Newcomers, such as Kleinworts, E. Erlanger, Morton, Rose & Co., Speyer Brothers, Seligman Brothers, J.S. Morgan & Co. and Lazard Brothers, emerged in London as cosmopolitan family banking firms.[5] Some of them were German-born Jews who came across from the United States. These Anglo-American houses opened London branches and began to take up foreign loan issues on a liberal scale. It is obvious that their new business strategy was to take advantage of organizing simultaneous loan issues in London and New York.

From about 1880, instead of the foreign government bonds common in the 1870s, colonial government bonds, and Indian, colonial and American railway debentures were highlighted on the market. Corporation bonds, domestic and colonial, were also newly introduced into the market from the late-1870s. Colonial government bonds, Indian and colonial railway guaranteed debentures and corporation bonds were gradually expanding the gilt-edged market.

The volume of new foreign government loan issues had cyclical fluctuations. There was another boom in them in the late-1880s ending in the Baring Crisis of 1890. Although their volume increased thereafter, foreign government bonds were no longer a promising market leader, but rather stable investment objects. The transactions of industrial securities now registered more rapid growth. By 1913 foreign government bonds had earned a reputation as a safe form of investment.[6]

Simon's calculation, the most precise one based on the *Investor's*

Monthly Manual, is too aggregated for an overview of foreign government loan issues on the London capital market.[7] For this purpose, information on individual, not overall, loan issues is needed. Appendix A shows the individual foreign government loan issues made wholly or partially through the London capital market in the period from 1870 to 1913. As mentioned in the notes, this contains several inevitable defects resulting from the dearth of data which is available only from the financial press.[8] Since appendix A includes many conversion loans and 'partials', amounts placed outside London simultaneously, it is not able to support a calculation of the amount of British foreign exports or of capital transfers from the London capital market. Its validity is strictly limited to a general overview of foreign government loan issues on the markets. Appendix A, therefore, must be treated most carefully. Despite these short-comings, however, it should be possible to gain an idea of the nature and the character of foreign government loan issues coming before the London capital market in the years from 1870 to 1913.

GEOGRAPHICAL DISTRIBUTION

Table 1.1 shows the geographical distribution (by country) of foreign government loan issues on the London capital market. Major developed European countries and the United States after 1896 were no longer large borrowers in London and raised necessary funds on their own domestic markets. Paris, rather than London, became the prime source of loans for Southern Europe, the Scandinavian countries, Romania, Switzerland and Russia.[9] Russia conducted large-scale financial operations in both London and Paris, but patronized the Paris capital market far more following the Franco–Russian entente of 1894. Russia did return to London in 1906 for a simultaneous loan issue.

The London capital market became especially receptive to South American and Far Eastern countries from the late-1890s. Their proportion of the total issue amount increased prominently, although South American government bonds had already been market leaders in the 1870s and late-1880s. From the outset, London was of paramount importance for Chinese government loan issues, but in 1895 China, as a result of Russia's diplomatic influence, tapped the Paris capital market to raise the Sino-Japanese War indemnity. China floated many simultaneous loans both in London and on the

Table 1.1 Foreign government loan issues in London 1870–1913 (by country) (£000; net proceeds) (%)(excluding % *) [index]

Country	*1870–74*	*1875–79*	*1880–84*	*1885–89*	*1890–94*	*1895–99*	*1900–04*	*1905–09*	*1910–13*	*Total*
Argentina	9370		9399	21418	9685	18715	9539	6297	2956	87379
	(1)(3)		(5)	(9)	(5)	(11)	(8)	(6)	(3)	(4)(9)
Austria	203259*	4000								207259*
	(27)(–)	(1)								(10)(–)
Belgium	1087									1087
	(0)(0)									(0)(0)
Bolivia	1156									1156
	(0)(0)									(0)(0)
Brazil	3079	5115	4093	30218	2957	14939	19555	10641	28468	119065
	(1)(1)	(2)	(2)	(12)	(2)	(8)	(17)	(10)	(33)	(6)(12)
Bulgaria				1746	1110		3756		3604	10216
				(1)	(1)		(3)		(4)	(1)(1)
Chile	2979	971		9343	2340	5690	260	7884	12307	41774
	(1)(1)	(0)		(4)	(1)	(3)	(0)	(7)	(14)	(2)(4)
China		2157		3680	1602	52016	2194	8852	14533	85034
		(1)		(2)	(1)	(30)	(2)	(8)	(17)	(4)(9)
Colombia	2000					2700				4700
	(0)(1)					(2)				(0)(1)
Costa Rica	1957			619					2000	4576
	(0)(1)			(0)					(2)	(0)(1)
Cuba				21576		6985	1086	2225		31872
				(9)		(6)	(1)	(3)		(1)(3)
Denmark			1648		1365	3989	630		2425	10057
			(1)		(1)	(2)	(1)		(3)	(0)(1)
Ecuador							52			52
							(0)			(0)
Egypt	32317	37705		11225	42498					123745
	(4)(11)	(12)		(5)	(23)					(6)(12)
Finland								1665		1665
								(2)		(0)(0)
France	240124*	2380								242504*
	(32)(–)	(1)								(11)(–)
Germany	14438		29500			3484				47422
	(2)(5)		(16)			(2)				(2)(5)
Greece		999	3939	6951	2621	6113	1659	419	2068	24769
		(0)	(2)	(3)	(1)	(3)	(1)	(0)	(2)	(1)(3)
Guatemala				922		1545				2467
				(0)		(1)				(0)(0)
Haiti						1800				1800
						(1)				(0)(0)
Hawaii				196						196
				(0)						(0)(0)
Holland	171	3525			4514	4432				12642
	(0)(0)	(1)			(3)	(3)				(1)(1)
Honduras	2000									2000
	(0)(1)									(0)(0)
Hungary	6750	3758	39556	5200		1634				56898
	(1)(2)	(1)	(22)	(2)		(1)				(3)(6)
Italy			25978							25978
			(14)							(1)(3)

Country	*1870–74*	*1875–79*	*1880–84*	*1885–89*	*1890–94*	*1895–99*	*1900–04*	*1905–09*	*1910–13*	*Total*
Japan	3200					13451	15209	39793	10450	82103
	(1)(1)					(8)	(13)	(36)	(12)	(4)(8)
Liberia	85							101		186
	(0)(0)							(0)		(0)(0)
Mexico				6702	7585	3787	7736			25810
				(3)	(4)	(2)	(7)			(1)(3)
Montenegro								243		243
								(0)		(0)(0)
Nicaragua				264				460		724
				(0)				(0)		(0)(0)
Norway		2889	859	4817	2166				2217	12948
		(1)	(0)	(2)	(1)				(3)	(1)(1)
Paraguay	1278			839						2117
	(0)(0)			(0)						(0)(0)
Persia					475				1206	1681
					(0)				(1)	(0)(0)
Peru	21310								1154	22464
	(3)(7)								(1)	(1)(2)
Portugal		3506	4438	14573						22517
		(1)	(2)	(6)						(1)(2)
Romania	805								1802	2607
	(0)(0)								(2)	(0)(0)
Russia	46680	13800	22897	93891	54175			16945		248388*
	(6)(15)	(4)	(13)	(38)	(30)			(15)		(11)(–)
Santo Domingo				502	2478	759				3739
				(0)	(1)	(0)				(0)(0)
Salvador				287				860		1147
				(0)				(1)		(0)(0)
Serbia						680	2160			2840
						(0)	(2)			(0)(0)
Siam								1580		1580
								(1)		(0)(0)
South Africa			100		2250					2350
			(0)		(1)					(0)(0)
Spain	20116	26515	12000							58631
	(3)(7)	(8)	(7)							(3)(6)
Sweden		3297	3918	1470	2950		928	2940		15503
		(1)	(2)	(1)	(2)		(1)	(3)		(1)(2)
Switzerland								2841		2841
								(3)		(0)(0)
Tonking						2784				2784
						(2)				(0)(0)
Turkey	29068	2500	14067	6027	21121		45155	2759		120697*
	(4)(9)	(1)	(8)	(2)	(12)		(39)	(2)		(6)(–)
USA	102375	205950				35709				344034*
	(14)(34)	(65)				(20)				(16)(–)
Uruguay	2520		8011	3510	19300	1192		164		34697
	(0)(1)		(4)	(1)	(11)	(1)		(0)		(2)(4)
Venezuela			2702					5229		7931
			(2)					(5)		(0)(1)
Total	748124	319067	183105	245976	181192	175419	115818	110759	87415	2166875
Total (excluding *)	304741									1003993
[index]	[100]	[100]	[100]	[100]	[100]	[100]	[100]	[100]	[100]	[100]

(Table 1.1 continues overleaf)

	1870–74	*1875–79*	*1880–84*	*1885–89*	*1890–94*	*1895–99*	*1900–04*	*1905–09*	*1910–13*	*Total*
Feinstein	385000	142000	271000	402000	338000	217000	155000	666000	818000	3394000
[index]	[51]	[45]	[148]	[163]	[187]	[124]	[134]	[601]	[936]	[157]
(excluding index *)	[126]									[338]
Simon	352600	158100	307600	451500	294400	379400	359700	653300	785300	3741900
[index]	[47]	[50]	[168]	[184]	[162]	[216]	[311]	[590]	[898]	[173]
(excluding index *)	[116]									[373]

Sources: Appendix A; C.H. Feinstein and S. Pollard (eds.), *Studies in Capital Formation in the United Kingdom, 1750–1920* (Oxford, 1988), table xvii (462–63); M. Simon, 'The pattern of new British portfolio foreign investment, 1865–1914' in A.R. Hall (ed.), *The Export of Capital from Britain 1870–1914* (1968), 38–39.

Notes: Germany includes North Germany and Prussia; South Africa includes Orange Free State;
* Only a fraction of these particularly large sums were raised in London;
Net proceeds were calculated as follows:
(net proceeds)=(total loan issue amounts) × (London issue prices, otherwise 100)/100;
These amounts do not mean actual capital transfers from the London capital market, and the data for the period before 1885, not based on *SEOI*, are perhaps insignificant because they include large partials;
Feinstein calculated UK investment abroad (net) on the indirect method and Simon British portfolio foreign investment (net) on the direct method.

Continent. Japan depended upon the London capital market for its first foreign loan issue in 1870. After a long interval, in the 1890s, it began to organize large loan issues in London. Japan briskly expanded a loan issue market from London to New York and Berlin during the Russo-Japanese War, and later reached Paris. The total Japanese government loan issues on the London capital market in the period from 1870 to 1913 amounted to £82,106,335 (net amount), 3.8 per cent of the total foreign government loan issues, but their proportion increased remarkably to 20.8 per cent in the period from 1900 to 1913 when transactions of foreign government bonds on the market were at a low ebb.

YIELDS

Anticipated returns and risks are the fundamental determinants of investors' demand. The promised yields of colonial and foreign government bonds were typically much higher than those of Consols,[10] but British investors did not always prefer these higher interest bonds because of perceived 'country risks'. In 1865 Viscount Goschen, in saying 'thousands of men, who, under the old system [the principle of unlimited liability], would rather have invested their money at 3 per cent. at home than risk it abroad for 50',[11] noted that not only high yields but also risks swayed the decision of British investors.

Dickson, who gives full treatment to eighteenth-century national debt problems, has paid attention to the aspect of safety in investment.[12] Kennedy has discussed British investors' preferences for safety, and explained the reasons for the apparent bias of the Victorian capital market towards foreign securities, as resulting mainly from a limited ability to achieve informed diversification of dangerous domestic ventures and the highly segmented, informationally inefficient structure of the various financial institutions of the London capital market.[13] Edelstein, taking risks in investment into consideration, calculated 'risk-adjusted returns' and confirmed a tendency for overseas 'risk-adjusted returns' to exceed those at home.[14] Edelstein's analysis of 'risk-adjusted returns' was similar to that of Bailey's analysis of Australian governments' bondholders.[15] Bailey emphasized that the importance of 'safe' investors or rentiers as colonial government bond investors.[16] The behaviour of Victorian investors is worth considering, but it is now almost impossible to trace bondholders because the loan issue banks held no subscription lists of their issued securities.[17] 'It has, in fact, proved to be extremely difficult to generalize about Victorian investors.'[18]

Table 1.2 shows the average realized yields of the foreign government bonds quoted on the London Stock Exchange at 5 year intervals from 1870 to 1910. The figures of these yields were made by dividing the annual nominal interest payments by the averages of the annual highest and lowest quotation prices of the bonds in the *Investor's Monthly Manual* and then averaged by country. Let

HQP_{ijt} = the annual highest quotation price of the ith loan of the jth country in the tth year,
LQP_{ijt} = the annual lowest quotation price of the ith loan of the jth country in the tth year,
NIP_{ijt} = the nominal interest payment (per cent) of the ith loan of the jth country in the tth year,

where

i = 1,.......,m, loans,
j = countries' number (Argentine,.......Venezuela),

and

t = the calendar year (1870, 1875, 1880, 1885, 1890, 1895, 1900, 1905, 1910).

The annual realized yield to the ith loan of the jth country in the tth year is calculated from:

$$r_{ijt} = \frac{NIP_{ijt} \times 100}{(HQP_{ijt} + LQP_{ijt})/2}$$

The averaged annual realized yield to the jth country of the tth year is also calculated from:

$$r_{jt} = \frac{\sum_{i=1}^{m} r_{ijt}}{m}$$

The contemporary market rate of interest and investors' assessment of the risk factors involved in the investment could affect the quotation prices. Obviously higher yields coincided with higher interest payments and lower prices.

The realized yields showed geographical patterns. In particular, South American countries' high-yield bonds deserved attention at the time. There were several notorious South American government loan issues which defaulted immediately after flotation. Without doubt, the fabulous promised yields enticed investors into perilous ventures and many disappointments. South European countries and Turkey manifested low creditworthiness on the market. Greece and Turkey had crucial debt problems from the late nineteenth century. Italy, after unification in 1870, steadily improved its borrowing position on the European financial markets and achieved first-rate standing by the 1880s. The yields of the bonds issued by East European and Far Eastern countries were not as high as those of the South American countries. Their creditworthiness was still middling even in 1910. Throughout the nineteenth century the more developed West European countries received a favourable assessment from investors. Just before the First World War the Scandinavian countries, where central governments relied on much foreign capital for their industrialization, attained similar levels of credit rating on the London capital market.

Silver loans were assessed at a discount under the gold standard mainly because of the depreciation of silver from the late nineteenth

Table 1.2 Realized yields of foreign government loans 1870–1910 (by country) (%)

Country	*1870*	*1875*	*1880*	*1885*	*1890*	*1895*	*1900*	*1905*	*1910*
Argentina	6.7	7.4	7.8	6.6	7.9	13.0	7.5	5.5	4.6
Austria	–	7.8	7.2	6.6	5.8	5.4	5.5	4.0	4.2
Belgium	4.5	4.2	3.9	3.5	3.1	3.1	–	–	–
Bolivia	–	27.0	24.0	–	–	–	–	–	–
Brazil	5.6	5.1	4.9	5.1	5.2	6.0	6.7	4.9	4.7
Bulgaria	–	–	–	–	–	6.6	7.1	5.8	5.1
Chile	6.1	5.8	6.8	5.2	4.7	4.8	5.6	4.9	4.8
China	–	–	7.6	5.8	6.2	6.3	6.1	5.3	5.2
Colombia	–	6.7	12.6	23.8	13.2	29.2	10.3	4.0	6.7
Costa Rica	–	37.3	36.9	39.6	5.0	16.9	10.4	12.2	12.5
Cuba	8.9	8.5	–	–	–	–	–	4.7	4.9
Denmark	3.3	4.5	–	4.0	–	–	3.6	3.3	3.5
Ecuador	10.3	14.3	10.4	12.1	4.9	18.5	–	–	–
Egypt	8.5	9.5	7.8	6.6	4.7	3.8	3.7	3.6	3.8
Finland	–	–	–	–	–	–	–	–	4.6
France	5.9	4.8	3.8	3.9	3.6	3.1	3.2	3.1	3.1
Germany	–	–	4.1	3.9	3.8	3.3	3.5	3.4	3.7
Greece	48.8	37.0	30.6	7.6	5.5	15.3	11.8	8.7	8.6
Guatemala	8.9	14.1	–	15.9	7.6	13.0	20.1	12.4	9.6
Hawaii	–	–	–	–	5.8	5.8	5.8	–	–
Holland	4.8	4.0	3.9	3.8	3.3	3.1	3.2	3.1	3.3
Honduras	12.7	200.0	181.2	210.5	74.4	143.0	190.5	97.3	83.3
Hungary	–	6.9	6.2	5.1	4.5	5.0	4.0	3.9	4.2
Italy	7.9	6.2	5.6	5.2	5.3	5.5	5.4	5.0	4.6
Japan	9.3	7.6	7.6	6.4	6.4	6.5	7.0	6.2	4.4
Mexico	32.5	32.2	32.4	26.2	7.2	8.4	8.4	6.2	6.2
Nicaragua	–	–	–	–	6.1	13.3	7.6	5.4	5.5
Norway	–	–	4.2	4.2	3.6	3.4	3.6	3.5	5.3
Orange Free State	–	–	–	6.1	5.8	–	–	–	–
Paraguay	–	51.0	61.5	133.3	4.8	19.7	17.0	5.7	5.6
Peru	6.7	10.2	26.6	50.0	–	–	–	–	–
Portugal	10.0	5.8	5.8	6.4	5.0	11.7	12.5	4.4	4.5
Romania	8.8	7.2	7.4	7.1	–	–	–	–	–
Russia	5.8	4.9	5.5	5.4	4.4	3.8	3.9	4.5	4.3
Salvador	–	–	–	–	–	9.1	–	–	6.8
Santo Domingo	9.9	66.7	5.6	44.4	13.6	–	–	–	–
Serbia	–	–	–	–	–	–	6.7	5.0	4.7
Siam	–	–	–	–	–	–	–	–	4.5
Spain	8.8	9.8	9.7	5.4	4.8	5.2	5.8	4.3	4.2
Sweden	5.0	4.7	4.4	4.1	3.7	3.2	3.6	3.5	3.9
Switzerland	–	–	–	–	–	–	–	3.5	3.6
Transvaal	–	–	–	–	–	4.5	–	–	–
Turkey	8.9	11.8	30.4	5.6	5.1	3.8	3.9	4.0	4.3
United States	6.8	5.3	4.5	3.6	3.7	3.6	3.2	3.3	3.4
Uruguay	–	13.0	20.0	10.3	8.8	1.0	7.7	5.2	4.9
Venezuela	29.3	43.9	36.5	10.0	6.0	7.1	10.7	5.9	5.3
Consols	3.2	3.2	3.1	3.0	2.9	2.6	2.8	2.8	3.1
Colonial governments	4.8	4.4	4.1	4.0	3.7	3.3	3.5	3.8	4.0

Source: *IMM*, 1872, 1875, 1880, 1885, 1890, 1895, 1900, 1905 and 1910; Consols – B.R. Mitchell, *British Historical Statistics* (Cambridge, 1988), 678; Colonial governments – M. Edelstein, 'The rate of return on UK home and foreign investment, 1870–1913' (1970), 295–6.

Notes: – implies no transactions; Excluding Treasury bills and provincial governments loan issues; Germany includes Prussia and Bavaria; Italy includes Sardinia; Romania includes Danube; Colonial governments' yields were calculated from 51 bonds.

Table 1.3 Japanese government loan issue terms (London) 1870–1910

Year	*(1) Nominal interest rate (%)*	*(2) Issue price (%)*	*(3) Nominal issue amount (£000)*	*(4) Borrowing period (year)*	*(5) Yield at issue (%)*	*(6) Yield on Consols (%)*	*(7) Yield difference (%)*
1870	9	98	1,000	13	9.2	3.2	6.0
1873	7	92½	2,400	25	7.6	3.2	4.4
1897	5	101½	4,385	53	4.9	2.5	2.4
1899	4	90	10,000	55	4.4	2.6	1.8
1902	5	100	5,104	55	5.0	2.9	2.1
1904	6	93½	5,000	7	6.4	2.8	3.6
1904	6	90½	6,000	7	6.6	2.8	3.8
1905	4½	90	15,000	25	5.0	2.8	2.2
1905	4½	90	10,000	25	5.0	2.8	2.2
1905	4	90	6,500	25	4.4	2.8	1.6
1907	5	99½	11,500	60	5.0	3.0	2.0
1910	4	95	11,000	60	4.2	3.1	1.1

Sources: (1)–(5) Part II; (6) B.R. Mitchell, *British Historical Statistics* (Cambridge, 1988), p.678.

Notes: (5)=(1)/(2) × 100; (7)=(5)–(6); The yields of 'Goschen' Consols (2¾%) were 2.0% (1897), 2.2% (1899) and 2.7% (1902) (C.K. Harley, 'Goschen's conversion of the national debt and the yield on Consols', *Economic History Review*, second series, xxix 1 (1976), 105.

century. The price of silver fell 20 per cent in the 1870s.[19] The establishment of the gold standard improved borrowing countries' creditworthiness on the foreign capital markets. The establishment of the gold standard in Russia attracted more foreign capital because of reductions in exchange risks.[20] In fact, after the adoption of the gold standard in 1897, the yields of Russian and Japanese government bonds plummeted as bonds prices rose.

Table 1.3 sets out the Japanese government loan issue terms in the period from 1870 to 1910. The rates of nominal interest reflect Japan's creditworthiness of the time, and the level of the yields at issue indicates the market's assessment of these loan issues. The risk factors were calculated roughly from the difference between the yields at issue and those on Consols, one of the relatively risk-free investments. The two early loans held large perceived risks for public investors since Japan was still an unknown country. Japan's borrowing position in London, however, improved remarkably as a result of both the adoption of the gold standard in 1897 and the conclusion of the

Anglo-Japanese alliance in 1902. Japan built closer relations with the London capital market. This obviously reflected the level of the yields at issue in 1899 and 1902. The two loan issues of 1904 involved the uncertainties and dangers of the Russo-Japanese War. The yields of Japanese government loans thus closely corresponded with the risks that the contemporary loan issue market perceived and the interest payments.

COMMISSIONS

Normally loan issue charges comprise the following commissions: loan issue bank, underwriting, brokerage (placing underwriting), brokerage (application), intermediary and miscellaneous commissions. The level of these commissions depends upon the risks which loan issuers undertake. The commissions on colonial government loan issues were low,[21] because colonial government loans were usually raised by tender.[22] In this loan issue method, the loan issue banks did not undertake loan issues at their own risk. On the other hand, foreign governments faced high commissions. Since most of the foreign government loan issues were guaranteed by the loan issue banks to take some or all of their issue amounts,[23] the loan issue banks demanded sufficient commissions to compensate for their risks.

Some of the South American government loan issues in the 1860s and 1870s, fully investigated by a parliamentary committee, revealed high loan issue commissions: the Honduras government 10 per-cent loan issue of 1867 paid about an 8.4 per-cent commission[24] and the Costa Rica government 7 per-cent loan of 1872 a 7.6 per-cent commission.[25] The Japanese government too paid a 7 percent commission in the 9 percent loan issue of 1870.[26] These loan issue commissions were extremely high in comparison with contemporary standards.

It was of importance to borrowing countries to free themselves from foreign financiers' high commissions. In fact, after the assiduous efforts by local financial institutions to use the most advantageous foreign capital markets, some of the borrowing countries successfully improved their subordinate position and became independent borrowers. For instance, Sweden carefully avoided over-dependence upon particular financiers and markets, and pursued the most favourable loan issue terms on the international capital markets. Throughout these operations, pre-eminent local banks always took the lead in loan issue negotiations with foreign financiers. The competitive background considerably lowered the level of commissions in Swedish government loan issues.[27]

Financiers, however, issued the loans of favoured foreign governments at remarkably low commissions especially when the loans were placed by tender. The London Joint Stock Bank tendered for the North German Confederation Treasury bonds issue in 1870 at a ½ per-cent commission;[28] in 1880 the bank also negotiated the re- sale of the Prussian government 4 per-cent domestic loan issue at a ⅓ per-cent commission.[29] In the Italian government 5 per-cent loan issues from 1880 to 1882, Hambros and Baring Brothers obtained only about a 2 3/10 per-cent profit with all charges included.[30] Hambros carried out the Swedish government 4 per-cent loan issue in 1880 at about a 2 3/5 per-cent profit.[31]

There was a tendency for loan issue commissions to diminish. Because of both the diffusion of underwriting[32] and keen competition on the loan issue market, financiers were forced to lower their loan issue commissions. In 1911 the London Rothschilds came to charge a 1 or 1¼ per-cent underwriting and a 1 per-cent loan issue bank commission for foreign government loan issues. This level was less expensive than contemporary standards, namely 2 or 1½ per cent of an underwriting and 1½ per cent of a loan issue bank commission. The London Rothschilds, therefore, felt proud that 'the underwriting commission we charged is less than all other governments had paid for their issues'.[33]

The commission of the Japanese government loan issues in the period from 1873 to 1913 are shown in Table 1.4. Except for the resales of domestic bonds in 1902 and the four loan issues during the Russo-Japanese War (1904–1905), the commissions charged by financiers were about 4 per cent. The costs of the four war loan issues were expensive to compensate for the risks of hazardous war loans.

MARKET LINKAGES

Borrowers who intended to obtain more favourable loan issue terms often sought to avoid over-dependence upon one market and turned more of their attention to other capital markets. Loan issue banks, for their part, became inclined to organize loan issues on plural markets because the wider dealings of securities enabled them to secure a

Table 1.4 Commissions of Japanese government loan issues (London) 1873–1910 (%)

Year	*1873*	*1897*	*1899*	*1902*	*1904 (6%)*	*1904 (6%)*	*1905 (4½%)*	*1905 (4½%)*	*1905 (4%)*	*1907*	*1910*
Underwriting	2	1½	2		2	2	2	2	½	1½	1½
Brokerage (placing underwriting)	½		½	½	½	½	½	½	½	½	½
Brokerage (application)	¼		¼		¼	¼	¼	¼	¼	¼	¼
Advertisement	¼		¼		¼	¼	¼	¼	¼	¼	¼
Loan issue bank	1		1		3½	3¾	2½	2½	1½	1½	1½
Total	4	4	4**	4¾	6½*	6¾*	5½*	5½*	4	4	4

Source: These sources will be mentioned in Part II.
Notes: Excluding the British stamp duty and intermediary commissions in Japan; * Russo-Japanese war loan issues; ** the commission to the actual issue amount on the market was 5%.

sufficient number of purchasers. It was a well-known fact that the Rothschilds would float many foreign government loans through their kin spread over the major European cities. From the 1890s the markets for foreign government loan issues came to include not only London but also Paris and other major Continental cities. After the turn of the century the New York capital market also began to deal with foreign loan issues. Simultaneous loan issues were a possibility and international market linkages were more important to borrowing countries.

Relationships between international capital markets, especially London and Paris, the largest markets of the time, in simultaneous loan issues is a key question here. The Berlin capital market did not transact a large number of foreign government securities,[34] but was concerned mainly with domestic industrial finance. The significance of the New York capital market in international finance was limited at that time and was subordinate to London.[35]

There was an increased number of security issues in France in the 1900s and the proportion of the foreign security issues ('valeurs étrangère') to the total rose to 66 per cent in 1904.[36] The Paris capital market was regarded as having 'completely regained its position as an

Table 1.5 Quotation prices of Russian and Japanese government bonds in London and Paris 1906–1913 (%)

Year	*Japanese government 4% bond (1905)*			*Russian government 5% bond (1906)*		
Year	*(1) Paris*	*(2) London*	*(3) Difference*	*(4) Paris*	*(5) London*	*(6) Difference*
1906	92.0	88.25	3.75	–	–	–
1907	88.0	82.0	6.0	94.75	90.25	4.50
1908	92.75	85.75	7.0	100.0	97.25	2.75
1909	99.50	93.25	6.25	103.50	101.50	2.00
1910	97.30	96.0	1.30	104.80	104.75	0.05
1911	94.85	92.0	2.85	104.65	104.0	0.65
1912	90.60	87.50	3.10	103.25	103.75	–0.50
1913	–	–	–	103.10	102.50	0.60

Sources: (1) and (4) from *Marché financier*, 1906–7, 204, 1907–8, 351, 1908–9, 333, 1909–10, 254, 1910–11, 247; 1911–12, 261, 1912–13, 283, 1913–14, 416; (2) and (5) from *IMM*, monthly.

Notes: % of the quotation prices; end of December; – implies no data; (3)=(1)–(2); (6)=(4)–(5).

international financial market, second only to London in its ability to absorb foreign loans.'[37]

In the 1900s, however, a partial isolation of the Paris capital market from London emerged. Comparing the prices of bonds quoted on the Paris Stock Exchange with those on the London Stock Exchange, *L'économiste français* commented in 1910: 'France is not the sole lender to the world but the one with the most favourable conditions. There is a difference of 2 or 3 points (that is to say, 2 per cent or 3 per cent), often of 5 or 6 and of from 7 to 8 in the capitalisation of the same government loans between France and London.'[38] The Russian government 5 per-cent bonds (1906) and the Japanese government 4 per-cent bonds (1905), issued simultaneously in Paris and London, showed such a tendency. As indicated in Table 1.5, there was a conspicuous and continuing difference in their quotation prices between Paris and London in the period from 1906 to 1909.[39]

During most of the period from 1890 to 1913 the discount rates at the Bank of France ('le taux d'escompte à la Banque de France') were lower than the bank rates in London.[40] Low interest rates in Paris might have caused a high capitalization of securities on the Paris capital market.

There was another, more important, reason for the higher quotation prices in Paris. It was the strict control by both the French government and great financiers of the Paris Stock Exchange that brought about the differences. The French government did not readily admit the quotation of bonds issued outside France on the Paris Stock Exchange, a practice referred to as the 'Frenchman's watertight system'.[41] The restricted supply of securities for the market necessarily led to higher capitalization on the Paris Stock Exchange. In fact, there were no marked differences between the quotation prices of the Japanese government 4 per-cent bonds of 1905 in London and Paris after 1910, when the French government admitted the quotation of London's tranche on the Paris Stock Exchange (Table 1.5). Labordère regarded high quotation prices in Paris as 'very inflated values' which whenever possible attracted foreign borrowers and companies to the Paris capital market.[42]

It is true that there was only slight official intervention in loan issue negotiations in Britain but, by contrast, in France foreign governments were not able to effect any loan issue without the authorization of the Ministry of Finance.[43] The French government invariably regarded foreign loans as a diplomatic implement directly reflecting its interests.[44] The French government put the power of authorizing a security quotation into the hands of the *Chambre Syndicale* at the Paris Stock Exchange on the condition that the government would make the final decision, taking into consideration diplomatic relations with a borrowing country.[45] On the other hand, it was the British government's established policy neither to control quotations on the London Stock Exchange nor to intervene in financiers' private transactions except in diplomatically important cases.[46] The General Purpose Committee of the London Stock Exchange assessed new quotation applications according to its own criteria.[47]

One factor in the selection of a loan issue market for borrowers lay in the difference of loan issue costs or commissions. It was pointed out in 1905 that loan issues in Paris required additional charges for the manipulation of the press and a higher rate of stamp duty.[48] Lysis, without giving a precise definition of the profit, pointed out the high profits earned by French financiers in foreign government loan issues.[49] Yet the level of the 'bénéfice syndic et commission (syndicate profit and commission)' in the Turkish government loan issues in Paris for the years from 1894 to 1914, calculated by Thobie, was less than 5 per cent after 1902[50] and the Japanese government 4 per-cent loan issues in 1905 and in 1910 were implemented at almost the same commission in London and Paris (about 4 per cent).[51] Kaufmann correctly estimated a net profit to a member of a syndicate, deducting various issue charges, at about 2 per cent.[52] It is difficult to generalize about the loan issue commissions in the Paris capital market on the basis of an insufficient number of loan issues, but one wonders if Lysis' figures might not be overestimated. As far as loan issue commissions were concerned, there was very little difference for borrowers between the London and Paris capital markets.

It is right to say, therefore, that it was mainly because of French government policy that the isolation of the Paris capital market from the London capital market occurred in some of the simultaneous loan issues. Both markets had no homogeneity in loan issues. Linkages between the world's main capital markets of the time were imperfect and differences in the quotation prices of securities occurred. These differences often hindered simultaneous loan issues on the international capital markets. As a result of the development of market linkages in later periods, however, the patterns of loan issues became diversified for borrowers. This made it possible for borrowers to select the most favourable loan issue terms on the international capital markets, either on one market or on multiple markets.[53]

2

Loan Issue Mechanism of the London Capital Market

A notable tendency in modern business development is to specialize and subdivide uncertainty and control in all possible degrees.
F.H. Knight, *Risk, Uncertainty and Profit*

It is important to understand the general character of loan issues on the London capital market before a particular country's loan matters are discussed. This chapter presents the development of the loan issue mechanism of the London capital market. The role, and the extent of the involvement, of a variety of financial institutions of the City in loan issue business for colonial and foreign governments will be examined.

It is useful to give an outline of the various stages by which an ultimate borrower (government), ultimate lenders (investors) and financial intermediaries were connected through the loan issue market, because the intervention of the financial intermediaries, which helped the borrower to find the lenders efficiently, often veiled the relationship between the ultimate borrower and the ultimate lenders. The capital market played a role 'to select the sources of highest yield, to capitalize these in the form of stocks and shares and to sell these securities to the public'.[1]

A government which intended to raise a loan first nominated a commissioner or an agent. He became the negotiator of the loan issue with the banks in the country where the government proposed to issue the loan. The commissioner or agent, at the next stage, looked for banks which would undertake the issue. The loan issue banks, in collaboration with stockbrokers, began to organize the loan issue for the market. They issued the prospectuses and informed the financial press of the loan issue; the stockbrokers also advertised to potential customers. Then the subscriptions took place. The relationship between the ultimate borrower (government) and the ultimate lenders (investors) was formed in this way. However, in most cases, before the offering of subscriptions, other financial intermediaries, namely the loan issue bank syndicate and the underwriters, temporarily intervened in the relationship between the ultimate borrower, the ultimate lenders and the loan issue banks.

The loan issue bank syndicate, the loan issue banks acting in union, undertook the loan issue for the ultimate borrower. The underwriters guaranteed to take the unsubscribed portion. Obviously these organizations helped to float the loan more efficiently on the loan issue market. It was through these intermediaries that the issued bonds were finally delivered to the ultimate lenders. All these interrelated operations between the ultimate borrower and the ultimate lenders together comprised the market loan issue mechanism.

DEVELOPMENT OF THE LOAN ISSUE MECHANISM

Market methods are developed so as to free loan issuers from the risks of loan issue activities. The creation of loan issue organizations, such as issue syndicates and underwriters, forms a part of this development.[2] Galbraith has rightly described 'the development of the modern business enterprise' as 'a comprehensive effort to reduce risk'.[3]

Loan Issues in the Early Nineteenth Century

The first peak of foreign government loan issues on the London capital market occurred in the early 1820s.[4] The independence of South American countries from Spain caused a large export boom in the British economy, and this excitement enticed many British investors to purchase South American government bonds.[5] These became market leaders but most of them quickly fell into default after 1825.

Jenks illustrated the foreign loan issue methods in the 1820s, and pointed out the co-operation among issue houses.[6] There is a reference to this in *The Times* in 1826 when J. & S. Ricardo & Co., a London merchant bank, was defending its high commission in the Greek government 5 per-cent loan issue of 1825.[7] Ricardo's letter, addressed to the editor of *The Times*, revealed the co-operation among financiers in this loan contract.[8] In the Colombian government loan issue of 1824, the financiers involved also co-operated; B.A.

Goldschmidt & Co., the issuer of this loan, prepared the list filled with merchants and men of great capital who were ready to take the bonds to share the risks and profits.[9]

The need for co-operation among financiers obviously stemmed from the increased size of the loan issues which were now too great for individual resources to bear the risks involved. Compared with the practice of the late nineteenth century, the loan issue organization of the 1820s simply meant participants' co-operation in taking a certain issue amount and sharing risks and profits. The terminology of a syndicate had not yet been used.

The sale organization for subscriptions in the 1820s was primitive. The success of loan issues depended almost entirely upon the loan issuers' narrow circle of friends and family. The most crucial matter was how loan issuers could ensure the solid support of purchasers. It must be emphasized that family and personal connections played a principal role. The Rothschilds frequently raised huge loans in London, Paris, Frankfurt-on-Main and Vienna simultaneously through their kin who acted as satellites.[10] Baring Brothers, one of the long-standing merchant banks in the City, also secured many correspondents for their transactions covering most of the main cities on the Continent and in the United States.

Loan issuers were often forced to take the remnant of the issue amount unless they could find sufficient purchasers. It was because of this uncertainty that loan issuers in the early nineteenth century received a large commission. In 1825 J. & S. Ricardo & Co. obtained a £60,000 commission (6 per cent) at least from the Greek government 5 per-cent loan issue.[11]

Syndication

At the end of the 1860s a loan flotation technique, syndication, was used for many of the new foreign government loan issues. A borrower made a contract for the loan issue with an agent who usually formed a syndicate. The syndicate purchased all or some of the unsubscribed bonds according to the contract, although there were possible variations in contracts of syndication. The forming of a syndicate to purchase unsubscribed bonds was in most cases applicable to foreign government loan issues because of their less creditworthy and more speculative nature.

So far little has been known about how foreign government loan issues were arranged on the London capital market. Lavington[12] and Hall[13] explained the mechanism of colonial government loan issues, depending upon Schilling.[14] It is true that Schilling has analysed the mechanism of colonial government loan issues, yet he neither disclosed his sources nor analysed them in the course of the development of the loan issue methods on the London capital market.[15] Furthermore, the techniques of syndication and capital underwriting[16] were developed largely in the field of foreign government loan issues,[17] since, as will be discussed later, colonial governments usually drew financial assistance from the British government, the Bank of England and other specific financial institutions in London.

It is possible to look at how particular foreign government loans of the 1860s and 1870s were floated on the market, from published sources such as British parliamentary papers and contemporary financial journals. Yet there have been no serious studies which made full use of them, although Jenks regarded the evidence taken before the parliamentary committee of 1875[18] as 'a storehouse of material upon the loan business'.[19]

With the marked increase of foreign government loan issues in the late nineteenth century, many financial journals referred to the loan issue mechanism. In 1873 the *Bondholder's Register* emphasized 'a considerable change during the last eight or ten years' in foreign government loan issues,[20] but the practice of syndication prevailing in the 1860s was not, in the sense of undertaking a loan issue in union at their own risk, very different from that of the 1820s. Syndication was not a new invention of the 1860s but had 'only recently come to the knowledge of the public'.[21] Large systematic operations among financiers on the stock exchange made people misunderstand it.

The primary role of a syndicate was to ensure a firm placement of the loan on the market. In other words, members of a syndicate jointly incurred risks in the loan issue by taking all or some of the issue amount on their own responsibility:

> the nature and object of a syndicate as I understand it is this: that any operation that is too large, either from the amount involved, or the risk involved for any one firm, rather than not be taken at all, should be subdivided by other firms in certain proportions, according to their means and importance. That is the primary object, to divide the risks of the operation, or to furnish guarantees

> to a Government for a certain portion of the loan being taken firm, as it is called, where any one individual firm would not be satisfactory to the Government, or not willing to take so large a risk themselves; therefore, they call in their friends and associates to join them in that operation.[22]

The contract of the Chilean government 5 per-cent loan issue syndicate in 1870 guaranteed to purchase unsubscribed bonds;[23] the syndicate of the Iquique & La Noria Pizaqua and Sal De Obispo and Junction Railways (Peru), formed in 1872, guaranteed to place half an issue amount of the 7 per-cent debentures.[24] The following quotation from the *Bankers' Magazine* of 1876 well describes how a syndicate secured a loan issue:

> when the preliminary arrangements had been completed between the borrowing government, or its authorised representatives in this country, and the firm who were to undertake the introduction of the loan to the public, the latter communicated to numerous capitalists, bankers, merchants, stockbrokers, private individuals and others, the terms on which they could enter the syndicate. An agreement was drawn up between the original agents, or contractors, and the members of the syndicate. The syndicate guaranteed the placing or disposal of a certain portion of the whole loan, perhaps one-third or even one-half; and the part so guaranteed was the first portion that might be placed among the public.[25]

Underwriting

The role of underwriting in ensuring firm purchasers of loan issues was of extreme importance, but so far historians have not explained its origin and development satisfactorily.[26] The contracts of syndication in foreign government loan issues during the 1860s and 1870s often included the *de facto* role of 'underwriting'. Since the syndicate guaranteed to purchase some of the loan issue amount at a certain price from the borrowers, members of the syndicate had to take unsaleable bonds at their own risk.[27]

The terminology of underwriting had not yet been used in the 1860s and 1870s, but underwriting was thus recognized as one of the roles of a syndicate. The development of underwriting was rather mysterious. Finnie believed that the practice of underwriting was

Chart 2.1 Development of syndicates and underwriting

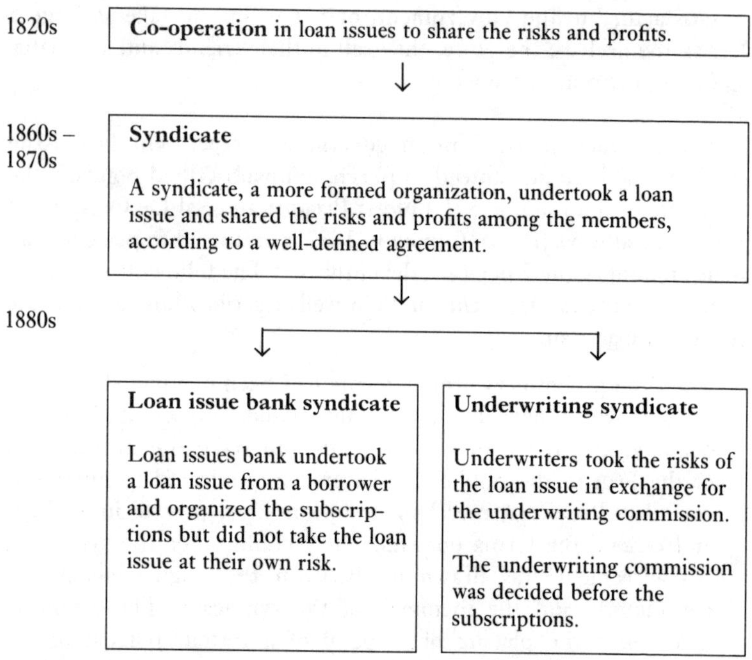

introduced to capital issues from marine insurance.[28] It is true that O'Hagan, an individual stockbroker, considered the question of why insurance could not be extended to capital issues.[29] When was underwriting institutionally split from the roles of a syndicate? In other words, when did a syndicate divide into an issue syndicate and an underwriting syndicate?[30] Unfortunately the origin of underwriting in foreign government loan issues can not be found in contemporary journals. Chart 2.1 shows the course of the development of syndicates and underwriting in the nineteenth century. At first, the separation of loan issue bank commissions from syndicate profits took place and the main role of syndicates became the guarantee of loan issues ('underwriting'). Subsequently, loan issue banks (loan issue bank syndicates) came to arrange the subscriptions alone and did not undertake loan issues at their own risk, although they organized underwriting syndicates; underwriters (underwriting syndicates), who were not involved directly in the subscriptions, guaranteed to purchase unsubscribed bonds in exchange for their commissions.

According to O'Hagan, he was the first person who followed the practice of underwriting in share and debenture issues. He wrote that:

> I began by approaching some of the larger trust and investment companies, and when I found them inclined to take shares or debentures in an undertaking I offered them, I persuaded them to risk having to take three or four times the amount they were contemplating if the capital was not fully subscribed, I paying them a commission for so doing.....I determined to put the business of underwriting or guaranteeing the subscription of the capital of limited liability companies on a legal and proper footing, and endeavoured to popularize the system to the extent that I should get the whole of my issues of capital underwritten or guaranteed.[31]

O'Hagan introduced underwriting into share and debenture issues and attempted to disseminate this practice to financial institutions. The practice of underwriting gradually came to be recognized as distinct from that of a syndicate. It seems certain that this separation necessarily drew smaller amounts of capital, compared with shares of a loan issue syndicate, into the underwriting business. The risks involved in issue could thus be dispersed to many underwriters, although the loan issuers did not obtain (or suffer) such large commissions (or heavy losses) as they took the loan issue at their own risks.

At the outset, large financiers were not in favour of underwriting but soon found it lucrative in well-organized projects.[32] Many financial institutions now regarded underwriting as a safe investment business, because they no longer needed to run great risks.

O'Hagan does not clearly mention when he carried out the first underwriting, but perhaps it was in the 1880s. In 1897 *The Statist* stated that 'underwriting has, with the more speculative concerns, almost taken the place of original subscriptions'.[33] It was after the guarantee of Baring Brothers' debts in 1890 that the Clydesdale Bank came to participate in Baring Brothers' underwriting.[34]

However, the introduction of underwriting into colonial government loan issues in the 1890s was extensively discussed by the financial press. The Bank of England and a stockbroker, usually

Mullens Marshall & Co., could always provide definite assistance by making advances to or selling unallotted balances at a reduced price[35] for colonial governments when the loan issues failed to secure the necessary issues by the tender method.[36] Yet the Bank of England replaced the tender method with the underwriting method because it came to consider that it could not support colonial government loan issues to an unlimited extent.[37] It is obvious that the underwriting method had the advantage of securing issue amounts on the market. In 1893 the Queensland government became the first colonial government to adopt underwriting in loan issues.[38] By the turn of the century, a terminology of underwriting took firm root in textbooks on investment,[39] and Lord Nathaniel Meyer Rothschild complained that 'the trouble was largely due to the excessive growth of the practice of underwriting, which made it fatally easy to bring out almost any loan.'[40]

The banks which made a contract for the loan issue nominated stockbrokers who organized underwriters and allotted the bonds. The stockbrokers informally called on various financial institutions in the City and invited them to underwrite at a certain commission. After this preliminary interview, the loan issue banks officially sent the underwriting letter stating the terms of the underwriting: i.e. the names of issuers, the issue amount, the underwriting commission and the responsibilities of the underwriters. The underwriters, in return, informed the loan issue banks of their underwriting amounts with deposits. Sometimes they had their secured amounts sub-underwritten.[41] Usually clearing banks, merchant banks, overseas banks, stockbrokers, discount companies, insurance companies, investment trust companies, merchants and interested individuals (correspondents, partners, staff and large clients) were nominated as underwriters. The scale of underwriting depended upon the strength and range of stockbrokers' market connections.

As shown in chapter 1, less creditworthy governments' loan issues, such as those of South American countries, usually demanded much higher underwriting commissions because of the greater concomitant risks in investment. A normal underwriting commission was between 1½ and 2½ per cent but declined to a 1 per-cent level after the First World War. Even so, underwriters still seem to have secured ample profits with comparatively small risks.[42]

FINANCIAL INSTITUTIONS AND LOAN ISSUES

Since the 'railway mania' during the 1830s, joint-stock banks hated business connected with share transactions.[43] They regarded such business as hazardous for sound banking. By the late nineteenth century, however, financial institutions developed the business organizations – a syndicate and underwriting – which could effectively disperse the concomitant risks of share and loan issues to underwriters. On the basis of the argument mentioned in the earlier part of this chapter, this section will examine how a variety of financial institutions in the City: clearing banks, overseas banks, foreign banks, merchant banks, the Bank of England and stockbrokers, became involved in colonial and foreign government loan issue operations.

Clearing banks

Before the Overend Gurney Crisis (1866), English clearing banks had developed and expanded on the basis of domestic transactions: discounting inland bills and short-term advances. By contrast, the business connected with colonies and foreign countries was mainly dealt with by merchant banks whose extensive correspondent networks played a prime part in their ability to conduct world-wide business. Yet merchant banks did not retain this exclusive position for long. In the latter part of the nineteenth century the London clearing banks, as well as overseas banks and foreign banks, began to encroach on this field.

It was the growth of acceptance business[44] which caused the first major change in the attitude of the London clearing banks towards overseas business.[45] As well as acceptance business, the London clearing banks regarded colonial and foreign loan issue business as another suitable area of activity, but loan issue business tended to lock up their deposits in illiquid investments, unsaleable bonds (mainly foreign ones). C. Gow, the general manager of the London Joint Stock Bank, emphasized that his bank's choice of portfolio investments depended entirely upon 'the essence of negotiability'.[46] It is true that in the 1870s the London Joint Stock Bank had been prohibited, by its byelaws, from investing funds in foreign bonds.[47] W. McKewan, of the London & County Bank, apologized to the committee on foreign loans of 1875 that his bank's role in the Honduras government loan of 1867 had by no means been that of a loan contractor but that of a subscription agent.[48] When the

Capital & Counties Bank was involved in the re-sale of the Japanese government 5 per-cent domestic bonds in 1897, *The Statist* raised the question of whether clearing banks, which received deposits from the public and paid them back on demand, should undertake foreign loan issue business.[49]

Traditional English banking practice hindered clearing banks from entering into loan issue business even as underwriters. Yet Goodhart revised this negative picture of the London clearing banks and in part threw new light upon their security issue business before the First World War, quoting that:

> they [clearing banks] were not only active as dealers in the market, but they had also come to play a major role in the new issue market, as underwriters, and in many cases taking on the main responsibility for the flotation of a new issue. Some of the banks' activity in the market came as a concomitant to their role as underwriters, selling off securities from their portfolios with which they had been stuck at the time of issue. The process of arranging and underwriting new issues was a lucrative one; banks were continually trying to keep up influential connections.[50]

So far very little has been mentioned about how the London clearing banks became involved in colonial and foreign government loan issue business.

The decline of the Crown Agents in colonial government loan business gave a great impetus to other financial institutions in the City. The Crown Agents were heavily involved in financial transactions with colonies, particularly in raising colonial government loans in the 1860s and 1870s. The efficiency of their office attracted loan issue business even from colonies which possessed responsible governments and agents of their own.[51] But in 1880 the Treasury considered that 'the transaction by the Crown Agents of the business of responsible Government Colonies is an arrangement which cannot be permitted to continue.'[52] Thereafter, opportunities for loan issue business for colonies with responsible governments were open wide to clearing banks and the Bank of England, because they had already established transactions in loan issues with these colonies.[53]

From the early nineteenth century, Glyn, Mills & Co.[54] aggressively raised loans to such an extent that Feis misleadingly grouped it among merchant banks.[55] It issued many Canadian government loans as one of the London agents of the Bank of Upper Canada from the 1830s.[56] After the 1880s the London & Westminster Bank undertook many colonial government loan issues for Australia (except for South Australia), Natal and the Cape of Good Hope. In 1876 the London Joint Stock Bank issued to the Quebec government a 5 per-cent loan[57] and, together with the London & Westminster Bank, became involved in Victorian government loan issues in the 1860s and 1870s.[58] Following the turn of the century the London Joint Stock Bank began to arrange the underwriting of colonial government loan issues on a large scale.[59] The Consolidated Bank, a London clearing bank, took up many Tasmanian government loan issues during the 1870s and 1880s, but from 1889 the London & Westminster Bank supplanted it.[60] In 1893 the Union Bank of London tendered a 3 per-cent loan for the Mauritius government and underwrote a New Zealand government 3½ per-cent loan.[61] By degrees the bank broadened its portfolio investments from domestic and colonial securities to foreign ones.[62]

The London clearing banks were also concerned with foreign government loan issues. They did not need to run great risks in foreign government loan issues if loan issues were underwritten fully. Yet foreign government loan issue business seemed to them in general a dangerous area, and the London clearing banks agreed to become loan issuers only when there were particular links, personal or commercial, with the borrowers.[63] As will be seen in chapter 4, there were particularly close personal connections between the Japanese government and Parr's Bank.

It is known that Glyn, Mills & Co. issued Portuguese government loans in the 1820s and 1830s.[64] In 1871 the London Joint Stock Bank undertook the North German Confederation 5 per-cent Treasury bonds issue for £6,000,000, in conjunction with the Royal Seehandlung Society of Berlin (Preussische Seehandlung), as a standard transaction.[65] In the 1880s the City Bank launched a number of Chilean government loan issues as the London agent of the Banco Nacional de Chile.[66] In 1885 the bank agreed to purchase the Chilean government 4½ per-cent loan, which had already been underwritten by a syndicate,[67] and underwrote the Nicaraguan government 6 per-cent loan issue in 1886.[68] From 1909 the London City & Midland Bank made large-scale Russian railway investments.[69] In 1889 the London & South Western Bank dealt with the Salvador government 6 per-cent loan, underwritten by Panmure

Table 2.1 Annual profits of Parr's Bank and Japanese government loan issues 1904, 1905 and 1907

Year	*(1) Parr's Bank's commissions earned from Japanese government loan issues (£000)*	*(2) Total annual gross profits (£000)*	*(3) (1)/(2) (%)*
1904	92	741	12.4
1905	210	770	27.3
1907	49	819	6.0

Sources: (1) WBA, D2469;
(2) T.E. Gregory, *The Westminster Bank through a Century* (1936), ii, 322–3.
Note: (3)=(1)/(2) × 100.

Gordon, Hill & Co.'s syndicate.[70] In 1895 the bank underwrote the Chinese government 4 per-cent war indemnity loan.[71]

Parr's Bank was particularly inclined towards foreign government loan issues. The bank was set up as a country bank at Warrington, and became a London clearing bank in 1891. Absorbing the Alliance Bank in 1892 and the Consolidated Bank in 1896, Parr's Bank paid much attention to foreign government loan issue business as well as acceptance business in Liverpool. In 1897 and 1903 the bank played a major role in effecting the Serbian government's 4 per-cent and 5 per-cent loan issues.[72] After 1899 Parr's Bank was intimately connected with many of the Japanese government loan issues, as will be discussed in Part II.

It is difficult to trace fully the exact amount of loan issue commissions in clearing banks' accounts.[73] Table 2.1 sets out Parr's Bank's commissions of 1904, 1905 and 1907 earned from the Japanese government loan issues and their proportion to the total annual gross profits, a fairly high one during 1904 and 1905.

The main reason for the London clearing banks increasing colonial and foreign government loan issue business in the 1890s was probably a desire to seek new businesses to compensate for a decline in their formerly lucrative activities of discounting inland bills and making advances to domestic industries.[74] Despite the fact that this new strategy jeopardized the liquidity of their resources, the extent of the risks which the London clearing banks ran in foreign loan issue business was not great because they always, in conjunction with stockbrokers, organized underwriting syndicates for the loan issues which they undertook.

Overseas banks

Before the Second World War there was an overall category of overseas banks which meant banks based in the British Empire, and contemporary writers did not make any distinction between those which raised equity and had their boards in a particular part of the British Empire (outside Britain), and those in Britain.[75] In this study the term 'overseas banks' means the overall category.

The names of overseas banks indicated their geographical relations, such as the Hongkong Bank with the Far East, the Bank of Montreal with Canada and the National Bank of Australasia with Australia. Their roles covered ordinary banking business (issuing bank notes, advancing and discounting bills), providing credit to international trade (acceptance and foreign exchange) and issuing securities.[76] Their loan issue business deserves more serious attention. Loan issue business was of significant importance in the areas with which some of the overseas banks were concerned. There was a regional distribution in the foreign government loan issues which the overseas banks undertook. They arranged loan issues mainly for the Far East, Persia and South America.[77]

The Oriental Bank played a leading role in Chinese and Japanese government loan issue business in the 1860s and 1870s, but went bankrupt in 1884.[78] The Hongkong Bank and the Chartered Bank were also active in making many loan issues for China, Japan and Siam as regular business. Because of some reluctance towards foreign loan issues on the part of the Chartered Bank,[79] after the turn of the century the Hongkong Bank carried out most of the Chinese government loan issues, facing no formidable competitor. It was more from a political viewpoint that the Hongkong Bank handled many Chinese government loan issues, its aim being to ensure the success of Britain's commercial interests in China.[80] As a consequence of the diplomatic conflict with other European powers in China, strong ties formed between the Hongkong Bank and the British Foreign Office. In 1898 the British Treasury, despite the Hongkong Bank's application,[81] refused to guarantee the Chinese government war indemnity loan,[82] but directed the Bank of England to accept an inscription of the bonds.[83] The Hongkong Bank's brilliant success in many foreign government loan issues for Far Eastern countries was ascribed partly to its close liaison with both the British Foreign Office and the foreign governments of those countries where the bank operated, and partly to the co-operation with the powerful stockbroker Panmure Gordon & Co. in loan issues.[84] Their co-operation in many Japanese government loan issues will be seen in Part II.

In Persia the Imperial Bank of Persia was invariably regarded as a guardian of Britain's commercial interests. In 1892 and 1911, it arranged two Persian government loans in London.[85] The bank clung to these operations and drew unusual assistance from the British government. After the Russian loan of 1901 to Persia, the British government came to give direct support to the Imperial Bank. The bank acted as 'the medium through which loans were passed' to the Persian government in 1903: an agreement that the Indian government was to lend up to £500,000 to the bank and that the bank was to lend this money to the Persian government, was concluded between the British government and the Imperial Bank of Persia.[86] From the loan issue negotiations in 1911 there is the more telling evidence of an officer at the British Foreign Office, showing favour to the bank: 'H.M. Government are bound to support [the] Imperial Bank [of Persia] in preference to other houses.'[87]

For South American countries, especially Argentina, Chile and Brazil, the eminent London merchant banks initially raised most of the loans, although the Oriental Bank was concerned with several Chilean government loan issues in the early 1870s. The London & River Plate Bank handled two Argentinian government loan issues in 1892 and 1903. In 1908 the London Bank of Mexico & South America issued the Salvador government 6 per-cent loan. In 1909 the Anglo-South American Bank undertook the Nicaraguan government 6 per-cent loan issue. But the activities of the overseas banks in this field were quite small in proportion to those of the merchant banks.

Keen competition with influential merchant banks, however, often forced overseas banks to switch their main business objectives to smaller operations, that is to say, Treasury bill and provincial government loan issues. The Bank of Tarapacá & London floated Chilean government Treasury bills in 1898[88] and 1902.[89] The London & Brazilian Bank issued a Pará government loan in 1901[90] and in 1904 raised a loan for the São Paulo government. The bank also arranged Bahia government loan issues in 1905 and 1910.[91]

In the 1860s and 1870s, the Bank of New South Wales, the National

Bank of Australasia and the Union Bank of Australia were involved in Australian government loan issues in London,[92] although most of them (except for South Australia) came to be dealt with by the Bank of England and the London & Westminster Bank after the 1880s. The Bank of Adelaide undertook many South Australian government loan issues. The Bank of Montreal acted as a loan issuer for the Canadian government.

Besides the income derived from foreign exchange business, loan issue commissions were one of the main earning sources for overseas banks. In an extreme case, the Hongkong Bank's profit from the Chinese government war indemnity loan issues of 1896 and 1898 reached around £130,000[93] and £220,971[94] respectively, which accounted for 22.0 per cent and 15.3 per cent respectively of its annual net earnings (deducting various expenses).[95] However, loan issue commissions were not always so remunerative to overseas banks as the Hongkong Bank's war indemnity loan issues. The Bank of New South Wales complained of 'the miserable commission' (¼ per cent) when it was involved in the Victorian government 4 per-cent loan issue in 1876;[96] in 1902 the Bank of Tarapacá & Argentina placed the Chilean government Treasury bills only with the £2,500 net profit (½ per cent of the issue amount).[97]

Overseas banks had wide branch networks spread over the world, but their loan issue activities for colonies (except for South Australia and Canada) and South America were limited. In these areas, well-defined financial channels had been formed between governments and particular financiers before the overseas banks embarked upon loan issue business. Merchant banks and banks with specific connections, such as the Bank of England and the London & Westminster Bank, had taken a firm grip on the business. On the other hand, in the Far East and Persia there was no formidable competitor to the overseas banks.

Foreign banks

Contemporaries defined foreign banks as the banks based outside the British Empire. In order to distinguish these banks from those based in the British Empire, this classification is adopted in this study. There were an increased number of foreign banks' branches in London between 1890 and 1895; accordingly they accepted large deposits and exerted more influence on the market.[98] In the 1890s the internationalization of the money market proceeded rapidly and

London became the largest financial centre for the settlement of trade bills and foreign borrowings.[99]

Foreign banks provided material assistance to their home countries' financial operations in London. There was 'so large a share of this [foreign securities] investment business done by the foreign branch banks.'[100] Keen competition between foreign banks and British banks (including clearing banks, overseas banks and merchant banks) occurred in loan issue business. In the Danish government 3 per-cent loan issue of 1894, Hambros, a London merchant bank and the loan issuer in London, did not authorize the Crédit Lyonnais's London branch as a loan issuer, even though the loan issue was arranged by the Crédit Lyonnais's head office.[101] On another occasion, however, foreign banks harmoniously collaborated with British banks as did the Yokohama Specie Bank and the Industrial Bank in Japanese loan issues in London.

Reputable French banks repeatedly made simultaneous loan issues in London and Paris. They were the earliest arrivals among foreign banks on the London money market. First, large banques de dépôts opened London branches: in 1865 the Comptoir National d'Escompte; in 1872 the Société Générale; in 1873 the Crédit Lyonnais,[102] and began to run their business in London. Subsequently, banques d'affaires[103] and banques coloniales came to issue foreign government loans on the London capital market.

German Kreditbanken also exercised great financial power in the London capital market. This obviously coincided with Germany's aggressive expansionist policy. The Deutsche Bank was founded in March 1870 and defined its business object as 'in particular to promote and facilitate trade relations between Germany, other European countries and overseas markets.'[104] The bank opened its London branch in 1873.[105] This branch, often simultaneously in Germany, arranged many loan issues to Germany and its dependencies. Other German banks also opened London branches: the Dresdner Bank in 1895 and the Disconto-Gesellschaft in 1899.[106]

A combination of British and French capital produced the Imperial Ottoman Bank in 1863.[107] Although the head office was registered in Constantinople, the bank's character was obviously an Anglo-French bank as its administration was governed by the two committees in London and Paris. The Imperial Ottoman Bank was authorized by the Turkish government (the Ottoman Empire) as the state bank, whose affairs were supervized by the government's commission.[108] Because

Table 2.2 Main earning sources of the Yokohama Specie Bank 1899 and 1901–1906

Earning	*1899*	*1901*	*1902*	*1903*	*1904*	*1905*	*1906*
From foreign exchange	6,852	4,960	5,349	6,280	6,261	7,352	9,772
(%)	(50)	(44)	(43)	(49)	(47)	(41)	(44)
From commission	433	149	238	232	1,041	1,923	1,324
(%)	(3)	(1)	(2)	(2)	(8)	(11)	(6)
Total earning	13,661	11,248	12,519	12,779	13,451	17,733	22,125
(%)	(100)	(100)	(100)	(100)	(100)	(100)	(100)

Source: Yokohama Specie Bank, *Yokohama Shōkin Ginkōshi Shiryō (History of the Yokohama Specie Bank)*, 4 (*Shiryō*) (Yokohama, 1920 reprinted 1976).
Notes: ¥000 (¥1=2s. ½d.);
No data for 1900.

of these relations, the Imperial Ottoman Bank was deeply involved in the Turkish government's finance, especially the reorganization of the national debt. Paris, since the loan issue in 1863, became a prime lender to Turkey but the Imperial Ottoman Bank introduced many Turkish government loan issues to London simultaneously.

The Russian Bank for Foreign Trade, the Swiss Bankverein and the Yokohama Specie Bank always played a very significant part in loan issues in London for their home countries. The Russian Bank for Foreign Trade opened a London branch in 1885.[109] The Yokohama Specie Bank was established in 1879 and opened the London branch as early as 1881.[110] In most of the Japanese government foreign loan issues after 1899, the Yokohama Specie Bank, without exception, co-operated with two major British banks, Parr's Bank and the Hongkong Bank. This combination of the loan issue banks including Panmure Gordon & Co., a stockbroker, became the backbone of Japanese government financial operations in London. Table 2.2 calculates the earning sources of the Yokohama Specie Bank. The proportion of the commission (including the loan issue commission) compared to the total earnings was not significant but was higher in the years when the bank undertook the Japanese government loan issues (1899, 1902, 1904 and 1905), although with a time lag.

Merchant banks

Merchant banks acted principally as acceptance and issue houses.

Their power and influence eventually raised London to being the world's largest financial centre in the nineteenth century. The relationship between merchant banks' loan issue business and their earning sources has never received a satisfactory explanation and will be considered here.

It is difficult to divide the amount of any loan issue among different types of co-issuers. Several scholars[111] have relied upon Brown's statistics on Britain's overseas new issues,[112] although he mentioned nothing about how to aggregate the amounts of the different types of co-issuers. Neither did Simon provide alternative statistics on foreign loan issues classified by financial institution.[113] Brown emphasized the drop in the merchant banks' proportion of the new overseas issues, from 43.7 per cent in the period 1885–1889 to 32.7 per cent in 1905–1909; in contrast with this, both the 'joint-stock banks' (clearing banks) and overseas banks, especially after the late 1890s, gained the share lost by the merchant banks. De Cecco consistently heralded 'the swan song of the power of the Bank of England and of the merchant banks'[114] after the Baring Crisis, by pointing to the rapid growth of clearing banks backed by large amounts of public deposits.[115]

Table 2.3 classifies foreign government loan issues by financial institution, showing the combination of co-issuers. According to this table, the share of merchant banks in the total foreign government loan issues dropped sharply after 1895: from 94 per cent in 1885–1889 to 39 per cent in 1905–1909. However, including the other types of loan issues in which merchant banks were concerned as one of the co-issuers, the share of merchant banks slightly recovered. It is true that after 1890 overseas banks, foreign banks and the London clearing banks began to issue many foreign government loans, and as a result merchant banks lost their shares on the loan issue market. Yet the merchant banks' key position on the loan issue market, especially in underwriting and linking one market with others in simultaneous loan issues, was firmly retained. Their roles in loan issue operations became more specialized. Merchant banks' experience and good sources of business information still made them significantly attractive to many foreign borrowers.[116]

Unlike clearing banks and overseas banks (public deposit banks), capital sources for merchant banks organized in a partnership were circumscribed by partners' capital and borrowing. This limitation often undermined their financial position. Partners' capital was

Table 2.3 Foreign government loan issues in London 1870–1913 (by financial institution)
(£000; net proceeds)
(per cent)

Combination of financial institutions	*1870–74*	*1875–79*	*1880–84*	*1885–89*	*1890–94*	*1895–99*	*1900–04*	*1905–09*	*1910–13*
Merchant bank	672173 (90)	244264 (77)	106112 (58)	231060 (94)	139282 (77)	79599 (45)	42051 (36)	42856 (39)	53001 (61)
Merchant bank Clearing bank						4432 (3)		1665 (2)	2217 (2)
Merchant bank Foreign bank	26960 (4)				990 (0)	3954 (2)	3756 (3)	6459 (6)	
Merchant bank Overseas bank							1273 (1)	860 (1)	
Merchant bank Clearing bank Foreign bank						3484 (2)			
Merchant bank Foreign bank Overseas bank							5104 (4)		
Merchant bank Clearing bank Foreign bank Overseas bank								17293 (15)	
Sub-total	(94)	(77)	(58)	(94)	(77)	(52)	(44)	(63)	(63)
Clearing bank	16438 (2)	2500 (1)	29500 (16)	4485 (2)	21694 (12)	6205 (4)	3140 (3)	164 (0)	0 (0)
Clearing bank Foreign bank								2841 (3)	
Clearing bank Foreign bank Overseas bank						13451 (8)	10105 (9)	22500 (20)	10450 (12)
Foreign bank	12029 (1)	31756 (10)	32067 (18)	7600 (3)	8586 (5)	21759 (12)	45786 (40)		
Foreign bank Overseas bank								478 (0)	
Overseas bank	4359 (1)	4126 (1)	100 (0)	2210 (1)	3438 (2)	34155 (19)	4604 (4)	10415 (9)	10504 (12)
Overseas bank Trust company									4750 (5)
Overseas bank Indefinite						2231 (1)			
Trust company				619 (0)					486 (1)
Government	16164 (2)	26515 (8)	15327 (8)		2035 (1)				
Indefinite		9905 (3)			5168 (3)	6148 (4)		5229 (5)	6008 (7)
Total	748123 (100)	319066 (100)	183106 (100)	245974 (100)	181193 (100)	175418 (100)	115819 (100)	110760 (100)	87416 (100)

Source: Appendix A.
Notes: Net proceeds were calculated as follows:
(net proceeds)=(total loan issue amounts) × (London issue prices, otherwise 100)/100;
The differences of the total with Table 1.1 are due to figures less than one thousand;
These amounts do not mean actual capital transfers from the London capital market.

the most reliable source of funding for merchant banks. It goes without saying that substantial capital would help to ensure the merchant banks' financial stability in business. In the 1880s Antony Gibbs, for example, suffered greatly from a lack of partners' capital resulting from both an excess of Australian investments and several eminent partners' withdrawal from the business.[117] Brown Shipley's business was also frequently upset by the retired partners' withdrawal of capital.[118] Merchant banks, in consequence, were subject to capital fluctuations effected by partners' withdrawal. This capital uncertainty often caused serious management problems. In an extreme case, the precariousness of the capital structure actually threatened a firm's existence.[119]

Table 2.4 compares the capital size of the various financial institutions: merchant banks; clearing banks; overseas banks; French banques de dépôts; French banques d'affaires; German Kreditbanken. With the exception of the merchant banks, the others were all joint-stock deposit banks. Many of the London clearing banks started from small country banks, whose capital size was much smaller than that of the eminent contemporary merchant banks, but, in the course of amalgamation, rapidly increased. On the other hand, most of the merchant banks carried out business with small capital, especially compared with the banks on the Continent which would take up security issue business, because merchant banks were organized as partnerships. As far as capital size was concerned, merchant banks were in a vulnerable financial position, their most important assets being their reputations and connections.[120] These well complemented lack of their capital size. However, merchant banks like Kleinworts and Brown Shipley specialized in acceptance business and enlarged their capital size. After 1910 they reached a capital figure almost equivalent to that of the London clearing banks and the banques d'affaires.

Merchant banks specialized in the businesses which stemmed mainly from their own historical backgrounds. For instance, from the late nineteenth century Kleinworts were seldom involved in security issues and concentrated on acceptance business.[121] R. Benson III, after his father's bankruptcy in 1875, rebuilt the firm (R. Benson & Co.) with small capital for carrying out retailing bonds and shares.[122] M. Samuel & Co. was engaged largely in merchant activities for Far Eastern countries.

Not all the merchant banks, therefore, were able to undertake foreign loan issues and the risks involved. Before the advent of

Table 2.4 Comparison of capital size of various financial institutions 1865–1910 (£000)

	1865	*1870*	*1875*	*1880*	*1885*	*1890*	*1895*	*1900*	*1905*	*1910*
Merchant Bank										
Baring Bros	–	–	–	–	–	1,000	*1891 1,025	1,025	1,025	1,025
Benson	–	–	–	–	–	265	60	117	192	198
Brown Shipley	–	–	1,270	1,196	1,106	1,399	1,276	–	–	–
Gibbs	–	–	–	–	419	1,060	543	420	716	919
Hambros	542	647	634	720	959	1,036	962	1,154	1,292	–
Kleinworts	654	914	845	759	822	892	1,174	1,718	2,330	3,419
J.S. Morgan	*1868 471	655	1,461	2,331	2,903	1,773	2,188	2,261	1,722	1,020
Schröder	655	891	1,686	1,423	672	1,149	1,174	1,435	*1901 1,979	2,530
Clearing Bank										
Parr's Bank	100	150	392	492	560	600	1,000	1,464	1,709	2,205
Westminster Bank	1,000	2,000	2,000	2,399	2,800	2,800	2,800	2,800	2,800	3,500
Overseas Bank										
Hongkong Bank	560	900	1,130	1,130	1,390	1,590	1,600	1,600	1,600	1,360
Banque de Dépôts										
Crédit Lyonnais	792	–	*1874 1,979	3,958	7,917	7,917	7,917	9,896	9,896	9,896
Société Générale	4,750	4,750	4,750	4,750	4,750	4,750	4,750	6,333	9,896	15,883
Banque d'Affaires										
Banques de Paris	2,454	2,454	2,454	2,454	2,454	2,454	2,454	2,454	2,454	2,969
Union Parisienne	–	–	–	–	–	–	–	–	2,375	2,375
Kreditbank										
Deutsche Bank	–	*1871 738	2,213	2,213	2,950	3,688	4,425	7,375	8,850	9,833
Disconto-Gesellschaft	1,672	1,672	2,950	2,950	2,950	3,688	5,654	6,392	8,358	8,358

Sources: *The Economist*, annually; K. Burk, *Morgan Grenfell 1838–1988* (1989), appendices ii and iii; R. Roberts, *Schroders* (1992), appendix IV(i); E. Baldy, *Les banques d'affaires en France depuis 1900* (Paris, 1922), annexes 1; E. Kaufmann, *La Banque en France* (Paris, 1914), tableaux; A. Bosenick, *Neudeutsche gemischte Bankwirtschaft* (Munich and Berlin, 1912), Anlage XVI Tabelle 1; BCA, Balance Sheets; AGA, Ms.11,042/1 and Ms.11,064/1; HA, Ms.19.033/17–29.

Notes: – implies no information; * the nearest year;
Rates of exchange (Fr1=9½d.; DM1=11⅘d.).

underwriting in the City, only those merchant banks with sufficient resources could run security issue business by purchasing all or some of the issue at their own risk. It is a well-known fact that the larger and long-standing merchant banks, such as Baring Brothers, the London Rothschilds and Hambros, frequently arranged many foreign government loan issues.

However, it is difficult to state in general to what extent loan issues contributed to merchant banks' earnings, for they covered a wide range of business and every merchant bank had its own character. In addition, their accounting figures cannot be formulated and standardized. It is merely apparent that loan issue commissions were one of the important earning sources for some of them. Fortunately the earning sources of several merchant banks can be deduced. In the case of J.S. Morgan Co. the gross earnings from security issues were rather irregular. The security transactions occupied a much larger proportion in the annual gross earnings but frequently caused heavy losses.[123]

Bank of England

It was clear that colonial governments could, from time to time, draw direct financial assistance from the British government. Parliament, given the recommendation of the Treasury, agreed to provide financial aid to colonies. The total amount of government funds disbursed in direct support of dependent colonies was £99,411 in 1879, but by 1900 had risen to ten times that sum.[124]

In comparison with foreign governments, colonial governments could float loans on the London capital market more easily. Certain financial institutions in the City, notably the Crown Agents, the Bank of England, and specific banks and stockbrokers with colonial connections, invariably looked after loan issues for colonial governments,[125] as previously stated.

In the late 1860s, the Bank of England regarded colonial government loan business as safe and well qualified. It was in 1866 that the Bank of England agreed to take the New Zealand government 6 per-cent bonds.[126] In 1876 the bank made arrangements for the management of the public debts for the Queensland government[127] and in 1878 for the first time undertook the New Zealand government 5 per-cent loan issue for £3,500,000.[128] Thereafter, at the Bank of England 'the era of colonial management has fairly opened.'[129] The

Bank of England undertook colonial loan issues for the Indian, New Zealand, Queensland, New South Wales (before 1902) and Transvaal governments. Colonial governments, for their part, could obviously derive an advantage from counting upon the Bank of England for their loan issue operations.[130] In addition, colonial government stocks inscribed at the Bank of England became favourable investment objects especially for safe investors.[131]

The Bank of England, in collaboration with Mullens Marshall & Co., a stockbroker, nicknamed 'Bank's Brother', implemented most of the colonial government loan issues by the tender method.[132] It was an established practice for the bank that a stockbroker actually made the necessary arrangements for loan issues on the market.

There were direct loan issue negotiations between the Bank of England and colonial governments. At first, an agent general for a colonial government sounded out market conditions at the bank when it wished to issue a new loan; the Bank of England, in conjunction with stockbrokers, reported to the agent general the assessment of the proposed loan issue and suggested a possible way. In the negotiations of the New South Wales government loan of 1891, W. Lidderdale, the governor of the Bank of England, informed S. Samuel, the agent general, that the intended loan could be placed privately among financial houses, but only at a much lower issue price than the current quotation prices of existing New South Wales government bonds because of the unfavourable market conditions for new loan issues.[133]

In 1892 the bank was deeply concerned with the Queensland government 3½ per cent loan issue. Originally this loan for £2,500,000 (the first issue) had been offered by a tender on the market at the minimum price of 94 per cent in 1891, but subsequently the unsubscribed balance was taken up again at 92 ¼ per cent.[134] Although Lidderdale was of the firm opinion that the Bank of England should not support colonial government loan issues to an unlimited extent nor even give any assistance unless the public accepted the loan,[135] Mullens Marshall & Co., on the terms of the agreement, urged the bank through the agent general to take some of the unsubscribed portion when the loan had been tendered on the market and only a small portion had been subscribed by the public.[136] By the end of the nineteenth century, however, the Bank of England had established the rules according to which it handled these government loan issues.[137]

The Bank of England never got involved directly in foreign government loan issues, as shall be seen in chapters 4 and 5. Under the guidance of the Treasury it only admitted to inscribe the stocks of diplomatically important foreign governments.

Stockbrokers

The important role of stockbrokers in loan issue operations has not been sufficiently discussed and is often underrated. Charles Duguid's famous textbook on the stock exchange mentioned the two important activities of stockbrokers related to loan issues: underwriting and broking.[138] Firstly, their activities were concerned with the broking of issued bonds. In order to encourage investors' demand for the bonds, stockbrokers supplied investment information to customers by circulars and information sheets.[139] More directly, stockbrokers sent the prospectuses with the stamped application forms and induced customers to purchase the issued bonds; they said we 'have pleasure in endeavouring to secure an allotment.'[140] Secondly, stockbrokers underwrote loan issues. The extent of their involvement in underwriting was varied, according to their position in loan issue operations. When stockbrokers, in collaboration with loan issue banks, arranged the loan issue, they played a positive role in organizing the underwriting and invited financial institutions to it.[141] Otherwise, they participated as commission-takers.

Large and pre-eminent stockbrokers often acted as *de facto* loan issuers, especially when the Bank of England, the Crown Agents and banks with little experience of loan issue business undertook loan issues. Although the fragmented structure of the London capital market often symbolized its 'deficiencies', compared with the German universal banking system,[142] stockbrokers inside the London capital market played a co-ordinated and integrated role in some of the loan issues. Schilling was the first to pay necessary attention to this aspect of stockbrokers' activities in colonial government loan issues.[143] Specific stockbrokers established direct and close relations with colonial governments' loan issues in London.[144] In these cases, the stockbrokers, rather than the loan issue banks, made preparations for loan issues on the market (underwriting and broking), and the loan issue banks acted simply as subscription agents because the loan issue banks were not experts in that business.

Three eminent stockbrokers: R. Nivison & Co., J.& A. Scrimgeour

& Co. and Mullens Marshall & Co., undertook colonial government loan issues almost as the sole operators. There were definite business boundaries among them: for colonies with responsible governments R. Nivison & Co. arranged loan issues; for the crown colonies J. & A. Scrimgeour & Co. and Mullens Marshall & Co. acted as the stockbrokers; Mullens Marshall & Co. usually organized loan issues which the Bank of England undertook.[145] In these loan issues, the loan issue banks including the Crown Agents put all the necessary arrangements of the loan issues into the hands of these stockbrokers.

J.A. Mullens, a partner of Mullens Marshall & Co., explained their roles in loan issues with the Crown Agents. J. & A. Scrimgeour & Co., the main stockbrokers of the Crown Agents,[146] 'generally go to the Crown Agents and see them, and then we discuss it more or less informally together; they [the Crown Agents] come down to our office and the thing [the loan issue] is settled.'[147] They, the financial experts to the Crown Agents,[148] decided the details of new loan issues: i.e. the issues of prospectuses, issue prices, the time of issues and so on.[149]

R. Nivison & Co., with 'its detailed knowledge of the sources of demand for Australia's government loans',[150] placed many loans in the London capital market. The company maintained direct and close relations with the Australian and Canadian governments. The London & Westminster Bank invariably employed R. Nivison & Co. as its stockbroker for colonial government loan issues.[151] The company also co-operated with the Bank of Adelaide for South Australian government loan issues and the Bank of Montreal for Canadian government loan issues.

In this way, the important role of stockbrokers as the organizers of underwriting, the core of a loan issue on the London capital market,[152] was gradually enhanced in many colonial government loan issues. They could find the demand for the underwriting and broking of newly-issued bonds on the market. 'London broking firms were the key to arranging finance'[153] for colonies.

Panmure Gordon & Co. floated many Japanese government loans on the London capital market. Whenever the Hongkong Bank, Parr's Bank and the Yokohama Specie Bank took up them, Panmure Gordon & Co. arranged the necessary things for loan issues because these loan issue banks (the banks with Far Eastern and Japanese connections) were not experts in loan issue business.[154] Panmure Gordon & Co.'s substantial role especially in the underwriting of Japanese government loan issues will be seen in Part II. However, it is an interesting fact that Harry Panmure Gordon, the founder of the company, had joined J. & A. Scrimgeour & Co., which was heavily involved in colonial government loan issues, as a junior partner in the 1860s.[155]

PART II
Japanese Government Loan Issues on the London Capital Market

Table 3.1 Total amounts of Japanese government loan issues 1870–1913

Loan issue place	*Nominal amount (£000)*	*(%)*	*Net amount (£000)*	*(%)*
London	87,893	48.4	82,106	48.6
New York	39,500	21.7	35,755	21.2
Germany	13,000	7.2	11,700	6.9
Paris	41,313	22.7	39,254	23.3
Total	181,706	100.0	168,815	100.0

Source: These sources will be referred to in chapters 3 to 7.
Notes: The issue places in Germany included Hamburg and Berlin;
The difference of £3,000 in the net amounts between Table 1.1 and Table 3.1 is due to the rate of exchange in the bond resale of 1897 (nominal amount £4,385,000 – appendix A and Table 1.1; nominal amount £4,389,000 – appendix B).

Table 3.1 shows the total loan issue amounts (nominal and net) of Japanese government foreign loan issues in London, New York, Germany (Hamburg and Berlin) and Paris, in the period 1870 to 1913, and appendix B their terms: rates of interest, issue amounts, issue prices (to the public), borrowing periods, objects and loan issuers. The following chapters 3 to 7 will discuss these financial operations mainly on the London capital market. Before mentioning details of the individual loan issues, their brief outline can be followed from these tables.

3

Early Loan Issues

The diplomatic representative makes speeches in a language utterly unknown to his fellow-guests. The financier, not the better for his dinner, confides in English equally unintelligible to the Finance Minister's relative that the loan, if successful, will be entirely owing to his – the financier's – abilities; that if unsuccessful, failure will only be attributable to the rotten and bankrupt state of the borrowing country. The relative and the diplomatic representative retire home perfectly satisfied with their relations with British finance, and calculating how many loans the Finance Minister can bring out before the unhallowed cabals of his opponents have forced His Excellency into resignation or exile.

Sir Henry Drummond-Wolff, *Rambling Recollections*

As a result of Japan's rapid industrialization after the Meiji Restoration (1868), substantial funds were required for the development of social institutions and infrastructures. The Tokugawa Shogunate government (*Bakufu*) and some feudal clans (*Han*) had previously borrowed money from foreign banks and merchant houses in Japan.[1] Yet the idea of a public loan was totally unfamiliar in Japan.

This chapter will examine the early Japanese government foreign loan issues in 1870 and 1873, the purposes of which were railway construction and the redemption of pensions for the old feudal knight class (*Samurai*). In the 1870s, however, Japan was still an unknown country to British public investors, without a sound borrowing record. British financial journalists regarded these Japanese bonds as almost as unreliable as Turkish and Egyptian bonds. Even in the 1890s, one British banker confessed that 'very shrewd people whom I know have bought Japanese stock [the 7 per-cent loan of 1873] to return 4⅞ per cent.'[2]

NINE PER-CENT LOAN ISSUE IN 1870

In 1870, just two years after the Meiji Restoration, the Japanese government first foreign loan issue was launched. This year was conspicuous for the number of foreign loan issues on the London capital market. The *Bankers' Magazine* described it as 'the epoch of foreign loans'.[3] Lowering of bank rate to 2½ per cent had encouraged foreign government loan issues, and under these rather unusually active circumstances financial journalists warned public investors against the dangers of highly remunerative foreign loans, nearly a 10 or 12 per-cent annual rate of interest.[4] Landes pointed out the 'lure of fabulous interest even more than the needs of trade that attracted British promoters and investors.'[5] Obviously the Japanese government 9 per-cent loan of 1870 was felt to be in this high-risk, high-return loan category.

In order to foster industrialization the new Meiji government, using Western capital and techniques, made great efforts to develop infrastructures as rapidly as possible. The impetus for railway construction in Japan came from A.L.C. Portman, the US minister in Japan (Chargé d'Affaires, 1865–1866). The Tokugawa Shogunate government had given him a railway building license in 1867, but the Meiji government had not recognized it.[6] At that time there were a number of proposals including British, French and American ones for railway construction.[7] H.S. Parkes, the British minister to Japan, therefore, advised the Japanese government to carry out the project with its own resources.[8] Parkes was doing his best to remove the American influence over the railway construction. In contrast with France, which bolstered the Tokugawa Shogunate government, Britain maintained intimate relations with the new Meiji government.

Horatio Nelson Lay,[9] a leading figure in the Japanese government loan issue of 1870, was very knowledgeable about China.[10] Initially he had acted as a supernumerary interpreter of the British government in China and from 1859 to 1863 had been the Inspector General of the Chinese Maritime Customs. He was one of the principals in the development of a European–Chinese naval force: the Lay–Osborn Flotilla.[11]

It was in about 1862 that Lay had the idea of a loan issue for the Chinese government which he brought to the Oriental Bank.[12] On his return to England, Lay collaborated with associates, directors of the Consolidated Bank, a manager of the Telegraph Construction & Maintenance Co. and a director of Fairbairn Engineering Co., to conduct mercantile business in China.[13] He became a speculator concerned with Chinese affairs and aimed to build railway telegraphs in China.[14] Lay soon saw the possibility of raising a Chinese government loan for the building of railway telegraphs and considered that close relations with Morrison Dillon & Co. and the Consolidated Bank could probably help him to raise the required money.[15] In 1869 Lay left for China to complete this project with the Chinese government, but it showed no interest.[16]

Lay then switched his attention to Japan as he had heard that the newly-established Japanese government (the Meiji government) needed a large amount of money for industrialization. Lay and his business partners held an optimistic view of Japanese investment business[17] and regarded it as 'a probable field for work'.[18]

In July 1869 Lay arrived in Japan. He was not confident of raising money for the Japanese government from his personal sources, and considered it indispensable to work with the Oriental Bank.[19] The bank had secured firm business opportunities in Japan since 1860, the year of the opening of the Yokohama branch, and in 1896 had been concerned with the establishment of the Japanese Mint.[20] Lay immediately explained to Parkes his plan of offering money to the Japanese government. Even to Parkes, Lay always pretended to be a representative of large British capital interests, asserting he had been sent to offer money to China and Japan.[21] E. Satow, an officer at the British Legation in Japan, arranged a meeting between Lay and S. Ōkuma, the vice-minister of home affairs (*Minbu Taiho*).[22]

In September 1869 Lay officially proposed the provision of £2 or £3 million to the Japanese government.[23] He also drew up many other ambitious business projects in Japan. Writing to T. Fairbairn he observed:

> We should not get only one loan but several loans and much business besides which if done thoroughly will quite ensure us the monopoly as the agents of the Japanese Government and we should in time literally 'coin money'. The field is here vast and capable of boundless development.[24]

Lay would have been one of the British pioneers in Japanese business if these projects had been successful.

In November 1869 Lay entered into negotiations with the Japanese government, dealing in particular with Ōkuma and H. Itō, the vice-minister of finance (*Ōkura Shōyu*).[25] The Japanese government intended to construct railways using money borrowed from Lay. Estimating the cost of the railway construction between Tokyo, Yokohama, Tsuruga and Hyōgo at approximately £3 million, Lay offered to raise £1 million of this amount from his friends in England on the security of the government's customs revenues and receipts from these railways. He also proposed that the Japanese government should leave all the necessary management of the railway construction in Lay's charge.[26]

Finally, in December 1869 the Japanese government agreed to make a loan contract with Lay on the following terms:[27]

(i) The Japanese government should raise £ million 'by a loan of that amount from any person or persons who may be willing to advance' at a 12 per-cent annual rate of interest repayable over 12 years.
(ii) The Japanese government should appoint Lay as the commissioner for raising and negotiating the loan.
(iii) The Japanese government should offer Lay all the customs revenues and net receipts of the railways constructed as the security of the loan.
(iv) The Japanese government should appoint Lay as its agent for buying materials for the railways.

It is obvious that this contract placed Lay 'in the double position of a contractor for the loan and a commissioner to raise the sum for the Japanese government.'[28] Subsequently, his intricate position would cause a serious difference between Lay and the Japanese government in understanding the character of the loan issue. It was almost beyond the Japanese government's understanding that Lay conceived a plan of 'putting this loan on the market',[29] that is to say, a public loan issued by subscriptions on the market rather than a private borrowing from his friends.

In March 1870 Lay returned to England and began to arrange the borrowing. Yet, as it happened, he was unable to count upon either the Consolidated Bank or Morrison Dillon & Co. as sources for the required money. Lay's project to borrow money on behalf of the Japanese government did not attract them. Lay then pursued the money by a public loan and looked for a financier in the City who was favourably disposed to the idea. He approached the London Rothschilds and Thomson, Bonar & Co., but these prominent merchant banks all declined to handle the matter.[30] The reputation of the new Japanese government was doubtful in British financial circles.

Lay and his partners became sceptical about the success of the intended loan issue on the market. As a consequence, some of them withdrew from the operation and Lay approached E. Erlanger, a Paris-based merchant banker. On 31 March 1870 Erlanger agreed to undertake the Japanese government loan for £1 million on the condition of being 'entitled to 3/8ths of the financial profits and 1/4th of the other profits of the combination' after deducting £50,000.[31] It is clear from this contract that Erlanger's share of the profit was enormous.

Yet Lay and Erlanger came to doubt the success of the loan issue and Erlanger wished to be free of his responsibility.[32] Lay, therefore, was forced to revise the previous contract and to ensure Erlanger more of the profit as follows:[33]

(i) Erlanger should receive £50,000 and one half of all profits arising from Lay's engagement with the Japanese government.
(ii) Erlanger and Lay should equally share all profits and losses from all future transactions in Japan.

On 23 April 1870 Erlanger issued a prospectus for the Japanese government 9 per-cent loan for £1 million at 98 per cent for 13 years.[34] J. Henry Schröder & Co., a London merchant bank, played a limited role in this loan issue. In response to Erlanger's proposal, the firm acted as the loan issuer at a 1 per-cent commission.[35] There is no clear explanation as to why Erlanger avoided producing this loan issue directly. Erlanger would issue many loans in London through J. Henry Schröder & Co.[36] because his head office was still in Paris.[37]

This loan issue was successful and the total amount of the subscriptions reached £1.7 million. The assessment of it was not altogether good, however. *The Economist* regarded it as questionable because of the lack of adequate financial information on Japan;[38] the *Financier* raised doubts about Japan's credibility by saying that 'Japan is more likely to prove another Turkey, another Egypt or an Argentine Republic . . . in the scrupulous fulfilment of her obligations

Table 3.2 Yields of foreign government loans issued during 1870

(1) *Country*	*(2)* *Interest rate (nominal) (%)*	*(3)* *Issue price (%)*	*(4)* *Yield at issue (%)*
Chile	5	83	6.0
Egypt	7	75	9.3
Honduras	10	80	12.5
Japan	9	98	9.2
Romania	7	86	8.1
Russia	5	80	6.3
Spain	5	80	6.3

Source: Appendix A.
Note: (4)=(2)/(3) × 100.

of a similar character'.[39] Yet public investors fully welcomed the loan issue because of its conspicuously high yield at issue, 9.2 per cent (also see Table 3.2).

In the meantime, it was found that there had emerged a crucial divergence between Lay's and the Japanese government's understanding of the loan contract. In June 1870 C.E. De Long, the US minister in Japan, informed the Japanese government that Lay had carried out the public subscriptions of the Japanese government 9 per cent loan in London by offering the customs revenues and railway receipts.[40]

The Japanese government had apparently expected a private borrowing. Parkes reported to Lord Clarendon, the British secretary for foreign affairs, that the Japanese government appeared to have been willing for a loan in a private form and had no intention of relying upon the market, but that the order of the Japanese government duly empowered Lay to raise the necessary fund in a public form.[41]

In addition, the exorbitant commission was a further cause of argument. There was a 3 per-cent difference between Lay's lending rate to the Japanese government (12 per cent) and the annual interest rate of the public loan (9 per cent). There was also a 2 per-cent balance between the par (100 per cent) and issue price (98 per cent). It was Lay's 'double position', acting as both the contractor of the loan and the commissioner of the Japanese government, that brought him this huge margin.[42]

Parkes, at first, felt satisfied to hear that British enterprises would be connected with the first Japanese railway construction,[43] but also informed the British Foreign Office that Japan would have preferred to make a loan from private sources rather than the stock exchange.[44] He regretted that the Japanese government could have enjoyed a loan issue on much better terms through an established financial channel such as the Oriental Bank.[45] Parkes had been concerned with the Oriental Bank in the Japanese government's borrowing of US$50,000 (£11,250) two years earlier.[46]

The reasons why the Japanese government desired to avoid a public loan on the foreign market were: firstly, it was afraid of revealing its financial difficulties, which might lower Japan's reputation in the ongoing tariff reform negotiations; secondly, the new government, which had been established only two years earlier, did not want to disclose its financial vulnerability to the public; thirdly, the government itself was not confident of carrying out a foreign loan issue because of limited knowledge of public loans.[47]

On 29 June 1870 the Japanese government informed Lay that it was cancelling the entire loan issue contract[48] and asked the Oriental Bank, instead of J. Henry Schröder & Co., to manage all the affairs of the loan.[49] The government also proposed that the Oriental Bank should make a new loan issue for £3 million for refunding the 9 per-cent one just issued.[50] The Oriental Bank refused because a further loan issue would damage the price of the bonds on the market.[51]

Lay brought an action in the court[52] but in December 1870 the Japanese government came to terms with him to pay £70,000 in total.[53] The Japanese government authorized all bonds issued by J. Henry Schröder & Co. and their management to be taken over by the Oriental Bank. The remaining amount for the railway construction (£2 million) was never raised.[54]

Out of the £70,000, Lay obtained only £13,000 and Erlanger £57,000.[55] This immense penalty alone amounted to 7 per cent of the total issue amount.[56] Foreign loan issue business at this time, especially with underdeveloped countries, could be very lucrative for financiers.

Ironically this loan issue revealed the fact that the Japanese government was ignorant of public loans. This gave a bitter lesson to the Japanese government when it launched a loan issue in 1873. Parkes, however, commented: 'I trusted the firm establishment of the Mikado's government [the Meiji government] would shortly enable them to enter the money market of the world whenever they needed funds for the development of the resources of their country.'[57]

SEVEN PER-CENT LOAN ISSUE IN 1873

In 1873 the Japanese government made a second foreign loan issue in London. After the Meiji Restoration, the new government granted pensions to the old feudal knight class (*Samurai*) in exchange for their fiefs. This charge, 27 per cent of the government annual ordinary expenditure in the years from 1868 to 1889, overloaded the government's finances.[58] The main purpose of this loan issue was to secure funds for the redemption of these pensions. After the first foreign loan issue in 1870, Japan's reputation in the City had improved to a certain extent: the Council of the Corporation of Foreign Bondholders, in response to many communications on Japan, noted its 'further elements of stability'.[59]

In the absence of T. Ōkubo, the minister of finance (*Ōkura Kyō*), K. Inoue, the vice-minister of finance (*Ōkura Taiho*), directed all the negotiations of this loan issue.[60] Reflecting upon the lessons of the first foreign loan issue in 1870, the Japanese government was now aware of the risks of leaving financial operations entirely to a foreign agent and took the lead in the loan issue negotiations. In March 1872 K. Yoshida was appointed as the Japanese government loan commissioner for this operation and ordered to raise a loan for from US$15 million (£3,375,000) to US$30 million (£6,750,000) at 7 per cent in either the United States or London.[61]

The Japanese government estimated the necessary redemption funds at US$10 million (£2,250,000) and also planned to invest the rest in mining and railway construction.[62] The reason why the Japanese government aimed at the US market first was that it was afraid of Lay's interference in the loan issue negotiations in London. In addition, Yoshida, who did not like the Oriental Bank's further involvement in Japanese government finance,[63] looked for a new financial source for the government.

Yoshida's diary and correspondence are apparently the only sources revealing the process of these loan issue negotiations between the Japanese government and foreign financiers. The Oriental Bank, the issuer of this loan, went bankrupt in 1884 and its records were probably destroyed.[64] A. & J. Scrimgeour, the stockbroker of this loan issue, has no records surviving concerning it.[65]

On 26 March 1872 Yoshida's mission including G.B. Williams, an American adviser to the Japanese government (*Oyatoi Gaijin*), left for San Francisco.[66] There they had an interview with the Bank of California on the general financial conditions in the US market. The Japanese government had dealt with this bank in connection with the refining of Japanese gold coins.[67] The Bank of California agreed on a small loan issue, but recommended that Yoshida should propose the intended loan issue to the Oriental Bank. The Bank of California, a correspondent of the Oriental Bank, set great store by the transactions between the Oriental Bank and the Japanese government, as shown previously. The Bank of California showed little interest in Yoshida's proposal because J. Robertson, the manager of the Oriental Bank's Yokohama branch, who developed the ambition of concluding the Japanese government loan issue, had warned the Bank of California that the Japanese government would not offer sufficient security for a new loan after the loan issue in 1870, and that nobody would lend money to Japan even at a 25 per-cent annual rate of interest.[68] Yoshida sent a telegram to the Oriental Bank's head office to the effect that the Japanese government would issue a new foreign loan for £4 million.[69]

Then Yoshida moved on to New York and C.E. De Long, the US minister to Japan, introduced J. Schiff, a German-born Jewish financier, to him.[70] Schiff soon acceded to a 7 per-cent loan for £4 million and suggested offering it directly to his 'head office' in Frankfurt-on-Main.[71] In his early days Schiff was thus involved in Japanese government loan affairs. As will be seen in chapter 5, he became a key person in arranging the Japanese government loan issues on the New York capital market during the Russo-Japanese War.

On 18 June 1872 Yoshida arrived in London. Many financiers there offered a loan issue to Yoshida and his diary tells us the contemporary practice of loan issue negotiations. He went to see C.J.F. Stuart, the chief manager of the Oriental Bank. His [Stuart's] assessment of the proposed loan issue was at a more than 8 per-cent annual rate of interest. This was calculated on the contemporary yield of the Japanese government 9 per-cent loan of 1870, about 8.1 per cent. Bischoffsheim & Goldschmidt, a London merchant bank, also made a similar assessment.[72] Bischoffsheim & Goldschmidt had been notorious in dealing with South American government loans during the 1860s and 1870s for fabulous commissions. Ernest Cassel, a London merchant banker, participated in Bischoffsheim &

Goldschmidt from 1871 to 1884[73] and Schiff had large transactions with it through Cassel because of their Jewish connections. Perhaps it was Schiff who introduced the Japanese government loan business to Bischoffsheim & Goldschmidt. Bischoffsheim & Goldschmidt offered the following loan issue terms to Yoshida:[74]

Issue amount	£4 million (£2 million for the moment)
Interest rate (nominal)	7 per cent
Issue price (to the public)	about 91 per cent
Issue charges	from 7 to 8 per cent

Yet these came to nothing. In July and August 1872 Yoshida stayed in Frankfurt and Paris but there were no negotiations with Schiff's 'head office'.[75]

An Anglo-American merchant bank, Morton, Rose & Co.[76] offered the most definite loan issue terms. At the end of August John Rose, one of the British partners, proposed the following alternatives to Yoshida:[77]

Issue amount	£2 million	£2 million
Interest rate (nominal)	6 per cent	5 per cent
Issue price (to the public)	85 per cent	70 per cent
Loan issue commission	7 per cent	6 per cent
Borrowing period	15 years	30 years

In September Morton, Rose & Co. again offered a 6 per-cent loan issue for £4 million (only £2 million would be transferred for the moment). Yoshida, who regarded Morton, Rose & Co. as at most an upper-second class merchant bank, suspended the negotiations.[78]

J.G. Walsh, a partner of Walsh Hall and Co. in Yokohama, who was dealing with imported merchandise in Japan, informed Yoshida that his elder brother in London (T. Walsh) was anxious to contact Yoshida about the loan issue. In June 1872, T. Walsh proposed to Yoshida putting the loan issue matter into the hands of the Netherlands Trading Co.[79] This company had financed feudal clans in Japan.

In November D.G. Van Polsbroek, an agent of the Netherlands Trading Co. and former Dutch minister in Japan, told Yoshida that he [Van Polsbroek], together with W. Van der Tak, the Dutch consul in Yokohama, would endeavour to arrange the Japanese government loan in Holland.[80] Van Polsbroek introduced this business to several Dutch financiers, but they could not raise the required money in Holland and brought it to eminent financiers in London and Paris. They acted only as an intermediary in this loan issue. Wercher-Bonverg, one of these Dutch financiers, sounded out Baring Brothers on the possibility of undertaking the Japanese government loan issue in London.[81] Failing to obtain the necessary assistance from London and Paris, in January 1873 Van Polsbroek and Van der Tak abandoned the proposed business.[82]

These loan issue negotiations with a variety of financiers show that the credibility of the Japanese government was low. The financiers who took notice of Japan's financial operation were 'second class' at best and notorious as takers of a large loan issue commission. The Japanese government had not yet been able to establish a sound rating in European financial circles.

Yoshida was reluctant to depend upon the Oriental Bank for the loan issue, but the Japanese government, especially Inoue, placed full confidence in the Oriental Bank. The bank had played a significant role in taking over the management of the previous Japanese government 9 per-cent loan from Lay. The Oriental Bank had built up close ties with the Japanese government.[83] In addition, it had the bank accounts of the Legations in the Far East run by the British Foreign Office. Parkes also had particular interests with the bank and helped the loan issue negotiations.[84]

The Oriental Bank showed a liberal attitude towards foreign loan issues. It was said that Stuart regarded a small loan as a principle of 'bad banking' and preferred a large loan when the bank aimed at a Chinese government loan issue in 1874.[85] Because of this expanding business policy, the Oriental Bank sustained heavy losses in the Chilean government loan issues in 1873 and 1875.[86]

In July 1872 Panmure Gordon, a junior partner of J. & A. Scrimgeour & Co., a stockbroker, proposed Yoshida that he [Panmure Gordon] should work with the Oriental Bank in forming a loan-issue syndicate for the Japanese government loan issue. Then, Yoshida received the Oriental Bank's own proposal: a 7 per-cent loan for £4 million (£4 million transferred for the moment and the other half within 6 months).[87] Inoue wrote to Yoshida that he should put more trust in the Oriental Bank when the loan issue took place in London, and Yoshida received it in September.[88] On this occasion, he seems to have seriously considered the possibility of the loan issue through the

Table 3.3 Commission of loan issue in 1873

	(per cent)
Loan issue bank	1
Syndicate	2½
Brokerage (application)	¼
Stamp duty	⅛
Others	¼
Total	4⅛

Source: Yoshida's Diary 4, *MZZKSS*, 146; *MZ*, 8, 640.

Oriental Bank. After the authorization of the government,[89] Yoshida approached the bank and decided to put the loan issue in the hands of the Oriental Bank,[90] although noting that there were other more favourable offers, as mentioned previously.

Because of the huge amount of the French war indemnity loan issues, the circumstances of the London capital market during 1872 showed themselves to be 'the most critical since the panic of 1866.'[91] Bank rate was at an unusually high 7 per cent in November 1872 and the market did not allow any new loan issues. On 4 January 1873, Yoshida re-opened the negotiations with the Oriental Bank. The bank agreed to act as the loan issuer and to engage J. & A. Scrimgeour & Co. for forming a syndicate for the loan issue.[92] The role of this syndicate was 'underwriting' because the loan issue bank commission was separated from the syndicate profit. On 9 January Stuart informed Yoshida that the market had turned favourably to new loan issues when bank rate fell from 5 to 4½ per cent. It is obvious that the Oriental Bank regarded bank rate as one of the indicators of the market conditions for new loan issues. The Oriental Bank and J. & A. Scrimgeour undertook the Japanese government loan issue at a 4⅛ per-cent commission (Table 3.3).[93] On 13 January 1873 Yoshida made a contract with the Oriental Bank and J. & A. Scrimgeour & Co.[94] The loan issue terms were as follows:[95]

Issue amount	£2,400,000
Interest rate (nominal)	7 per cent
Yield at issue	7.6 per cent
Issue price	92½ per cent (to the public)
	90 per cent (to the government)

Security	400,000 *koku*[96] of rice per annum
Borrowing period	25 years
Redemption	the loan should be redeemed every year after 1875, 2 per cent of the principal by drawings.

By 16 January the subscriptions had reached £9,664,900, approximately 4 times oversubscribed.[97] The Union Bank of London purchased £150,000 of the bonds in its portfolio investments but immediately resold.[98] Mainly because of their high remuneration, 7.6 per cent at issue, the Japanese government bonds proved very attractive to public investors.

British financial journals, however, published unfavourable comments on this operation. *The Economist* again pointed out the concomitant risks of the Japanese government loan issue as saying that 'the result, we fear, is likely to be as unfortunate for the lenders as similar borrowings by new countries which wished to develop their resources.'[99] In fact, in the financial year of 1873, large deficits occurred in the Japanese government's revenue.[100]

The two early Japanese government foreign loan issues successfully ensured the issue amounts mainly due to the high interest rates and yields at issue. In comparison with contemporary standards, these were extremely advantageous to investors, while the Japanese government bore heavy costs. The fact that the Japan of the day was a totally unknown country to many Western investors led to such an unfavourable assessment of the loan issue terms on the foreign capital market. It must be noted, however, that despite the high interest rate and yield at issue, the Oriental Bank charged a standard level loan issue commission.

The Japanese government of the 1870s had no specific knowledge of foreign loan issues. It is no exaggeration to say, therefore, that the government at this time put full trust in the Oriental Bank when it embarked upon financial operations abroad. After an interval of twenty-four years, in 1897, the Japanese government would return to the London capital market for foreign loan issues. During that period, in 1879, the bank which would specialize in foreign business, the Yokohama Specie Bank, was established under the patronage of the Japanese government.

4

Sino-Japanese War Loan Issues

The financial troubles were a measure of the strain which the rapid growth of a modern industrial system accompanied by territorial expansion was imposing on a poor country. The expansionist policy was, in other words, endangering financial stability; but to that policy Japan was irrevocably committed.

G.C. Allen, *A Short Economic History of Modern Japan*

During the period from 1874 to 1896 Japan did not draw upon foreign capital markets. In this interval of nearly a quarter of a century, Japan financed its rapid industrialization, mainly in textile industries, from domestic savings. Modern financial institutions were created in that period. The National Bank Act of 1872, modelled on the National Currency Act of 1863 in the United States, provided considerable facilities for setting up 'national banks (*Kokuritsu Ginkō*)'.[1] These 'national banks' (private commercial banks) took a significant part in financing industries. The Mitsui Bank, the first private commercial bank, not based on the National Bank Act, was established in 1876. In 1878 the Tokyo Stock Exchange was opened on the new Securities and Exchange Act. The following year the Yokohama Specie Bank was set up with authorized capital of ¥3,000,000 (£306,250) for financing Japanese importers and exporters.[2] The Bank of Japan, the central bank, was finally founded in 1882. The Japanese government at this stage saw no sound reason to invite foreign capital to the industrialization process, although there was possibly a shortage of capital in the industrial private sector.

After the Sino-Japanese War (1894–95), however, the government rapidly increased military expenditure. As a result, the balance of the Japanese government's revenue and expenditure deteriorated markedly. The surplus ratios fell from 9.7 per cent in 1896 to 0.1 per cent in 1898, and in 1899 revenue became equivalent to expenditure.[3] At first, domestic loans were the main source of funding, but the increased military expenditure soon led to severe trade deficits because most of the military goods were imported. As Japan's trade balance went into the red almost every year after 1896,[4] the Japanese government had to secure gold (or foreign currency on the gold standard) for settling the trade deficits. It was in the late-1890s that the Japanese government inevitably came to rest on foreign loans, because domestic loans were utterly incapable of achieving this purpose. This chapter will view three Japanese government loan issues after the Sino-Japanese War, the purpose of which was the settlement of the adverse trade balances caused by heavy military expenditure.

ESTABLISHMENT OF GOLD STANDARD

Apart from the early foreign loans in 1870 and 1873 (sterling bonds – gold standard ones), the Japanese government domestic bonds (yen bonds – silver standard ones) had not yet been quoted on the London Stock Exchange. In 1884 S. Yoshihara, the Governor of the Bank of Japan, approached the Committee of the London Stock Exchange, but failed to win quotation mainly because of silver standard bonds.[5] In 1896 T. Katō, the Japanese minister in London, agreed with the London Stock Exchange on the quotation of 5 per cent domestic bonds for ¥60,838,250 (£6,210,571).[6] Yet, being silver standard bonds, their daily transactions were very small and prices were low.[7]

Before 1897, the yen was based principally on the silver standard. As shown in chapter 1, silver standard bonds were valued unfavourably on the market because of exchange risks. The silver standard in Japan became a distinct impediment to conducting smooth transactions with the City. Japan needed the same standard as Britain. In fact, one British merchant pointed out in 1884 that Japan could borrow money more favourably in London with gold standard bonds.[8] It is hardly surprising, therefore, that Japan, the same as other countries, aimed to adopt the gold standard.

During the years from 1895 to 1898 Japan received a considerable amount of war indemnity money (£32,900,980) from China. On the basis of this M. Matsukata, the Japanese Minister of Finance, adopted the gold standard in Japan. The Japanese Gold Standard Act operated from October 1897 at the rate of ¥1 to 24.58 d. Obviously this was to 'command higher credit, and be able to borrow on more favourable terms in foreign countries' as a gold standard country.[9] This currency reform brought a stable rate of exchange with gold standard countries.[10]

RESALE OF 5 PER-CENT DOMESTIC BONDS IN 1897

In 1894 war broke out between China and Japan. The war was financed mainly by domestic loans and funds transferred from the exchequer. After the war, in 1896, the Deposit Money Bureau (*Yokinbu*)[11] at the Ministry of Finance had temporarily taken a large quantity of 5 per-cent military bonds,[12] because the domestic capital market had insufficient capacity to absorb all the loans issued by the public. The government considered reselling some of these bonds abroad.

In 1896 the Japanese government ordered the Bank of Japan to resell the military bonds, held by the Deposit Money Bureau, for ¥43 million (£4,389,583) on a foreign market. In November 1896 the bond re-sale negotiations started. K. Fukuma, a manager of S. Samuel & Co. in Kobe, informed the Japanese Ministry of Finance that his London house M. Samuel & Co. (Marcus Samuel),[13] a London merchant bank, wanted to purchase the 5 per-cent domestic bonds, held by the Deposit Money Bureau, for ¥30 million (£3,062,500).[14] Samuel Samuel, Marcus Samuel's younger brother, ran a merchant house (S. Samuel & Co.) in Yokohama and Kobe as an agent of M. Samuel & Co., and did a brisk business importing machinery, tools, textiles and petroleum into Japan and exporting curios and rice.[15] S. Samuel & Co. emphasized probable assistance from the London Rothschilds.[16]

In December 1896 Katō (the Japanese minister in London) entered into preliminary negotiations with M. Samuel & Co. Marcus Samuel proposed buying ¥30 million of the bonds, but soon found it difficult to purchase such a large quantity of silver standard bonds. He had mistakenly believed that these bonds were gold standard ones. They only agreed that W.F. Mitchell, a partner of M. Samuel & Co., would continue the negotiations in Japan.[17]

In the middle of April 1897, however, an abrupt bid by the Chartered Bank quickened proceedings. The Chartered Bank proposed to the Bank of Japan the purchase of the military bonds for ¥40 million (£4,083,333) at £100 per ¥1,000 (97.9 per cent to par),[18] which was subsequently raised to £101 (98.9 per cent to par).[19] While the

Chartered Bank hesitated at the final stage, in May S. Samuel & Co., together with the Hongkong Bank, offered to the Bank of Japan the purchase of bonds to the nominal value of ¥35 million (£3,572,917) at £102 per ¥1,000 (99.9 per cent to par). The Bank of Japan, of course, accepted this more advantageous offer.[20] The Chartered Bank finally agreed to participate in S. Samuel & Co.'s syndicate.[21] The re-sale amount increased to ¥43 million (£4,389,583) and the principal and interest were guaranteed to pay in gold. The following contract was made between the Bank of Japan, S. Samuel & Co. and the Hongkong Bank on 28 May 1897:[22]

Re-sale amount	¥43 million (£4,389,583)
Interest rate (nominal)	5 per cent[23]
Resale price	£102 per a nominal price of the ¥1,000 (99.9 per cent to par)
Borrowing period	53 years
Others	the government should guarantee to pay the principal and interest in gold at the rate of 2s. ½d. per ¥1; the government, for one year, should not issue any loan in Europe except through S. Samuel & Co. and the Hongkong Bank.

S. Samuel & Co.'s success in the loan issue negotiations was a result of the Chartered Bank's reluctance to launch a foreign loan issue. Perhaps the bank, under the direction of J.H. Gwyther, may have regarded such business as extremely risky.[24]

The syndicate of this bond resale included a variety of City banks: the Capital & Counties Bank (a clearing bank); the Hongkong Bank (an overseas bank); the Chartered Bank (an overseas bank); the Yokohama Specie Bank (a foreign bank).[25] Why did the Capital & Counties Bank participate in this loan resale as one of the loan issue banks? The bank was founded in 1877 as the Hampshire & North Wiltshire Banking Co. and expanded its business mainly in the southwest of England.[26] The bank acted as an agent of M. Samuel & Co.[27] To ensure a firm basis for subscriptions on the market, M. Samuel & Co., which was engaged largely in merchant activities, put this resale operation into the hands of the Capital & Counties Bank.[28] The Capital & Counties Bank only undertook two foreign government loan issues before 1914: the Santo Domingo government 6 per-cent

Table 4.1 Application and allocation of 5 per-cent bond resale in 1897

Loan issue bank	*Application* (£)	*Allocation* (£)	(¥)
Capital & Counties Bank	9,500,000	1,637,200	(16,400,000)
Hongkong Bank	8,500,000	1,217,900	(12,200,000)
Chartered Bank	7,750,000	1,138,100	(11,400,000)
Yokohama Specie Bank	2,000,000	306,800	(3,000,000)
Total	27,750,000	4,300,000	(43,000,000)

Source: CCBA, A53b/76.
Note: ¥1=2s. 1/2d.

loan in 1889 and the Japanese government 5 per-cent bond resale in 1897. *The Statist*, however, cast doubts on whether a clearing bank could become involved in foreign loan issue business.[29]

From 1 June 1897 the subscriptions started at £103 12s. 4d. per ¥1,000 (101½ per cent to par). The syndicate received the 2 1/2 per-cent coupon of June 1897[30] and a 1½ per-cent underwriting commission. Panmure Gordon, Hill & Co., a stockbroker, mainly arranged the underwriting.[31] The applications amounted to £27,750,000, 6.5 times oversubscribed (Table 4.1).

This resale operation was sufficiently lucrative to the syndicate. On a rough estimate its profit, including the 2½ per-cent half-yearly interest of June 1897, amounted to at least 4.1 per cent of the whole resale amount. In comparison with the Japanese government loan issues of later periods, however, this level of commission was not as high as the Japanese government had feared.[32] Yet Japanese journalists were critical, saying that the high interest (5 per-cent) bonds would injure government finances[33] and that the resale price was much lower than the quotation prices of similar bonds on the domestic market.[34]

In the City these bonds were welcome. On 15 May 1897 bank rate fell to 2 per cent and the 5 per-cent interest bonds were particularly deserving of investors' attention. The yield of the bonds at issue was approximately 4.9 per cent. In fact, after the subscriptions, the Chartered Bank attempted to purchase Japanese government 5 per-cent domestic bonds for resale in London.[35] The issuers of this bond resale were not leaders in the field of foreign government loan issue business,[36] but it was on this occasion that the Japanese government first used, after a quarter century interval, the City for a financial operation.

FOUR PER-CENT LOAN ISSUE IN 1899

The balance between the Japanese government's revenue and expenditure deteriorated markedly following the Sino-Japanese War. Increased military expenditure because of the menace of Russia in Manchuria put the government's finances in an awkward position.[37] The domestic capital market became filled with government bonds, the issue amount of which was increased to about ¥391 million (£39 million) in 1898,[38] and could bear no more new loan issues. In fact, due to a slump caused by bad crops the Japanese government failed to raise three public works loans for ¥79,282,028 (£8,093,374) in 1898. The Japanese Ministry of Finance postponed them and temporarily transferred some of the Sino-Japanese War indemnity money to the required funds.[39] To offset these difficult financial conditions in the domestic capital market K. Inoue, the Japanese Minister of Finance, was firmly in favour of raising a new foreign loan.[40]

In 1898 Inoue ordered K. Takahashi, the deputy-governor of the Yokohama Specie Bank, to scrutinize foreign capital markets for a future foreign loan issue.[41] It was the first time that Takahashi was involved in government foreign loan business. Just 6 years later he would fulfill an important mission to float a considerable amount of government loans abroad during the Russo-Japanese War.

In April 1898 Takahashi met Alexander Allan Shand (a sub-manager of Parr's Bank), W. Dun (a director of Parr's Bank) and R.W. Whalley (an assistant manager at the head office of Parr's Bank) in London.[42] Shand, who had been the manager at the Yokohama branch of the Chartered Mercantile Bank of London, India & China and had also been engaged as a Japanese government's Honourable Foreign Adviser (*Oyatoi Gaijin*) in his early business career in the Far East, became a major influence in the Japanese government loan issues at Parr's Bank. Takahashi had served in a junior capacity under Shand in Yokohama. Shand had returned to London to join the Alliance Bank, which amalgamated with Parr's Bank in 1892, but maintained extensive relations with Japan.[43] For instance, in 1881 he introduced S. Hihara, of the Yokohama Specie Bank, to the Alliance Bank's Bartholomew Lane branch for the opening of a private account, and in 1885 an account for the Yokohama Specie

Bank itself.[44] After the amalgamation with the Alliance Bank, Parr's Bank took over this relationship and favourably admitted unsecured advances to the Yokohama Specie Bank.[45] Obviously Takahashi depended upon his personal relations with Shand in researching the market.[46]

From these interviews Takahashi made the following outline of a future foreign loan issue and reported it to Inoue:[47]

(i) A 4 per-cent or 4½ per-cent loan for less than £5 million at 90 per cent.
(ii) The loan issue should be divided into a three-year consecutive operation.
(iii) The Japanese government should create a standing post of loan commissioner in the Legation in London to keep close communications with the City.[48]

Takahashi also advised putting loan issue matters, in collaboration with the Yokohama Specie Bank's London branch, into the hands of Katō (the Japanese minister in London).[49]

Inoue aimed to raise ¥70 million (£7,145,833) abroad by either a resale of 5 per-cent domestic bonds or a new 4½ per-cent loan issue.[50] The Japanese government, which regarded M. Samuel & Co.'s commission from the previous bond resale in 1897 as 'exorbitant',[51] attempted to employ other financiers in the City. Katō approached the Union Bank of London and Parr's Bank, London clearing banks.[52]

Parr's Bank offered 'the cheapest and safest issue terms' and Katō finally brought the negotiations with Parr's Bank to the Yokohama Specie Bank's London branch.[53] The new S. Ōkuma cabinet, however, sought a Treasury bill issue for £2 million at 3½ or 4 per-cent interest.[54] Parr's Bank agreed to undertake this at a ⅛ per-cent commission,[55] but was not able to conclude the issue mainly because of the Japanese cabinet's wavering commitment.

In 1899 Matsukata (the minister of finance in the A. Yamagata cabinet) embarked upon the foreign loan issue. To meet the government budget deficit he increased the issue amount to ¥100 million (£10,208,333).[56] Matsukata, though, being uneasy about dependence upon foreign borrowings for meeting the financial deficits,[57] issued the following guidelines for the loan issue at a cabinet meeting of January 1899:

Issue amount	£10 million (according to the market conditions, half the amount should be placed in the first year)
Interest rate (nominal)	less than 4½ per cent
Redemption	within 40 years
Purpose	railway construction and improvement; establishment of steel works; expansion of the telephone service.[58]

In March 1899 the Japanese government ordered the Bank of Japan to arrange this loan issue in London.[59] Its assessment of the loan issue was based on Takahashi's previous research. K. Matsui, the Japanese minister (chargé d'affaires) in London, conducted all the loan issue negotiations. On behalf of the Bank of Japan, S. Hayakawa, the secretary of the Japanese Ministry of Finance (*Ōkura Shokikan* and *Sanjikan*), and Y. Nakai, the manager of the Yokohama Specie Bank's London branch,[60] became the principal negotiators of this loan issue with British financiers.[61] This was the first time that the Yokohama Specie Bank was concerned with a Japanese government loan issue.

Hayakawa approached many banks in the City. M. Samuel & Co. proposed a loan issue at favourable terms, a 4 per-cent loan at 95 per cent,[62] but the Japanese government found the condition of offering a mortgage on the loan totally unacceptable.[63] One American merchant in Japan described the character of the Japanese hating borrowing on security as:

> the Japanese do not like the idea of being called upon to give security for a loan. It hurts their pride to be classed with the Chinese. They consider the guarantee of their Government equal to any security than can be offered, . . . they will not negotiate with us if we announce that security must be given. They consider the faith of this Government equal to any in the world.[64]

Hayakawa's original plan was to form a large loan issue syndicate inviting the Union Bank of London, the London Joint Stock Bank and Parr's Bank, but only Parr's Bank accepted the offer. Parr's Bank became the main issuer and Panmure Gordon, Hill & Co. arranged the other issuers.[65] Of the Far Eastern trade connections the Hongkong Bank and the Chartered Bank also participated in the loan issue syndicate.[66]

Although the Japanese government desired a 95 per-cent issue price,[67] Hayakawa agreed on a 4 per-cent loan at 90 per cent (86 per cent to the government).[68] The loan issue commission was 4 per cent, the standard level for contemporary loan issues.[69] The Japanese Ministry of Foreign Affairs confirmed that many underwriters secured the whole issue amount.[70]

The forming of the syndicates in this loan issue was as follows: Parr's Bank, the Yokohama Specie Bank, the Hongkong Bank and the Chartered Bank (the loan issue banks) formed the loan issue bank syndicate, the role of which was to undertake the loan issue from the Japanese government; subsequently, Panmure Gordon, Hill & Co. (the stockbroker) assisted the loan issue banks in forming their underwriting syndicates and also organized their own; these underwriting syndicates guaranteed the loan issue should the public subscriptions not absorb the issue amount. The role of the stockbroker in organizing the underwriting was of extreme importance, and this loan issue mechanism would be followed in Japanese government loan issues of later periods.

By 29 May 1899 the loan issue banks and the Japanese government had reached the following accord on the impending loan issue:[71]

Amount	£10 million (£8 million to the public)
Interest rate (nominal)	4 per cent
Yield at issue	4.4 per cent
Issue price	90 per cent (to the public) 86 per cent (to the government)
Borrowing period	55 years
Loan issue commission	4 per cent
Other	the Bank of Japan should apply for £2 million of the bonds before the public subscriptions;[72] the loan should be redeemable after 1909 by drawings at the option of the Japanese government on giving 6 months' previous notice.

The Japanese government believed that 'the terms offered are quite favourable especially when compared with [the] market value of bonds of several other countries.'[73] The 4 per-cent loan issue

Table 4.2 Commission of 4 per-cent loan issue in 1899

Underwriting	2
Loan issue bank	1
Brokerage (placing underwriting)	½
Brokerage (application)	¼
Advertising	¼
Total	4

Note: per cent.

Underwriting syndicate	*Underwriting amount*	*Underwriting commission (2%)*	*Brokerage commission (1/2%)*	*Loan issue bank commission (1%)*
Panmure Gordon	5,106,000	102,120	25,530	
Hongkong Bank	1,146,400	22,928	5,732	18,750
Chartered Bank	547,500	10,950	2,737.5	18,750
Yokohama Specie Bank	2,491,000	49,822	12,455.5	31,250
Parr's Bank	709,000	14,180	3,545	31,250
Total	9,999,900	200,000	50,000	100,000

Source: WBA, D2469.
Notes: £; There was a shortage of the underwriting for £100.

commission was nearly equivalent to those of the 1897 resale (Table 4.2).[74]

The market assessed this loan issue as very dubious. For example, the *Investors' Review* was scathing, saying that Japan's deteriorating financial situation did not permit such an enormous loan issue amount (£10 million) given the current market conditions; the high issue price would deter many subscribers.[75] Indeed, the yield of this loan (4.4 per cent at issue) was less favourable to investors than that of the 5 per-cent military bonds resold in 1897 (yielding about 4.8 per cent at market at the end of June 1899).[76]

The subscriptions were carried out on 6 June but only £980,000, 9.8 per cent of the total issue amount, was applied for. The remainder was taken by the underwriters. The quotation price of these bonds on the unofficial market sank immediately to 88½ per cent.[77] The Japanese government decided to purchase a further £2,500,000 of the bonds mainly from Sino-Japanese War Indemnity Special Account funds.[78] As a result, in addition to £2 million which was purchased in advance by the Bank of Japan, around 45 per cent of the total issue amount was taken by the Japanese government and the Bank of Japan. Table 4.2 indicates the commissions and underwriting amounts at the loan issue banks and stockbrokers. It is clear that Panmure Gordon, Hill & Co. largely arranged the underwriting.

Even in September 1899 the underwriters held most of the unsubscribed bonds. Panmure Gordon, Hill & Co., through J.S. Morgan, proposed to J.P. Morgan & Co. (New York) that they should organize a group for selling these bonds in New York. Yet J.P. Morgan & Co. saw no opportunity of doing so.[79] Parr's Bank kept many of the bonds (£316,558) in its investments.[80] The underwriters suffered seriously from the lack of a market for the bonds.[81]

Why did this loan issue fail to attract public investors' attention? The Japanese government concluded that the causes of this failure were: (i) the issue amount was too large; (ii) the yield of the bonds was disadvantageous in comparison with that of the 5 per-cent military bonds of 1897; (iii) public investors had misgivings about the stability of Japan's national finance; (iv) there was competition with other countries' loan issues on the market.[82] The contemporary market conditions, especially high bank rate, discouraged new loan issues.

Up to that time the Japanese government had relied, for its foreign loan issues, upon specific financiers such as the Oriental Bank, the Hongkong Bank, the Chartered Bank and M. Samuel & Co., which had occupied an influential position in Far Eastern trade. This time Takahashi exploited a new channel, based on his personal relations with Shand, and Parr's Bank played a leading part in the loan issue. However beneficial these loan issue terms were to the Japanese government, the financial operation itself did not generate interest among investors.

The outcome of this loan issue revealed Japan's low creditworthiness in the City: the Japanese government was overestimating this when it said that 'Japan is now rated at between Germany and Italy.'[83] The newly exploited financial channel, Parr's Bank (a clearing bank), was not so effective in Japan's foreign loan issue operation as the government had expected. The Japanese government realized that foreign loan issues on the London capital market would require the assistance of merchant banks as well as clearing banks. In fact, the eminent merchant banks, such as Baring Brothers, J.S. Morgan & Co., Schröder and the London Rothschilds, showed no great interest in this operation.[84]

RESALE OF 5 PER-CENT DOMESTIC BONDS IN 1902

The Japanese government's financial position had not improved remarkably even after the foreign loan issue in 1899. The government still accumulated debts, both domestic and foreign. Further new loan issues were not acceptable on the sluggish domestic market and the government, in fact, failed to float domestic loans. To raise the required funds there was no other recourse left but a foreign loan. In 1901 the Japanese government started negotiations on the resale of the 5 per-cent domestic bonds for ¥50 million (£5,104,000), held by the Deposit Money Bureau at the Ministry of Finance.[85] The Japanese government ordered K. Takahira, the Japanese minister in Washington, to arrange this in the United States, but the negotiations with American financiers proved futile.[86]

After the Anglo-Japanese alliance concluded on 30 January 1902, however, public opinion in Britain became more amicable to Japan. The alliance was for an exchange of benefits for both Japan and Britain in the Far East, especially against Russia's menace in Manchuria. The conclusion of the alliance produced close relations between Japan and the London capital market. It is true that this would encourage foreigners' investment in Japan.[87]

In the summer of 1902, in response to the Hongkong Bank's offer through the Industrial Bank,[88] the Japanese government decided to sell these domestic bonds to British financiers. The government immediately directed the Deposit Money Bureau at the Ministry of Finance to sell the bonds abroad and to purchase in their place the new ones, scheduled for issue in the financial year of 1902. The resale of domestic bonds abroad produced the same effects as a new foreign loan issue to the government.

At that time there were two Japanese financial institutions, the Yokohama Specie Bank and the Industrial Bank, capable of arranging a foreign loan issue. These two banks stood in a special relation to the Japanese government. Since its foundation in 1879 the Japanese government directly controlled the management of the Yokohama Specie Bank; the minister of finance had the power to intervene in the bank's business and to nominate the governor and directors. The Japanese government and the Bank of Japan also exceptionally made large deposits and advances to the Yokohama Specie Bank for using foreign exchange transactions.[89] After 1899 the Yokohama Specie Bank was connected with most of the government's foreign loan issues as one of the loan issue banks.

On the other hand, in March 1900 a special act to establish the Industrial Bank was promulgated. Two years later, with ¥2,500,000 (£255,208) paid-up capital (¥10 million [£1,020,833] authorized capital) the Industrial Bank was set up. The Japanese government provided several privileges for the bank, as will be seen in chapter 8. The Hongkong Bank undertook the management of share subscriptions when the Industrial Bank was founded in 1902 and thereafter they maintained close business relations.[90]

In the period before the Russo-Japanese War (1904–5), the Japanese government fixed no definite boundary between the Yokohama Specie Bank and the Industrial Bank in foreign loan issue business. Therefore, the Yokohama Specie Bank regarded the Industrial Bank as a formidable competitor which was 'squeezing into the foreign loan issue business.'[91] In such an entangled situation, the Industrial Bank, in collaboration with the Hongkong Bank, took the initiative in the resale of the 5 per-cent domestic bonds.

In October 1902 the Japanese government decided to resell ¥50 million (£5,104,166) of the 5 per-cent domestic bonds to the Hongkong Bank through the Industrial Bank. The Hongkong Bank considered inviting two eminent merchant banks: Baring Brothers and the London Rothschilds, and one eminent merchant banker, Ernest Cassel, to the bond resale. The London Rothschilds inquired of the British Foreign Office whether the proposed Japanese government loan business would be acceptable, both politically and commercially, to them.[92] F. Bertie, the British under-secretary of state for foreign affairs, admitted that it was 'a matter of political importance that Japan should be able to raise in this country rather than elsewhere the money which she requires' and explained the Foreign Office's non-intervention policy towards private transactions. In this resale operation the London Rothschilds only agreed to become a major underwriter. Baring Brothers, which had growing interests in the Far East, agreed to become the main issuer.[93] Cassel played an important part in also taking much of the underwriting.

In September 1902 the Hongkong Bank embarked upon the loan issue negotiations with the Industrial Bank. The Hongkong Bank's role was, in substance, to be an intermediary between Baring Brothers and the Japanese government. The proposed terms were as follows: the bonds should be delivered to London at 98 per cent per ¥1,000 (96 per cent to par); the Hongkong Bank and the Yokohama Specie Bank should become an issuer of this resale; the total issue amount should be at most ¥50 million (£5,104,000) which, according to market conditions, could be reduced to ¥30 million (£3,063,000); the Japanese government should not withdraw gold directly from the Bank of England but would be allowed to purchase it on the open market; the intermediary commission to the Industrial Bank should be ¾ per cent of the total resale amount.[94]

The Japanese Ministry of Finance approved most of these terms.[95] On 30 September 1902 the Hongkong Bank, with Baring Brothers' consent, concluded the negotiations with the Industrial Bank and the Japanese government. The outline of the contract was as follows:[96]

Resale amount	¥50 million (£5,104,000)
Resale price	£98 per a nominal price of the ¥1,000 bond (96 per cent to par)
Interest rate (nominal)	5 per cent[97]
Borrowing period	55 years
Others	the Japanese government should guarantee to pay the principal and interest in sterling at the rate of ¥1=2s. ½d.; the Japanese government should desire the Hongkong Bank to fix the resale price in London at more than £103, based on the quotation price of Japanese government 5 per-cent bonds.

The Hongkong Bank invited the Yokohama Specie Bank to this resale as one of the issuers when the negotiations with the Japanese government were concluded. The Yokohama Specie Bank agreed to this.[98] The Yokohama Specie Bank, because it set great store by its business relations with Parr's Bank, persuaded the Industrial Bank to include Parr's Bank as well in this bond resale as one of the loan issuers.[99] Yet The Hongkong Bank only allowed Parr's Bank to be an underwriter.[100] Parr's Bank underwrote ¥1 million (£102,083) of the bonds.[101]

The Hongkong Bank's original idea of forming a syndicate for this resale can be seen from the letter addressed by E. Cameron, the Hongkong Bank's London manager, to Lord Revelstoke, the head of Baring Brothers:

> if New Court [the London Rothschilds] and the Banque de Paris take 1 million, we then have 4½ millions assured, as follows, Yourselves and the Bank [the Hongkong Bank] 2 millions, C.J. Hambro Co. 1 million (of which they have booked £350,000), Cassel, New Court and the Banque de Paris £1,500,000. I think one of the conditions with the syndicate should be that each member applies, when the lists are open, for the full amount of their subscription, and be prepared to take their full proposition of the allotment. In that way the issue would be bound to be a success as no one, either of the public or of the syndicate would get an allotment in full. That would give back bone to the market and would much more than compensate members of the syndicate for the extra amount they would have to hold. If the public applied very largely, the syndicate might be consulted and asked how much stock they would like to keep and we would allot accordingly.[102]

Baring Brothers, the Hongkong Bank and the Yokohama Specie Bank formed syndicates to invite 'leading Stock Exchange firms' to participate. Panmure Gordon, Hill & Co. acted as the stockbroker for this resale. The character of this syndicate was an 'underwriting' syndicate, but the commission was not decided in advance and the profit of the syndicate was distributed among members according to their shares, after deducting the loan issue bank commission and miscellaneous charges.

In October Baring Brothers immediately started organizing their own syndicate for guaranteeing the placement of the bonds on their world-wide business correspondent network, from the Continent to the United States. In regard to the Paris capital market, Baring Brothers informed the Banque de Paris of this resale. Their proposal was that the Banque de Paris should guarantee £250,000 of the bonds on the condition that it would be allowed to share in the rest of the profit after deducting a 1 per-cent loan issue bank commission charged by the Hongkong Bank and Baring Brothers.[103] The Banque de Paris was at first adverse to the proposed business because of the political climate there, namely hostility towards Japan under the alliance with Russia,[104] but, after the French government's authorization, agreed to participate in the syndicate for £250,000.[105] Baring Brothers offered Hottinguer, an old private financier in Paris, £25,000 of the share.[106] Baring Brothers also invited Hope & Co., a long-established financial house in Amsterdam, to join the syndicate for £50,000[107] and the Banque Federal in Zurich for £10,000.[108]

Since early in the nineteenth century, Baring Brothers had had firm relations with the United States markets. Kidder, Peabody & Co. in Boston[109] shared £100,000 of the bonds.[110] They also informed Baring, Magoun & Co. in New York[111] of reserving the share for £50,000.[112] In London many merchant banks, overseas banks, stockbrokers and merchants showed interest in this resale: Hambros, for instance, took £100,000 of the bonds;[113] Cassel £500,000; the London Rothschilds £300,000.[114]

In this way, by 8 October Baring Brothers had completed their own syndicate for £2,100,000. Table 4.3 shows the names, shares and profits of Baring Brothers' syndicate. The Hongkong Bank and Baring Brothers asked the British government to inscribe the bonds at the Bank of England. In general, the method of inscribing stocks afforded several facilities to bondholders: transfer of inscribed stocks was exempt from the stamp duty, the payment of dividends could be posted and dividends could be invested automatically.[115] In 1891 there were at least thirty-five colonial government inscribed stocks quoted on the London Stock Exchange.[116] The practice of inscribing stocks could be an impetus to public investors; Cameron acknowledged that 'it will be a great encouragement to subscribers'.[117] This method was a characteristic of colonial government loans, but was often employed also in important foreign loans, such as the Chinese government 5 per-cent loan in 1896 and the 4½ per-cent one in 1898, when the British government regarded them as diplomatically important. Because of the conclusion of the Anglo-Japanese alliance, the Foreign Office and the Treasury recognized the political importance of this Japanese government 5 per-cent bond resale[118] and the Bank of England agreed to inscribe the bonds for ¥5,731,000 (£585,039), 11.7 per cent of the resale amount.[119]

On 7 October 1902 the Hongkong Bank, Baring Brothers and the Yokohama Specie Bank published the prospectus. The issue price was fixed at £102 1s. 8d. per ¥1,000 (100 per cent to par). This was slightly lower than the price of more than £103, which the Japanese government had been hoping for in the negotiations. The subscriptions took place from 7 to 9 October. *The Statist* assessed that 'the high interest loving public' favourably received the subscriptions.[120] The total amount of the applications reached ¥97,993,000 (£10,003,000), 1.96 times the issue amount (Table 4.4).

Table 4.3 Baring Brothers' syndicate for 5 per-cent bond resale in 1902 (£)

Name	*Occupation*	*(1) Share of syndicate*	*(2) Profit*
E. Cassel	merchant banker	500,000	16,250
N.M. Rothschild	merchant bank	300,000	9,750
Banque de Paris	foreign bank	250,000	8,125
C.J. Hambro	merchant bank	100,000	3,250
Kidder Peabody	foreign bank	100,000	3,250
Hope & Co.	foreign bank	50,000	1,625
H.J. Lefevre & Co.	merchant	50,000	1,625
Baring Magoun	foreign bank	50,000	1,625
(No 2)		50,000	1,625
Frühing & Goschen	merchant bank	25,000	812
Glyn Mills, Currie	clearing bank	25,000	812
Hottinguer	foreign bank	25,000	812
Cunliffes	merchant bank	25,000	812
A. Wagg	stockbroker	25,000	812
Derenberg Meyer	merchant bank	10,000	325
Lord Farquhar	member of parliament	10,000	325
J. Birch & Co.	merchant	10,000	325
W. Bisset	retired civil servant	10,000	325
F. Huth & Co.	merchant bank	10,000	325
L. Messel & Co.	stockbroker	10,000	325
J.C. & C.W. Morrice	stockbroker	10,000	325
Steer Lawford & Co.	stockbroker	10,000	325
J. & A. Scrimgeour	stockbroker	10,000	325
Baring Brothers	merchant bank	375,000	12,187
Banque Federal	foreign bank	10,000	325
Lord Rothschild	merchant banker	10,000	325
Senior Perugid	–	10,000	325
W. Betzold	foreign banker	10,000	325
Morris Prevost	merchant bank	10,000	325
Total		2,090,000	67,922

Syndicate profit: £3 5s. per ¥1,000

Sources: BBA, 302, 70 and 146c;
London Post Office Directory, 1903.

Notes: (1) 8 October 1902;
(2) 11 November 1902;
– implies no information.

Table 4.4 Subscriptions of 5 per-cent bond resale in 1902 (¥; ¥1=1s. ½ d.)

Loan issue bank	*Application*	*Allotment*
Hongkong Bank	45,525,000	22,330,000
Baring Brothers	44,986,000	24,590,000
Yokohama Specie Bank	7,482,000	3,080,000
Total	97,993,000	50,000,000

Source: BBA, 302, 112.

On 20 October the scrips for ¥50 million (£5,104,166) was quoted on the official price list of the London Stock Exchange.[121]

The Industrial Bank received a 1¼ commission (¾ per cent from the syndicate and ½ per cent from the Japanese government) in total; a 3¼ per-cent profit was paid to the members of the syndicate; the Hongkong Bank, Baring Brothers and the Yokohama Specie Bank received a 1 per-cent loan issue bank commission; the total commission of this bond resale amounted to 5½ per cent (Table 4.5). The cost of this bond resale seemed expensive to the Japanese government, the level of the loan issue commission being higher than the previous loan issues in 1897 and 1899 (about 4 per cent).

It was the first time that the Japanese government was successful in attracting the pre-eminent London merchant banks to its financial operations. Although the outcome was not fully satisfactory to the Japanese government, this bond resale, without doubt, broadened the range of financiers for Japanese government foreign loan issues. The Japanese government could now depend upon the Hongkong Bank's wide-ranging business relationships in the City, especially with many

Table 4.5 Commission of 5 per-cent bond resale in 1902 (per cent)

Loan issue bank commission	1
Brokerage (placing underwriting)	¼
Brokerage (application)	¼
Industrial Bank	¾
Syndicate profit	3¼
Total	5½

Source: BBA, 302, 2.

pre-eminent merchant banks. The Hongkong Bank, in co-operation with Panmure Gordon, Hill & Co., had formed these relationships during the negotiations of Chinese government loan issues. The Hongkong Bank's successful invitation of the first-class merchant banks and banker (Baring Brothers, the London Rothschilds and Cassel)[122] to the bond resale was a goal that the Japanese government had pursued for a long time. The happy combination of the financial institutions, including both the banks with Far Eastern and Japanese connections (the Hongkong Bank and the Yokohama Specie Bank) and the merchant banks (Baring Brothers, the London Rothschilds and Cassel), on the loan issue market paved the way for Japan's further large-scale financial operations on the international capital markets during the Russo-Japanese War period.

5

Russo-Japanese War Loan Issues (1)

> *Sir Ernest Cassel was the last of the new breed of financiers, mainly of Jewish and mostly of German origin, who played such a pre-eminent part in English social, political and economic life of the Edwardian age, a position they owed to the unprejudiced, if not disinterested, patronage of King Edward. None contributed more to the fruitful flow of capital and diffusion of trade at a time when the industrial strength of Great Britain was ebbing;*
>
> A. Allfrey, *Edward VII and His Jewish Court*

The Japanese government needed to raise a considerable amount of money abroad during the Russo-Japanese War (1904–1905). Japan had to fight another 'war' with foreign financiers in London as Russia did in Paris.[1] K. Takahashi, now the deputy-governor of the Bank of Japan, conducted all these loan issue negotiations. It is no exaggeration to say that it was Takahashi who established the definitive pattern of the Japanese government's foreign loan issues which his successors would follow. Up to the present time, Takahashi's autobiography[2] and diary[3] have been the only detailed sources of these important financial operations on the international capital markets.[4] It must be noted, however, that his autobiography and diary had a decisive fault: Takahashi, because of his position as the Japanese government special loan commissioner, was shut out completely from the financiers' internal negotiations. His autobiography and diary cannot tell the whole story of the negotiations.

Takahashi firmly believed that 'a stroke of good fortune' won him success with the loan issues,[5] but it was the merchant banks' world-wide business network that enabled the Japanese government to manage the huge loan issue operations in London, New York, Berlin and Paris. In this chapter, material from hitherto little-explored British and Japanese archival records will be used to illuminate the first foreign loan issue made by the Japanese government during the Russo-Japanese War.

Since the Boxer Rebellion of 1900 Japan had been exposed to the growing menace of Tzarist Russia in Manchuria and Korea. At the end of 1903 the futile negotiations in St Petersburg resulted in a diplomatic rupture. The Japanese government began to make full-scale preparations for war against Russia. It is fair to say that the Japanese government financed the Russo-Japanese War largely by public loans. The total war expenditure amounted to ¥1,826,290,483 (£186,433,819); 77.7 per cent of which, approximately ¥1,418,731,000 (£144,828,789), was raised by public loans and borrowings both abroad and in Japan.[6]

In March 1904 the Japanese government implemented the first domestic war loan (Exchequer bonds) issue 'under very favourable feelings'.[7] At the same time, it aimed to issue a foreign loan to obtain gold (or gold.standard currency), because Japan's trade balance at that time suffered severely from constant deficits and there was a continued drain on gold. From the outbreak of the war in February 1904, the Bank of Japan's gold reserves sank rapidly. For Japan, it was obvious a foreign loan was the most convenient and immediate way for obtaining gold on a large scale. C.M. MacDonald, the British minister in Tokyo, predicted: 'I cannot but think that the drain of gold must continue in such proportions as to render a foreign loan an absolute necessity'.[8]

DIPLOMATIC NEGOTIATIONS

The Japanese government needed to secure funds when a Russo–Japanese War appeared inevitable in October 1903. Under the Anglo–Japanese alliance of 1902 Japan could expect some financial assistance from Britain, although Britain's strict neutrality was stipulated in the treaty unless allied countries began war with Japan.[9] T. Hayashi, the Japanese minister in London, learnt that Lord Lansdowne, the British secretary of state for foreign affairs, had confidentially told Marcus Samuel, a senior partner of M. Samuel & Co. (a London merchant bank),[10] to take into serious consideration the possibility of Britain's guaranteeing a Japanese government loan.[11]

The Japanese government, at the onset of the diplomatic negotiations, expected that Marcus Samuel's influence over the British government could help Japan's loan issue, intended as part of the preparations for the imminent Russo-Japanese conflict.[12] His idea was for a loan of £20 million to be raised by the British government and afterwards to be lent to the Japanese government at a 4 per-cent rate of interest. Marcus Samuel was reasonably confident that Baring Brothers and the Hongkong Bank would co-operate with him in this loan issue. Yet Lord Lansdowne considered that the British government would not accept such an offer because of the current unfavourable market conditions for borrowings.[13] Marcus Samuel made a revised proposal: a loan guaranteed by the British government to pay 4 per-cent annual interest for only £10 million. Lord Lansdowne, though, held out no hope of obtaining the British government's guarantee.[14]

These negotiations clearly show the British government's attitude towards the Russo-Japanese War. The British prime minister A.J. Balfour, who had a policy of avoiding direct interference in other countries' affairs, declared that 'we must be most careful not to give any advice to the Japanese to which, in case of war, they might point and say "you must help us, for it was through following your lead that we find ourselves in this mess"'.[15] In the cabinet, J.Austen Chamberlain, the chancellor of the exchequer, also upheld this opinion.[16] As early as 26 December 1903 the British government, through the Hongkong Bank, was informed of the likelihood that the Japanese government would invoke the British government's financial assistance. Lord Lansdowne replied: 'I suppose a favourable answer is out of the question, and there seems no object in sending our unfavourable one'.[17] E. Cameron, the Hongkong Bank's London manager, was afraid that the current market conditions were not favourable to the prospect of issuing a large Japanese government loan.[18]

The Japanese government started rather impetuous diplomatic negotiations with the British government on this matter. On 27 December J. Komura, the Japanese minister for foreign affairs, ordered Hayashi to try to ascertain Lord Lansdowne's opinion on whether Japan would be able to obtain some financial assistance from the British government on the basis of the Anglo-Japanese alliance.[19] Lord Lansdowne considered that the British government could probably only allow Japan to use British fleet coaling stations and colonial communications facilities. This reply was far from what the Japanese government hoped. Hayashi told Lord Lansdowne that the Japanese government desired assistance from the British government in raising money in London, and that for this purpose it had already authorized

Marcus Samuel to negotiate informally with Lord Lansdowne. Yet the matter was too serious for the British Foreign Office to decide on its own and Lord Lansdowne saw reason to consult other cabinet members.[20]

At the end of 1903 Lord Lansdowne reluctantly received from the Japanese government the direct proposal of a loan guarantee. Immediately Lord Lansdowne told Balfour that 'what she [Japan] most wants is money. . . . I do not suppose that there is any chance of our finding the £20,000,000 for which they ask.'[21] Balfour considered it unfeasible to find the £20 million for Japan. He was of the firm opinion that Britain's guarantee of the Japanese government war loan would be construed as an act of war against Russia.[22] Chamberlain desired Lord Lansdowne to deal with the matter in the same spirit as Balfour had, and pointed out the unfavourable conditions of the money market for a new loan issue.[23]

On 1 January 1904 Hayashi again discussed the subject of financial assistance with Lord Lansdowne.[24] Hayashi, although not explicitly, explained a plan for converting Japanese government domestic bonds to more favourable terms on the British government's guarantee.[25] Chamberlain, who thought that the current market would be unable to absorb the proposed Japanese government war loan issue because of an excess of loans issued during the Boer War, gave an unwilling reply to Lord Lansdowne. Thus the success of the diplomatic negotiations for securing the financial assistance of the British government is questionable. It seems to have achieved nothing so far.

Foreign governments and British financiers often requested that the British government should guarantee payment of their intended loans. Yet this was completely against the practice of the British government and before the First World War only three foreign government loans enjoyed such unusual backing, as indicated in Table 5.1.

Also the Bank of England never dealt with any foreign loan issue business. A letter, addressed to the Serbian government from the bank, declared that it was not its practice to undertake foreign loan issues as the bank invariably acted for the British government, India and the British colonies.[26]

In the middle of January 1904, as an alternative to Marcus Samuel, the Japanese government looked around for financiers who could make favourable arrangements for its loan issue without the British government's guarantee.[27] The Japanese government courted

Table 5.1 British government's guaranteed loans before 1914

Year	*Act*	*Guaranteed loan*	*Loan issuer*
1855	18 & 19 Vict. c.99	Turkey £5,000,000	Bank of England
1885	48 Vict. c.11	Egypt £9,424,000	the London Rothschilds
1898	61 Vict. c.4	Greece £6,800,000	Bank of England

Source: T.168/55, Memorandum.

the favour of the London Rothschilds,[28] but Alfred Rothschild, the second son of Lionel Nathan Rothschild (younger brother of Nathaniel Meyer Rothschild), merely indicated his house's possible support at a later occasion.[29] The London Rothschilds could not openly participate in Japan's financial operations during the war because of Jewish concerns in Russia.[30]

Meanwhile, Hayashi requested the Japanese government to send a financial expert as a government special loan commissioner to conduct loan issue negotiations in London directly.[31] He also reported that some of the eminent financiers in the City would take up the loan issue on certain securities such as customs or railway revenues, instead of the British government's guarantee.[32]

Apart from these diplomatic links, the Hongkong Bank desired to undertake the Japanese government war loan issue through its own channels. On 8 January 1904 the Hongkong Bank's Yokohama branch proposed to the London office an issue of £5 million Japanese government Treasury bills for less than 5 years.[33] The London office, after communicating with Baring Brothers, took a wait-and-see attitude and dispatched the following telegram to the Yokohama branch:

> our opinion is that a loan for a moderate amount can be floated if they are prepared to hypothecate some revenues as security. Probably five years Treasury Bills with holders' option to convert later on into 5% Bonds. It is impossible to say now what the terms would be, but fear onerous. If unwilling to hypothecate in Japan probably Formosa would do. Others are now trying to float [a] loan, consequently we would do Japanese government more harm than good by our trying the market at the present moment.[34]

In this way, the Hongkong Bank's London office by no means rejected the possibility of the Japanese government loan issue on the London capital market.

BARING BROTHERS AND WAR LOAN ISSUE

Before Takahashi's loan issue negotiations, Baring Brothers, together with the Hongkong Bank, had played a leading role in the early war loan issue negotiations with the Japanese government, although their all-out efforts came to naught. However, Baring Brothers' original idea of developing the New York capital market for international loan issues under London's primacy was to be realized in the first Japanese government war loan issue of May 1904, as will be seen later.

The Hongkong Bank and Baring Brothers were looking for attractive opportunities for the Japanese government war loan issue. In February 1904 the Hongkong Bank started loan issue negotiations. The Hongkong Bank's Yokohama branch mediated the loan issue negotiations between the Japanese government and Baring Brothers. The Hongkong Bank's Yokohama branch suggested the following loan issue terms to the London office: a £10 million 6 per-cent loan for 5 years at 85 per cent without any security.[35] Given the negative prospect for Japanese government bonds on the London Stock Exchange, the Hongkong Bank's London office considered it imperative to take prompt action and told the Yokohama branch 'to advise [the] Japanese government [that] do not delay [in] accept[ing] any money we can offer now[,] as [a] temporary reverse will occasion [a] heavy fall [of] Japanese government bonds rendering [a] new loan impossible on any terms.'[36]

The Hongkong Bank, together with Baring Brothers, agreed to offer the following preliminary terms for the Japanese government war loan issue:

Issue amount	£10 million
Interest rate (nominal)	6 per cent
Government proceeds	85 per cent per £100
Borrowing period	10 years
Security	£2 million of the proceeds to be retained in London
Redemption	option of repayment after 2 years
Others	the Japanese government should not issue any more foreign loans for 12

> months except through Baring Brothers and the Hongkong Bank.[37]

This was the most definite proposal of any submitted by the British banks before Takahashi's loan issue negotiations. Yet, even given that a war loan was regarded as extremely risky among financiers, the terms were in every respect highly unfavourable to the Japanese government: i.e. the 6 per-cent high rate of interest; the low proceeds; the security condition. They were not acceptable.

Meanwhile, Baring Brothers took several diplomatic actions. Since Britain took a strictly neutral attitude towards the Russo-Japanese War, they were afraid of sowing discord between their business strategy and the British government's diplomatic policy by becoming publicly connected with the Japanese government loan affairs. Lord Revelstoke, the head of Baring Brothers, contacted Count Alexandre Benckendorff, the Russian ambassador in London, about this matter.[38] Lord Revelstoke also frankly asked Lord Lansdowne whether it would be inconvenient to the British government if they dealt with the Japanese government war loan. Because of the delicate character of the business, Baring Brothers considered it desirable to obtain the British government's official approval before embarking upon it. Lord Lansdowne perfunctorily said 'that I could not see that we had any business to object, but that of course we could take no official cognizance of the matter and that we would be able to say that we had not been in any way concerned in it.'[39] Lord Lansdowne only reiterated the Foreign Office's established rule – no intervention in private transactions.

Baring Brothers scrutinized the loan issue markets on the Continent, particularly the Paris capital market for the proposed Japanese government loan issue. Lord Revelstoke immediately contacted E. Noetzlin, administrateur (director) of the Banque de Paris, on whether it could take some part in the impending Japanese government loan issue. In spite of the antagonistic feelings to Japan there, Baring Brothers expected the Paris capital market to act as a buffer should the London capital market fail to take a sufficient amount.

Noetzlin declined this offer, saying that 'you are right to foresee that political considerations would undoubtedly prevent the Banque de Paris doing so, however tempting such a business might be . . . it would put us in the most awkward position if it became known here that the Banque de Paris has an interest in providing money for the Japanese.'[40] At that time the Banque de Paris was negotiating an issue of the Russian government Treasury bills in Paris. Public sentiment in Paris showed itself 'tellement surchauffé en faveur des russes (really overheated in favour of the Russians).'[41]

Baring Brothers found it impossible to arrange the proposed Japanese government loan issue in London alone, without the co-operation of Continental financiers, and subsequently, did similar market research in the United States. They paid much attention to the New York capital market which at that time had not yet developed sufficiently for foreign loan issues. Baring Brothers asked Baring, Magoun & Co. in New York whether it could take the Japanese government war loan for £5 million there. Baring Brothers also made an urgent contact with several pre-eminent financiers in the United States: J. Stillman, the president of the National City Bank (New York), who had close connections with the Rockefellers; J. Schiff, a senior partner of Kuhn, Loeb & Co.; Kidder Peabody & Co. (Boston).[42]

F.A. Vanderlip, the vice-president of the National City Bank, relayed Stillman's message to the effect that he [Stillman] admitted the probability of being able to underwrite £5 million of the bonds in the US markets, but felt very dubious about a large amount of the loan being taken by public investors. Vanderlip also communicated with W.G. Rockefeller, son of William Rockefeller, and J.A. McCall, the president of the New York Life Assurance Co., who had been expected to become large takers of this operation. Yet the proposed Japanese government loan business did not attract them partly because of neutral feelings in the United States towards the war and partly because of the great risks. Furthermore, Vanderlip strongly recommended that Baring Brothers should approach Kuhn, Loeb & Co., which had acquired much experience in dealing with railway securities, about the business.[43]

Baring, Magoun & Co., however, was optimistic about the proposed loan issue on the US market saying 'there must be a fair chance of attracting the public'. They considered that underwriting of the loan issue for £5 million would be feasible and public subscriptions at 90 per cent would take £2 million of the bonds on the condition of the principal and interest being paid in New York.[44] Baring, Magoun & Co. was keen to launch the Japanese government war loan issue in New York. Even after Baring Brothers' withdrawal from the business early in March, it was still willing to handle it when the Hongkong Bank requested placing some of the loan directly in the United States,[45] but Baring Brothers did not like their name [Baring] to be connected with any Japanese government borrowings during the Russo-Japanese War.[46]

On 4 March 1904 Baring Brothers, taking into consideration all the factors surrounding the Japanese government loan issue business, finally found a reason to postpone involvement in it. Lord Revelstoke's letter addressed to Hugo Baring, a partner of Baring, Magoun & Co., adduced his reasons for reaching such a conclusion:

> we have decided, after mature deliberation, not to take part in a public issue at the present moment. The fact is that there is a feeling here among the highest people that it would be well to preserve a more or less neutral attitude, in spite of the fact that the Japanese are our allies; and as it is obvious that these Japanese are not averse to raising a Loan, and that if things go against them they might have to come again for a still further issue: you will understand how averse we should be to making an issue which might go to a discount, and how much we are convinced that we had better await a probable conclusion of hostilities before embarking on a large responsibility, which we should have to carry through without any help from the Continent. We have explained our attitude fully to the Hongkong & Shanghai Bank, who are on the most friendly terms with us, and who quite recognised the wisdom and soundness of our views. They are evidently in a different position from ourselves: they have a large business with the East, and are above all things anxious that no competitor should wrest any good business from them. To this consideration we do not attach so much importance, and have, therefore, informed the Hongkong & Shanghai Bank that we consider they were quite justified in proceeding to arrange any negotiations they may have in hand with fresh partners.[47]

Obviously there were several reasons for Baring Brothers' faltering in the business. Firstly, they were sensitive about the Russo–Japanese War and had still retained close connections with the Russian government as a London agent. In terms of business strategy, it was more prudent by far for Baring Brothers to maintain strict neutrality than to play an aggressive role in the Japanese government war loan issue.

Secondly, and more importantly, Baring Brothers were afraid of being involved in a perilous loan issue, because they would have to carry out the Japanese government war loan issue without any assistance from the Paris capital market; their estimate of the US market was that it could absorb at most £2 million. Thirdly, Baring Brothers, unlike the Hongkong Bank, had no large volume of transactions with the Far East. In this situation they showed no inclination to plunge into such a risky venture. In fact, when Takahashi arrived in London toward the end of March 1904, Lord Revelstoke explained the impossibility of undertaking public subscriptions of the Japanese government loan issue and proposed a private borrowing to the extent of £60,000 in the form of Japanese government Treasury bills.[48]

However, when Baring Brothers as well as the London Rothschilds desired to become one of the loan issuers of the Japanese government 4 per-cent loan in 1905, R.H. Whalley, the general manager of Parr's Bank, censured this conduct. He emphasized that even when hostilities to Japan had already commenced, Baring Brothers had felt that they could not have their name, which would have been of value to the Japanese government, publicly connected with any Japanese loan issue.[49]

The London Rothschilds' attitude towards the Russian government was different. Despite an amicable letter from the Russian Ministry of Finance,[50] since the 3½ per-cent loan issue in 1893 the London Rothschilds had refrained from involvement in Russian government loan issues and were acting only as a paying agent because of the ill-treatment of Jews in Russia.[51] The London Rothschilds no longer placed trust in Russian government finance and Alfred Rothschild rightly depicted it as a 'juggler'.[52]

Although the Japanese government had embarked upon the loan issue negotiations with the Hongkong Bank's Yokohama branch, on 3 March 1904 the government appointed K. Takahashi as the special loan commissioner.[53] This meant that the Japanese government had decided to negotiate the intended loan issue not through the Hongkong Bank's Yokohama branch but directly in London.

Cameron was unwilling to give up this lucrative business opportunity and persuaded Lord Revelstoke to reconsider the previous decision.[54] Although the Hongkong Bank's original plan of issuing the Japanese government loan in conjunction with Baring Brothers had reached an impasse, Cameron believed it feasible, saying: 'Our [the Hongkong Bank's London office's] opinion is that danger is exaggerated, but we do not feel confident that money can be got here, in any case it is certain not without American help.'[55] The Hongkong Bank considered that the Japanese government war loan issue was, perhaps, possible with 'American help'.

TAKAHASHI'S MISSION

On 6 February 1904 Japan broke off diplomatic relations with Russia and the Russo-Japanese War broke out. Initially M. Matsukata, a senior statesman, who was in charge of the management of the war finance, nominated Takahashi to be the Japanese government loan commissioner.[56]

The Japanese government decided to raise war loans for ¥200 million (£20,417,000) at the cabinet meeting held on 17 February 1904,[57] and ordered the Bank of Japan to arrange a foreign loan for £10 million on the following terms:

Issue amount	£10 million
Interest rate (nominal)	less than 5 per cent
Redemption	within 45 years
Security	customs and railway revenues
Issue charges	less than 4 per cent excluding the British stamp duty
Others	resale of existing domestic bonds should also be taken into consideration.[58]

On 19 February 1904 Takahashi left for London via New York. Towards the end of March Takahashi began loan issue negotiations with financiers in the City and looked for a loan issue bank which could favourably undertake the intended war loan. He considered it best to approach the Yokohama Specie Bank's correspondents for the loan issue. First, Takahashi sounded out A.A. Shand, a manager of Parr's Bank, on the possibility of the loan issue for £10 million. Shand introduced him to Cecil P. Parr, the chairman of Parr's Bank, and John Dun, former general manager and now a director of Parr's Bank.[59] Takahashi continued interviews on the loan issue with several banks and stockbrokers, such as Cameron,[60] W.M. Koch and A. Levita, partners of Panmure Gordon & Co.,[61] J.H. Gwyther, the chairman of the Chartered Bank,[62] and the Union of London & Smiths Bank's directors.[63]

Takahashi made the acquaintance of several pre-eminent merchant bankers, such as Lord Revelstoke[64] and Alfred Rothschild.[65] Meanwhile, H.R. Beeton,[66] a stockbroker in the firm of Woolston, Beeton, Brodrick & West, suggested to Takahashi that the Japanese government should employ its financial agent in London, in considering the way of colonial government loan issues, and depend upon influential financiers such as Ernest Cassel who was able to arrange Anglo–American loan issues by inviting the Rothschilds, J.S. Morgan and so on.[67] Ernest Cassel was a string-puller of huge financial operations in the City and an intimate friend of King Edward VII. Cassel seems to have played an important role in the series of Japanese government war loan issues during 1904 and 1905, even though his name never became public. In fact, Takahashi often relied upon Cassel's paramount influence over financiers as a last resort, when difficulties occurred in the loan issue negotiations.[68] It must be noted that from the early stage of the Japanese government loan issue negotiations, financial experts in the City paid much attention to the possibility of an Anglo–American loan.

Takahashi did not make headway in the loan issue negotiations easily. Not only because of the ominous market conditions for a large new loan issue, but also because of misgivings over Japan's supremacy in the war, the British banks cast doubt upon the success of the proposed loan issue on the market. Since the outbreak of the war (6 February) the prices of Japanese government bonds on the London Stock Exchange had fallen considerably, while those of Russian government bonds had remained more stable.[69] The Russian government secured firm financial assistance from France. Unlike the French government, the British government did not make its attitude clear towards the Russo-Japanese War. There were serious debates on the neutrality under the Anglo-Japanese alliance and some bankers even considered that raising money for Japan might violate it.[70]

Takahashi had to hasten completion of the loan issue. The drain of gold from Japan being so immense since the outbreak of the war, the specie reserves at the Bank of Japan were rapidly diminishing, far more in fact than had been anticipated. In May the reserves reached a bottom of ¥68,087,261 (£6,951,000).[71] The Japanese government was afraid of depleting gold stocks reserved for settlement of the trade balances. Takahashi lost no more time in bringing about the loan issue, even though the terms proposed by British financiers in the loan issue negotiations were not fully satisfactory.

So imperative was it to ensure financial resources for the war that on 9 April 1904 Komura informed Hayashi that if it should prove impossible to conclude the loan issue negotiations immediately, the Japanese government gave permission even for making temporary private borrowings and afterwards converting them to public bonds when the market showed a favourable turn.[72]

In spite of Takahashi's proposal of the loan issue to the City financiers, only three banks: Parr's Bank, the Hongkong Bank and the Yokohama Specie Bank, accepted this. The Chartered Bank which had participated in some of the Japanese government loan issues in the past, after long deliberation, refused to undertake the proposed loan.[73] Because of the unfavourable outcome of the previous loan issue in 1899, it came to hold to a conservative policy towards the Japanese government war loan issue.

Why was Parr's Bank involved in this operation? For it is true that Shand took the initiative in Takahashi's loan issue negotiations with Parr's Bank. On the basis of the established business relationship with the Japanese government, Takahashi persuaded Parr's Bank to become the main loan issuer.[74] Hayashi described it thus 'he [Takahashi] had approached several financiers on the subject [the loan issue] . . . but all of them declined to take the matter up, except Mr. Dun of the Parr's Bank. He . . . succeeded in forming a group of issuing banks and in floating the loans.'[75]

The Hongkong Bank was looking for a new partner in the Japanese government war loan business after Baring Brothers' withdrawal. At the next stage, Takahashi and Shand mediated between the Hongkong Bank and Parr's Bank, and successfully formed a group of loan issue banks.[76]

Takahashi considered the three following methods of raising money on the market: (i) an issue of Treasury bills for 1 or 2 years; (ii) an issue of new bonds; (iii) a resale of domestic bonds. Given the bad market circumstances, Takahashi at first supposed that either an issue of Treasury bills or a resale of domestic bonds would be more feasible. The Japanese government instructed him to attempt an issue of Treasury bills rather than a resale of domestic bonds.[77]

However, Japan's victories at the onset of the war brought about favourable changes in the ongoing negotiations. This is clear from the fluctuations in the prices of Japanese government bonds on the London Stock Exchange, which suddenly began rising in the middle of April 1904.[78] Given these improved circumstances, Takahashi now proposed to issue a new secured loan for £10 million, not Treasury bills, and the loan issue banks finally agreed to this for half the proposed amount.[79] On 27 April 1904 Takahashi informed the Japanese government of the following provisional terms reached with the loan issue banks:

Issue amount	£5 million (half of the total amount of £10 million)
Interest rate (nominal)	6 per cent
Borrowing period	7 years
Security	revenue of the customs duty (nominal)
Issue price	93 per cent (to the public) 88 per cent (to the government)
Others	every month one twelfth of the total yearly payment of the principal and interest should be paid to the representative bank of bond holders in London.[80]

In response to this proposal, the Japanese government directed Takahashi to re-negotiate on the following points: (i) to raise the government proceeds closer to 90 per cent from 88 per cent; (ii) to remove the clause of the remittance of the principal to London. S. Matsuo, the governor of the Bank of Japan, urged him to complete the negotiations as soon as possible.[81] It seemed likely that the Japanese government would accept the terms of the loan issue.

Takahashi raised the proceeds to 90 per cent from 88 per cent.[82] In the final stages, the Japanese government, through Cameron, received confirmation of the British government's favourable views towards this financial operation in London.[83] In this way, by 3 May 1904 the loan issue negotiations between Takahashi, Parr's Bank, the Hongkong Bank and the Yokohama Specie Bank were closed, leaving the other half of the £5 million issue amount reserved for the future. However, the ongoing loan negotiations with the loan issue banks effected a significant change. Baring Brothers, probably as a result of Cassel's influence, had almost persuaded J. Schiff, a senior partner of the Kuhn, Loeb & Co. in New York, to become a loan issuer of the other £5 million. The 'team activity' nature of merchant banks produced an international linkage of the loan issue markets to the Japanese government loan issue.

LOAN ISSUE IN NEW YORK

Early in March 1904 Baring Brothers had withdrawn from the loan issue negotiations. At the end of March Lord Revelstoke, in accordance with the progress of Takahashi's negotiations with the loan issue banks, directed G. Farrer, a director of Baring Brothers and then temporarily in the United States, to make contact again with Stillman on the possibility of floating the Japanese government war loan on the New York capital market.[84] Stillman, however, was not keen to issue it.[85]

However, as a consequence of Cassel's strong influcncc in the City, the other half of the Japanese government war loan (£5 million) was to be arranged on the New York capital market. Cassel always acted as a co-ordinator behind the scenes among financiers involved in a connection, and it is difficult to know to what extent Cassel was actually concerned in this operation. E. Fukai, Takahashi's secretary in the loan issue negotiations, inferred in his reminiscences that Cassel would persuade Schiff to take part in the Japanese government war loan issue in the United States,[86] although he [Schiff] had already been approached by Baring Brothers. Following a trip to Egypt in May 1904, it is certain that Cassel and Schiff met in Frankfurt.[87] Both were Jewish emigrants from Germany. There is no definite evidence but probably they would discuss the possibility of a Japanese government war loan issue in the United States.[88] It should be noted that the Japanese government war loan issue in the United States was thus promoted by a merchant bankers' network connected by filial, ethnic and religious ties.

Schiff had moved to the United States from Frankfurt in 1865 when he was 18 years old, and ten years later threw himself energetically into the affairs and operations of Kuhn, Loeb & Co. founded by Abraham Kuhn and Solomon Loeb in 1867.[89] Schiff had made substantial transactions in American railway investment with Cassel and their relations were so intimate that Cassel always retained his own account at Kuhn, Loeb & Co.[90] It was said that 'he [Schiff] had the advantage of the guidance of that distinguished financier [Cassel]'.[91] It was the second time that Schiff was involved in Japanese government loan issue business. In 1873, although it had been fruitless, the young Schiff had attempted to raise money for the Japanese government in Frankfurt, as seen in chapter 3.

No evidence survives showing the negotiations between Schiff and Cassel but perhaps Cassel, who was looking for a loan issuer for the other half of the Japanese government war loan, persuaded Schiff to introduce it on the US market. This idea of Cassel accidentally coincided with Baring Brothers' business strategy to develop the New York capital market for foreign loan issues. Cassel probably mediated between Lord Revelstoke and Schiff. It is confirmed that Lord Revelstoke met Schiff towards the end of April 1904.[92]

The negotiations between Lord Revelstoke and Schiff seemed to go well and Lord Revelstoke immediately despatched a telegram to Farrer that '[I have] seen Schiff who is anxious [to] take £5,000,000 loan . . . [as a] part of the £10,000,000 issue here and in America – Schiff [is] very confident.'[93] It was on that evening that Schiff first met Takahashi in London at a dinner given by Arthur Hill.[94] Hill, a former partner of Panmure Gordon, Hill & Co. and then a partner of Hill & Sons and also of Speyer Brothers, may have arranged this so as to introduce Schiff to Takahashi.

On 4 May Takahashi informed the Japanese government that Schiff had agreed to undertake the other half amount of the loan in New York and by this, he had successfully completed the war loan issue for £10 million. Hayashi strongly advised Komura to accept this offer promptly by pointing out 'not only financial but also political benefits'.[95] The Japanese government approved this proposal[96] and declined M. Samuel & Co.'s offer of a loan for £12 or £13 million on the same terms as the loan issue banks'.[97]

The negotiations were nearing the final stage. Baring Brothers agreed to prepare marketing for the loan issue in New York. Lord Revelstoke offered the business to Stillman and expected him to 'choke off' the probable competition among financiers there.[98] The terms of the loan issue in New York arranged between Lord Revelstoke, Schiff and Cameron were as follows:

(i) The London issue banks (Parr's Bank, the Hongkong Bank and the Yokohama Specie Bank) should purchase the Japanese government 6 percent bonds for £10 million.

(ii) The London issue banks should pay a 90 per-cent price of the bonds with a half-yearly coupon payable 5 October 1904.

(iii) Kuhn, Loeb & Co. should agree to purchase bonds to the value of £5 million from the London issue banks at 90 per cent and pay a ½ per-cent commission to Baring Brothers.
(iv) The bonds and coupons should be payable in sterling and dollars otherwise at the rate of exchange of US$4.87 to £1.
(v) Issue price was to be 93½ per cent and an underwriting syndicate was to be formed at a 2 per-cent commission. The London issue banks and Kuhn, Loeb & Co. should place £5 million of the bonds separately for underwriting but the London issue banks should have an interest of £1 million in the bonds underwritten in American.[99]

These terms of the New York issue banks were almost the same as the London issue banks', except for paying the ½ per-cent intermediary commission to Baring Brothers. Baring Brothers' position in this agreement was rather ambiguous. Baring Brothers were the intermediary of this loan issue in New York. The loan issue banks, especially Parr's Bank, from the outset to the end, regarded Baring Brothers' role as 'Kuhn, Loeb & Co.'s agent'.[100]

Why was Schiff so ardent to tackle the Japanese government war loan issue in the United States? As an investment banker he seems to have sufficiently assessed the potential of this business.[101] In addition, Schiff, as the president of the American Jewish Association, had a particular interest in the outcome of the Russo-Japanese War. Takahashi, in his contribution to Schiff's biography, explained what he felt to be Schiff's subconscious intention as 'he [Schiff] felt sure that if defeated, Russia would be led in the path of betterment, whether it be revolution or reformation, and he decided to exercise whatever influence he had for placing the weight of American resources on the side of Japan'.[102] Schiff referred to the Russian government privately as 'the enemy of mankind'.[103] Ill-treatment of Jews in Russia may have influenced Schiff's final decision to embark upon the Japanese government war loan issue.

In this loan issue the London issue banks were somewhat pressed to find a partner for the other half of the amount. It was their established business practice, in the first place, to look to the Continent, especially the Paris capital market. Yet the Russo-Japanese War frustrated Paris financiers' desire of taking up the Japanese government war loan business. Instead of Paris, Baring Brothers switched their attention to the New York capital market. However, there had been 'a harbinger of change'[104] in 1900 when the Chancellor of the Exchequer (M.Hicks Beach), on the basis of J.S. Morgan & Co.'s London–New York axis, turned more of his attention to the New York capital market for issuing the Boer War loans.

Baring Brothers' efforts to introduce the Japanese government war loan issue to New York were of great importance in the history of foreign loan issues in the United States. Cassel was highly appreciative of Baring Brothers' conduct in this loan issue.[105] Up to about the beginning of the century the New York capital market had only worked in an underwriting capacity, in conjunction with London, for large-volume Continental securities, and sold bonds especially for German and Swedish governments. The Japanese government war loan issue in New York accelerated the rise of a foreign loan issue market in the United States.[106] Carosso in his general history of American investment banking depicted this as 'one of its [Kuhn, Loeb & Co.'s] largest and most important flotations up to this time [1904].'[107] All things considered, it is fair to say that this loan issue altered the contemporary structure of the international loan issue markets, over-centralized as they were on Europe, and assisted New York's rise.

Meanwhile, the loan issue in New York held another significance for Britain, in a political sense. The British government did not like to be seen giving direct assistance to Japan and desired to keep a strictly neutral attitude towards the Russo-Japanese War. The Japanese government loan issue in London would surely have presented a crucial problem for the British government even though there had been no official intervention.[108] Such worry was now ended by the American banks' participation. The co-operation of the two markets, Schiff wrote, prepared for the success of the subsequent Japanese government war loan issues during 1904 and 1905.[109]

PERFORMANCE

By 6 May 1904 the loan issue negotiations for £10 million, equally split between London and New York were completed. The final terms of the loan issue contract with the loan issue banks were as follows:

Issue amount	£10 million
Issue place	London and New York equally
Issue price	93½ per cent (to the public)

Table 5.2 London issue banks' underwriting (May 1904, London) (£)

Underwriting syndicate	*Underwriting amount*	*Underwriting commission (2%)*	*Brokerage commission (½ %)**
Panmure Gordon	2,500,000.00	50,000.00	50,000.00
Hongkong Bank	1,152,666.66	23,053.33	
Yokohama Specie Bank	646,666.66	12,933.33	
Parr's Bank	1,000,666.66	20,013.33	
Total	5,300,000.00	106,000.00	50,000.00

Source: WBA, D2469.
Notes: £300,000 over-underwritten;
* ½ per cent of £10 million (total issue amount).

	90 per cent (to the government)
Interest rate (nominal)	6 per cent
Yield at issue	6.4
Borrowing period	7 years
Security	first charge on the customs revenues
Others	the Japanese government should pay 1/12 of the sum required for the interest every month to the Hongkong Bank and the Yokohama Specie Bank; the principal should be first charge on the secured customs revenues if the principal of the loan is not paid at least 14 days before the due date; Kuhn, Loeb & Co. should pay a ½ per-cent commission to Baring Brothers; the Japanese government should reserve the right to redeem at par, all or any of the bonds, at any time after 1907, on giving 6 months' previous notice.[110]

Yet the Japanese government was not entirely satisfied with these terms. In fact, Y. Sakatani, the Japanese vice-minister of finance, complained of the low issue price and the high rate of interest.[111]

The loan issue in London and New York was to be underwritten fully by the separate syndicates[112] at a 2 per-cent commission. In

London the loan issue banks organized their own syndicates, as indicated in Table 5.2. The underwriting syndicate in New York included many of largest banks and insurance companies there. Kuhn, Loeb & Co. completed the underwriting syndicate for US$25 million (£5 million).[113] On 11 May 1904 the prospectuses were issued simultaneously both in London and New York.[114] Kuhn, Loeb & Co. persuaded the National City Bank and the National Bank of Commerce in New York to take part in this loan issue as the loan issuers.[115] Enthusiasm for Japanese government bonds on the London Stock Exchange began and their prices suddenly and steeply rose after the announcement of the new 6 per-cent war loan issue. Many financial papers made a very favourable assessment and had an optimistic view of placing the loan on the market. *The Statist*, from the viewpoint of public investors, pointed out the following advantages of this loan issue: the low rate of the issue price, an excellent security on the loan and the high rate of interest.[116]

The number of the subscribers was enormous: the *Financial Times* described them as 'expecting to receive no more than 2 per-cent, of their subscriptions'[117] and the London & Brazilian Bank reported that '[the] Japanese war loan applications were made for £100,000,000 within a few hours of the publication of the prospectus.'[118] A clerk at the Hongkong Bank's London office depicted the rush of the subscriptions as 'when the door was opened the crowd pushed the Bobbies inside and bent many of our railing in their scramble to get application forms. It was necessary to call out all the Rugger players.'[119] In London the total amount of the applications reached £151,975,500, almost 30 times oversubscribed, and the total number was 30,022.[120] One of the prominent features of these subscriptions was a large number of small applicants. The London Rothschilds recommended to their Continental clients to purchase the bonds, saying that they were better secured than the Japanese government 4 per-cent loan of 1899.[121] Thus the operation in London showed great success. Temporary pressure on the money market, caused by the subscriptions, had been feared, but the money requirements for them brought about only a slightly higher rate of interest than usual.[122]

The subscriptions in New York were also over-subscribed fivefold. The closing price on the kerb market (an unofficial market) amounted to 94¾ per cent, 1¼ per cent above the issue price.[123]

The first Japanese government war loan issue in 1904 deserved

Table 5.3 Yields of foreign government loans issued in London during 1904 (per cent)

(1) Month	*(2) Government*	*(3) Interest rate (nominal)*	*(4) Issue price*	*(5) Yield at issue*
February	Ecuador	4	68	5.9
May	Japan	6	93½	6.4
May	Cuba	5	97	5.2
June	Greece	4	84	4.8
July	China	5	97½	5.1
November	Japan	6	90½	6.6
December	Mexico	4	94	4.3

Source: Appendix A.
Note: (5)=(3)/(4) × 100.

many investors' especial interest.[124] The reason was that, compared with other foreign government loans issued on the London capital market in 1904, the yields of the two Japanese government war loans (6.4 per cent and 6.6 per cent) were the most advantageous (Table 5.3), and the loan issue was firmly underwritten by many first-class merchant banks, which undoubtedly gave some assurance to public investors.[125] Owing to the enormous amount of the subscriptions, the applications were cut off in the allotment.[126]

In comparison with the bond resale in 1902 (the 5½ per cent) and the loan issue in 1899 (the 4 per cent), the 6½ per-cent loan issue commission, partly deriving from the balance of the interest paid in October 1904,[127] was very expensive to the Japanese government

Table 5.4 Commission of 6 per-cent loan issue (May 1904, London) (per cent)

Underwriting	2
Brokerage (placing underwriting)	½
Brokerage (application)	¼
Advertising	¼
Coupon paying	1 23/48
Issue banks	2 1/48
Total	6½

Source: WBA, D2469.
Notes: Balance of the interest of October 1904 was included in the commission.

(Table 5.4). Undoubtedly the financiers considered the character of this war loan to be parlous.

The Japanese government, depending upon the merchant banks' widely scattered network of correspondents, successfully accomplished the first foreign war loan issue, even though the loan issue terms themselves were not favourable. Now the New York capital market came to be included in Japanese government financial operations. The collaboration of the Anglo–American markets would lead the Japanese government to success in further loan flotations on the international capital markets. Without doubt, this newly-established loan issue pattern was born of the combination of the loan issue banks which had been formed in the previous Japanese government loan issues. At first, the banks with Far Eastern and Japanese connections, such as the Hongkong Bank, Parr's Bank and the Yokohama Specie Bank, brought loan issues to the London capital market and floated them in conjunction with the merchant banks (Baring Brothers and Cassel) and the stockbroker (Panmure Gordon & Co.). The banks with Far Eastern and Japanese connections, however, were not experts in international financial operations and played only a limited role in linking the international capital markets. Subsequently, the merchant banks, although their names did not appear publicly, prepared the expansion of the loan issue markets for the Japanese government loan issue. The merchant banks brought off the Japanese government loan issue in London and New York simultaneously.

6

Russo-Japanese War Loan Issues (2)

Western Europe financed its [Japan's] armaments, its wars, and its economic development, drawing it in to its system of alliance. The growing strength obtained from the use of that capital made Japan a better credit risk for investors and a more important ally.

H. Feis, *Europe the World's Banker 1870–1914*

Japan's unprecedented financial experience during the Russo-Japanese War (1904–1905) is of great use for a study of foreign loans on the international capital markets. In a very short span of time (19 months), Japan floated a series of five foreign loans in London, New York, Germany and Paris. The large scale of financial operations on the international capital markets, especially the expansion and integration of the loan issue markets, was unique in the world's financial history.

The first Japanese government foreign war loan was floated on the London and New York capital markets in May 1904, as shown previously. In November the second one was made by the same banks. This loan was placed on practically the same terms as the first. The Japanese government, however, reconsidered the excessive reliance on the Anglo–American capital markets. In the third loan issue of March 1905 German banks approached the London issue banks: i.e. Parr's Bank, the Hongkong Bank and the Yokohama Specie Bank, to participate in this loan issue, but the London issue banks refused this. The pattern of the fourth war loan issue in July 1905 did not follow the previous three and the loan issue places came to include Germany. Through Kuhn, Loeb & Co.'s business channel the German banks floated the Japanese government war loan in Germany.

After the Russo-Japanese War, in November 1905, the French government came to agree to the Japanese government loan issue in Paris. The Paris and London Rothschilds were finally involved in this large financial operation as the main loan issuers. This became a landmark in the history of Japanese government foreign loan issues. Now, with London's profound influence on Japan's borrowing undermined, the Japanese government held to a new policy of systematically seeking to concentrate loan issues on the international financial centre offering the most attractive terms.

Borrowing countries, pursuing more favourable loan issue terms, could move from one capital market to another through merchant banks' correspondent networks.[1] The expansion of the loan issue markets for Japanese government loans during 1904 and 1905, which brought 'the greatest possible freedom in dealing' to both the borrower and investors,[2] become a key question in this chapter.

SIX PER-CENT LOAN ISSUE IN NOVEMBER 1904

The Japanese government, which nervously anticipated accelerated military expenditure in accordance with the progress of the war, attempted to bring out a new war loan after the first in May 1904. In July 1904 A. Sone, the Japanese minister of finance, drew up a plan for raising money for either £10 million or £20 million within 1904.[3] His initial idea was to resell Japanese government 5 per-cent domestic bonds endorsed to pay the principal and interest in sterling.[4] K. Takahashi suggested a new 5 per-cent loan issue because the 5 per-cent domestic bonds had not yet been quoted on the New York Stock Exchange.[5] Yet he was forced to accept a 6 per-cent loan.[6] The allure of Japanese government bonds on the London Stock Exchange was not sufficiently strong and their quotation prices had temporarily plummeted. Public investors expected a new more advantageous (higher interest) loan issue.[7]

Towards the beginning of October Takahashi reached a preliminary accord with the London issue banks on a new 6 per-cent loan issue for £12 million.[8] However, Kuhn, Loeb & Co. had no confidence in placing the insufficiently secured long-term bonds on the market,[9] since the popularity of the first Japanese government war bonds had temporarily faded in New York and the quotation price was always much lower than in London.[10] The demand for Japanese government bonds in New York was limited. This cleavage in the quotation prices between the two markets decisively impeded the smooth conclusion of the second war loan issue negotiations.

Ernest Cassel began to co-ordinate various interests among the loan issue banks behind the scenes.[11] By lowering the issue price Kuhn, Loeb & Co. finally agreed to take half the issue amount (£6 million) in much the same way as before.[12] On 17 October Kuhn, Loeb & Co. and the London issue banks agreed on the following loan issue terms:

Issue amount	£12 million (split equally between London and New York)
Rate of interest (nominal)	6 per cent
Yield at issue	6.6 per cent
Issue price	91 per cent (to the public) 87½ per cent (to the government)
Borrowing period	7 years
Security	remainder of the customs revenues
Loan issue commission	nearly 4⁷⁄₁₀ per cent including the half yearly interest.[13]

Takahashi immediately reported these to the Japanese government,[14] but the government did not readily assent to them because they were very different from what Sone and Takahashi had previously concurred. In particular, the low government proceeds (87½ per cent) were unsatisfactory and S. Matsuo, the governor of the Bank of Japan, ordered Takahashi to raise them[15] and to postpone finalizing the present negotiations, unless more favourable terms were offered.[16] As things turned out, however, this wait-and-see attitude of the Japanese government proved wrong. The movement in rates of interest was upwards and they rose sharply from November;[17] accordingly the quotation prices of the Japanese government bonds began to fall steeply, especially on the New York Stock Exchange. Once it perceived the exacerbated market conditions, the Japanese government authorized Takahashi to conclude the negotiations promptly on the previous terms,[18] but the loan issue banks had by then withdrawn the offer.

Loan issue terms are always regulated by current market conditions and a definite tender cannot be valid for long.[19] The Japanese government's mistaken appreciation of the contemporary market conditions frustrated Takahashi's procuring the advantageous loan issue terms which they could have enjoyed.

British public opinion also showed a considerable change. At the beginning of October, S. Ōkuma's pessimistic speech at the Tokyo Clearing House, in which he stressed the need for further foreign loan issues for the war, caused a considerable decline in the prices of the Japanese government bonds in both London and New York.[20] In addition, the Russian Baltic fleet's brutal attack on British fishing boats in the North Sea raised the British war fears.[21]

On 26 October Kuhn, Loeb & Co. informed the London issue banks that the critical downfall in the prices of the first Japanese government war bonds on the New York Stock Exchange made it impossible at 91 per cent for them to place any Japanese government loan for the moment.[22] Kuhn, Loeb & Co. wished to reduce the issue price reflecting the market conditions in New York.[23] In general, new loan issue prices are determined by the prices of existing bonds on the market.[24] The quotation price of the first 6 per-cent war bonds sank to 91⅞ in New York, only a ⅞ surplus to the new issue price. Obviously the 91 per-cent issue price was too high for the New York capital market.

On 3 November Takahashi and the loan issue banks, again, agreed on the second war loan issue for £12 million:

Issue amount	£12 million (split equally between London and New York)
Rate of interest (nominal)	6 per cent
Yield at issue	6.6 per cent
Issue price	90½ per cent (to the public) 86½ per cent (to the government)
Borrowing period	7 years
Others	the excess of the issue price above 90 per cent, namely ½ per cent, should be divided between the loan issue banks and the Japanese government; the proceeds raised in New York should be kept there at the disposal of the Japanese government and not be transferred to London; the Japanese government should reserve the right to redeem at par, all or any of the bonds, at any time after 1907, on giving 6 months' previous notice.[25]

In the middle of October, however, Speyer Brothers, an Anglo-American bank, suddenly asked the Hongkong Bank to introduce them to the Japanese government war loan business.[26] Speyer Brothers had maintained intimate connections with the Hongkong Bank through Panmure Gordon & Co. Speyer Brothers, until that time, had had no direct relations with Japan, but were perhaps attracted by the success of the first war loan issue.

Speyer Brothers were set up in London in 1861 and closely linked with their sister firms: Speyer & Co. in New York and Lazard Speyer-Ellissen in Frankfurt-on-Main. Speyer Brothers, with a correspondent network covering the United States, the Continent and London, would be most effective in placing a loan simultaneously in major financial centres.[27] It was likely that Speyer Brothers would become Kuhn, Loeb & Co.'s most formidable competitor in New York. Kuhn, Loeb & Co. was to organize a loan issue on the New York capital market alone, but Speyer Brothers were capable of arranging a loan issue internationally through their sister firms.[28]

Merchant bankers' business conduct was no longer strictly competitive and co-operation was often preferred.[29] Lord Revelstoke advised Kuhn, Loeb & Co. to make a political offer to Speyer Brothers, that is to say, Speyer Brothers would undertake a certain amount of the loan issue on the same terms as the London issue banks.[30] Kuhn, Loeb & Co. only agreed to offer Speyer Brothers £500,000 of the bonds at a 1 per-cent commission in New York and London respectively,[31] but Speyer Brothers refused this.[32]

The underwriting syndicates were organized on a 2 per-cent commission.[33] The loan issue banks authorized the Swiss Bankverein to receive the subscriptions in Switzerland.[34] In New York, Kuhn, Loeb & Co. did not form an underwriting syndicate and the loan issue banks (loan issue bank syndicate) underwrote the whole amount. On 14 November the prospectuses were published and the public subscriptions implemented. All the subscriptions were oversubscribed. In London the total sum amounted to £80,533,800, 13⅖ times oversubscribed;[35] in New York the oversubscription was 1½ times;[36] in Hamburg there were subscriptions for £101,000.[37]

Takahashi and the loan issue banks had much difficulty in fixing the issue prices, which resulted mainly from the different quotation prices of the first war bonds in London and New York. In addition, the rise in interest rates also frustrated the smooth loan issue. However, the terms of the loan issue still seemed too expensive to the Japanese government and incurred much criticism in Japan: the 6 per-cent interest rate was too high and the 90½ issue price was less than the first by 2 per cent. Perhaps most Japanese expected that the second war loan issue would have obtained a more favourable assessment from foreign investors on the basis of the victories against Russia in Manchuria.[38] The Japanese government reconsidered its current policy of counting so heavily upon the Anglo-American capital markets alone for war finance. Sone ordered the Japanese minister in Paris to investigate the likelihood of a Japanese government war loan issue there.[39] Furthermore, the Japanese government attempted to approach other notable American financiers, for instance the Morgan group, which was often in opposition to Kuhn, Loeb & Co. in railway investment business.[40] The Japanese government was looking around for more favourable loan issue facilities.

FOUR-AND-A-HALF PER-CENT LOAN ISSUE IN MARCH 1905

The Japanese government had not obtained really advantageous foreign loan issues so far. In order to ensure more favourable loan issue terms for the third war loan issue, it intended to extend a loan issue to the markets on the Continent, but I. Motono, the Japanese minister in Paris, reported that it would be absolutely impossible to place any Japanese government war loan on the Paris capital market during the Russo-Japanese War.[41] France had built up close relations with Russia under the Franco–Russian entente of 1894. The diplomatic situation in France thus frustrated Japan's financial operations there.

Germany's political posture towards the Russo-Japanese War was a contrast to France's. Initially Germany had maintained strict neutrality in the war but in January 1905 Russia floated a loan for DM325 million (£15,979,166) under the auspices of the leading Berlin banks such as Mendelssohn, the Disconto-Gesellschaft, S. Bleichröder and the Berliner Handels-Gesellschaft.[42] In this situation, Bernhard von Bülow, *Reichskanzler* (chancellor), asserted that Japan was equally free to borrow money on the German capital markets.[43] Katsunosuke Inoue, the Japanese minister in Berlin, reported that it would be feasible to bring about a Japanese government war loan issue in Germany because Oswald von Richthofen, the German foreign minister, would allow it.[44]

Japan needed further foreign loans because it had to import much of its military equipment. In January 1905 a Japanese cabinet meeting decided, for the moment, to issue a new foreign loan for ¥200 million

(£20,416,666).[45] On 10 February 1905 Sone ordered Takahashi to arrange a new foreign loan, one at less than 6 per cent, for £20 million.[46]

From early in 1905 the conditions of the London capital market improved remarkably for new loan issues; money was extremely plentiful and bank rate was brought down to 2½ per cent on 9 March. The Japanese government 6 per-cent high interest rate war bonds then began attracting much investor attention not only in London and New York but also on the Continent, and this growing demand resulted in their price soaring. Due to these favourable market conditions, the loan issue banks became optimistic about flotation of the third war loan and considered the possibility of a 5 per-cent loan on the security of either the tobacco monopolies or railway revenues.[47] Takahashi proposed a 5 per-cent loan for either £20 million or £30 million on the security of the tobacco monopolies at 90 to 92½ per cent. He was keen to invite German banks to participate in this loan issue.[48]

On 20 March Takahashi started the negotiations with the loan issue banks involving Baring Brothers. They submitted the following two alternatives:

Issue amount	£30 million	£30 million
	(£15 million in London and New York respectively)	
Rate of interest (nominal)	5 per cent	4½ per cent
Issue price		
(to the government)	96 per cent	90 per cent
(to the public)	92½ per cent	85½ per cent
Yield at issue	5.2 per cent	5.0 per cent
Borrowing period	25 years	25 years
Security	Tobacco monopolies	Tobacco monopolies
Redemption	the Japanese government should reserve the right to redeem at par, all or any of the bonds, at any time after 1910, on giving 6 months' previous notice.[49]	

Takahashi opted for the second proposal. The Japanese government desired to raise the issue price by 1 or 2 per cent and to reduce the loan issue commission which it still considered too high. The negotiations were concluded immediately: the government proceeds were raised from 85½ to 86¾ per cent; the borrowing period was fixed at 20 years.[50] As early as 24 March Takahashi made a contract with the loan issue banks.[51] In addition to the favourable market conditions, the vying tender from the German banks and Speyer Brothers may perhaps have made the loan issue negotiations go smoothly.

The loan issue banks again encountered Speyer Brothers' keen competition. By mid-March Speyer Brothers asked the loan issue banks whether they could take part in the forthcoming loan business as a co-issuer.[52] Except for Germany's participation, Takahashi and the loan issue banks had already agreed to conduct the loan issue through the usual business channels.[53] The loan issue banks refused to authorize Speyer Brothers as a loan issuer.

The loan issue banks, in fact, paid more attention by far to an offer from two other groups of German banks. Without doubt the Japanese government aimed to spread out the loan issue markets to the Continent. J. Schiff, who understood that the German government would no longer be opposed to a Japanese government loan issue there, suggested to Takahashi that a Japanese government war loan issue could be made in Germany through Warburg in Hamburg. Schiff maintained close relations with Warburg – more than the usual business correspondence.[54] At that time the Japanese government foreign loan issue became a delicate matter in Germany, because some of the eminent Berlin banks had substantial interests in the Russian government loan business, as shown previously. Schiff considered it expedient to ask Warburg in Hamburg, in conjunction with the Hongkong Bank's Hamburg agent M. Brüssel, to float the Japanese government loan in Germany.[55]

In addition to Warburg, the German bank group headed by the Deutsch-Asiatische Bank attempted to place the Japanese government war loan on the Berlin capital market.[56] They, with the consent of the German government, made a firm proposal to undertake £10 million worth of the bonds out of the total amount (£30 million). This group included the leading German credit banks, such as the Deutsche Bank and the Dresdner Bank.[57] The Hongkong Bank and the Deutsch-Asiatische Bank had maintained close relations since the Chinese government war indemnity loan issues in 1896 and 1898.

The Japanese government considered allocating £10 million or even £15 million worth of the bonds to the Deutsch-Asiatische

Table 6.1 Commission of 4½ per-cent loan issue (March 1905, London) (per cent)

Underwriting	2
Brokerage (placing underwriting)	½
Brokerage (application)	¼
Advertising	¼
Coupon paying	29/30
Loan issue banks	1 8/15
Total	5½

Source: WBA, D2469.

Bank group, but the London issue banks strenuously opposed it on the same terms as theirs.[58] The London issue banks, pioneers of the Japanese government war loan business, did not see the necessity of inviting an additional partner and had full confidence in being able to place the present loan issue on the Anglo-American markets alone. The loan issue banks only authorized the Deutsch-Asiatische Bank group as underwriters and agents for public subscriptions in Germany.[59] The Deutsch-Asiatische Bank group, however, refusing to play such a secondary role,[60] withdrew from the business.[61]

In consequence, the loan issue banks organized public subscriptions in Germany through Warburg alone. Warburg, confirming that the attitude of the German Foreign Office was favourable, participated in the business as an agent for public subscriptions in Hamburg.[62] Although the loan issue banks' network thus covered most of the Continent except for France, it was still difficult for the Japanese government to effect a loan issue on the Continent with an independent loan issuer, not a subsidiary of the London issue banks.

The subscriptions started from 29 March 1905.[63] The loan was oversubscribed elevenfold in London and sevenfold in New York.[64] The total amount of applications in Hamburg reached £4,121,500.[65] As shown in Table 6.1, the loan issue commission was significantly reduced this time. The loan issue banks, which now felt safe about Japan's borrowing for the war, agreed to lower them to 5½ per cent. In addition, competition with Speyer Brothers and the German banks in the loan issue negotiations also helped to bring about this reduction. It is also worth noting that the National Provident Institution purchased £32,000 of the bonds.[66] This investment, made by an insurance company, meant that the Japanese government war bonds were now recognized as a respectable investment venture among conservative financial institutions in the City.

In the third war loan issue negotiations, the loan issue banks were confronted with keen competition from the German banks which had not occurred previously. Japan, since its first foreign loan issue in 1870, had depended mainly upon the London capital market for raising funds, and London, therefore, had become established as the main market. But this time, the Japanese government approached the German market to float the loan as the eagerness of the Continental markets for Russian government loans had diminished.[67]

FOUR-AND-A-HALF PER-CENT LOAN ISSUE IN JULY 1905

The Battle of Tsushima on 27 May 1905 paved the way for peace-making between Russia and Japan. Early in June Theodore Roosevelt, the president of the United States, played a leading part in the diplomatic negotiations for peace.[68] On 8 July 1905 J. Komura, the Japanese minister of foreign affairs, left for the peace negotiations at Portsmouth [New Hampshire].

The outlook for peace seemed good in June 1905 when Takahashi started negotiations on the fourth war loan issue. In order to meet deficits from the military expenditure budget in the financial year of 1905, the Japanese government decided to raise ¥300 million (£30,625,000) by a further foreign loan.[69] The Japanese government, always fearing the exhaustion of specie reserves abroad for the settlement of trade deficits, was keen to seek funds for the continuation of the war, reasoning also that, in the event of peace being concluded, these funds could be used for the military expenditure on the evacuations from Manchuria and for the redemption of domestic war bonds.

It was barely two and a half months since the third war loan had been floated. Schiff reluctantly agreed to this prompt action.[70] Considering the current enthusiasm for Japanese government bonds, he advised Takahashi to raise the loan issue as soon as possible.[71] Lord Revelstoke and Cassel unwillingly acceded to this proposal.[72] According to A. Levita, a partner of Panmure Gordon & Co. and known as 'Willy Koch's right- hand man', the London issue banks were of the firm opinion that the intended loan for £30 million might possibly be feasible, provided that 'the Mediterranean horizon [the diplomatic tension in Morocco between France and Germany] clears'.[73]

Takahashi's initial idea was for a £30 million loan to be placed equally in London, New York and Germany. This constrained the loan issue banks to include some eminent German banks in the operation.[74] Fearing that Japan would overload the Anglo-American markets, Schiff strongly recommended that Takahashi should approach the Deutsch-Asiatische Bank through Warburg.[75] From a diplomatic viewpoint, the Japanese government welcomed German banks' full participation in the war loan issue.[76]

However, W.M. Koch, a partner of Panmure Gordon & Co. and a key figure of the previous Japanese government war loan issues, was unwilling to authorize any German banks as a loan issuer. It seems likely that he intended to place a Japanese government loan on the Paris capital market after the war. He believed that Germany's participation would discourage his ambitious plan.[77] The London issue banks were also averse to Germany's new participation.[78] They were afraid of a reduction in their loan issue commission by sharing a loan issue with German banks. Finally the London issue banks admitted Germany's participation on the same terms as Kuhn, Loeb & Co.'s.[79]

Warburg introduced the Deutsch-Asiatische Bank to this business through Max von Schinckel, a *Geschäftsinhaber* (owner) of the Norddeutsche Bank and the Disconto-Gesellschaft.[80] He was also a *Geschäftsinhaber* of the Deutsch-Asiatische Bank. The Deutsch-Asiatische Bank was set up in 1889 to boost German overseas banking in the Far East. The bank had a composite character: most of its stock being held by the major private and credit banks in Germany which constituted the bank's board of directors.[81] Warburg and the Deutsch-Asiatische Bank, in combination, formed a syndicate for the flotation of the fourth Japanese government war loan in Germany. About half of the founders of the Deutsch-Asiatische Bank became involved in this operation (Table 6.2).

The other group, Mendelssohn, the Disconto-Gesellschaft, S. Bleichröder and the Berliner Handels-Gesellschaft, which had taken part in bringing out the Russian government loan in January 1905, declined to participate in the Japanese government loan issue.[82] In 1906 A. Schoeller, a *Geschäftsinhaber* of the Disconto-Gesellschaft apologized to Takahashi for his conduct of 1905, saying that at that time he had had to be mindful of financial relations with the

Table 6.2 Amounts of 4½ per cent loan issue (July 1905, Germany) (£000)

Loan Issue Bank	*Amount*
Bank für Handel und Industrie	972
Bayerische Hypotheken und Wechsel Bank	342
Born und Busse	342
Delbrück, Leo & Co.	563
Deutsch-Asiatische Bank	972
Deutsche Bank	1,458
Dresdner Bank	972
National Bank für Deutschland	729
Norddeutsche Bank	850
Sal. Oppenheim Jr. & Co.	342
A. Schaaffhausenscher Bankverein	729
Jacob S.H. Stern	729
M.M. Warburg & Co.	1,000
Total	10,000

Source: PBA, D6804, Agreement, 7 July 1905.
Note: £1=DM20.45.

Russian government.[83] Warburg became an independent issuer in Hamburg.[84] By 4 July 1905 the German issue banks and Warburg provisionally agreed with the London issue banks on the placement of the loan for £10 million in Germany.[85]

This loan issue, however, caused debate among German industrialists as to what extent the money raised there would be used for purchasing German manufactured goods. They were afraid that the Japanese government would promptly transfer the loan proceeds to London and purchase British military goods.[86]

On 3 July Takahashi started the fourth war loan issue negotiations with the London issue banks. On 4 July they agreed on the following terms:

Issue amount	£30 million (£10 million in London, New York and Germany respectively)
Rate of interest (nominal)	4½ per cent
Issue price	90 per cent to the public 86¾ per cent to the government
Issue commission	5½ per cent
Yield at issue	5.0 per cent

Borrowing period	20 years
Security	receipt of the second charge on the tobacco monopolies
Redemption	the Japanese government should reserve the right to redeem at par, all or any of the bonds, at any time after 1910, on giving 6 months' previous notice.[87]

These were practically identical to those of the third loan issue. The prospectuses were issued on 11 July and the public subscriptions started in London, the United States and Germany simultaneously.

The first simultaneous loan issue in the three major countries was successfully implemented. The loan was heavily oversubscribed: by 10 times in London, 4½ times in the United States and 10 times in Germany.[88] Japanese government bonds had now become very popular especially in London, so much so that many shrewd premium hunters deceived the loan issue banks by applying several times over for small amounts.[89]

Germany's participation gave a considerable jolt to the established pattern of the Japanese government loan issues depending upon the Anglo-American markets, although London still retained a more or less leading role in the Japanese government loan issue negotiations. From a strictly economic point of view, this new policy of expanding the loan issue markets would benefit the Japanese government, which was now able to obtain more favourable loan issue terms on the international capital markets.

FOUR PER-CENT LOAN ISSUE IN NOVEMBER 1905

On 5 September 1905 Komura and S. Witte, the representative of the Russian government, signed the Russo-Japanese peace treaty at Portsmouth.[90] This treaty was not entirely satisfactory to the Japanese who expected considerable indemnity money from Russia, as had been the case with the Sino-Japanese War.

The Japanese government was left with enormous national debts mainly from the huge military expenditure during the war. The foreign debts outstanding amount rose as high as 9.9 times the figure in 1901 and the ratio of the borrowing to the total government general account revenue remained at over 394 per cent in 1905.[91]

In September 1905 the Japanese government sounded out Takahashi on the possibility of a new 4 per-cent conversion loan issue in

Britain, the United States, Germany and France simultaneously, for redeeming the first and the second 6 per-cent foreign war loans for £22 million and the fifth 6 per-cent domestic Exchequer bills for ¥100 million (£10,208,333). The Japanese government instructed him to produce an unsecured 4 per-cent loan issue for between ¥300 million (£30,625,000) and ¥400 million (£40,833,333) at more than 90 per cent.[92]

Since 1903 the Japanese government had desired to float a loan on the Paris capital market.[93] In 1904 M. Arakawa, Japanese consul in London, pointed out that probable competition between British and French financiers would restrict the London issue banks' initiative in loan issue negotiations and allow Japan to obtain more favourable loan issues. He suggested inviting the Paris Rothschilds to a Japanese government loan issue.[94] Motono (the Japanese minister in Paris) was, on the other hand, pessimistic in this regard, learning that the Paris Rothschilds had declared that during the Russo-Japanese War no Japanese government loan issues in France would have been feasible. But he was confident that this attitude would change after the war.[95]

Meanwhile, Takahashi himself intended to establish a channel to the Paris capital market through Koch. Koch, through his kinship, introduced Takahashi to M. de Verneuil, *Syndic des Agents de Change* (Paris Stock Exchange), and M. Rouvier, the French minister of finance.[96] On 28 March 1905 Takahashi had an interview with Verneuil and he gave Takahashi a message from Rouvier to the effect that he [Rouvier] wished to build up much closer economic relations with Japan after the Russo-Japanese War.[97] This action of Rouvier's obviously meant that the French government would no longer object to a Japanese government loan issue on the Paris capital market once the peace negotiations between Japan and Russia were concluded.

In July 1905 Takahashi contacted the French government,[98] since without governmental authorization it was impossible to make any foreign loan issues there. On 16 September Takahashi and Koch discussed the new Japanese government loan issue with Verneuil and Jacque de Günzbourg, the head of Günzbourg et Cie and of the Société Générale de Crédit Industriel et Commercial. Takahashi proposed a 4 per-cent loan issue for £50 million in Britain, the United States, Germany and France.[99]

Verneuil and Günzbourg agreed on most points saying, however, that it remained difficult for the French government to authorize the new Japanese government loan issue before the Russian government loan issue which had been pending since March 1905. Although Takahashi and Koch confirmed Rouvier's approval for placing the Japanese government loan on the Paris capital market, French diplomatic relations with Russia greatly influenced the progress of the Japanese government loan issue in Paris.[100]

In addition to the channel through Koch, Takahashi, through the London Rothschilds, approached the Paris Rothschilds. During the Russo-Japanese War the London Rothschilds had never become involved in the Japanese government war loan business except as underwriters. It was a long-established policy for them to avoid war lendings.[101] Following the Russo-Japanese War Takahashi asked the London Rothschilds to introduce him to the Paris Rothschilds for a new loan issue in Paris.[102] The Rothschilds were in a paramount position to form an international loan issue consortium on the basis of their strong family ties covering most of the main European cities: Frankfurt-on-Main, Vienna, Paris, Naples and London.[103]

A series of correspondence between the London and the Paris Rothschilds unequivocally indicates their involvement in the Japanese government loan issue. In the middle of September 1905 the London Rothschilds informed the Paris Rothschilds of the Japanese government's intention to place a new loan in Paris. The Paris Rothschilds of course showed '*un grand intérêt* (a great interest)' but also pointed out difficulties in this business: firstly, political discord between France and Germany might prevent a simultaneous loan issue in France and Germany; secondly, the imminent Russian government loan issue in France would profoundly influence the progress of the Japanese government loan issue, since the French were much more familiar with Russia; thirdly, it was indispensable to obtain the French government's authorization for a new loan issue in Paris.[104] The Paris Rothschilds also emphasized that they were not able to undertake any Japanese government loan in Paris without the London Rothschilds' participation in the London issue.[105] The London Rothschilds eventually agreed to be included in the new Japanese government loan in London as one of the loan issue banks.[106]

Notwithstanding Takahashi's successful approach to the Paris capital market, it is clear that the Japanese government could launch no operation before the Russian government loan issue. The Japanese government loan issue in Paris depended entirely upon the progress of the Russian government loan issue negotiations.[107] Furthermore, until the end of September, nothing had been decided on the German banks' participation in this loan issue.[108]

On the other hand, the London issue banks were unanimously opposed to the new Japanese government loan issue. They felt that Japan had already borrowed a huge amount, and saw no reason to borrow further even after the war. At this stage Takahashi found no way of completing the loan issue and his negotiations with the London issue banks were at a stalemate.

In October, however, the London issue banks came to agree to issue the new loan and Takahashi started the negotiations.[109] Interest in Japanese government bonds was still high everywhere and the loan issue banks wanted as large a share of the new loan as possible. The major problem in the loan issue negotiations was how to distribute the issue amount to the members equitably. Lord Revelstoke, in fact, feared that the inclusion of the Paris capital market would lead 'either to a diminution in the amount available for London, New York and Germany, or possibly to the transfer of the German interest to Paris.'[110] The London issue banks were of the firm opinion that Kuhn, Loeb & Co.'s and Germany's shares should be reduced.[111] Kuhn, Loeb & Co. was, for its part, dissatisfied with such an inequitable allocation.[112] Warburg would have great difficulty in persuading the German issue banks unless the share of the German banks' participation were equivalent to that of New York issue banks'.

On 14 November Kuhn, Loeb & Co. asked the London issue banks to postpone the loan issue for the time because it wanted to negotiate its share of the new loan issue,[113] although the Japanese government wished for an immediate conclusion.[114] Yet the London issue banks were about to launch the immediate loan issue in London, Germany and Paris alone, excluding New York.[115] They informed Kuhn, Loeb & Co. that they were unable to increase the share to Kuhn, Loeb & Co., and finally it acquiesced.[116]

As demand for the Japanese government bonds in the United States was limited and their quotation prices on the New York Stock Exchange were always lower than in London, the Japanese government war bonds often flowed out from the United States to Britain.[117] The fact that the bonds, even issued in New York, were sterling ones accelerated their outflow to Britain.[118] It was revealed in 1907 that most of the first 6 per-cent war bonds, issued in London

Table 6.3 Main position of first 6 per-cent bonds in 1907

Country	*Amount (£)*	*(%)*
Belgium	223,025	2.2
Britain	8,706,875	86.5
France	394,875	3.9
Germany	177,075	1.8
Holland	99,500	1.0
Italy	115,550	1.1
Japan	50,000	0.5
USA	4,650	0
Others	298,675	3.0
Total	10,070,225	100.0

Source: JMFA, K. Shōda Papers, 28-6.
Note: Based on the interest payment at the Yokohama Specie Bank in 1907; Bonds were issued in June 1904 in London and New York for £10 million but the actual issue amount was £10,070,225.

and New York, were in British investors' hands, as shown in Table 6.3. It is true to say that except for from a political viewpoint, the subscriptions in New York were 'always somewhat fictitious, and based to a great extent on the desire for a hastily snatched premium.'[119]

These phases of the negotiations revealed that an international loan issue consortium was vulnerable to the entangled interests of the members involved and the different market circumstances. Once the Paris capital market was opened to Japanese government loan issues, the position of the New York capital market became relatively insignificant. Available funds for foreign investment in the New York of that time were nowhere near the level of London and Paris. Paris had still retained the second place in the world's financial markets. It was certain that the Japanese government could raise much cheaper money there than in New York. Now the London issue banks, as well as the Japanese government, turned more of their attention to the Paris capital market.

However, the Russian government loan issue negotiations made no progress. As a result of disagreement among the financiers, the new Russian government loan was eventually to be issued in the following year.[120] The diplomatic hinderance towards the Japanese government loan issue in Paris was removed.

Hearing rumours of the postponement of the Russian government loan issue, early in November the Japanese government ordered Motono to discuss with Rouvier an immediate issue of the Japanese government loan on the Paris capital market.[121] The French government agreed to issue the Japanese government loan before the Russian one[122] and the Russian government had no objection to this.[123]

In the final stage Takahashi had an interview with the Paris Rothschilds on the loan issue in Paris.[124] On 15 November Takahashi and Koch called at 'Rue Laffitte'.[125] Meyer Alphonse de Rothschild had died in May 1905[126] and the whole burden of the Paris Rothschilds' direction fell upon James de Rothschild, a nephew of Meyer Alphonse de Rothschild, because Edouard de Rothschild, the head of the Paris Rothschilds, was ill.[127] In these negotiations Takahashi and the Paris Rothschilds agreed on the following outline of the loan issue:

Issue amount	half the amount of the total issue
Sale price (to the Paris Rothschilds)	89½ per cent
Rate of exchange	£1 to Fr25–25
Date of the issue	within November 1905.[128]

Subsequently, the Paris Rothschilds came to terms with the banks engaged in the Russian government loan business[129] and had a conference to co-ordinate a smooth placement of the Japanese government loan on the market.[130] Verneuil had approached the Crédit Lyonnais and obtained its assurance to collaborate with the Paris Rothschilds in the forthcoming Japanese government loan issue, although the Crédit Lyonnais had declined to become the chief issuer in Paris because of its close relations with Russia.[131] As shown in Table 6.7, the two large banques de dépôts (the Crédit Lyonnais and the Comptoir National d'Escompte), which had been leading members of the pending Russian government loan issue syndicate, decided to participate in the Japanese government loan issue with the Paris Rothschilds.[132] Once the French government removed the restriction on a Japanese government loan business, many Paris financiers began to take it up openly, deeming it most advantageous.[133]

From 15 November the loan issue banks, with 'usual worry', started underwriting for this loan issue.[134] The London issue banks accepted most of the agreement which Takahashi and the Paris Rothschilds had reached,[135] and authorized the Paris Rothschilds as the principal issuer in Paris. On 24 November the London issue banks, Kuhn, Loeb & Co. and Warburg agreed to undertake the loan issue.[136] The following contract between the Japanese government, Parr's Bank, the Hongkong Bank, the Yokohama Specie Bank, the London Rothschilds and the Paris Rothschilds was made:[137]

Issue amount	£50 million present issue amount should be £25 million (other £25 million to be reserved for a future issue for the redemption of the 6 per-cent foreign loans of 1904) £12 million in Paris £6.5 million in London £3,250,000 in New York[138] £3,250,000 in Germany
Issue purpose	redemption for the 6 per-cent domestic war Exchequer bills
Rate of interest (nominal)	4 per cent
Issue price	90 per cent to the public 88 per cent to the government
Yield at issue	4.4 per cent
Borrowing period	25 years
Security	nil
Redemption	the Japanese government should reserve the right to redeem at par, all or any of the bonds, at any time after 1921, on giving 6 months' previous notice.

As far as the London issue was concerned, the whole amount of £6.5 million was underwritten at a 1½ per-cent commission (Tables 6.4 and 6.5). At that time underwriting was already regarded as sufficiently sound and remunerative to financial institutions. Notwithstanding Lord Rothschild's (Nathaniel Meyer Rothschild's) censure,[139] the London Rothschilds themselves organized an underwriting syndicate. This underwriting list included many companies or persons firmly linked with them such as South African financial groups, merchant banks, merchants and stockbrokers.[140]

The prospectuses were issued on 27 November and the public subscriptions were carried out simultaneously in London, New

Table 6.4 Commission of 4 per-cent loan issue (November 1905, London) (per cent)

Underwriting	1½
Brokerage (placing underwriting)	½
Brokerage (application)	¼
Advertising	¼
Loan issue Banks	1½
Total	4

Source: WBA, D2469.

York, Germany and Paris.[141] In London 'a giant rush for the loan' took place[142] and the subscriptions were oversubscribed by 28 times (Table 6.6). The subscriptions in New York were also oversubscribed by 5 times and those in Germany by 10 times.[143] Parr's Bank earned the £34,958 profit from this loan issue;[144] its profit (£209,632) earned from the three Japanese government loan issues during 1905 amounted to 27.3 per cent of its annual gross profit (£769,000).

In Paris there were no public subscriptions. The syndicate purchased the whole issue amount of the loan and placed it directly to their clients through '*guichets* (counters)'.[145] As indicated in Table 6.7, the Paris Rothschilds established the '*syndicate de prise ferme*

Table 6.5 London issue banks' underwriting (November 1905, London) (£)

Underwriting syndicate	*Underwriting amount*	*Underwriting commission (1½%)*	*Brokerage commission (½%)**
Panmure Gordon	2,375,000	35,625	32,500
London Rothschilds	1,125,000	16,875	
Hongkong Bank	1,000,000	15,000	
Yokohama Specie Bank	700,000	10,500	
Parr's Bank	1,300,000	19,500	
Total	6,500,000	97,500	32,500

Source: WBA, D2469.
Note: * ½ per cent of the issue amount in London (£6.5 million).

Table 6.6 Application and allotment (November 1905, London)

Loan issuer	*Applications (£)*	*Allotment (£)*	*Allotment (number)*
Parr's Bank	77,000,660	2,878,500	28,789
Hongkong Bank	51,604,600	1,410,100	13,509
Yokohama Specie Bank	28,330,700	1,295,600	15,158
London Rothschilds	25,803,550	915,800	3,223
Total	182,739,510	6,500,000	60,679

Source: HSBA, LOHI/47.

et de placement',[146] which encompassed eminent banques de dépôts and banques d'affaires such as the Crédit Lyonnais, the Comptoir National d'Escompte, the Société Générale, the Société Générale de Crédit Industriel et Commercial and the Banque de Paris. The '*prise ferme*' (to take the loan firm) was a 1.5664 per cent and the '*placement*' (to place the loan) a 1½ per-cent commission. The shares of the Crédit Lyonnais and the Paris Rothschilds in the placement were particularly larger than others. In Paris, the loan issue banks had

Table 6.7 4 per-cent loan issue (November 1905, Paris) (Fr; Fr1=9 1/2d.)

Loan issue bank	*[Prise ferme]* *Amount*	*Benefit (1.5664%)*	*[Placement]* *Amount*	*Benefit (1.5%)*
Crédit Lyonnais	40,000,000	626,560	97,565,000	1,463,475
Vernes et Cie	30,000,000	469,920	18,309,000	274,635
Comptoir d'Escompte	20,000,000	313,280	32,282,500	484,237.5
Société Générale	20,000,000	313,280	32,282,500	484,237.5
Crédit Industriel et Commercial	10,000,000	156,640	6,631,000	99,465
Banque Française	7,000,000	209,648	4,000,000	60,000
Banque de Paris	56,500,000	885,016	24,430,000	366,450
Syndicat des Agents	21,000,000	328,944	21,000,000	315,000
Participants	12,000,000	187,968		
M.M. Rothschilds	83,500,000	1,307,944	63,500,000	952,500
Total	300,000,000	4,699,200	300,000,000	4,500,00

Source: AN, 132/AQ/69, B–13–1/8, Syndicat Emprunt Japonais 4% (1905).

Table 6.8 Syndicate account of 4 per-cent loan issue (November 1905, Paris)

	(%)	*Amount (Fr)*
Payment to the Japanese government		
(deducting the interest)	88.5	265,584,000
Commission to Panmure Gordon	(0.5)	1,509,000
Various charges	(0.2)	709,539.90
Commission (*placement*)	(1.5)	4,500,000
Syndicate profit (*ferme*)	(1.6)	4,699,200
(Commissions total)	(3.8)	
Total	92.3	277,001,739.90
Proceeds of the bonds (Fr300,000,000)	89.9	269,700,000
Half yearly interest from 1 January 1906	2.0	6,036,000
Other interests	0.4	1,265,739.90
Total	92.3	277,001,739.90

Source: AN, 132/AQ/70, B–14–1/4.
Note: Fr1=9 1/2d.

to pay some charges to manipulate the press and political parties to smooth the placement.[147] The 3.8164 per-cent loan issue commission in Paris was a little cheaper than in London. In Germany the same banks, headed by the Deutsch-Asiatische Bank and Warburg, which took up the 4½ per-cent loan issue of July, again organized the subscriptions.[148]

In the loan issue of November 1905 the Japanese government finally organized a loan issue operation in the Paris capital market. During the Russo-Japanese War such a facility had been totally denied to Japan, and therefore it had had to rely excessively upon the Anglo–American markets.[149] This ingress into the Paris capital market led the Japanese government to establish a new pattern of foreign loan issues, one which Takahashi's successors would follow in the future, of counting upon simultaneous loan issue markets. Now the Japanese government became relatively independent of the London financiers' strong influence and was able to pursue the most favourable loan issue terms on the international capital markets. As a result, it was able to float the loan at the minimized commission, about 4 per cent (Table 6.4 and 6.8), because of the element of competition

As a result of the expansion and integration of the loan issue markets, however, the Japanese government had to take diplomatic situations into consideration when it launched a loan issue in France where the government invariably regarded foreign loan issues as a kind of a diplomatic implement. These new loan issue circumstances necessarily made the Japanese government pay more attention to diplomatic matters which it had not fully experienced so far in the loan issues on the Anglo–American markets.

7

Loan Issues After the Russo-Japanese War

foreign loan issues are serious matters for a state. Unlike the projects that individual people, unconcerned with the state, privately depend upon low rate foreign capital, the state's direct borrowing abroad will cause the responsibility of paying it off at the sacrifice of the state. This is very different from the case that an individual goes into bankruptcy or fails in business. Nevertheless, if the state ventures to raise foreign loans, it should not only consolidate its [financial] foundation but also firmly ensure sources of specie for the payment of principal and interest of the loans.

Meiji Zaiseishi (History of Japanese Finances in the Meiji Era)

The Japanese economy after the Russo-Japanese War maintained a marked growth in the formation of fixed capital. The first Saionji cabinet (1906–1908) increased national expenditure on several governmental undertakings: the expansion of armaments; the nationalization and the new construction of railways; the extension of steelworks and the telephone. In contrast with the first Katsura cabinet (1901–1906), which made an effort to redeem the national debt, this first Saionji cabinet financed these undertakings hurriedly by both domestic loans and increased taxation.[1] As a result, the Japanese government came to pay an immense sum on the national debt. The expenditure related to the national debts in the government general account rose rapidly from 1906.[2]

The increase in government expenditure led to increased imports and caused severe trade deficits. It was imperative, therefore, that the Japanese government should secure gold, in any way, for settling the trade deficits. The imposition of a newly-revised tariff of 1906 attempted to conserve gold by restricting rising imports.[3] However, the Japanese government came to consider the reduction of interest payments on foreign debts by the conversion of outstanding issues to new issues bearing smaller coupons.

Japan, now on the verge of becoming a heavy-debtor country, was encouraged to follow this course. From the standpoint of debt burden by country, represented by public debt per head of population, the rate at which Japan's debt burden multiplied from £1.2 in 1900 to £5.2 in 1910 was remarkable.[4]

This chapter will examine two Japanese government conversion loan issues in London and Paris after the Russo-Japanese War. As a consequence of the rise of the Paris capital market, London's unchallenged lead in Japanese government loan issue business was being undermined and the loan issue markets were decentralized. Now the Japanese government was in the position of being able to find the most favourable loan issue terms by moving between the London and the Paris capital markets. However, both diplomatic affairs in France and the different market conditions often hindered Japan's financial operations there.

FIVE PER-CENT LOAN ISSUE IN 1907

According to the agreement of November 1905 with the loan issue banks: i.e. Parr's Bank, the Hongkong Bank, the Yokohama Specie Bank, Kuhn, Loeb & Co., the London Rothschilds and the Paris Rothschilds, the Japanese government was obliged to fulfill immediately another 4 per-cent loan issue for the remaining amount (£25 million). In August 1906 the Japanese government instructed K. Takahashi, the government loan commissioner, to arrange it. The purpose of this loan issue was to convert the high interest rate (6 per-cent) war bonds (£22 million) of 1904, issued in London and New York, to lower ones (4 per cent). Takahashi and the government agreed on the following outlines of the new loan issue:

(i) to issue £25 million 4 per-cent sterling bonds in Britain, the United States, France and Germany for conversion or redemption of the £22 million 6 per-cent loan of 1904.

(ii) the loan issue should be based on the loan issue terms of the 4 per-cent loan in November 1905.

(iii) a new syndicate for this loan issue should be formed, should the loan issue banks refuse to take up the loan issue.

(iv) Treasury bills should be issued temporarily if market conditions were unfavourable, and afterwards these should be converted into bonds.[5]

The enthusiasm for Japanese government bonds which had surged during the Russo-Japanese War now ebbed everywhere, and many foreign investors became apprehensive about the predicament of Japan's finances after the Russo-Japanese War.[6] In 1906, especially its closing quarter, the conditions of the London money market became very tight: in the early part of the year the withdrawal of gold from London to the United States, stemming from the San Francisco earthquake and a boom on the New York Stock Exchange, gradually narrowed the market; in November the Bank of England raised bank rate to 6 per cent; in December there was a danger of an unprecedented 7 per cent. Most of the central banks on the Continent followed a similar high interest rate policy to maintain their gold reserves.[7] Bond prices fell sharply.

The extraordinarily high interest rate had a dampening effect upon new loan issues.[8] In fact, on the London capital market there were new loan issues for £167,187,400 during 1905, but during 1906 these rapidly decreased to £120,173,200.[9]

Under these adverse circumstances Japan's efforts to reorganize the national finances did not, of course, receive favourable attention from foreign financiers. The London Rothschilds and the Paris Rothschilds considered it quite out of question to issue any Japanese government conversion loan for the moment.[10] Therefore, Takahashi had to wait for a recovery of the loan issue markets. Taking into full consideration the different quotation prices of the Japanese government 4 per-cent bonds of 1905 in New York, London, Germany and Paris, Takahashi prepared for the following three loan issue alternatives:

(i) a 4 per-cent simultaneous loan issue in London and Paris.
(ii) a 4 per-cent loan issue in Paris alone.
(iii) a 4 per-cent loan issue in Paris and 5 per-cent in London separately.[11]

Takahashi had formulated the definite intention of floating a simultaneous loan equally in London and Paris. Because of the low quotation prices in New York and Germany, he cast doubts on arranging the simultaneous loan issue there.[12] The high interest rate on the market, as mentioned previously, hampered his immediate negotiations with the London issue banks. The banks took a wait-and-see policy as the London Rothschilds had noted that there was no chance of placing a Japanese government loan then.[13]

In Paris Takahashi found that it was the French government's diplomatic policy, rather than financial matters,[14] which entangled the loan issue negotiations. In the middle of November 1906 Takahashi and S. Kurino, the Japanese ambassador in Paris, had an interview with S. Pichon, the French minister of foreign affairs, and J. Caillaux, the French minister of finance, on the Japanese government loan issue in Paris.[15] Pichon, in return for the loan issue, demanded a certain quid pro quo, namely an entente for protection of their mutual interests in the Far East. Pichon made the following definite proposals:[16] (i) Japan should co-operate with the Anglo–French group in the China Central Railways construction; (ii) Japan should guarantee the security of the French Indo–China colonies. Caillaux was keen to take up the loan issue in Paris and promised Takahashi to introduce other eminent financiers in Paris, should the Paris Rothschilds decline it.[17] Perhaps Caillaux, who had particular interests with the Banque de l'Indo–Chine, intended to put the loan issue into the hands of the banque.[18]

However, P. Cambon, the French ambassador in London, had a major impact on the negotiations between Pichon and Takahashi by warning that the Japanese government loan issue in Paris would probably upset diplomatic relations between France and Russia.[19] Pichon, who paid much attention to affiliations with Russia, confirmed the Russian government's posture towards the Japanese government loan issue in Paris.[20] The Russian government, for its part, insisted that the matters should proceed in accordance with the Portsmouth treaty, and desired the French government not to allow any Japanese government loan issue in Paris until a treaty of amity with Japan was to be concluded.[21] Japan and Russia were, at that time, negotiating a commercial treaty and fishery convention.[22]

On 10 January 1907 Pichon told Kurino that the French government was not able to disregard Russia's opinion.[23] After the Russo-Japanese War in which Russia had been the aggressor, Japan now conversely became a menace to Russia in the Far East. Likewise, the United States was nervous of Japan's foreign loan issues which might be used to expand its armaments. M. Bompard, the

French ambassador in St Petersburg, gave assurance to the Russian government that the French government would never open the Paris capital market to Japan until the Russo-Japanese amity treaty was signed.[24]

Meanwhile, there was serious diplomatic confrontation between France and Germany. The French government and financiers showed unanimous irritation towards Takahashi's visit to Germany in December 1906. They suspected that he attempted to draw some financial assistance from Germany.[25] The growing antagonism to Germany seriously deterred the smooth progress of Takahashi's loan issue negotiations in Paris.

As mentioned in chapter 1, the Japanese government 4 per-cent bonds of 1905 (sterling bonds) were sustained artificially at a much higher price in Paris, in contrast with those in London and New York. There was a significant and continuous difference between London, New York and Paris in the quotation prices (Chart 7.1). On the 'Frenchman's watertight system'[26] the Paris Stock Exchange admitted quotation only of the securities issued in France. The restricted supply of securities on the Paris capital market accordingly pegged the quotation prices at higher levels than in London and New York. Hence, the Japanese government, at the outset, aimed to place the intended 4 per-cent loan on the Paris capital market.[27] Takahashi, in fact, considered that the 4 per-cent loan issue was feasible in Paris alone or in Paris and London simultaneously on the condition that the quotation of the London and New York tranche of the 4 per-cent bonds of 1905 was admitted on the Paris Stock Exchange.[28] However, as he set great store by the established relations with the London issue banks, he finally pursued the possibility of the 4 per-cent simultaneous loan issue in London and Paris rather than a franc loan in Paris alone. In order to do so, it was unavoidable for the Japanese government to level off the different quotation prices of these bonds in London and Paris.

In June 1906 Kurino had desired the French government to admit the quotation of the tranche of the 4 per-cent bonds of 1905, issued outside France, on the Paris Stock Exchange.[29] The London Rothschilds considered that no large number of the 4 per-cent bonds would flow from London to Paris because of the high quotation price there.[30] Yet M. de Verneuil, *Syndic des Agents de Change*, and the Paris Rothschilds disagreed on the quotation because of the probable damage to French public investors.[31]

Chart 7.1 Quotation prices of 4 per-cent bonds of 1905 in London, New York and Paris 1906–1913

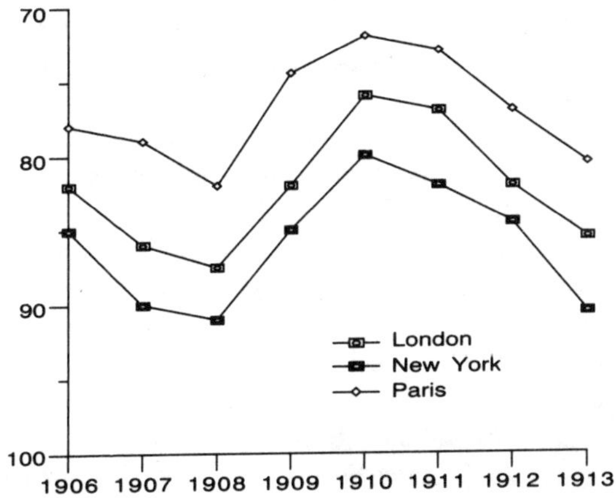

Sources: IMM; Compagnie des Agents de Change, *Annuaire des valeurs admises à la cote officielle, années 1915–1917*, i (Paris, 1917), 259; *Commercial and Financial Chronicle*.

Note: The highest and lowest prices of the years were averaged.

On 9 January 1907 Kurino made the following apologies to Pichon for the misapprehensions concerning Japan's intentions, explaining that: (i) the Japanese government had no intention of waging war on Russia or the United States, and the purpose of the loan was not for armaments but for the conversion of the 6 per-cent foreign loans of 1904; (ii) for a simultaneous loan issue in both Paris and London the French government should admit the quotation of the Japanese government 4 per-cent bonds of 1905, issued outside France, on the Paris Stock Exchange; (iii) in accordance with this the Bank of Japan could purchase £3 million of the 4 per-cent bonds, issued in London.[32]

On 16 January the 6 per-cent bank rate came down to 5½ per cent and the market conditions became more favourable to new loan issues. I. Motono, the Japanese minister in St Petersburg, was attempting to persuade the Russian government to agree on Japan's loan issue in Paris,[33] but the Russian government insisted that the Japanese government should delay the present loan issue until the remainder of the Russian government's previous loan issue was fulfilled.[34] Takahashi, fearing to lose an opportunity, firmly objected to this postponement.[35] On 15 February Pichon finally agreed to float an immediate issue of the Japanese government loan.[36] The matter was put into the hands of the French minister of finance (Caillaux) and Caillaux conceded the new 4 per-cent loan issue on the Paris capital market in March.[37]

Caillaux authorized the new loan issue, but did not give permission to quote the tranche of the 4 per-cent bonds of 1905, issued outside France, on the Paris Stock Exchange. The French government feared that these low price bonds would flow into France so as to damage French investors' benefits.[38] Without such permission, in practice, it was impossible to average the different quotation prices and this would ultimately hinder the loan issue banks from fixing the issue price of the new 4 per-cent simultaneous loan, because the quotation prices of existing bonds on the market usually determine the issue price of a new loan. Takahashi was thus forced to abandon the new 4 per-cent loan issue in Paris.[39]

Takahashi immediately switched the intended 4 per-cent loan issue to a 5 per-cent loan issue in London and New York.[40] It was impracticable for Takahashi, who intended to issue the new loan at as high a price as possible (nearly par),[41] to arrange a new 4 per-cent loan issue in London and New York, because at that time the quotation prices of the Japanese government 4 per-cent bonds of 1905 were hovering around low levels in London (88¼ per cent, yielding 4½ per cent at market)[42] and New York (84 per cent, yielding 4⅘ per cent at market).[43]

At the beginning of 1907, the London Rothschilds and the Paris Rothschilds were fully aware of the awkward situation surrounding the Japanese government loan issue negotiations. The London Rothschilds pointed out that: the 6 per-cent bank rate did not allow any new loan issues on the market; the diplomatic conflicts between Japan, Russia and the United States had repercussions on the loan issue negotiations.[44] As for the quotation of the London tranche, the Paris Rothschilds were not agreeable to it,[45] despite the London Rothschilds' support for Takahashi.[46]

This hesitancy on the part of the Paris Rothschilds seemingly coincided with the policy followed by the French government. Had the French government exceptionally admitted the Japanese government's 4 per-cent bonds of 1905, it would, no doubt, have been forced to do the same for others.[47] On 15 February 1907 the Paris Rothschilds wrote to the London Rothschilds that the Japanese government should withdraw the proposal of quoting the London tranche of the 4 per-cent bonds of 1905 on the Paris Stock Exchange; the Paris Rothschilds suggested a 4 per-cent simultaneous loan issue in Paris and London, based on the quotation price of the London Stock Exchange, for £25 million.[48] It was obvious that French investors would gain a considerable advantage from such a low issue price (accordingly a high quotation price). As the Paris Rothschilds could not agree to quoting even the London tranche (£6.5 million), Takahashi broke off the 4 per-cent loan issue negotiations, informing them that he intended to arrange a new 5 per-cent loan with the London issue banks.[49]

From 20 February 1907 Takahashi started the 5 per-cent loan issue negotiations with the London issue banks anew. Although the Paris Rothschilds were still committed to the 4 per-cent loan issue in Paris,[50] the London Rothschilds advised Takahashi to invite the Paris Rothschilds to the 5 per-cent loan issue.[51] Takahashi, who considered the 5 per-cent loan issue for £18 million mainly in London, agreed that the Paris Rothschilds could act as underwriters in this loan issue.[52] The London Rothschilds enquired of the Paris Rothschilds as to what extent they could involve themselves in the underwriting of the 5 per-cent loan issue,[53] and Takahashi through the London Rothschilds contacted the Paris Rothschilds on the possibility of the loan issue in Paris.[54] On 26 February 1907 the Paris Rothschilds agreed to participate in it as loan issuers in Paris.[55] Thus the Paris capital market again showed interest in the Japanese government loan business. The London Rothschilds told the Paris Rothschilds that 'no doubt when the time comes everyone will want to participate [in it]'[56] and emphasized that the 5 per-cent loan would be very alluring.[57]

After the *rapprochement*, from 1 March 1907 the Paris Rothschilds and Takahashi started direct negotiations.[58] Both provisionally agreed to issue the 5 per-cent loan for £11.5 million in Paris[59] without mentioning the quotation of the London tranche of the 4 per-cent bonds of 1905 on the Paris Stock Exchange.[60]

The Japanese government had to negotiate with Kuhn, Loeb & Co., the main issuer of the 6 per-cent loan of 1904 in New York, as well. Since Kuhn, Loeb & Co. appraised the proposed issue price (at par) as too high for the New York capital market,[61] it decided to accept subscriptions there in 6 per-cent bonds of 1904 only and gave up subscriptions in cash.[62] Kuhn, Loeb & Co. participated in the loan issue (underwriting) in London for £1 million on the original issuer's terms.[63] The German banks: the Deutsch-Asiatische Bank and Warburg, refused to be involved in this operation in any form because the market conditions in Germany were not acceptable.[64]

On 6 March the contract of the Japanese government 5 per-cent loan issue was made between Takahashi, Parr's Bank, the Hongkong Bank, the Yokohama Specie Bank, the London Rothschilds and the Paris Rothschilds. The outline of the loan issue terms was as follows:

Issue amount	£23 million (£11.5 million in London and £11.5 million in Paris)
Issue purpose	redemption of the Japanese government 6 per-cent sterling loans issued in 1904 for £10 million and £12 million in London and New York
Rate of interest (nominal)	5 per cent
Issue price	99½ per cent (to the public) real issue price included interest should be 98½ per cent (to the public) 95½ per cent (to the government)
Yield at issue	5.0 per cent
Borrowing period	40 years
Rate of exchange	Fr25–25 per £1 and at the current rate of exchange on London in New York
Redemption	the Japanese government should reserve the right to redeem at par, all or any of the bonds, at any time after 1922, on giving 6 months' previous notice.[65]

The London issue banks started organizing the underwriting at a 1½ per-cent commission.[66] Table 7.1 shows the London issue banks' shares in underwriting. The London Rothschilds completed their underwriting syndicate for £725,000 including South African connections, merchant houses and stockbrokers.[67]

From 9 March the subscriptions were implemented in London and Paris simultaneously. In London, despite 'rather a poor opening',[68]

Table 7.1 Underwriting of 5 per-cent loan issue (1907, London) (£)

Underwriting syndicate	*Underwriting amount*	*Underwriting commission (1½%)*	*Brokerage commission (½%)**
Panmure Gordon	4,926,000	73,890	52,500
London Rothschilds	1,500,000	22,500	
Kuhn, Loeb & Co.	1,000,000	15,000	
Hongkong Bank	1,150,000	17,250	
Yokohama Specie Bank	1,000,000	15,000	
Parr's Bank	1,424,000	21,360	
Warburg	500,000	7,500	
British syndicate			5,000
Total	11,500,000	172,500	57,500

Source: WBA, D2469.
Note: * ½ per cent of the issue amount in London (£11.5 million).

the amount of the applications was over £11 million and the total numbers of the applicants and amount are indicated in Table 7.2. The total loan issue commission in London amounted to 4 percent, including a 1½ percent underwriting and a 1½ per-cent loan issue bank commission (Table 7.3). The loan issue in Paris also firmly secured the issue amount[69] and Table 7.4 calculates the French issue banks' shares in this operation. They formed a syndicate for taking 'firm' and placing the loan, and carried out the placement directly through their '*guichets* (counters)' at a 1½ per-cent commission.[70] In addition to the Paris Rothschilds, the Banque de Paris and the Crédit Lyonnais became main loan issuers and these three banks mainly placed the bonds. The total commission paid to the members of the Paris syndicate amounted to 3.5566 per cent.[71] For the Japanese government, the total cost of this conversion amounted to about £1,104,923 (£920,000 for the commissions to financiers and £184,923 for other charges),[72] but it could reduce the annual payment of interest for £220,000.

Initially the Japanese government aimed at Paris as the main market for this conversion loan issue. Because of the artificial price manipulation on the Paris capital market, the Japanese government 4 per-cent bonds of 1905 were being traded at a much higher price there

Table 7.2 Subscriptions of 5 per-cent loan issue (1907, London) (£)

Loan issue bank	*[Cash] Application*	*Allotment*	*[Bond] Application (Allotment)*	*[Total] Application*	*Allotment*
Parr's Bank	2,815,340	1,985,300	2,480,700	5,296,040	4,466,000
Hongkong Bank	1,176,900	841,700	1,534,400	2,711,300	2,376,100
Yokohama Specie Bank	1,327,000	987,600	1,475,100	2,802,100	2,462,700
London Rothschilds	354,480	243,900	793,300	1,147,780	1,037,200
New York	91,400	64,000	385,000	476,400	449,000
Switzerland	484,800	386,900	241,100	725,900	628,000
Hamburg	90,600	70,400	10,600	101,200	81,000
Total	6,340,520	4,579,800	6,920,200	13,260,720	11,500,000

Source: LRA, XI/111/36.

Notes: Allottees who paid in 6 per-cent bonds (converted ones) should receive the following for each £100 of 6 per-cent bonds: (i) £100 new 5 per-cent bonds; (ii) £1 (being equivalent to the advantage obtained by cash subscribers); (iii) 10 s. (the difference between the issue price of new 5 percent bonds [99½] and the redemption of 6 per-cent bonds at par [100]).
Allottees who paid in 6 per-cent bonds should have priority in the subscriptions.

Table 7.3 Commission of 5 per-cent loan issue (1907, London) (%)

Underwriting	1½
Brokerage (placing underwriting)	½
Brokerage (application)	¼
Advertising	¼
Issue banks	1½
Total	4

Source: WBA, D2469.

than in London and New York. The Japanese government could not easily conclude the 4 per-cent loan issue negotiations with the French financiers in part because of the French government's diplomatic relations with Russia, and in part because of the difficulty in fixing the issue price resulting from the French government's refusal to quote

Table 7.4 5 per-cent loan issue (1907, Paris) (Fr)

	[Prise ferme]			*[Placement]*	
Loan issue bank	*Amount*	*Benefit (1½%)*	*Benefit (0.5566%)*	*Amount*	*Benefit (1½%)*
Banque de Paris	71,623,645	1,074,354	398,657	45,030,850	675,462
Crédit Lyonnais	38,715,320	580,729	215,489	62,188,225	932,823
Hottinguer et Cie	29,036,490	435,547	161,617	13,782,460	206,736
Société Générale	19,357,660	290,364	107,744	31,094,365	466,415
Comptoir d'Escompte	19,357,660	290,364	107,744	31,094,365	466,415
Crédit Industriel et Commercial	9,679,335	145,190	53,875	6,387,240	95,808
Banque Française	5,807,500	87,112	32,324	4,000,105	60,001
M.M. Rothschilds Syndicate					
(Rothschilds)	86,297,390	1,294,460	480,331	61,447,390	921,710
(Others)	10,500,000	157,500	58,443	–	–
(Crédit Lyonnais)	–	–	–	35,350,000	530,250
Total	290,375,000	4,355,625	1,616,227	290,375,000	4,355,625

Source: AN, 132/AQ/69, B–13–2/1.
Notes: Fr1=9½d.;
– implies no transactions.

on the Paris Stock Exchange the tranche of the 4 per-cent bonds of 1905, issued outside France. The French government finally agreed to float the 4 per-cent loan in Paris but never permitted the quotation of the London tranche and the Paris Rothschilds also paid little attention to it. Owing to this impediment, Takahashi made up his mind to depart from Paris and counted largely upon the London issue banks for the new 5 per-cent loan issue. Finally the Paris Rothschilds, under the leadership of the London issue banks, agreed to be involved in this operation. For the Japanese government, this loan issue became the one in which diplomatic situations intervened most.

FOUR PER-CENT LOAN ISSUE IN 1910

Apart from the ¥476,318,800 (£48,624,210) 5 per-cent domestic loans issued in 1908 and 1909 for the railway nationalization,[73] there had been no significant increase in Japan's national debts in the period between 1906 and 1910. Yet the burden of these railway nationalization debts placed a heavy load on the national finances because the government had to create 5 per-cent bonds in exchange for the nationalized railway companies' shares. In January 1910, the amount of the debts outstanding (long-term) reached approximately ¥2,650,355,000 (£270,557,070) and the annual government's debt expense ¥154,270,000 (£15,748,395).[74] In particular, the proportion of relatively higher rate of interest (5 per-cent) bonds to the total national debts occupied 63 per cent.[75]

The second Katsura cabinet (1908–1911) tended to convert these higher interest rate bonds to lower ones, as had been done in 1907. Early in 1910 the cabinet decided on a huge financial reorganization scheme, namely the conversion of ¥595 million (£60,739,583) 5 per-cent domestic bonds to new ones bearing smaller coupons. The Japanese government carried out the following separate financial programme in 1910: two 4 per-cent domestic loan issues for ¥200 million (£20,416,666) and two 4 per-cent foreign loan issues in London and Paris.[76]

In February 1910 T. Katsura, the Japanese prime minister, ordered K. Mizumachi, the Japanese vice-minister of finance and government loan commissioner, to issue a 4 per-cent loan in London and Paris either simultaneously or separately. After the conversion loan issue in 1907, the Japanese government had little wish to arrange a loan issue on the New York capital market because it could raise the required funds in London and Paris more cheaply.

Market conditions in London, however, became more and more sluggish and 'the financial deadlock' appeared: on 8 January 1910 bank rate declined to 4 per cent and sank lower to 3 per cent on 9 February.[77] At the beginning of the year, financial deficits occurred in the British government's finance and the political confusion in Britain (the general election and parliamentary reform) also affected the conditions of the loan issue market.[78] Under these circumstances, Mizumachi's proposal of a Japanese government 4 per-cent conversion loan issue was not readily accepted by the London issue banks.[79]

In April Mizumachi and several London issue banks agreed on the following preliminary loan issue terms: (i) they, in coalition with Paris, should undertake the Japanese government loan issue; (ii) the probable lowest issue price should be fixed at 94 per cent on the basis of the lowest quotation prices of the Japanese government 4 per-cent bonds of 1905 in London.[80] Mizumachi obviously regarded the Paris capital market as playing a competitive role in the loan issue negotiations. The London Rothschilds informed the Paris Rothschilds that the Japanese government aimed to place a conversion loan in both London and Paris simultaneously for between £20 million and £25 million.[81]

From 18 April Mizumachi started the negotiations with the Paris Rothschilds. Their broad outline of their agreement was as follows:

(i) to issue a 4 per-cent franc loan for less than Fr450 million (£17,812,500) in Paris.
(ii) the issue price should be fixed at 95 per cent to the public and at 91 per cent to the government.
(iii) the loan issue should be carried out at the beginning of May 1910.[82]

The Paris Rothschilds strongly insisted on a franc loan issue in Paris, separated from London, although Mizumachi pursued the possibility of a simultaneous loan issue and tried to raise the issue price.

This time, however, he encountered no diplomatic conflicts with the French government in floating the loan on the Paris capital market,[83] because there were no German banks in this loan issue, and the Franco-Japanese agreement and the Russo-Japanese convention had been concluded in 1907. The Balkans, rather than the Far East, deserved serious diplomatic attention at that time. French manufacturers only requested the Japanese government to purchase their goods in return for the loan issue.[84] The French Ministry of Finance admitted the quotation of the tranche of the Japanese government 4 per-cent loan of 1905, issued in London, on the Paris Stock Exchange, which the Japanese government had for long desired.[85] On 25 April Mizumachi and the Paris Rothschilds agreed to the 4 per-cent franc loan issue on the following conditions:

Issue amount	Fr450 million (£17,812,500)
Rate of interest (nominal)	4 per cent
Yield at issue	4.18 per cent
Borrowing period	60 years
Issue price	(to the public) 95½ per cent
	(to the government)91½ per cent
Redemption	the Japanese government should reserve the right to redeem at par, all or any of

the bonds, at any time after 1920, on giving 6 months' previous notice.[86]

Financiers in Paris were keen to take up this loan issue and the Paris Rothschilds successfully organized a syndicate: the Crédit Lyonnais, the Banque de Paris, the Société Générale, the Comptoir National d'Escompte, the Société Générale de Crédit Industriel et Commercial and Hottinguer et Cie participated in it.[87] The prospectus was published on 5 May when the loan issue negotiations in London had been concluded.[88] The seven banks, including banques de dépôts, banques d'affaires and haute banques, agreed to take up the loan at a 2½ per-cent commission and to place it directly to their clients at a 1½ per-cent commission.[89]

In London, it was anticipated that the London issue banks would probably take up the loan issue by the beginning of May. Yet their assessment of the loan issue market in general made it difficult to conclude the new loan issue,[90] and eventually the London Rothschilds withdrew from the business.[91] The London Rothschilds predicted in 1906 that the boom in Japanese bonds, especially during the Russo-Japanese War, would end. They had said, 'the day [the end of the boom] will come, and is probably not far distant when the conversion of the sixes [6 per-cent loans of 1904] may take place.'[92] The main reason for their withdrawal from the negotiations was perhaps to be ascribed to the unfavourable assessment of the Japanese government loans on the market and partly also to the separation of the loan issue in Paris from that in London, which freed the London Rothschilds from co-operating with the Paris Rothschilds in this business. Yet the London Rothschilds' withdrawal from the loan issue negotiations startled the Japanese government.

On 5 May Parr's Bank, the Hongkong Bank and the Yokohama Specie Bank arranged the 4 per-cent loan issue on almost similar terms as in Paris:

Issue amount	£11 million
Rate of interest (nominal)	4 per cent
Yield at issue	4.21 per cent
Borrowing period	60 years
Issue price	(to the public) 95 per cent
	(to the government) 91 per cent
Issue commission	4 per cent

Redemption	the Japanese government should reserve the right to redeem at par, all or any of the bonds, at any time after 1920, on giving 6 months' previous notice.[93]

From 6 May the London issue banks invited subscriptions, but out of the £11 million only £8.5 million had been applied for by 18 May.[94] The underwriters took the unsubscribed portion (£2,437,370, approximately 23 per cent of the issue amount).[95] Such an unexpected outcome had not been experienced in the Japanese government loan issues since 1899. The market conditions of that time were not appropriate for new loan issues: for instance, in February 1910 even the British government failed to float £4 million British Treasury bills (2⅛ per cent interest).[96] The dull market conditions did not improve markedly and the rate of interest was still dropping. The official history of the Yokohama Specie Bank explained the reasons for the unsatisfactory conditions thus:[97] King Edward VII's death had temporarily depressed the market; the loan issue in Paris attracted many British investors; most importantly, the issue terms themselves, especially the 95 per-cent issue price (yielding 4.21 per cent at issue), were not sufficiently alluring to public investors, in comparison with the prices of the existing Japanese government 4 per-cent bonds of 1905 on the market (yielding 4.18 per cent at market).[98]

The predominance of the London issue banks in Japanese government loan issue business had declined after 1905 because of the rise of Paris. The London and Paris capital markets were no longer dependent upon each other. Now the Japanese government could have access to Paris directly, not just through the London issue banks. This competitive market structure enabled the Japanese government to arrange its loan issue on more favourable terms.

The rise of the Paris capital market after the Russo-Japanese War produced a flurry of activity among the financiers concerned with the Japanese government loan issues. London's unchallenged lead, which had been established since the first foreign loan issue in 1870, was lost. This decisively effected the loan issue markets for the Japanese government. The market linkages became relatively decentralized, although the markets were not really separate and there was much potential for co-operating in simultaneous loan issues. As a result of both the development of markets and the improvement in Japan's borrowing position abroad, Japan could have access to the world's

Chart 7.2 Linkages of loan issue markets

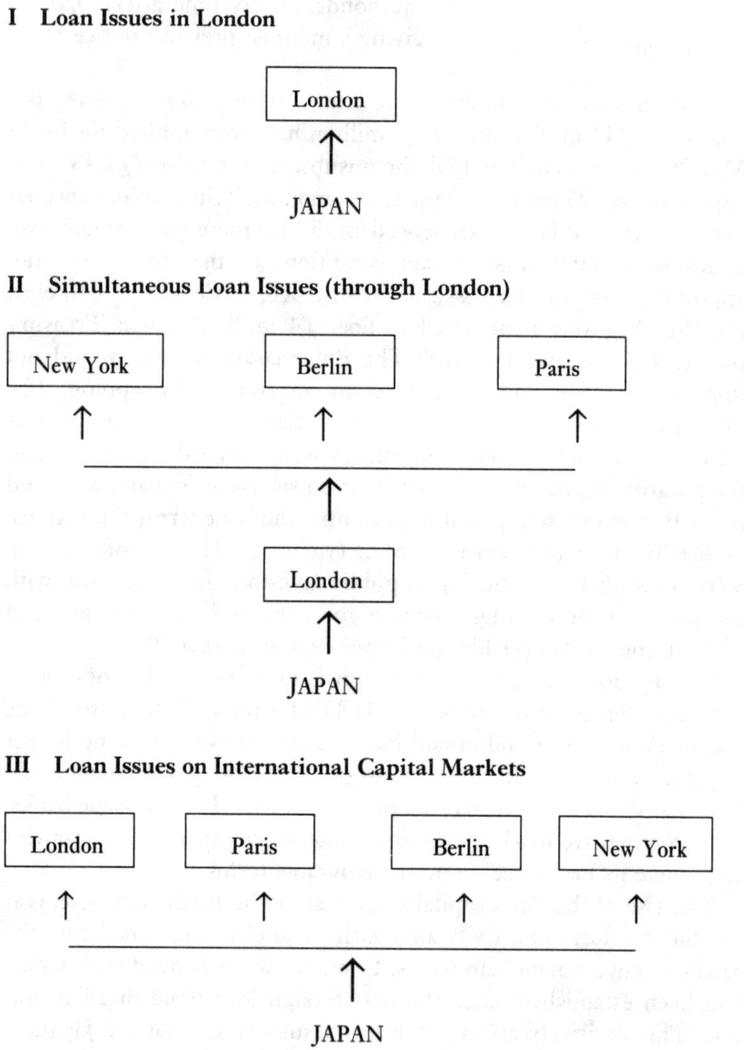

principal capital markets directly, not through the main market (London). With the increased competition among the markets, the Japanese government could now pursue the most advantageous loan issue on the international capital markets, and the patterns of loan issues for the Japanese government became more diversified. In this sense, the market linkages became closer for borrowers (see Chart 7.2).

Until 1923, when the severe earthquake (*Kantō Daishinsai*) occurred,[99] however, the Japanese government had no need to float foreign loans, mainly because Japan enjoyed large trade surpluses during and after the First World War. Had not the continuous trade deficits improved remarkably, the Japanese government would probably have depended upon more foreign loan issues after 1914 and would have been thrown into a debt crisis.

8

Municipal and Company Loan Issues

Every industrial and commercial undertaking, however, involves a certain amount of risk, and its success presupposes investigation into the circumstances connected with it. It cannot be imagined that foreign capitalists will lend their money without such investigation and without a certain amount of control as is now provided for by Japanese law.

H. Dyer, 'Japanese industries and foreign investments', *The Financial Review of Reviews*

Many British financiers paid heed to the Japanese economy as an attractive field of investment. From the turn of the century *British Diplomatic and Consular Reports* began to mention foreign investments in Japan: in 1901 a scarcity of available capital in Japan was revealed and the question of seeking investment was raised;[1] in 1902 it was pointed out that many Japanese companies needed cheap foreign capital.[2] The Anglo-Japanese Corp., an investment company for promoting enterprises in Japan with British capital, was projected in 1904.[3]

American investors also sought to invest in Japan. In August 1906 J. Schiff, a senior partner of Kuhn, Loeb & Co., who had played a prime part in the Japanese government foreign loan issues during the Russo-Japanese War, visited Japan with E.H. Harriman, who was at that time called the 'American railway king'.[4] Schiff emphasized that investment in Manchuria, where Japan was creating a new market after 1905, should be open to foreign capital.[5] Paris financiers such as Albert Kahn also encouraged Japanese investment by French capital after the conclusion of the Franco-Japanese agreement in 1907.

As a consequence of the enthusiasm for the Japanese government war bonds on the foreign capital markets, investment in Japanese industries and enterprises received more attention among foreign investors. Obviously government foreign loan issues paved the way for company ones. A series of articles written by Henry Dyer, the first principal of the Imperial College of Engineering in Tokyo, advocated industrial investment in Japan, saying that the opportunities for it were numerous and highly remunerative.[6]

Foreign investment in Japan peaked after the Russo-Japanese War. Several British financiers started an intensive investigation of Japanese investments. They even considered the possibility of direct investments which were regarded as having 'a higher yield for their money than debentures would offer'.[7]

The contemporary Japanese economy needed much capital for its rapid industrialization. Japanese chambers of commerce welcomed low interest-rate foreign capital.[8] Meanwhile, the Japanese government itself regarded municipal and company foreign loans, as well as the government ones, as an important source of funds for paying trade deficits.[9] In fact, K. Takahashi, the Japanese government loan commissioner, admitted in 1906 that the Japanese government had no intention of raising a further foreign loan because of its heavy borrowing abroad, but that there would be the possibility of municipal and company foreign loan issues.[10]

This chapter examines municipal and company foreign loan issues in the period from 1902 to 1913. It also compares them with the government foreign loan issues, especially with respect to the investment channels between Japanese borrowers and the London capital market.[11]

INDUSTRIAL BANK AND FOREIGN LOAN ISSUES

The Japanese government took a strictly defensive posture towards foreign capital on the '*Prinzip der Erziehung der Nation zur Selbständigkeit* (principle of bringing up a nation for independence)'.[12] On 21 August 1906 a cabinet meeting decided the following policy for the import of foreign capital:

(i) municipalities and companies which intended to import foreign capital (or to issue debentures abroad) should consult the government.

(ii) the Industrial Bank, the most eligible financial institution for importing foreign capital to Japan, should invariably mediate it.[13]

The Japanese government intended to control fully the import of foreign capital to municipalities and private sectors.[14] For this purpose it immediately reorganized the Industrial Bank as an intermediary of capital imports.

In March 1902 the Industrial Bank was founded with ¥10 million (£1,020,833) authorized capital (¥2.5 million [£255,208] paid-up capital) under a special act of parliament. The governor and directors were all appointed by the Japanese government. The bank also retained several privileges: a 5 per-cent annual dividend upon the share capital was guaranteed by the government for 6 years from the foundation; the bank was empowered to create debentures to the extent of 5 times its paid-up capital.[15] At the outset, the ambiguously stipulated business object was that the bank should provide long-term capital for borrowers.[16] Therefore, its character was regarded simply as a Japanese 'Crédit Mobilier'. Yet it was also understood that in the near future the bank would begin the business of importing capital into Japan.[17]

Although a channel for government foreign loan issues in London: i.e. the Yokohama Specie Bank, Parr's Bank and the Hongkong Bank, had been established during the Russo-Japanese War, the Japanese government created another for municipal and company ones. K. Inoue, a senior statesman, turned more of his attention to the Industrial Bank.[18] In February 1905 A. Sone, the Japanese minister of finance, directed Takahashi in London to promote the Industrial Bank to the City as a new joint venture for Japanese investment.[19] For this purpose, the Japanese government intended to invite eminent foreign financiers to become directors of the Industrial Bank.

Baring Brothers, which had been examining the possibility of Japanese private railway investments since 1902, were informed by Sale & Frazer Co., their correspondent in Yokohama, of the reorganization of the Industrial Bank.[20] C.V. Sale had set up Sale & Co. in London for Anglo-Japanese trade in 1882 and afterwards Sale & Frazer Co. was established in Yokohama as a sister firm.[21] Sale & Frazer Co. acted as Baring Brothers' correspondent in Japan from 1903.[22]

In April 1905 Takahashi approached Baring Brothers and explained that the Industrial Bank was the most eligible financial institution to mediate between Japanese borrowers and the City. He invited Baring Brothers to nominate a foreign director for the Industrial Bank.[23] Yet Baring Brothers considered that such a financial intermediary (the Industrial Bank) would impede direct transactions between

Japanese companies and foreign investors and have an ill effect on foreigners' investment.[24] They refused even Sale's participation in the Industrial Bank.[25] Perhaps Baring Brothers were anxious to deal with the Japanese private railway investments by themselves.[26]

Subsequently, Takahashi invited Panmure Gordon & Co., a stockbroker, to this reorganization project, but W. Koch, a partner of Panmure Gordon & Co., proposed the following conditions for its participation:

(i) The unpaid capital (¥7.7 million [£765,625]) of the Industrial Bank, out of the ¥10 million (£1,020,833) authorized capital, should be paid up immediately and the paid up capital should be increased to ¥20 million (£2,041,666).

(ii) Panmure Gordon & Co. should undertake the issue of the newly increased stock (¥10 million [£1,020,833]).

(iii) The Industrial Bank should engage Panmure Gordon & Co. exclusively as the bank's sole stockbroker, and Panmure Gordon & Co. should take up security issues in London at a ½ per-cent commission.[27]

Koch obviously aimed to reform the Industrial Bank into an Anglo-Japanese joint venture to share the stock equally. But Takahashi and the Japanese government responded that: the payment of the unpaid capital was to be fulfilled by June 1906; Panmure Gordon & Co. had only a priority of the security issues; out of the newly-increased stock, only ¥7 million (£714,583) should be sold abroad.[28] They were firm in minimizing foreign influences on the Industrial Bank's management.

On 23 October 1905 the provisional contract was made between them, and the Industrial Bank appointed Panmure Gordon & Co. as its London agent.[29] Similar agent contracts would be placed with Günzbourg et Cie (Paris) and Warburg (Hamburg) in 1907.[30] Yet the Japanese government was not entirely successful in transforming the Industrial Bank into joint venture because the contract omitted a stipulation that the bank should nominate foreign directors. These agent contracts, however, played an important role in placing abroad at a low commission the foreign loans which the Industrial Bank undertook. Through these channels the Industrial Bank ensured that foreign loan issue markets could arrange loan issues effectively. The Industrial Bank was, thus, successful in minimizing loan issue costs in many of the municipal and company foreign loan issues. In fact, J. Soyeda, the first governor of the Industrial Bank, admitted that he made great efforts to carry on direct transactions with foreign financiers so as to avoid additional intermediary commissions.[31]

The Industrial Bank was formidable for foreign financiers in Japanese loan issue business. After 1906 the bank was deeply concerned with many municipal and company foreign loan issues, so much so that foreign financiers were very wary of its advantageous position. Foreign financiers often blamed the Japanese government's unfair intervention, through the Industrial Bank, in private transactions. In fact, foreign merchants in Japan complained that Japanese municipal foreign loan issues were almost unavailable except through the Industrial Bank.[32] C.M. MacDonald, the British ambassador in Tokyo, commented that the Japanese government gave too much favour to the Industrial Bank 'at the expense of its [foreign] rivals'.[33]

In February 1906 an amendment of the Industrial Bank Act was brought into effect: the bank's paid-up capital increased to ¥6,250,000 (£638,020) out of the ¥10 million (£1,020,833) authorized capital; then the bank increased the authorized capital to ¥17.5 million (£1,786,458); the ¥7.5 million (£765,625) newly-increased stock was all placed abroad and paid up fully. As a result, the bank's paid-up capital now became ¥13,750,000 (£1,403,645) and the proportion of the capital, held by foreigners, reached 43 per cent.[34]

MUNICIPAL LOAN ISSUES

After the Russo-Japanese War Japan entered a new era of foreign loan issues for municipalities and companies. The loan issues were concentrated in 1908 and 1909 in particular (appendices C and D). Municipalities were willing to introduce low interest rate foreign capital into their infrastructure establishments. Owing to the low capital accumulation, interest rates in Japan were much higher than those in Western developed countries. There were large interest rate differentials (4.3 per cent at the end of December 1904) between Japan and Britain.[35]

At that time there were the following three common channels of municipal foreign loan issues:

(i) by foreign financiers directly (through correspondents in Japan).
(ii) by foreign financiers through the Industrial Bank.

(iii) by foreign financiers through other Japanese banks.

Before July 1902 the Japanese government had not yet followed any definite guideline for municipal foreign loan issues. In July 1899 the City of Kobe negotiated on an issue of ¥1 million (£102,083) 6 per-cent bonds with J.M. Morse, the president of the American Trading Co. in Yokohama and Kobe.[36] They agreed to issue ¥500,000 (£51,042) of the 6 per-cent bonds. Morse purchased ¥250,000 (£25,521)[37] in sterling. This was the first municipal foreign loan issue in Japan, although the character was very different from public loans placed through subscriptions on the market. In 1902 the 6 per-cent City of Yokohama waterworks foreign loan for £90,000 was arranged by S. Samuel & Co. in Yokohama and M. Samuel & Co. placed it in London.[38]

Thereafter, in July 1902 the Japanese Ministry of Home Affairs gave notification that municipalities should invariably inform both the Ministry of Home Affairs and the Ministry of Finance of loan issues before commencing negotiations with foreign financiers.[39] The aim of this was obvious. The Japanese government intended to control the import of foreign capital to municipalities. Although foreign financiers were never shut out wholly, there was only a little room for them to vie effectively with the Industrial Bank in municipal loan issue business. In order to escape censure of its unfair trade interventions, the sagacious Japanese government reserved a limited number of municipal foreign loan issues for foreign financiers. For instance, it was under the Japanese government's administrative guidance that Sale & Frazer Co. took the City of Nagoya 5 per-cent loan issue in 1909.[40]

The municipal foreign loan issues before the Russo-Japanese War period were arranged mainly by British merchants in Japan. They did not always offer favourable loan issue terms. The City of Osaka 6 per-cent harbour loan contract in 1902 between the Daisan Bank, the Yasuda Bank and S. Samuel & Co. exemplifies one of the early unfavourable municipal foreign loan issues.

(i) The Daisan Bank should purchase ¥3.5 million (£357,292) of the bonds from the municipality.

(ii) S. Samuel & Co. should sell them in London through M. Samuel & Co. at a 7½ per-cent commission including all the charges.

(iii) The Yasuda Bank should underwrite half the issue amount (¥1,750,000 [£178,646]) and S. Samuel & Co. the other half.

(iv) S. Samuel & Co. should pay a 2½ per-cent underwriting commission to the Yasuda Bank.[41]

It must be noted that the municipality paid a large loan issue commission, 7½ per cent. S. Samuel & Co.'s real commission amounted to nearly 8 per cent including the balance between the issue price (99 per cent) and the purchase price from the municipality (about 97¾ per cent). The reason for the 6 per-cent rate of interest was ascribed to the character of a domestic loan. ¥3.5 million [£357,292], out of the ¥17,038,000 [£1,739,296] bonds issued, were offered to the subscriptions abroad.[42] S. Samuel & Co. agreed to underwrite only half the amount (¥1,750,000) and the Yasuda Bank was to sell the other half in the domestic market should the subscriptions in London fail. S. Samuel & Co. also obtained a 10 per-cent commission in the City of Yokohama 6 per-cent waterworks loan of 1902.[43] These show that the Japanese municipalities did not enjoy really favourable foreign loan issues before the Russo-Japanese War.

In view of these unfavourable loan issue circumstances, in August 1906 the Ministry of Finance gave notification that small municipal loans (less than ¥1 million [£102,083]) should either be floated on the domestic market or aggregated to the form of Industrial Bank foreign debentures; municipal foreign loan issues should be made through the Industrial Bank.[44] Although the Japanese government announced that it had no intention of interfering in transactions, it was obvious that this was the virtually inevitable result for municipalities.[45]

How could British merchants in Japan find a loan issue market for municipalities? In other words, how could they mediate between municipalities and the City? Correspondence between Sale & Frazer Co., Baring Brothers and Antony Gibbs[46] in the City of Tokyo loan issue negotiations of 1906 provides a rich source of information on this matter. It reveals practice in contemporary foreign loan business.

In July 1905 Sale & Frazer Co. (Yokohama), through its sister firm Sale & Co. (London), offered the City of Tokyo harbour loan issue to Baring Brothers. Yet Baring Brothers showed little interest in it because their Japanese investment business was confined strictly to government or first class private railway company loan issues. Baring Brothers, therefore, exhorted Sale & Co. to take this business to

Antony Gibbs. Brien Cokayne, a partner of Antony Gibbs, and Lord Revelstoke met to discuss it and Lord Revelstoke assured him that this would be as sound as a government loan issue. Cokayne was afraid of locking up capital in a loan issue and hesitated to launch such a risky venture without full knowledge of its character. Vicary Gibbs, another partner of Antony Gibbs, was, however, rather keen to seize the proposed loan issue[47] and consulted Panmure Gordon & Co. on the possibility.[48] Despite the information supplied being very imprecise and no statistics being available on the City of Tokyo, by the end of July Gibbs had decided on the following tentative loan issue terms:

	(%)
Rate of interest	6
Issue price	97 (to the public)
	90 (to the municipality)
Commission	7

(%)	
2	to Antony Gibbs
1	to Sale & Frazer Co.
2	to underwriters
½	brokerage
1	printing and advertising
½	the stamp duty.[49]

The loan issue commission amounted to 7 per cent and there was a 1 per cent intermediary commission to Sale & Frazer Co.

It seems likely that Sale & Frazer Co. had not yet firmly grasped the business opportunity. Antony Gibbs became sceptical about the progress of the negotiations in Japan, and in September it proposed either a 6 per-cent loan at 95½ per cent or a 5½ per-cent one at between 90 per-cent and 88 per cent.[50]

Ultimately Antony Gibbs' bid ended up unfulfilled. In June 1906 the Industrial Bank and the City of Tokyo agreed to issue a 5 per-cent loan for £1.5 million through Parr's Bank, the Hongkong Bank and the Yokohama Specie Bank. The 5 per-cent rate of interest and 3½ per-cent commission were much better than Antony Gibbs' offer.[51] Sale & Frazer Co. reported to Baring Brothers that 'it is a triumph for the Industrial Bank of Japan, and for those Japanese who insisted that their credit has now reached such a standard that foreign intermediaries are no longer required.'[52] Foreign financiers, however, were dissatisfied with this outcome. In particular, S. Samuel & Co. complained that the City of Tokyo had an obvious motive for putting the loan issue into the hands of the Industrial Bank, disregarding many foreign financiers' more advantageous offers.[53] The Industrial Bank took the initiative in underwriting the loan issue through Panmure Gordon & Co.[54] The result of this loan issue was undersubscribed and the underwriters took £283,840 of the bonds, 18.9 per cent of the issue amount.[55]

Sale & Frazer Co. often mediated loan issues between Japanese borrowers and the City. Lazard Brothers placed the loans Sale & Frazer Co. undertook in Japan, on the London capital market. Through these business connections, both the City of Nagoya 5 per-cent loan of 1909 and the City of Yokohama 5 per-cent one of 1912 were floated. The City of Nagoya 5 per-cent loan was issued at a 5½ per-cent commission.[56] In comparison with the loan issues undertaken by the Industrial Bank, the terms were slightly less favourable to the municipality.

Appendix C shows that in the period from 1906 to 1913 there were four municipal foreign loan issues which the Industrial Bank undertook. Their cumulative amount in that period comprised nearly 80 per cent of the total municipal foreign loan issues. As shown, the bank ensured a firm business channel with Panmure Gordon & Co. through its agent contract, and the usual Japanese government loan takers in London: i.e. Parr's Bank, the Hongkong Bank and the Yokohama Specie Bank, invariably placed all of them.

In 1909 the City of Osaka issued a 5 per-cent loan for £3,084,940 in London through the Industrial Bank. £1,250,000 of the bonds had been purchased in advance and the balance of £1,834,940 was subscribed on the market.[57] The 5 per-cent loan issue commission excluding miscellaneous charges[58] was more expensive to the municipality than the 3½ per cent in the City of Tokyo loan issue of 1906. In the same year the Industrial Bank also took the City of Yokohama 5 per-cent waterworks loan issue for £716,500. Parr's Bank, the Hongkong Bank and the Yokohama Specie Bank floated it at a 4 per-cent commission through Panmure Gordon & Co. It was oversubscribed fivefold.[59]

In February 1912 the City of Tokyo raised a £9,175,000 foreign loan for purchasing private electric tramway companies. Despite many foreign financiers' vigorous offers, the Industrial Bank finally took it. The loan was placed on the three major capital markets: London, New York and Paris, simultaneously. The Industrial Bank completed these operations through Panmure Gordon & Co. and Günzbourg et Cie.[60] Parr's Bank, the Hongkong Bank and the Yokohama Specie Bank undertook the loan issue in London, Kuhn, Loeb & Co. in New York, and the Société Générale, the Banque de Paris and the Comptoir National d'Escompte in Paris. K. Mori, the Japanese government financial commissioner, conducted all these negotiations on behalf of the Industrial Bank.[61] He assessed the capacity of the Anglo–American markets at £6 million at most and included Paris in this operation.[62] According to the different market conditions, the following separate loan issue terms were prepared:

Loan issue amount	£9,175,000	
London	£3,175,000	
Paris	£4,000,000	
New York	£2,000,000	
Rate of interest (nominal)	5 per cent	
Loan issue prices	(to municipality)	(to the public)
London	93 per cent	98 per cent
Paris	92 per cent	96¾ per cent
New York	93½ per cent	98 per cent
Yields at issue		
London	95.1 per cent	
Paris	5.2 per cent	
New York	5.1 per cent.[63]	

The outcome of the subscriptions in London was poor and only £1,523,600, 48 per cent of the London issue amount, was taken by the public.[64]

French investors also paid much attention to investments in Japan after the conclusion of the Franco-Japanese agreement in 1907. In the very same year the Banque de Paris sent Horace Finaly, *sous-directeur* (sub-director), to Japan to look into the possibility of Japanese investments.[65] Japanese businessmen were also willing to build up commercial relations with French financiers. In 1907, Soyeda (the governor of the Industrial Bank) on a business trip, approached several financiers in Paris through J. de Günzbourg[66] and T. Masuda, a director of the Mitsui Zaibatsu, contacted the Paris Rothschilds and Vernes et Cie.[67]

In 1909 and 1912 the City of Kyoto floated 5 per-cent loans on the Paris capital market through the Mitsui Bank. The main figure of these loan issues was Kahn, an influential French financier, who had established close connections with the Mitsui Zaibatsu.[68] In 1906 the City of Kyoto decided to construct waterworks, roads and an electric tramway on borrowing. Initially the City brought this business to the Industrial Bank, but the bank failed to float the loan in Europe because of adverse market conditions. K. Saigō, the mayor, approached the Mitsui Bank, instead of the Industrial Bank, and in 1908 made temporary borrowings of ¥2.7 million (£275,625) from the Mitsui Bank. The Mitsui Bank, which was at that time considering redirecting its business from deposit to investment banking,[69] intended to raise further necessary funds abroad.[70]

In March 1909 the City of Kyoto agreed with the Mitsui Bank to issue a 5 per-cent loan in France for ¥17 million (£1,735,417).[71] S. Watanabe, the manager of Mitsui Bussan Kaisha in London, became a prime negotiator.[72] Kahn mediated between Watanabe and the loan issue banks in Paris: the Banque de l'Union Parisienne and the Société Marseillaise de Crédit Industriel et Commercial et de Dépôts.[73] On 28 June 1909 Watanabe concluded the following loan issue terms:

Issue amount	Fr45 million (£1,781,250)
Rate of interest (nominal)	5 per cent
Issue price	99 per cent (to the public)
	93 per cent (to the municipality)
Yield at issue	5.4 per cent
Borrowing period	30 years.[74]

The total issue amount was purchased by the syndicate.[75] The contract stated that the syndicate could re-purchase 20 per cent of the issue amount from the market to manipulate the market price of the bonds properly.[76] The 6 per-cent loan issue commission, including miscellaneous charges, was not particularly advantageous to the municipality. The distribution of the commission among the concerned financial institutions is indicated in Table 8.1.

The syndicate successfully secured the issue amount[77] and the French government immediately admitted the quotation of the loan on the Paris Stock Exchange.[78] The syndicate desired the City of Kyoto to use French manufactured goods for the works which the loan financed.[79] In 1912 an additional 5 per-cent loan for Fr5 million

Table 8.1 Distribution of loan issue commissions in the City of Kyoto 5 per-cent loan issue in 1909

	(%)
Mitsui Bank (intermediary)	½
Kahn (intermediary)	½
Banque de l'Union Parisienne (loan issue bank)	½
Société Marseillaise (loan issue bank)	½
Syndicate profit	4
Total	6

Source: MA, Ginkō 13–6, T. Toyama, Mitsui Ginkō Ō-Bei Schucchion Hōkokusho (Report of an officer dispatched by the Mitsui Bank to Europe and America) (1909), 121–2.
Note: Syndicate profit included miscellaneous charges.

(£197,917) was issued at a 5 per-cent commission through the same channel.[80]

Perhaps it was in these two financial operations that French financiers gained a firm foothold in Japanese loan issue business and fully eliminated Britain's strong sway over their activities.[81] Meanwhile, the Mitsui Bank was proud of accomplishing these issues without any British intermediary.[82]

COMPANY LOAN ISSUES

Japanese industries and enterprises needed cheap foreign capital. The Osaka Merchant Shipping Co. intended to issue low interest rate foreign debentures in 1900.[83] Baring Brothers' experimental operations to scrutinize the possibility of Japanese private railway investments started from 1902 but a defect in the Japanese law frustrated its progress. Baring Brothers considered that 'everything [in this business] depends upon confidence in the security offered'[84] to debentures because British railway investors, who drew 'a marked distinction between investments of an industrial nature and railway investments',[85] paid much attention to the security for their money. Hence Baring Brothers advised the Japanese government to legislate a mortgage law[86] and the Japanese railway mortgage law was enacted on 26 February 1905.[87] As a result of railway nationalization in 1906, however, all the efforts to introduce foreign capital into the Japanese private railway companies were wasted.[88]

Like the municipal foreign loan issues, it was after the Russo–Japanese War that company foreign loan issues reached a peak. It is obvious from appendix D that the proportion of the railway company foreign debenture issues to the total foreign ones from 1905 to 1913 was well over 75 per cent, and would probably have been higher, had not the railway nationalization taken place. British investors regarded railway, mining and electricity in particular as their appropriate investment objects.[89]

The attitude of the Japanese government towards company foreign loan issues was almost the same as that towards municipal ones. The previous announcement of 1906 was also applicable to company foreign loan issues. In addition to this, the Japanese secured debentures trust law stipulated that a company which intended to enter a trust agreement with foreigners should file an application with the Ministry of Finance.[90] On these grounds the Japanese government could legally intervene in private transactions.

Several foreign merchants resident in Japan, such as Birch, Kirby & Co., S. Samuel & Co. and Sale & Frazer Co., played a leading role in placing company loans, especially the earlier ones, abroad as agents or correspondents of London merchant banks. These merchant houses dispatched useful business information directly to the City. In 1904 R.J. Kirby, a former partner of Birch, Kirby & Co., set up a Japanese business intelligence office in Tokyo, the purpose of which was to furnish British firms with a monthly report of Japanese business.[91]

Apart from the large-scale company loan issues patronized by the Japanese government, merchant houses were able to take part effectively in company foreign loan issues. In particular, S. Samuel & Co. was involved most deeply in company foreign loan business. It undertook the Kansai Railway Co. debenture issue in 1905 and in 1908 made a private borrowing for ¥3 million (£306,250) for the Keihan Railway Co. on the Daiichi Bank's guarantee.[92] These transactions resulted in many concomitant orders for British manufactured railway goods. In 1910 Sale & Frazer Co. arranged the ¥5 million (£510,416) Hokkaidō Colonial Bank 5 per-cent foreign debentures, the purpose of which was conversion of high interest rate domestic debentures to lower foreign ones.[93]

Overseas banks also became involved in Japanese company foreign loan issues. The Hongkong Bank, since the resale of the Japanese government domestic bonds in 1902, collaborated with Baring Brothers in Japanese investment business. Its Yokohama branch often supported Sale & Frazer Co., the Baring Brothers' agent in Japan, in several Japanese private railway debenture issues. The Hongkong Bank, however, switched the partner of its Japanese investment business from Baring Brothers to the Industrial Bank after the Industrial Bank made an agent contract with Panmure Gordon & Co., as mentioned previously. In 1905 the Chartered Bank issued the 5 per-cent Hokkaidō Colliery & Coal Railway Co. debentures through Faber & Pigot Co., a merchant house in Japan.[94]

French financiers had stakes in several Japanese company loan issues. In 1908 Kahn mediated the Kanegafuchi Cotton Spinning Co. 7½ per-cent debenture issue between the Mitsui Bank and banks in Paris.[95] In 1909 Gysin Frères in Paris mediated the 6½ percent debenture issue in Paris for the Matsui Muslin Spinning Co.[96] In 1913 the newly established Banque Franco-Japonaise, in co-operation with the Industrial Bank, placed the first Oriental Colonial Corp. 5 per-cent debentures, guaranteed by the Japanese government, on the Paris capital market.[97]

The Industrial Bank played a key role in mediating large-scale company foreign loan issues for the South Manchurian Railway Co.[98] and the Oriental Colonial Corp. Its business network, covering London (Panmure Gordon & Co.), Paris (Günzbourg et Cie) and Hamburg (Warburg), enabled the bank to issue more favourable foreign loans than any foreign merchants in Japan could arrange. The Industrial Bank made eight out of the eleven company foreign loan issues during the period from 1906 to 1913.

Many investment companies (or 'promoting companies') for Japanese investment were set up.[99] The principal role of these companies was to 'investigate and arrange preliminaries for any class of investment or enterprise.'[100] Yet as the prospectus of the Japanese Eastern Corp. announced a 25 per-cent premium on the debenture stock,[101] their character was speculative and they could not secure firm footings among investors. It seems likely that British investors were reluctant to channel money through a financial intermediary specializing in Japanese investment. As the Anglo-Japanese Bank did not gain a high reputation in the City,[102] merchant banks invariably took the initiative with Japanese investment.

By contrast, French financiers, much behind the British in Japanese investment business, set up a specific intermediary for Japanese investments. In 1913 the Société Générale, together with the Industrial Bank, founded the Banque Franco-Japonaise, the purpose of which was to establish direct financial linkages between France and Japan, not through British intermediaries.[103]

DIRECT INVESTMENT

Japan, as mentioned, imported most of its foreign capital in the form of loans (portfolio investment). Direct investment in 1912 was estimated roughly at ¥29,521,000 (£3,013,602) – only 1.6 per cent of the total foreign capital in Japan (government foreign bonds, government domestic bonds [exported], municipal foreign bonds, company foreign debentures and direct investment).[104] Why was the proportion of direct investment to the total foreign capital in Japan so low? In other words, what was the hindrance to direct investment to Japan? The explanation of loan issues is not applied straight to direct investment. Compared with loan issues, both investment objects and the behaviour of foreign investors will be scrutinized here.

Because of the dearth of information[105] it is difficult to trace precisely the direct investments, especially the ingress of multinational companies and banks into the Japanese market. Surviving records reveal only a limited number of the direct investments in manufacturing sectors.[106] It was estimated in 1907 that 20.2 per cent of the total capital of companies which were newly projected or had increased their capital was jointly held with interested foreigners.[107]

Although foreign capital suppliers would bear the concomitant risks of their investment, the Japanese government often intervened in these transactions and aimed to 'divert all the import foreign capital into one channel',[108] namely debenture issues through the Industrial Bank. Baron Iwasaki (Yanosuke Iwasaki), brother of Yatarō Iwasaki (the founder of the Mitsubishi Zaibatsu), was of the firm opinion that direct investment in Japan should not be permitted freely from the viewpoint of protectionism; he thought that 'the economy of Japan is not yet advanced to such a stage as to allow foreign capitalists to hold half the amount, or more, of the whole stock of a company, and to take entire control.'[109] As rightly indicated, 'only those foreign companies whose presence could contribute to the nation's industrialization process were permitted to operate.'[110]

The high yield of Japanese investment, however, attracted foreign investors as *The Times* correspondent pointed out that 'investments which sound almost incredible in English ears go a-begging in Japan.'[111] In 1900 the Japanese minister in Washington received an enquiry into the possibility of direct investment in Japan.[112] M. Arakawa, the Japanese consul in London, who had an intimate knowledge of foreign investment, suggested to the Japanese government that: (i) the import of foreign capital should be made with the introduction of new technology; (ii) an eligible institution for capital import such as the Industrial Bank of Japan should be established; (iii) conflict between the management of a company and foreign investors (share and debenture holders) should be avoided; (iv) fair treatment should be required of foreign investors.[113]

Some direct investments caused conflicts and frictions between foreign investors and the Japanese. The Anglo-Japanese Syndicate launched a large-scale joint undertaking for the supply of water power (the Anglo-Japanese Hydro-Electric Co.) in 1908. This water-power scheme was assessed 'as a safe and good form of investment'[114] but did not proceed satisfactorily mainly because of financial difficulties. The British banks involved in this scheme were reluctant to take the responsibility of raising funds for the Japanese banks.[115] It was generally reported that the form of investment in promoting industrial enterprises was 'to provide profits for the Japanese, while leaving the risks for the foreigners' and very little success was attained.[116]

A British agent in Japan gave an example of why foreigners had much difficulty in controlling the management of a Japanese company: most Japanese thought that if foreign investors were allowed to take one half of the whole amount of the shares, they might pass a vote against the interest of the Japanese shareholders who were invariably inclined to propose setting apart large reserves for the company, not for the shareholders.[117] It is true that Japanese investors, from the viewpoint of financial stability, paid more attention to the reserves of the company they invested than their drawing dividends.[118]

There were serious conflicts between the foreigners and the Japanese in the Osaka Gas Co., 65 per cent of whose capital was held by A.N. Brady, an American engineer and capitalist: the foreign officers found the Japanese workers and officers hostile towards them; labour troubles such as attacks on the foreign officers occurred frequently.[119]

The legislation of the new commercial law in 1899 and of the mortgage laws in 1905 paved the way for encouraging investment by foreigners. Although an article of the *Anglo-Japanese Gazette* insisted on foreigners being treated as partners, not as mere money-lenders, foreign investors should not put their money into Japanese industries and enterprises unless they came to superintend the management in Japan.[120] There were still legal[121] and ethnic discriminations against foreigners. So, all in all it is fair to conclude that the 'Japan [of that time] was a profitable, but sometimes difficult, market'[122] for foreign investors and firms.

Foreign investors, for their part, would regard debenture issues, rather than direct investment, as safe investment in Japanese industries and enterprises.[123] As far as the Japanese investment before 1914 was concerned, the attitude of foreign investors would be risk-averse.[124]

9

Effects of Japanese Government Loan Issues

To guard against a possible drain of gold abroad, a complicated mechanism has been developed which in the details of its working is peculiar to this country. . . . When we come to consider how this can best be done, it is to be noticed that the position of a country which is preponderantly a creditor in the international short-loan market is quite different from that of a country which is preponderantly a debtor.

J. M. Keynes, *Indian Currency and Finance*

Chapters 3 to 8 dealt with the development of Japanese government (including municipal and company) borrowing abroad, mainly, but not exclusively, in London. The argument there laid stress upon the mechanism of Japanese government loan issues on the London capital market. This chapter, however, throws light upon two other important facets of Japanese government foreign loan issues: firstly, the role of the Japanese government's loan proceeds in the working of the gold standard before the First World War;[1] and secondly, the repercussions of the loan issues on Japan's trade structure with Britain. These matters are not concerned directly with the loan issue mechanism on the market but with the influence of the loan issues on the international financial and trade system. It is hoped that the explanation in this chapter will supplement the argument in the previous chapters, especially from the viewpoint of Japan's relations with the world economy of that period under the gold standard.

JAPANESE GOVERNMENT'S FOREIGN FUNDS

After the Sino-Japanese War (1894–95) the Japanese government obtained large indemnity money (£38,083,000) from China and temporarily held it in London.[2] The City feared the sudden withdrawal of the indemnity money from London to Japan might seriously diminish reserves at the Bank of England and cause sharp fluctuations in the London money market,[3] even though the great Franco–Prussian indemnity loan issues in 1872 passed without serious reaction.[4] The court of the Bank of England cautiously observed Japanese government deposits in London. B.B. Greene, a director of the bank (the deputy-governor from 1870 to 1871 and the governor from 1873 to 1875), warned that 'we must consider the Japanese Deposit as quite abnormal'[5] and 'I am concerned to see what is to happen to the Japanese Money, no doubt we shall lose control of the greater part of it.'[6]

Some countries would hold money in the world's financial centres – London, Paris, Berlin and New York. It was an established practice for British dominions to keep loan proceeds in London and manage them from there.[7] Whale gave explanations on how this system worked with reference to borrowing countries' domestic currencies:

> There is, however, another way in which these monetary transfers may be brought about: that is, by creating additional money in the borrowing country on the basis of money held in the lending country. There is evidence, I think, that this was commonly done by the banks in many of the countries in which Britain invested – the Dominions and British colonies, the South American countries, and Japan. The lending country is in this way spared the loss of gold, yet the borrowing country gets increased supplies of money. If the banks in the borrowing country treat their foreign (or overseas) balances as being exactly equivalent to gold reserves, and proceed to make them the basis for a multiple expansion of their notes or deposits.[8]

Lindert pointed out that before the First World War several central banks, in Austria–Hungary, Greece, Japan, Romania, Russia, Switzerland, the Scandinavian countries and Chile, tended to prefer foreign exchange to gold in their official reserves.[9] It was a well-known fact that Russia held large funds in Paris, Berlin and London which were transferred from its loan proceeds, and managed them on the international money markets.[10] The Chilean government, from 1906, also kept deposits mainly in Berlin and London under the name of the 'Conversion Fund'.[11] Lindert further revealed that not only British colonies but also the two foreign countries, Greece and Japan, held more reserves in foreign exchange than in gold.[12]

In the pre-1914 world 'London was the predominant world credit, clearing and gold center.'[13] Most international transactions were invoiced by pound and financed by bills on London.[14] For clearing purposes, overseas and foreign banks kept working balances of sterling in London. Credit countries gave to debt countries long-term lendings from their trade surpluses.[15] These capital movements helped the smooth working of the contemporary gold standard by cushioning vast trade deficits and surpluses between the credit and debt countries.

In a lending country, like Britain, a bank rate policy could regulate the outflows and inflows of capital, especially of short-term funds, through small interest changes, as Beach and Bloomfield have confirmed.[16] A bank rate policy made it possible for the Bank of England to regulate the value of the domestic currency – the volume of note issue which corresponded with its gold reserves.

In contrast, a borrowing country had to follow a more direct policy of regulating the value of the domestic currency. A very different form of the gold standard was built there: there was no circulation of gold coins; in practice the central bank in a borrowing country was often reluctant to convert its bank notes into gold,[17] while people in Britain could freely draw gold (coins or bullion) from circulation (the Bank of England) and export such amounts to other countries. Specie holdings abroad, in the form of foreign exchange bills or sterling balances, provided an easily-obtained means for a borrowing country to settle its trade balances directly, without causing the trouble of actual gold movements and serious fluctuations in the rate of foreign exchange.[18] By selling specie holdings abroad or purchasing foreign exchange bills, the central bank in a borrowing country could conduct official operations in the foreign exchange markets. It intended to control the markets directly for sustaining fluctuations in foreign exchange rates within the zone of the gold points, especially when the rates moved to the gold export point.[19] Keynes addressed this practice in his famous writing on the Indian currency and finance: a peripheral [borrowing] country's government or central bank kept gold or other resources abroad for regulating the value of its domestic currency in terms of the gold exchange standard system.[20]

It was not during the inter-war period that the idea of the gold exchange standard was produced. The structure and actual form of the gold standard before 1914 was 'far from the simple and uniform thing' and 'differed considerably from country to country'.[21] Its working was by no means 'automatic'[22] but 'managed'.[23] Central banks in borrowing countries needed to regulate their monetary conditions so as 'to shield domestic economic activity from external disturbances'[24] created under the gold standard. Nurkse found the 'Pre-War [before the Second World War] antecedents of the gold exchange standard' in Russia, the Scandinavian countries, India, the Philippines, Argentina, Japan and so on.[25] These countries kept funds in the world's financial centres as 'reserve currencies' which acted as '"cushions," "buffers" or "insulators"' to actual gold movements.[26]

The Austro–Hungarian Bank after 1896 adopted a foreign exchange policy (*Devisenpolitik*), the purpose of which was to stabilize fluctuations in the foreign exchange market.[27] Russia as well adopted a similar policy. Since the 1870s Berlin had been a major place of foreign exchange transactions for Russian currency (paper ruble). The Russian government aimed to end speculation in these transactions by intervening in the market. After the introduction of the gold standard in 1897, the State Bank, the central bank after 1897, purchased and sold exchange (gold) bills to maintain fluctuations in foreign exchange rates within the gold points. The primary source of these operations was the government's borrowing abroad. The bank purchased foreign loan proceeds from the government and kept working balances in foreign currencies in the world's financial centres.[28]

Even under the pre-1914 gold standard, foreign exchange operations were of great importance to Sweden. The Riksbank, the central bank, held large foreign assets (balances) for reserve requirements and as an international means of payment. Foreign loans were the most reliable source of these foreign assets. The bank often discouraged outflows of gold from Sweden, performing foreign exchange operations. Jonung, therefore, regarded the Swedish gold standard before 1914 as 'a managed gold standard'.[29]

For Japan, a debt country located far distant from the world's financial centres, it was impossible to depend upon a bank rate policy to attract gold in the form of short-term funds. So, the Japanese government obviously regarded a foreign exchange policy as a major weapon to prevent sharp fluctuations in the foreign exchange market, when a drain of gold caused by trade deficits took place.[30]

In terms of transferring money from one country to another, the practice of holding specie abroad in these gold standard countries was analogous to India's gold exchange standard.[31] However, from 1893 rupee notes no longer had silver convertibility and the value of one rupee (par) was fixed rigidly at 1s. 4d. The Council of India in London established the Gold Standard Reserve (sterling) on the proceeds of Council bills and profits of the Indian Mint. In addition, there were other reserves (balances) held in London: the Paper Currency Reserve and the Indian government's treasury balances. From these funds the Indian government paid home charges and interest on its sterling debts.

The close economic relations between Britain and India caused the development of a bilateral money payment system. Council bills played a role in transferring money from Britain to India; those who needed to make payments in India, purchased council bills (denominated in rupees) for sterling and sent them to India; the Indian government and others who needed to make payment in sterling purchased these bills with rupees. Conversely, those who transferred money from India to London, bought bills (on London) with rupees in India and sent them to London; the Council of India in London purchased these bills with sterling. The issue of Council bills enabled the Indian government to settle the balance of payments with Britain and to control exchange rates between Britain and India on the markets.[32]

With the spread of the gold standard to many countries, however, British bankers feared an efflux of gold from the London money market.[33] Financial institutions in London became more and more nervous about possible ill effects of foreign loan issues on the market. From the viewpoint of defending the gold reserves at the Bank of England, the practice of keeping most of the loan proceeds in London was very desirable to Britain, because these proceeds were still under the control of the London money market. This practice spared Britain a loss of gold.[34]

Loan proceeds kept at financial institutions in London formed sterling balances. These balances, as 'international reserve assets', could provide the London money market with international liquidity.[35] In fact, Kindleberger understood the character of these balances from the viewpoint of 'old-fashioned principles of lending long and borrowing short'.[36] It was true that the City held relatively large funds for clearing international transactions, but gold reserves at the Bank of England were always considered to be insufficient to meet the demand of transactions on the market. Viner declared that 'the outstanding feature of English gold reserves during the nineteenth century was their inadequacy not only for this global task but even to preserve convertibility of sterling.'[37]

Japan's specie holdings in London (both the government's and the Bank of Japan's) were of great assistance to the Bank of England in adjusting constant fluctuations on the money market. Until the turn of the century, the London balances held by the Council of India had produced a similar effect to the market. As the Council kept large sums in London (the Gold Standard Reserve), the Bank of England often counted upon them from the 1890s.[38] In the following twenty years, however, the Bank of England regarded the Japanese government's funds in London, rather than the Council of India's London balances, as a more stable and reliable source for regulating money demand in the market and borrowed from them on a large scale. According to Sayers, there were at least five occasions during 1905 that the Bank of England borrowed between £500,000 and £1,600,000 from the Bank of Japan.[39]

In the period before the Russo-Japanese War (1904–1905), the Japanese government had not yet established the practice of leaving funds abroad as *Zaigai Seika* (specie holdings abroad or specie reserves abroad).[40] Until March 1903 most of the deposit was paid out in London or transferred to Japan in gold and silver bullion. Only £1,132,864 was retained for further payment of various claims on the Japanese government.[41]

The cumulative issue of the foreign loans during the Russo–Japanese War brought large foreign funds to Japan. It was imperative under the gold standard that the Japanese government should secure funds abroad for settling the trade balances which were substantially in deficit almost every year from 1896 to 1913. Owing to the extraordinarily increased military imports, in 1904 the Japanese government established a new rule for managing foreign loan proceeds: for its payments abroad the government chose to hold most of these proceeds permanently in the world's financial centres, such as London, Paris, Berlin and New York; the government could sell some of the loan proceeds to the Bank of Japan and receive these payments in yen notes in Japan.[42]

Chart 9.1 indicates the distribution of loan proceeds among the Japanese government, the Bank of Japan, the Yokohama Specie Bank and other foreign exchange banks. Japan's specie holdings rose rapidly from 1905 and its main source obviously lay in foreign

Chart 9.1 Distribution of Japanese loan proceeds

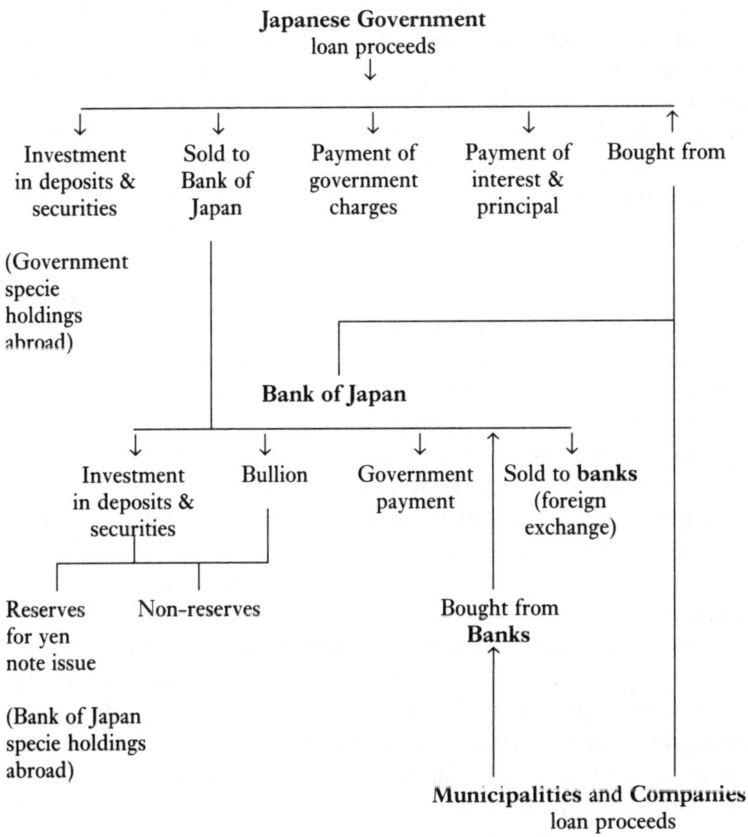

Note: For the figures from 1903 to 1913, see JMFA, Shōda Papers, 49–1,14, 16 and 23.

loan proceeds.[43] In the years of 1904, 1905, 1906, 1907 and 1910 the Japanese government obtained large loan proceeds. Out of the specie holdings abroad, the government paid the principal and interest on the foreign loans; after 1906 all the payments connected with the foreign loans amounted to well over 30 per cent of the government's total annual payments abroad; the government also paid from the specie holdings abroad its various import charges, mainly armaments for the navy. Some of the specie holdings abroad were sold to the

Bank of Japan for settling trade balances in the form of foreign exchange. The remains were invested in deposits with financial institutions in the world's financial centres or in short-term securities (usually British Treasury bills).[44] From a standpoint of liquidity, most of the investments were retained in deposits at the Bank of England and London clearing banks. The government also kept accounts in New York, Paris and Berlin but London was the nucleus, 55.3 per cent of the total government's foreign funds (31 January 1908),[45] because the government transferred funds from New York, Berlin and Paris to London.[46]

There were transactions in specie holdings abroad between the Japanese government, the Bank of Japan, the Yokohama Specie Bank and other foreign exchange banks. The Bank of Japan bought loan proceeds from the Japanese government, municipalities and companies which issued foreign loans. Payment was made in yen. The Bank of Japan resold most of its specie holdings abroad to foreign exchange banks which needed to make payments abroad, in the form of foreign exchange. The Bank of Japan usually invested the specie holdings abroad in deposits at the Bank of England and the Yokohama Specie Bank's London branch or in British Treasury bills,[47] dividing them into the note-issue-reserves and the non-note-issue-reserves accounts.[48]

There were relationships between specie holdings abroad and the domestic money supply.[49] Chart 9.2 portrays their relations. Under the gold standard the Bank of Japan could influence the value of the domestic currency through the operation of selling and purchasing specie holdings abroad in the form of foreign exchange, even when the rate of foreign exchange did not reach a gold shipment point and gold conversion was not presented to the Bank of Japan. The Bank of Japan could, to a certain extent, control the rate of foreign exchange on the market by selling (or purchasing) specie holdings abroad (or bills of exchange) to (or from) exchange banks. It was obvious that the Bank of Japan regarded a foreign exchange policy as one of the monetary policies for regulating the value of the domestic currency, because an official discount rate [bank rate] policy, as mentioned, was ineffective for Japan to attract gold from abroad.[50] It was revealed that the Bank of Japan would resell foreign exchange (pound sterling bills on London) at about the gold export point, ¥1=2s. 1/4d.[51]

In order to discourage or avoid gold conversion the Bank of Japan always depended upon large sellings of foreign exchange bills (pound

Chart 9.2 Specie holdings abroad and foreign exchange

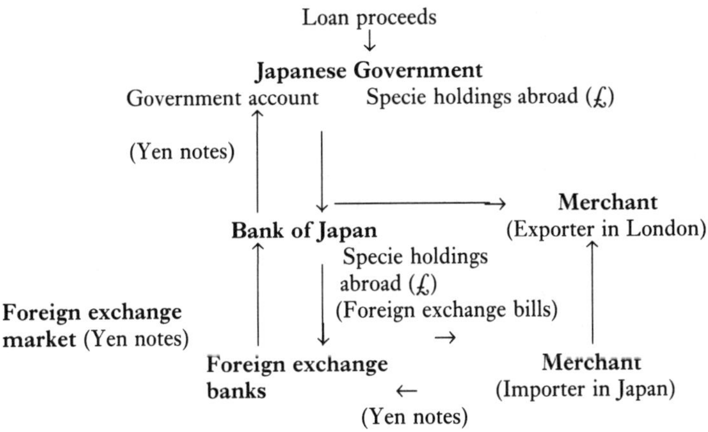

sterling bills on London), especially to foreign banks, at a little higher rate than that of the gold export point. The funds for such transactions were paid mainly from the non-note-issue-reserves abroad.[52] This practice, however, raised scathing criticism that the selling of the cheaper foreign exchange bills by the Bank of Japan would bring foreign exchange rates of yen on the market up and finally encourage more import to Japan.

The Japanese government kept large specie holdings abroad which were replenished from the foreign loan proceeds and not linked directly with the domestic money supply.[53] The Japanese government often sold these specie holdings abroad to the Bank of Japan and received yen notes in Japan, when it met the financial deficits.[54] These operations necessarily increased the money supply in Japan, but the settlement of the trade deficits would soon (not immediately), through the decrease of specie reserves at the Bank of Japan, return the domestic money supply. When the settlement was made directly with the government's specie holdings abroad or the Bank of Japan's non-note-issue-reserves, there was no influence on the domestic money supply.

While the benefit of the practice of holding specie abroad to the British economy or the working of the international gold standard has been shown, it is also true that the Japanese government, for its part, benefited from this. The practice of holding specie abroad avoided the cost of gold movements from the world's financial centres to Japan when the specie was used directly for settling the trade balances. The Anglo-Japanese alliance played a pivotal role in ensuring the safety of these funds in London.

The investment of specie holdings abroad earned Japan much income.[55] This motive was significant to the Bank of Japan. As Milner once indicated 'what is the benefit of the Bank of England holding a large reserve of bullion, if no part of it is to be used',[56] it was always too expensive for note issue banks to set aside large bullion for their note-issue-reserves in vault. In consequence, the Bank of Japan did not become inclined to transfer the purchased loan proceeds to Japan in gold. To yield income the bank would invest them, as specie holdings abroad, in the world's financial centres. The average proportion of the income from the investment of specie holdings abroad reached nearly one third of the Bank of Japan's annual net profits from 1906 to 1912.[57] This form of investment not only brought huge income to the bank, but also acted as note-issue- reserves. Even though the practice of specie holdings abroad had such an advantage, the Bank of Japan could not use them for gold conversion in Japan.[58]

Furthermore, Japan's practice of holding specie abroad played a role of softening the influence of large foreign borrowings on the domestic economy. It enabled the Japanese government to absorb foreign borrowings indirectly – without causing actual movements of gold or serious fluctuations in foreign exchange rates.[59]

As Chart 9.3 suggests, the trade balances in Japan did not directly and immediately reflect the Bank of Japan's note issues to such an extent as the price-specie-flow-mechanism of the classical gold standard model implied.[60] The settlement of the trade balances from the specie holdings abroad did not effect the immediate decrease of the money supply in Japan, even when the severe trade deficits, which would have worsened the Bank of Japan's reserve position, occurred. Hence, Keynes depicted the working of the gold exchange standard (including the practice of holding specie abroad) as one of the national systems which 'develop devices and maintain large liquid reserves with the express object of having the power to maintain internal equilibrium over the short period, without too sensitive a regard for external events.'[61]

Even after the Russo-Japanese War Japan continued to maintain substantial funds in London, but British banks feared that Japan would seek control or influence over the London money market more

Chart 9.3 Trade balances and bank note issues 1897–1913

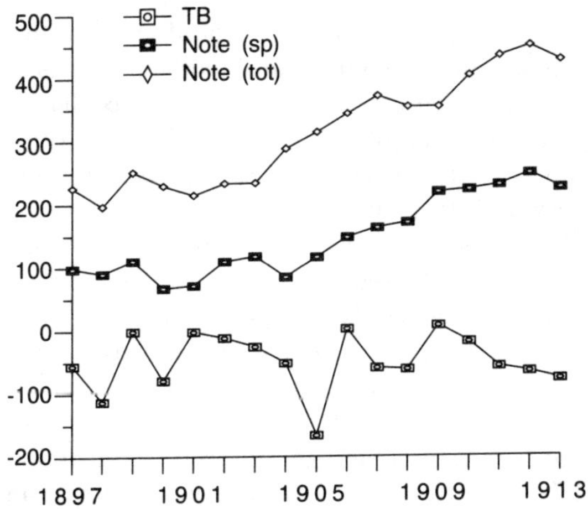

Source: *NGKHS*, Shiryō, 326–9; *MHSKT*, 278–9.
Notes: TB – trade balance; Note (tot) – Bank of Japan note issue (specie reserve and securities for fiduciary issue); Note (sp) – Bank of Japan note issue (specie reserve issue).

directly.[62] The City enquired of the British Foreign Office about Japan's credit balance in London.[63] Now British financiers became worried about further Japanese foreign loan issues because Japan already retained large funds in London. The London Rothschilds considered that it would be easy for Japan to provide money for Korea and Manchuria out of its funds abroad, when the Japanese government embarked upon the South Manchurian Railway Co. debenture issue in 1908.[64] More strongly, the British Foreign Office questioned Japan's practice of maintaining huge funds in London, saying that it seemed to be more economical to buy foreign exchange bills on London than to pay interest on foreign bonds when the Japanese government needed to pay abroad.[65] Although it was difficult for foreign financiers to understand Japan's strenuous attempts to keep such large funds in London, the Japanese government always had misgivings about the constant shortage of gold for making up the trade deficits. Therefore, the specie control always became a crucial and inevitable problem for the Japanese government in the period from 1896 to 1913.

FOREIGN LOANS AND TRADE BALANCES

From the end of the nineteenth century there was a serious argument about how capital exports influenced the British economy.[66] However, these still continuing and important debates – the merits and demerits of capital exports to the British economy before 1914 – are beyond the scope of this study.[67] Here the consideration is strictly limited to the effects of Japan's foreign borrowings on its trade balances with Britain.

Generally the repercussions of foreign borrowings on borrowing countries' economies flowed through two main channels.[68] Firstly, direct use of loan proceeds for purchasing goods from lending countries, as in the case of tied loans, increased imports in the borrowing countries. Secondly, funds transferred from loan proceeds generated consumption and related expenditures in the borrowing countries' economies and, through this process, imports were boosted indirectly. In the latter case, however, the lending countries could not always increase exports to the borrowing countries, because multilateral trade structures[69] with the borrowing countries would finally decide whose exports were increased.[70]

It is of importance to analyse the repercussions of Japan's large foreign borrowings during 1904 and 1905. This unique experience provides a typical example of a relationship between foreign loans and trade balances in a borrowing country. In fact, Saul, formulating the patterns of multilateral trade in the world economy, described the reaction of Japan's trade balances to the foreign loans as 'most interesting' but 'without making any pretence at an exact calculation'.[71] It is useful to extend his analysis with further calculations.

Japan's trade balance from 1896 to 1913 was in deficit almost every year with a peak in 1905.[72] The Japanese government was always forced to obtain gold or foreign currency to cover these trade deficits. The main purpose of the Japanese government foreign loans, therefore, lay in the settlement of these trade deficits. Table 9.1 shows Japan's international payments in the period from 1904 to 1913. In terms of the absolute value, the total of long-term capital movements (mostly foreign borrowings) is equivalent to the total of the trade and invisible balances (including the large foreign loan interest payments and repayments), short-term capital movements, gold (specie) movements and changes of specie holdings abroad.[73] It is sufficient here to confirm that the basic trade structure in the

Table 9.1 Japan's balance of payments 1904–1913 (¥ million; ¥1=2 s. ½d.)

Year	*(1) Trade balance*	*(2) Invisible balance*	*(3) Long-term capital movements*	*(4) short-term capital movements*	*(5) Total*	*(6) Gold (specie) movements*	*(7) Specie holdings abroad changes*
1904	52.4	–77.2	97.2	10.5	–21.9	–73.6	51.7
1905	–167.1	–157.3	591.0	119.7	386.3	14.4	371.9
1906	4.0	–27.9	119.9	–74.4	21.6	23.1	–1.5
1907	–60.1	67.1	25.6	–82.7	–50.1	–9.8	–40.3
1908	–61.6	–1.3	64.2	–57.0	–55.7	15.2	–70.9
1909	6.5	–2.8	128.9	–58.8	73.8	74.3	–0.5
1910	–18.8	–66.5	102.1	–14.2	2.6	–5.0	7.6
1911	–58.4	–45.6	–4.4	–6.5	–114.9	–9.3	–105.6
1912	–66.1	–41.9	34.4	49.4	–24.2	–7.7	–16.5
1913	–78.6	–17.1	95.6	16.8	16.7	–14.8	31.5
Total	–552.6	–370.5	1254.5	–97.2	234.2	6.8	227.4

Sources: Calculated from I. Yamazawa and Y. Yamamoto, *Chōki Keizai Tōkei 14, Bōeki to Kokusai Shūshi (Estimate of Long-term Economic Statistics of Japan)*, 14, (Foreign Trade Balance of Payments) (Tokyo, 1979), table 16 (223–4). H.G. Moulton, *Japan: An Economic and Financial Appraisal* (1932) gives the brief sketch of Japan's international account from 1899 to 1913 (500–10); M.S. Gordon, 'Japan's balance of international payments, 1904–1931' (E.B. Schumpeter [ed.], *The Industrialization of Japan and Manchukuo* [New York, 1940], appendix) calculated the 'balance of payments of all Japan 1904–1936, including Korea and Formosa' (end table) but the invisible items which these pioneering works used are incomplete, because the details of Japan's invisible items in the period from 1902–1945 were published in 1950 (Japanese Ministry of Finance, *Zaisei Kin-yū Tōkei Geppō [Monthly Report of Financial and Monetary Statistics]*, no.5 [Tokyo, 1950], 38–55).

Notes: Invisible balance includes non-monetary gold, travel, freights, insurance, investment income (interest and dividends on securities and income on undertakings), government receipts and payments, other services and transfer (government and private);
Long-term capital movements include portfolio investments and their repayments, and direct investments and their collections;
Long-term capital movements show an aggregated item and cannot be broken down by portfolio and direct investments;
Short-term capital movements are a residual item, the net balance calculated from all other items, and include errors and omissions;
Specie (gold) movements mean the movements of gold for monetary use;
(1)+(2)+(3)+(4)=(5)=(6)+(7).

Japanese economy of the time was to obtain the funds from foreign loans to meet trade deficits and to pay the principal and interest of these loans; the rest of the funds were kept in store in the form of specie holdings abroad. The practice of holding specie abroad, however, complicated the relationship between the loan proceeds and trade balances to a considerable extent. Demand for imports was created indirectly through an expansion of credit and fulfilled itself in a later period, because the Bank of Japan purchased specie holdings abroad from the government and used them for reserves for issuing bank notes.

Japan had trade deficits with Britain, India and Germany; surpluses with the United States, China, France and Italy.[74] Japan exported food and textiles to China, and substantial quantities of raw silk to the United States, Italy and France, the United States being the largest importer from Japan over all. Japan imported raw cotton from India, oil from the United States, and manufactured goods from Britain and Germany.

During the Russo-Japanese War Japan's inherent trade structure: i.e. the constant and large deficit in foreign trade financed by foreign loan proceeds, was exaggerated. In this period Britain acted as the largest exporter, of both goods and capital, to Japan, and its share in Japan's total annual imports, at almost one third, was very noticeable. Britain increased its exports to Japan to a much higher degree than any of the other countries (the United States, Germany and France) which were involved in the simultaneous issues of the Japanese government loans. In particular, imports of war-related goods from Britain increased greatly,[75] and British exporters of iron, steel, coal, steamships, boilers and railway equipment occupied the largest shares of the Japanese import markets in this period.[76] In these cases, British loans increased further the demand for those British exports that already enjoyed substantial market penetration. It may also be noted that these were Britain's 'well-established industries', which retained competitiveness in exports markets.[77]

The total net (to the government) amount of the foreign loan issues during 1904 and 1905 amounted to £36,925,000 in Britain, £34,065,000 in the United States, £11,535,000 in Germany and £10,560,000 in France (see chapters 5 and 6). Japan's trade balances, loan proceeds, repayments of loan principal, and payments of interest need to be tabulated by country, in order to compare the relationship between loan issues and trade balances.[78] Table 9.2

Table 9.2 Britain's trade balances, loan issues and loan payments with Japan 1903–1911 (£ million)

Year	*(1) Trade balance*	*(2) Gold & silver movement*	*(3) Total*	*(4) Change proceeds*	*(5) Loan*	*(6) Change payment*	*(7) Loan*	*(8) Change change*	*(9) Total*
1903	2.4	–2.5	–0.1	–	0.3	–	0.9	–	–
1904	2.7	0	2.7	2.8	9.6	9.3	1.6	0.7	–5.8
1905	7.9	0.1	8.0	8.1	28.1	27.8	3.0	2.1	–17.6
1906	10.2	–1.7	8.5	8.6	2.3	2.0	3.2	2.3	8.9
1907	9.0	–0.1	8.9	9.0	*4.0	3.7	4.0	3.1	8.4
1908	7.2	–	7.2	7.3	4.8	4.5	4.7	3.8	6.6
1909	4.4	–	4.4	4.5	4.3	4.0	5.0	4.1	4.6
1910	5.6	0.7	6.3	6.4	*6.7	6.4	5.0	4.1	4.1
1911	8.8	0.6	9.4	9.5	5.3	5.3	5.3	4.4	8.6
Total			55.3	56.2	65.4	63.0	32.7	24.6	17.8

Sources: (1) and (2) *Statistical Abstract for the United Kingdom in Each of the Latest Fifteen Years from 1896 to 1910*, 72–3, 248–9 and 254–5;
(5) and (7) calculated from Appendix B,C and D.

Notes: Included re-exports;
Japan included Formosa;
Base year for changes is 1903;
* The balances, deducting the redemption amounts from the issue amounts, were divided according to London's shares;
Loan proceeds and repayments were calculated from their issue prices (to government, municipalities and companies) and nominal interest rates; Repayments of principal and payments of interest were assumed to make uniformly, starting in the first years of the loan;
(3)=(1)+(2); (9)=(4)+(8)-(6);
The British exports–imports data are used here because the Japanese data do not show gold and bullion movements by country.

shows Britain's trade balances (merchandise and bullion) with Japan, Japan's proceeds from loans floated in London, Japan's repayments of loan principal and payments of interest, and their changes (the base year is 1903). It is noted that the amounts of the loan issues during 1904 and 1905 were extremely large; after 1906 these became much smaller. Except for 1904 and 1905 the sum of the trade balance, loan proceeds, repayments of loan principal and payments of interest showed a surplus to Britain. The most fundamental character of these trade relations was that Britain's loans, to a considerable degree, unilaterally settled the trade balances with Japan. The interlocking settlement structure of trade between Britain and Japan of this time was direct, although India slightly increased exports to Japan. Given the advantageous trade structure, Britain's loans significantly contributed to the increase of its exports to Japan. Britain's overall trade balance showed a deficit and was made up by invisible trade items, but its trade balance with Japan was still kept in surplus. In this respect, Britain's capital exports to Japan paid returns.

On the other hand, the trade structure of the United States with Japan in this period was an extreme contrast. The Japanese government loans of 1904 and 1905 issued in New York improved the position of the United States in trade with Japan remarkably, being the largest importer from Japan, but after 1906 the effects of the loan issues ceased. The United States' exports to Japan tended to fall, increasing Japan's trade surpluses with the United States. Every year the balance of trade showed a large deficit for the United States. The United States' loans to Japan were settled multilaterally. Indeed, some of the funds supplied from the United States, Germany and France in 1904 and 1905 were used to buy British exports. This was perhaps due to the fact that Japan could not find any other import channel of military goods than the British one.[79]

From 1897 to 1902 all (six) of the battleships of the Imperial Japanese Navy were built in Britain (Thames Iron Works, John Brown, Vickers and Armstrongs); from 1899 to 1901 four armoured cruisers, out of six, in Britain (Armstrongs).[80] Up to 1912 Japan built 19.8 per cent of the warships and other armed vessels at W.G. Armstrong Whitworth and its predecessor companies.[81] At Vickers (Barrow) as well Japan's share (36.29 per cent) of the distribution of foreign orders by market was the largest from 1903 to 1916. Trebilcock has confirmed the export competitiveness of the British armament industry before the First World War.[82] Germany feared, in fact, that Japan would not purchase enough manufactured goods from it to cover the loan issue amount.[83]

Given the multilateral trade settlement system, Britain, the largest lender to Japan, significantly increased its exports to Japan because of its overwhelming competitiveness in some Japanese import markets, particularly those for military equipment. Britain's loans to Japan finally brought surpluses to Britain without a loss of gold.

Conclusion

Table 3.1, at the beginning of Part II, summarized the overall level of the Japanese government foreign loan issues in the period from 1870 to 1913. The total loans issued on the London capital market amounted to £82,106,335 (net amount), around 3.8 per cent of the total foreign government loan issues in that period. However, the proportion in the period from 1900 to 1913 increased sharply to 20.8 per cent because Japan's foreign loan operations took place mainly after 1900. Paris rapidly increased its share in Japanese loan business, despite only becoming concerned with it after 1905.

A 'SUCCESSFUL' BORROWER

The history of the Japanese government foreign loan issues has suggested a number of reasons for Japan's growth in creditworthiness on the foreign capital markets.

Firstly, the Japanese government, after 1899, learned to avoid over-reliance upon one particular foreign financier and market, a practice which tended to impose a high rate of commission on borrowers. The Japanese government never allowed itself to fall easy prey to aggressive foreign financiers who often urged borrowers to take more loans, although in the 1870s it had been a dependent borrower. In order to take the initiative in loan issue negotiations with foreign financiers, the Japanese government prepared multiple markets and financiers for its foreign loan issues. From this point of view, the Paris capital market played a significant role in sharpening competition among financiers and effectively improved Japan's borrowing position on the international capital markets. It seems, in the long run, that the geographical expansion of the loan issue markets produced a certain market mechanism in loan issue negotiations. As a consequence, the Japanese government could obtain more favourable loan issue terms.

Secondly, considerable emphasis needs to be placed on the role of the leading local financial institutions in Japan, notably the Yokohama Specie Bank and the Industrial Bank, which took the initiative in negotiating loan issues with foreign financiers after 1899. By developing a protective economic policy against foreign capital, the Japanese government had a definite plan to set up those banks with privileges. Both banks established close business ties with the eminent foreign financiers, through which they placed many loans efficiently on the international capital markets at lower costs.

Thirdly, the Japanese government developed a keen appreciation of the structure of the London capital market, and knew how to operate a variety of financial institutions in the City to maximize their effects in its loan issue operations. The loan issue mechanism for Japanese government loans may be described as a harmonious combination of various financial institutions.[1] At first, the banks with Far Eastern and Japanese connections, such as Parr's Bank, the Hongkong Bank, the Yokohama Specie Bank and the Industrial Bank, introduced a loan issue to the London capital market. These banks acted as loan issue banks (except for the Industrial Bank), but were not really such because they were not experts in loan issue business. Subsequently, their business ties drew in merchant banks (Baring Brothers, the London Rothschilds and Ernest Cassel) and a stockbroker (Panmure Gordon & Co.), whose role was essential in organizing the loan issue on the London capital market. At the final stage, the merchant banks, through their correspondent network, linked other major international capital markets, especially New York, Berlin and Paris, for the simultaneous loan issue.

Unlike South American countries, where close ties between governments and City financiers had existed since the early 1820s and where excess funds in European money markets flowed cyclically,[2] Japan tended to be neglected by foreign financiers as it had been isolated for so long. From the macro-economic viewpoint, however, the adoption of the gold standard in Japan in 1897, as in other countries, was important in its borrowing abroad. A standard for economic transactions was needed. The gold standard was a prerequisite for Japan to build up close effective relations with the City, for without it, it was difficult to make favourable and smooth borrowings in London.

Japan's practice of holding specie abroad, which enhanced the working of the international gold standard system, represented its links with the City. The practice of holding specie abroad contributed considerably to the adjustment of constant fluctuations on the London money market, because the Bank of Japan could often lend the specie reserves in London to the Bank of England. This could provide international liquidity for the London money market. For Japan, this practice could reduce the influence of large borrowings abroad on the domestic economy by regulating the rate of foreign exchange on the market. The holding of specie abroad pegged Japan's currency through sterling balances in London (not directly through gold) to the pound sterling, the international currency, and Japan could absorb large foreign loans without considerably disrupting its foreign trade and commerce. Foreign loans enabled Japan to secure a large amount of specie, which was also used to increase the Bank of Japan's note issue, despite the cumulative trade deficits. This finally caused prosperous conditions in the Japanese economy.[3]

In wider perspective, it is necessary to state the fundamentals of Japanese economic and political development in this era, related to the improvement of its creditworthiness.

Political stability fostered the smooth process of industrialization in Japan, and this finally improved Japan's creditworthiness on the foreign capital markets. After the Meiji Restoration in 1868, the newly-established government achieved political stability in Japan. This government initiated a deliberate programme of modernization in the country by adopting Western culture and techniques.[4]

The economic development in the Japan of the time was connected directly to the military strength of the state. The state pursued policies, such as restricting inward direct investment, which maintained Japan's independence and hastened its development as an imperialist country after the Russo-Japanese War. Often described as 'armament loans', the character of the Japanese government foreign loans had a military purpose above all. At least 75 per cent of the total loan issue amount (net amount and excluding the conversion loans) was used for military outlay. The increased armaments raised Japan to the status of a great military power.

LOAN ISSUE MECHANISM

The loan issue mechanism of the London capital market, especially the important role of stockbrokers in loan issues, has not been emphasized sufficiently in the previous literature and needs to be highlighted here. The fragmented structure of the London capital market included a variety of financial institutions in foreign loan issue operations, but the activities of stockbrokers co-ordinated their interests in loan issues and enabled various financial institutions, even lacking the necessary expertise, to become loan issue banks.

Undoubtedly, the leading figures of the London capital market were merchant banks, and they had dealt with most of the large foreign government loan issues since the early nineteenth century. Other banks, such as clearing banks, overseas banks and foreign banks, encroached gradually on the field of foreign loan issue business in the late nineteenth century. But lack of experience did not allow them to effect loan issues on the market easily. They needed to co-operate with merchant banks or stockbrokers, who were experts in loan issue business.

Most of the loan issues on the London capital market were carried out by the method of public subscription. If the loan issue was underwritten fully, the loan issue banks did not run great risks, except for their own underwriting amounts. The loan issue banks were not always required to be experts in loan issue business and often were simply subscription agents, allowing other financial institutions, such as stockbrokers, to make the necessary arrangements for the loan issue. This is why various banks, other than merchant banks, could act as loan issue banks in the London capital market when they had reasons for business, namely specific linkages with borrowers.

Underwriting could effectively disperse the risks of loan issues to underwriters and became the core of loan issue operations on the London capital market. Such a structure in the loan issue market could free financial intermediaries involved in loan issues from the large risks. Stockbrokers played a substantial role in organizing the underwriters of loan issues, except when the loan issues were arranged by merchant banks, most of which would form underwriting syndicates mainly by themselves or undertake the loan issues at their own risk. In Germany and France, on the other hand, loan issue banks (Kreditbanken and banques de dépôts) often undertook loan issues at their own risk. In most cases, they, as universal banks, took the issue and placed them directly with their clients and correspondents by the method of direct placement.

For financial institutions, loan issue commissions were important earning sources. Both loan issue bank and underwriting commissions fluctuated with borrowers' creditworthiness on the market. Less creditworthy borrowers faced more expensive commissions which were imposed by loan issue banks and underwriters in order to compensate their risks adequately. Brokerage (placing underwriting and handling applications) and intermediary commissions were fixed. Loan issue commissions became one of the criteria for borrowers to select loan issue banks and markets, as did costs of loan issues. The competitive market structures enabled borrowers to issue loans at lower costs.

The expansion and integration of loan issue markets are important in considering loan issues on the international capital markets, such as London, Paris, Berlin and New York. The mechanism of market linkages has not been satisfactorily analysed so far because of the lack of information on loan issue negotiations.

Before the First World War, only specific financial intermediaries, with established business connections over a range of national markets, could take up international loan issue business. Typically merchant banks, on their extensive correspondent networks, frequently linked the markets together for loan issues. At the outset, market linkages occurred in simultaneous loan issues under the influence of the main market. As a result of the development of the other capital markets, London's unchallenged lead declined and the relationships between the world's major capital markets became relatively decentralized. But each market was not really separate. The national capital markets, parts of the international capital markets, would co-operate in many simultaneous loan issues. In addition, borrowers improved their borrowing position on foreign markets and could have access to any international capital markets directly, not through their main market. The patterns of loan issues became more diversified for borrowers. Now borrowers could select the most favourable loan issue either on one market (a separate loan) or on multiple markets (a simultaneous loan). The market linkages reached a new stage.

DEBT REWARDED

Most of this study has been devoted to the Japanese government loan issue operations *on the London capital market*. It is right to conclude, from this viewpoint, that the Japanese government's foreign loan issue activities were 'successful', because Japan could raise itself from the position of a doubtful borrower in the 1870s to a respected one after the Russo-Japanese War. However, no straightforward answer to the larger question – whether Japan's foreign borrowings were really successful with respect to its domestic economy – is possible unless their consequence is closely examined. The import of Japan's foreign borrowings in this sense is beyond the scope of this study, but a few final words should be said.

Japan's early industrialization before the 1890s was financed mainly by domestic sources, not foreign borrowings. From 1897, Japan began to depend upon heavy foreign borrowings. The foreign capital in the Japanese economy of this time played a limited role mainly in alleviating the strain of the foreign trade deficits incurred to support rapid militarization. The import of foreign capital in the form of government loans in this period neither contributed directly to the industrial development of Japan nor positively changed the basic structure of its economy.

The Japanese economy, just on the eve of the First World War, was almost thrown into a debt crisis which resulted from the large loan issues during the Russo-Japanese War. The cost of serving debts would often impoverish borrowing countries. In 1914, the Japanese government, exhausting a huge amount of its specie holdings abroad, had to make an urgent agreement with the Bank of Japan and the Yokohama Specie Bank that the latter should offer the government its export bills for the payment of the government's charges abroad. Yet the outbreak of war made it unnecessary.[5] Increased exports, stimulated by war demand, secured Japan sufficient trade surpluses.[6] Otherwise it would have suffered considerably from the payment of the outstanding debts and trade deficits. Japan was lucky because the exceptional and unexpected circumstances of a world war saved it from the most obvious problem of large foreign borrowings – the cost of servicing the debt.

Appendix A

Foreign Government Loan Issues in London 1870–1913

Appendix A has the following inevitable defects because its primary sources are based on the financial press: (i) not all the loan issues on the London capital market were found in the table and there were ones missing, especially privately placed loans; (ii) loans (loan issue amounts) issued on the London capital market are listed in this table whenever possible but this distinction was not always possible even from prospectuses, and loans (loan issue amounts) issued outside the London capital market and partials are inevitably included; (iii) loans (loan issue amounts) issued outside the London capital market are listed in the table when the primary sources regarded them as London's tranches; (iv) the tracing of loan issue purposes (conversion, redemption and so on), loan issuers and market relations are incomplete; (v) only central government loans are collected because it is difficult to follow Treasury bill and provincial government loan issues from the financial press; (vi) some government guaranteed loan issues are included in the table as government loan issues; (vii) resales of domestic loans (loans which had been issued internally and afterwards resold abroad) are included in the table; (viii) differences of information, especially on loan issue amounts, among the financial press are referred to in footnotes unless there are decisive grounds for selection; (ix) careful treatment is needed with respect to as above such as Argentina, Egypt, Greece, Mexico, Portugal, Russia, Spain and Turkey; their repeated conversion operations often obscured the real extent of their loan issues.

Some remarks should be made about loan issue information collected from the financial press. (i) *IMM* covers the full period (1870–1913) but includes only loans quoted on the London Stock Exchange. The tables of 'British Capital Created' and of 'British

Capital Called up' give accurate loan issue amounts in London mostly, but their coverage is limited and there are large omissions. (ii) *Stock Exchange Official Intelligence, Stock Exchange Year-Book* and *Fenn's Compendium* provide most extensive information on loan issues by country, but do not always separate London's issue amounts from total amounts (issued or created) and often include loan issue amounts outside the London capital market (partials). (iii) The London Rothschilds' official history (*A Century of Finance 1804 to 1904*) provides the most precise information of their loan issues, but loan issue amounts include other Rothschilds' tranches and coverage ended in 1903. (iv) *The Economist* no longer gave individual loan issue information after the year of 1881 because *IMM* played this role. After 1903 it published British capital created and called up – the same figure as *IMM*. (v) The London Stock Exchange Archives (Ms.18,001 [quotation applications] and Loan and Company Prospectuses) were concerned only with loans quoted on the London Stock Exchange but provide the most accurate loan issue terms. (vi) *Annual Report of the Council of the Corporation of Foreign Bondholders* gives useful information on countries with heavy borrowing.

Abbreviations:

C	Continent (places outside of Paris and Germany)
Cl	Clearing banks
Ec	*The Economist*
F	Foreign banks
FBH	*Annual Report of the Council of the Corporation of Foreign Bondholders*
Fn	*Fenn's Compendium*
G	Germany
Gn	Government
HA	Hambros Archives
I	Indefinite
IMM	*Investor's Monthly Manual* (British Capital Created)
LA	London Stock Exchange Archives
LCP	Loan and Company Prospectuses (London Stock Exchange [Guildhall Library])
LJSBA	London Joint Stock Bank Archives
M	Merchant banks
N	New York
O	Overseas banks

P	Paris
RA	London Rothschilds Archives
RH	The London House of Rothschild [J.Ayer], *A Century of Finance*
SEOI	*Stock Exchange Official Intelligence*
SEY	*Stock Exchange Year-Book*
T	Trust companies

Notes: – implies no information;
( ) Original issue year;
'Issue amount (nominal)' means the London issue amount (nominal);
'Market relations' shows the linkages of loan markets;
'Issue patterns' shows the combination of financiers in issue;
Loan issue prices were not fixed in most of the conversion loan issues because the payments were made by the exchange of old bonds for new ones.

Year	*Country*	*Interest rate (nominal) (%)*	*Issue price (nominal) (%)*	*Issue amount (£000)*	*Market relations*	*Issue patterns*	*Loan issuers*
1870	Argentina[1]	6	88	1034[2]		M	C. de Murrieta
1870	Austria	5	–	97548[3]	P	M	London Rothschilds
1870	Austria	5	–	105711[4]	P	M	London Rothschilds
1870	Chile	5	83	1012[5]		M	J.S. Morgan
1870	Egypt	7	78½	7142[6]	P	M	Bischoffsheim & Goldschmidt
1870	France	6	85	10000[7]		M	J.S. Morgan
1870	Honduras	10	80	2500[8]		M	Bischoffsheim & Goldschmidt
1870	Japan	9	98	1000[9]		M	Schröder
1870	North Germany	5	96½[10]	7500[11]		Cl	London Joint Stock Bank
1870	Peru	6	81¼[12]	11920[13]	C	M	Schröder
1870	Romania	7	86	434[14]		M	C. Devaux
1870	Romania	7½	72	600[15]	C	F	Anglo–Austrian Bank
1870	Russia	5	80	12000[16]	P	M	London Rothschilds
1870	Spain	5	80	2318[17]	P	M	London Rothschilds
1870	Spain	3	29½	34300[18]		Gn	Spanish Financial Commission
1870	Turkey	6	60½	22000[19]	C	M	L. Cohen
1871	Argentina	6	88½	6122[20]	P	M	C. de Murrieta
1871	Brazil	5	89	3459[21]		M	London Rothschilds
1871	Costa Rica	6	72	500[22]		M	Bischoffsheim & Goldschmidt

Year	*Country*	*Interest rate (nominal) (%)*	*Issue price (nominal) (%)*	*Issue amount (£000)*	*Market relations*	*Issue patterns*	*Loan issuers*
1871	Costa Rica	6	74	500[23]		M	Bischoffsheim & Goldschmidt
1871	France	5	82½	11111[24]		M	Baring Bros; London Rothschilds
1871	Holland	5	90½	189[25]		M	S. Montagu
1871	Hungary	5	81	3000[26]	C	M	Raphael
1871	Liberia	7	85	100[27]		M	Holderness, Nott
1871	North Germany	5	96[28]	7500[29]		Cl	London Joint Stock Bank
1871	Paraguay	8	80	1000[30]		M	Robinson & Fleming
1871	Russia	5	81½	12000[31]	P	M	London Rothschilds
1871	Spain	6	80	2622[32]		M	Stern Bros
1871	Spain	3	31	6375[33]	PC	Gn	Spanish Financial Commission
1871	Turkey	6	73	5700[34]		M	Dent Palmer
1871	USA	5	102⅜	40000[35]	P	M	Baring Bros; London Rothschilds
1871	Uruguay	6	72	3500[36]		M	I. Thomson, T. Bonar
1872	Argentina	6	76	1225[37]		M	Stern Bros
1872	Bolivia	6	68	1700[38]		M	Lumb. Wanklyn
1872	Costa Rica	7	82	1496[39]		M	Knowles & Foster
1872	France	5	84½	165622[40]	C	M	Baring Bros; London Rothschilds
1872	Paraguay	8	85	562[41]		M	Robinson & Fleming
1872	Peru	5	77½	15000[42]	P	M	Schröder; Stern Bros
1872	Russia	5	89	15000[43]	C	M	London Rothschilds
1872	Spain	3	28¾	9000[44]	PC	Gn	Spanish Financial Commission
1873	Argentina[45]	6	89½	2040[46]		M	Baring Bros
1873	Chile	5	94	2276[47]		O	Oriental Bank Corp
1873	Colombia	4½	–	2000[48]		Cl	London & County Bank
1873	Egypt	7	84¼	32000[49]	PC	FM	Imperial Ottoman Bank; Bischoffsheim & Goldschmidt
1873	Hungary	5	80	5400[50]	C	M	Raphael
1873	Japan	7	92½	2400[51]		O	Oriental Bank Corp
1873	Russia	5	93	15000[52]	P	M	London Rothschilds
1873	Spain	3	–	1482[53]		Gn	Spanish Financial Commission
1873	Turkey	6	58½	8000[54]	P	F	Imperial Ottoman Bank
1873	USA	5	102⅜	60000[55]	P	M	Baring Bros; London Rothschilds
1874	Argentina	6	80	357[56]		M	Stern Bros
1874	Belgium	3	75½	1440[57]	C	M	Baring Bros
1874	Turkey	5	43½	15900[58]	P	F	Imperial Ottoman Bank
1875	Brazil	5	96½	5301[59]		M	London Rothschilds
1875	Chile	5	88¼	1100[60]		O	Oriental Bank Corp
1875	China	8	95	327[61]		O	Hongkong Bank

Year	*Country*	*Interest rate (nominal) (%)*	*Issue price (nominal) (%)*	*Issue amount (£000)*	*Market relations*	*Issue patterns*	*Loan issuers*
1875	France	3	–	2380[62]	C	I	–
1875	Russia	4½	92	15000[63]	P	M	London Rothschilds
1875	Spain	3	–	13302[64]		Gn	Spanish Financial Commission
1875	Sweden	4½	98¾	982[65]	C	M	Erlanger
1876	China	8	10	0274[66]	C	O	Hongkong Bank
1876	Norway	4½	96½	1320[67]	P	M	Hambros
1876	Portugal	5	83½	306	P	F	Société de Dépôts et de Comptes Courants
1876	Sweden	4½	96½	1500[68]		M	Hambros
1876	USA	4½	103½	60000[69]	P	M	London Rothschilds; J.S. Morgan; Seligmans
1877	China	8	98	1601[70]		O	Hongkong Bank
1877	Egypt	5	–	10800[71]	P	F	Comptoir National d'Escompte
1877	Egypt	6	–	20700[72]	P	F	Comptoir National d'Escompte
1877	Hungary	6	83½	4500[73]	PGC	M	London Rothschilds
1877	Portugal	3	50	4000[74]	P	M	Baring Bros
1877	Spain	2	par	13213[75]	P	Gn	Spanish Financial Commission
1877	Turkey	5	50	5000[76]		Cl	Glyn Mills, Currie
1877	USA	4	102¾	140000[77]	P	M	London Rothschilds; J.S. Morgan; Seligmans; Morton Rose
1878	Egypt	5	73	8500[78]	P	M	London Rothschilds
1878	Holland	4	98⅜	3583[79]	C	I	B.W. Blydenstein; Exchange & Investment Bank; Jordaan & Co.
1878	Norway	4½	95	1700[80]	P	M	Hambros
1878	Portugal	3	50	2500[81]	C	M	Stern Bros
1878	Sweden	4	88	1000[82]	P	M	Hambros
1879	Austria	4	–	4000[83]	C	I	–
1879	Greece	5	–	999[84]		O	Ionian Bank
1880	Denmark	4	–	1648		M	Hambros
1880	Norway	4	97½	881[85]	P	M	Hambros
1880	Portugal	3	50½	2200[86]	PC	M	Stern Bros
1880	Prussia	4	–	29500[87]		Cl	London Joint Stock Bank
1880	Russia	4	75	24000[88]	C	F	Russian Bank for Foreign Trade
1880[89]	Sweden	4	97½	2200[90]	PC	M	Hambros
1881	Argentina	6	91	2450[91]	P	M	C. de Murrieta
1881	Greece	5	74	1250[92]	P	M	Hambros
1881	Hungary	4	75½	16000[93]	PG	M	London Rothschilds
1881	Italy	5	90	14600[94]	C	M	Hambros; Baring Bros
1881 (1880)	Sweden	4	98½	700[95]	C	M	Hambros
1881	Turkey	5	83	5000	P	F	Imperial Ottoman Bank

Year	*Country*	*Interest rate (nominal) (%)*	*Issue price (nominal) (%)*	*Issue amount (£000)*	*Market relations*	*Issue patterns*	*Loan issuers*
1881	Venezuela	3	–	2702[96]		M	Robarts, Lubbock
1882	Argentina	6	92½	817[97]	C	M	Morton, Rose
1882	Italy	5	88	14589[98]	C	M	Hambros; Baring Bros
1882 (1880)	Portugal	5	92¼	2460		Gn	Portuguese Government Financial Commission
1882	Russia	3	55	8904[99]	PGC	M	Baring Bros
1882	Spain	4	–	12000[100]		Gn	Spanish Government Financial Commission
1882	Turkey	5	83	3000[101]	P	F	Imperial Ottoman Bank
1883	Brazil	4½	89	4599[102]	P	M	London Rothschilds
1883	Hungary	4	–	5096[103]	PGC	M	London Rothschilds
1883 (1880)	Sweden	4	98½	1100[104]	P	M	Hambros
1883	Uruguay	5	72	11127[105]		M	I. Thomson, T. Bonar
1884	Argentina	5	84½	1673[106]	P	M	Baring Bros
1884	Argentina	4	84	5952[107]		M	J.S. Morgan
1884	Greece	5	68½	4400[108]	P	M	Hambros
1884 (1881)	Hungary	4	77⅜	16000[109]		M	London Rothschilds
1884	Hungary	4	–	10000[110]	PGC	M	London Rothschilds
1884	Orange Free State	6	par	100[111]		O	Standard Bank
1884 (1880)	Portugal	3	50½	2095[112]	PC	Gn	Portuguese Government Financial Commission
1884 (1881)	Turkey	5	–	7427[113]	PC	F	Imperial Ottoman Bank
1885	Chile	4½	89	808[114]		Cl	City Bank
1885	China	7	98	1505[115]		O	Hongkong Bank
1885	China	6	98	750[116]		O	Hongkong Bank
1885	China	6	98	1500[117]		M	Baring Bros; Matheson
1885 (1880)	Egypt	3	95½	9424[118]	PG	M	London Rothschilds[119]
1886[120]	Argentina	5	80	4000[121]	P	M	Baring Bros; J.S. Morgan
1886	Brazil	5	95	6431[122]		M	London Rothschilds
1886	Chile	4½	98½	6010[123]		M	London Rothschilds
1886	Costa Rica	4 (5)	92½ 96½	655[124]		T	River Plate Trust
1886	Cuba	6	87	24800[125]		M	Baring Bros
1886	Hawaii	6	98	200		M	Matheson
1886	Mexico	3	60	4650[126]		Cl	Glyn Mills, Currie
1886	Nicaragua	6	92½	285[127]		Cl	City Bank
1886	Norway	3½	98	1700[128]	P	M	Hambros
1886	Paraguay	2,3 and 4	–	839[129]		M	Robarts, Lubbock
1887 (1886)	Argentina	5	85½	4290[130]	P	M	Baring Bros; J.S. Morgan
1887[131]	Argentina	5	91½	1300[132]		M	C. de Murrieta

Year	*Country*	*Interest rate (nominal) (%)*	*Issue price (nominal) (%)*	*Issue amount (£000)*	*Market relations*	*Issue patterns*	*Loan issuers*
1887	Chile	4½	97½	1160[133]		M	London Rothschilds
1887	Greece	4	78½	1780[134]	PC	M	Hambros
1888	Argentina	4½	87	3933[135]	G	M	Baring Bros
1888 (1887)	Argentina	5	94	1500[136]		M	C. de Murrieta
1888	Brazil	4½	97	6297[137]	PGC	M	London Rothschilds
1888 (1887)	Egypt	4½	95½	2330[138]	G	M	London Rothschilds
1888[139]	Greece	6	81½	673	C	M	Antony Gibbs
1888	Guatemala	4	–	922[140]		M	Hambros; I. Thomson, T. Bonar
1888	Mexico	6	78½	3700[141]	GC	M	Antony Gibbs
1888	Norway	3	88½	3560[142]	P	M	Hambros
1888	Portugal	3	–	7761[143]		M	Baring Bros
1888	Russia	4	86⅖	19775[144]	PGC	M	Baring Bros; Hambros
1888	Santo Domingo	6	–	76[145]		M	Peter, Lawson
1888	Santo Domingo	6	83½	475[146]		Cl	Capital & Counties Bank
1888	Sweden	3	–	1470[147]	P	M	London Rothschilds
1888	Turkey	5	77	7827[148]	PG	F	Deutsche Bank
1888	Uruguay	6	82½	4255[149]	PC	M	Baring Bros
1889 (1887)	Argentina	5	97	1168[150]		M	C. de Murrieta
1889	Argentina	4½	90	5263[151]	PG	M	Baring Bros; C. de Murrieta
1889	Argentina	3½	par	2659[152]		M	Stern Bros
1889	Brazil	4	90	20000[153]	P	M	London Rothschilds
1889	Bulgaria	6	–	1746[154]		M	Robart, Lubbock
1889	Chile	4½	101¾	1546[155]	G	F	Deutsche Bank
1889 (1888)	Greece	6	96¼	277		M	Antony Gibbs
1889	Greece	4	72	1200[156]		M	Hambros
1889	Greece	4	77½	5000[157]	G	M	Antony Gibbs
1889	Hungary	4½	–	5200[158]	P	M	London Rothschilds
1889	Mexico	5	77½	1300[159]	G	M	Seligmans
1889	Portugal	4½	–	6812[160]	P	M	Baring Bros
1889	Russia	4	–	27685[161]	PGC	M	London Rothschilds
1889	Russia	4	–	49120[162]	P	M	London Rothschilds
1889	Salvador	6	95½	300		Cl	London & South Western Bank
1889 (1888)	Santo Domingo	6	70	42[163]		Cl	Capital & Counties Bank
1890 (1889)	Bulgaria	6	92½	1200		F	Imperial Ottoman Bank
1890	Egypt	3½	91	29400[164]	PGC	M	London Rothschilds
1890	Egypt	4	99¼	7299[165]	P	M	Stern Bros
1890	Greece	5	93	2400[166]	GC	M	Hambros

Year	*Country*	*Interest rate (nominal) (%)*	*Issue price (nominal) (%)*	*Issue amount (£000)*	*Market relations*	*Issue patterns*	*Loan issuers*
1890	Mexico	6	65	325[167]		I	Home & Colonial Assets & Debenture Corp
1890	Mexico	6	93½	6000[168]		M	Antony Gibbs
1890	Russia	4	93	14238[169]	PGC	M	Baring Bros; Hambros
1890	Russia	4	79¼	11865[170]	P	M	London Rothschilds
1890 (1868)	Russia	4	98⅞	1651[171]	P	M	Schröder; London Rothschilds
1890	Santo Domingo	6	77	575[172]	C	I	Westendorp
1890	Sweden	3½	–	1960[173]	P	M	London Rothschilds
1890	Turkey	4	78½	1372[174]	PGC	F	Imperial Ottoman Bank
1890	Turkey	4	81¾	7827[175]	P	F	Imperial Ottoman Bank
1891	Argentina	6	–	2000[176]	P	M	J.S. Morgan
1891	Russia	3	79 7/10	19775[177]	PC	M	Hambros
1891	Russia	4	–	12656[178]		M	London Rothschilds
1891	Turkey	4	93½	6316[179]	P	M	London Rothschilds
1892	Argentina	5	–	1361[180]		O	London & River Plate Bank
1892	Argentina	5	–	6324		M	Baring Bros
1892	Chile	5	95	1800[181]		M	London Rothschilds
1892	Holland	3½	100½	4492[182]	C	I	Agency of Financial Ministry
1892	Persia	6	95	500[183]		O	Imperial Bank of Persia
1892	South Africa	5	90	2500		M	London Rothschilds
1892	Uruguay	3½	–	19300[184]	P	Cl	Glyn Mills, Currie
1893	Brazil	5	80	2650		M	London Rothschilds
1893	Chile	4½	–	630		Cl	City Bank
1893	Egypt	4¼	–	8500[185]	P	M	London Rothschilds
1893	Greece	5	–	389[186]		M	Hambros
1893	Santo Domingo	4	–	2035[187]		Gn	DominionFinancialAgency
1894 (1893)	Brazil	5	79	1060		M	London Rothschilds
1894	China	7	98	1635[188]	GC	O	Hongkong Bank
1894	Denmark	3	96⅜	1388[189]	P	M	Hambros
1894	Mexico	6	68	2594[190]	C	Cl	Glyn Mills, Currie
1894	Norway	3½	99	2188[191]	P	M	Hambros
1894	Russia	3½	94 4/6[192]	15820[193]	P	M	London Rothschilds
1894	Sweden	3	–	990[194]	P	FM	Crédit Lyonnais; Hambros; London Rothschilds
1894	Turkey	3½	94¼	8212[195]	P	M	London Rothschilds
1895	Brazil	5	85	7442[196]	P	M	London Rothschilds
1895	Chile	4½	93½	2000[197]		M	London Rothschilds
1895	China	6	96½	3000[198]		O	Hongkong Bank
1895	China	6	106	1000[199]		O	Chartered Bank

Year	*Country*	*Interest rate (nominal) (%)*	*Issue price (nominal) (%)*	*Issue amount (£000)*	*Market relations*	*Issue patterns*	*Loan issuers*
1895	China	4	98⅘	15820	PC	F	Crédit Lyonnais; Comptoir National d'Escompte; Russian Bank for Foreign Trade
1895	Guatemala	4	–	1545[200]	G	F	Deutsche Bank
1895	Hungary	3	87⅛	1875[201]	P	Cl	Lloyds Bank
1895	USA	4	110	12463[202]		M	London Rothschilds; J.S. Morgan
1896	Chile	5	95½	4000[203]	GC	M	London Rothschilds
1896	China	5	98¾	16000[204]	G	O	Hongkong Bank
1896	Haiti	6	90	2000[205]	P	F	Société Générale
1896	Tonking	2½	87	3200[206]	P	F	Banque de l'Indo-Chine
1896	Uruguay	5	71½	1667		Cl	Glyn Mills, Currie
1896[207]	USA	4	110	20000		M	London Rothschilds; J.S. Morgan
1897	Argentina	4	–	6385[208]	PG	M	Baring Bros
1897	Colombia	1½					
		3	–	2700		Cl	London & County Bank
1897	Denmark	3	99 1/16	3992[209]	P	FM	Crédit Lyonnais; Hambros
1897	Japan	5	101½	4385[210]		ClFO	Capital & Counties Bank; Yokohama Specie Bank; Hongkong Bank; Chartered Bank
1897	Santo Domingo	4	66	1150[211]		M	Brown Jansen
1897 (1895)	Serbia	4	68	1000[212]	P	Cl	Parr's Bank
1898	Argentina	4	–	1527[213]		M	Baring Bros
1898	Argentina	4	–	6746[214]		M	Baring Bros
1898	Argentina	4	–	4057[215]		M	Baring Bros
1898	Brazil	5	–	8613[216]		M	London Rothschilds
1898	China	4½	90	16000[217]	G	O	Hongkong Bank
1898	Greece	2½	101½	6023[218]	PC	I	Bank of England
1898	Holland	3	92	4817[219]	C	ClM	Union Bank of London; Speyer Bros
1899	China	5	97	2300[220]	P	IO	British Chinese Corp; Hongkong Bank
1899	Denmark	4	–	35[221]		I	–
1899	Germany	3	92	3787		ClFM	London Joint Stock Bank; Deutsche Bank; Stern Bros
1899	Japan	4	90	10000[222]		ClFO	Parr's Bank; Yokohama Specie Bank; Hongkong Bank
1899	Mexico	5	–	3787[223]	PGCN	M	J.S. Morgan
1900	Argentina	6	–	2000		M	Baring Bros
1900	Argentina	4	–	2828[224]	P	M	Baring Bros
1900	Argentina	4	–	1028[225]		M	Baring Bros
1900	Chile	4½	–	260[226]		M	London Rothschilds

Year	*Country*	*Interest rate (nominal) (%)*	*Issue price (nominal) (%)*	*Issue amount (£000)*	*Market relations*	*Issue patterns*	*Loan issuers*
1900	Denmark	3½	94¾	665	P	F	Crédit Lyonnais
1900	Sweden	4[227]	98	947[228]	P	Cl	Lloyds Bank
1901	Brazil	4	–	14605[229]		M	London Rothschilds
1902	Bulgaria	5	89½	4197[230]	PC	FM	Imperial Ottoman Bank; Stern Bros
1902[231]	Greece	4	83½	880[232]	PG	M	Hambros
1902	Japan	5	par	5104[233]		FMO	Yokohama Specie Bank; Baring Bros; Hongkong Bank
1902	Turkey	4	86	7818[234]	P	F	Imperial Ottoman Bank
1903	Argentina	5	89	1430[235]		MO	Baring Bros; London & River Plate Bank
1903 (1890)	Argentina	5	87	2770[236]		O	London & River Plate Bank
1903[237]	Brazil	5	90	5500[238]	PGC	M	London Rothschilds
1903	Serbia	5	90	2400	P	Cl	Parr's Bank
1903	Turkey	4	–	38432[239]		F	Imperial Ottoman Bank
1904[240]	China	5	97½	2250[241]		O	Hongkong Bank
1904	Cuba	5	97	7201[242]	PGCN	M	Speyer Bros
1904	Ecuador	4	68	77[243]		Cl	Glyn Mills, Currie
1904 (1902)	Greece	4	84	870[244]	C	M	Hambros
1904 (1902)	Greece	4	84	230	PG	M	Hambros
1904	Japan	6	93½	5000[245]	N	ClFO	Parr's Bank; Yokohama Specie Bank; Hongkong Bank
1904	Japan	6	90½	6000[246]	NG	ClFO	Parr's Bank; Yokohama Specie Bank; Hongkong Bank
1904	Mexico	4	94	8230[247]	PCN	M	Speyer Bros
1905 (1903)	Brazil	5	96½	3000[248]		M	London Rothschilds
1905	Chile	5	95½	1350[249]		M	London Rothschilds
1905	China	5	97	1000[250]	PG	O	Hongkong Bank
1905	Japan	4½	90	15000[251]	N	ClFO	Parr's Bank; Yokohama Specie Bank; Hongkong Bank
1905	Japan	4½	90	10000[252]	GN	ClFO	Parr's Bank; Yokohama Specie Bank; Hongkong Bank
1905	Japan	4	90	6500[253]	PGN	ClFMO	Parr's Bank; Yokohama Specie Bank; London Rothschilds; Hongkong Bank
1905	Siam	4½	95½	500[254]	P	FO	Banque de l'Indo-Chine; Hongkong Bank; Chartered Bank

Year	*Country*	*Interest rate (nominal) (%)*	*Issue price (nominal) (%)*	*Issue amount (£000)*	*Market relations*	*Issue patterns*	*Loan issuers*
1905	Venezuela	3	–	5229[255]	P	I	Council of Foreign Bondholders
1906	Brazil	5	96	1100		M	London Rothschilds
1906	Chile	4½	par	3700[256]	PGC	FM	DeutscheBank;SpeyerBros
1906 (1902)	Greece	4	83½	270[257]	G	M	Hambros
1906	Russia	5	89	13101[258]	P	M	Baring Bros
1906	Switzerland	3½	99	2200[259]	P	ClF	Glyn Mills, Currie; Swiss Bankverein
1906	Uruguay	5	96¼	170[260]	P	Cl	Glyn Mills, Currie
1907	Argentina	5	97½	2580[261]	PG	M	Baring Bros; J.S. Morgan
1907	Brazil	5	95	3000		M	London Rothschilds
1907 (1904)	China	5	94	650		O	Hongkong Bank
1907	China	5	par	1500		O	Hongkong Bank
1907	Japan	5	99½	11500[262]	P	ClFMO	Parr's Bank; Yokohama Specie Bank; London Rothschilds; Hongkong Bank
1907	Siam	4½	98	1125[263]	PG	O	Hongkong Bank
1907	Switzerland	3½	99½	666[264]	PG	ClF	Glyn Mills, Currie; Swiss Bankverein
1908	Argentina	4	–	818[265]		M	Baring Bros
1908	Brazil	5	96	4000	P	M	London Rothschilds
1908[266]	China	5	98¾	1110[267]	G	O	Hongkong Bank
1908	China	5	99	1500[268]		O	Hongkong Bank
1908	China	5–4½	98	2500[269]	P	O	Hongkong Bank
1908	Greece	5	97	200[270]	PGC	M	Hambros
1908	Liberia	6	101	100[271]		M	Erlanger
1908	Salvador	6	86	1000		MO	Chalmers, Guthrie & Co. London Bank of Mexico & South America
1908	Sweden	4	98	3000[272]		M	Hambros
1909	Argentina	5	98	2960[273]	PGN	M	Baring Bros; J.S. Morgan
1909	Chile	5	96½	3000[274]		M	London Rothschilds
1909 (1908)	China	5	par	740[275]	G	O	Hongkong Bank
1909[276]	Cuba	4½	96	1131	N	M	Speyer Bros
1909	Finland	4½	92½	1800	C	ClM	Union of London & Smiths Bank; Hambros
1909	Montenegro	5	97	250		M	Boulton Brothers
1909	Nicaragua	6	92	500[277]	C	O	Anglo–South American Bank
1909	Russia	4½	88¾	5955[278]	PG	M	Baring Bros
1909 (1908)	Turkey	4	89½	1094[279]	PG	FM	Imperial Ottoman Bank; Stern Bros

Year	*Country*	*Interest rate (nominal) (%)*	*Issue price (nominal) (%)*	*Issue amount (£000)*	*Market relations*	*Issue patterns*	*Loan issuers*
1909	Turkey	4	89	2000[280]	P	FM	Imperial Ottoman Bank; Morgan Grenfell
1910	Argentina	5	101	1209		M	Baring Bros; Morgan Grenfell
1910	Argentina	4	–	411		M	Baring Bros
1910	Brazil	4	90	1000		M	London Rothschilds
1910	Brazil	4	87½	10000[281]	P	M	London Rothschilds
1910	Bulgaria	4½	91	3960	GC	M	Schröder
1910	Chile	5	99	2600[282]		M	London Rothschilds
1910	China	7	108	450		T	London City & Midland Executor Trustee Co.
1910	China	5	100½	1110[283]	G	O	Hongkong Bank
1910 (1909)	Cuba	4½	98	1131	N	M	Speyer Bros
1910	Greece	5	99	1588[284]	PC	M	Hambros; Erlanger
1910	Japan	4	95	11000[285]		ClFO	Parr's Bank; Yokohama Specie Bank; Hongkong Bank
1911	Brazil	4	92	4500	C	M	London Rothschilds
1911	Brazil	4	83½	2400	P	I	South American Railway Construction
1911	Chile	5	98½	2452	PG	M	London Rothschilds
1911	Chile	5	98½	5000[286]	PG	M	London Rothschilds
1911	Chile	4½	–	275		M	London Rothschilds
1911	China	5	100½	1500[287]	PGN	O	Hongkong Bank
1911	Costa Rica	4	–	2000[288]	P	I	M.C. Keith
1911 (1909–10)	Cuba	4½	98¾	1131	N	M	Speyer Bros
1911	Greece	4	86½	573[289]	C	M	Hambros; Erlanger
1911	Norway	4	100¾	2200		ClM	Union of London & Smiths Bank; Hambros
1911	Persia	5	96½	1250[290]		O	Imperial Bank of Persia
1911	Peru	5½	98½	1172[291]	G	M	Schröder
1912	Brazil	4	83½	2400		I	South American Railway Construction Co. (Lloyds Bank)
1912	Chile	3	95	1099[292]	GC	M	Schröder
1912	China	5	95	5000[293]		OT	British Bank for Foreign Trade; British International Investment Trust
1912	Denmark	4	97	2500[294]	P	M	Hambros
1913	Argentina	5	99	1000[295]		M	Baring Bros
1913	Argentina	5	98	341[296]		M	Baring Bros
1913	Brazil	5	97	11000[297]		M	London Rothschilds
1913	Chile	5	96	1118[298]	P	M	Schröder
1913	China	5	90	7416[299]	PGC	O	Hongkong Bank
1913	Romania	4½	91	1980[300]	GC	M	Schröder

Sources:

Primary sources of the table were as follows:

1870–8 *5th Annual General Report of the Council of the Corporation of Foreign bondholders*;

1878–84 *Stock Exchange Year-Book and Burdett's Official Intelligence* (Quotations);

1885–1913 *Burdett's Official Intelligence and Stock Exchange Official Intelligence* (retitled from the 1899 edition) (British, Foreign and Colonial Loans issued in London);

1870–1913 *Investor's Monthly Manual* (British Capital Created).

These data were modified on the basis of the following journals, books and archival records:

Fenn's Compendium of the English and Foreign Funds, Debts and Revenues of all Nations, 14th ed. (by R.L. Nash) (1889) and 16th ed. (by S.F. Van Oss) (1898);

The London House of Rothschild [J. Ayer], *A Century of Finance 1804 to 1904* (1905), 52–81;

The Economist ('Commercial History and Review');

Burdett's Official Intelligence and Stock Exchange Official Intelligence (retitled from the 1899 edition) (main part) (1885–1914);

Thomas Skinner, *Stock Exchange Year-Book* (for the years of 1880, 1890, 1901, 1912 and 1916);

Annual Report of the Council of the Corporation of Foreign Bondholders, 1877–1913;

Hambros Archives, Loan Issue Papers;

Loan and Company Prospectuses (London Stock Exchange [Guildhall Library]);

London Joint Stock Bank Archives, Loan Issue Papers;

London Stock Exchange Archives, Ms.18,001 (Index of Quotation Applications);

London Rothschilds Archives, Loan Issue Papers.

Appendix B

Japanese Government Loan Issues 1870–1913

Year	*Rate of interest (nominal) [Yield at issue] (%)*	*Issue amount (£000)*	*Issue price (public) (%)*	*Borrowing period (year)*	*Object*	*Loan issuers*
1870	9 [9.2]	1,000 (London)	98	13	railway construction	Schröder
1873	7 [7.6]	2,400 (London)	92½	25	redemption of pension fund	Oriental Bank
1897	5 [4.9]	4,389 (London)	101½ (resale)	53	military	Capital & Counties Bank Hongkong Bank Chartered Bank Yokohama Specie Bank
1899	4 [4.4]	10,000 (London)	90	55	railway steelworks telephone	Parr's Bank Chartered Bank Hongkong Bank Yokohama Specie Bank
1902	5 [5.0]	5,104 (London)	100 (resale)	55	military steelworks telephone tobacco	Baring Bros Hongkong Bank Yokohama Specie Bank
1904	6 [6.4]	10,000 London (5,000) New York (5,000)	93½	7	military Yokohama Specie Bank	Parr's Bank Hongkong Bank
1904	6 [6.6]	12,000 London	90½	7	military	Parr's Bank Hongkong Bank

		(6,000) New York (6,000)				Yokohama Specie Bank
1905	4½ [5.0]	30,000 London (15,000) New York (15,000)	90	25	military	Parr's Bank Hongkong Bank Yokohama Specie Bank
1905	4½ [5.0]	30,000 London (10,000) New York (10,000) Germany (10,000)	90	25	military	Parr's Bank Hongkong Bank Yokohama Specie Bank
1905	4 [4.4]	25,000 London (6,500) New York (3,250) Germany (3,250) Paris (12,000)	90	25	conversion	Parr's Bank Hongkong Bank Yokohama Specie Bank London Rothschilds Paris Rothschilds
1907	5 [5.0]	23,000 London (11,500) Paris (11,500)	99½	40	conversion	Parr's Bank Hongkong Bank Yokohama Specie Bank London Rothschilds Paris Rothschilds
1910	4 [4.2]	17,813 (Paris)	95½	60	conversion	Paris Rothschilds
1910	4 [4.2]	11,000 (London)	95	60	conversion	Parr's Bank Hongkong Bank Yokohama Specie Bank

Source: These sources have been referred to in chapters 3 to 7.
Notes: The issue places in Germany included Hamburg and Berlin;
Short-term loan issues in 1913 were excluded.

Appendix C

Japanese Municipal Foreign Loan Issues 1899–1913

Year	*Municipality (Object)*	*Issue amount (nominal) ¥000)*	*Interest rate [Yield at issue] (%)*	*Issue price (to the public) (%)*	*Intermediary (issue place)*	*Issuers*
1899	Kobe (Waterworks)	250	6 [6.5]	92	Morles (Yokohama)	Morles (Yokohama) (possibly in London)
1902	Yokohama (Waterworks)	900	6 [6.1]	98	S. Samuel	M. Samuel Capital & Counties Bank (London)
1902	Osaka* (Harbourworks)	3,085	6 [6.1]	99	Daisan Bank Yasuda Bank	M. Samuel Capital & Counties Bank (London)
1906	Tokyo** (Harbourworks, Street Improvements	14,580	5 [5.0]	100	Industrial Bank	HongkongBank Parr's Bank Yokohama Specie Bank (London)
1907	Yokohama*** (Harbourworks)	3,108	6 [6.1]	99	S. Samuel	M. Samuel (London)
1909	Yokohama (Gasworks)	648	5 [5.1]	97½	Hongkong Bank	HongkongBank (London)
1909	Osaka+ (Waterworks, Electric Tramway)	30,320	5 [5.2]	97	Industrial Bank	HongkongBank Parr's Bank Yokohama Specie Bank (London)
1909	Nagoya++ (Waterworks)	7,816	5 [5.2]	95½	Sale & Frazer Co.	Lazard Bros (London)

1909 Kyoto+++ (Waterworks, Electricity and others)	17,550	5 [5.1]	99	Mitsui Bank (Kahn)	Banque de l'Union Parisienne (Paris)
1909 Yokohama*+ (Waterworks)	7,000	5 [5.1]	98	Industrial Bank	HongkongBank Parr's Bank Yokohama Specie Bank (London)
1912 Kyoto*++ (Waterworks, Electricity and others)	1,950	5 [5.1]	98½	Mitsui Bank (Kahn)	Banque de l'Union Parisienne (Paris)
1912 Tokyo**+ (Electricity)	89,564	5 [5.1]	98	Industrial Bank	HongkongBank Parr's Bank Yokohama Specie Bank (London)
		5 [5.1]	97¾		Kuhn, Loeb (New York)
		5 [5.1]	96¾		Société Générale (Paris)
1912 Yokohama (Gasworks)	1,200	5 [5.1]	97½	Sale & Frazer Co.	Law Debenture Corp. (London)

Sources: *MTZ*, 12, 721; Finance Bureau of Japanese Ministry of Finance, *Kin-yū-Jikō Sankōsho (Annual Reference Bulletin on Financial Matters)*, for the year of 1920 (Tokyo, 1920), 27; Industrial Bank of Japan, *Nihon Gaisai Shōshi (Short History of Japanese Foreign Loans)* (Tokyo, 1948); *GKS*, 2; *SEOI*, annually; London Stock Exchange (Guildhall Library), Loan and Company Prospectuses.

Notes: The issue amounts were based on Japanese records and not converted at the fixed rate of exchange (for instance, ¥1=2s. ½d. and ¥1=Fr2 11/19),
* according to the contract, the amount was ¥3,500,000;
** the original amount was £1,500,000;
*** the original amount was £317,000;
+ the original amount was £3,084,940;
++ the original amount was £800,000;
+++ the original amount was Fr45,000,000;
*+ the original amount was £716,500;
*++ the original amount was Fr5,000,000;
**+ the original amounts were £9,175,000 (London), £5,175,000 (New York) and Fr100,880,000 (Paris).

Appendix D

Japanese Company Foreign Loan (Debenture) Issues 1905–1913

Year	*Company*	*Issue amount* (¥000)	*Interest rate (nominal) [yield at issue]* (%)	*Issue price (to the public)* (%)	*Kind of loan*	*Intermediary*	*Loan issuer (issue place)*
1905	Kansai Railway	9,763*	4½ [4.6]	97½	debenture (trustee: Debenture Corp.)	S. Samuel	M. Samuel (London)
1906	Hokkaidō Colliery & Coal Railway	9,763*	5 [5.1]	98½	debenture (trustee: Industrial Bank)	Chartered Bank	Chartered Bank (London)
1907	South Manchurian Railway	39,052**	5 [5.2]	97	government guaranteed debenture (1st)	Industrial Bank	Hongkong Bank Parr's Bank Yokohama Specie Bank (London)
1908	South Manchurian Railway	19,526+	5 [5.1]	98	government guaranteed debenture (2nd)	Panmure Gordon	Privately placed (London)
1908	Kanegafuchi Cotton Spinning Co.	2,000	7½	–	debenture	Mitsui Bank	Banque Française pour le commerce et l'Industrie [A. Gysin] (Paris)
1908	South Manchurian Railway	19,526+	5 [5.1]	97½	government guaranteed debenture (3rd)	Industrial Bank	Hongkong Bank Parr's Bank Yokohama Specie Bank (London)

1908	Industrial Bank	19,526+	5 [5.2]	97	government guaranteed debenture (13th)	Industrial Bank	Panmure Gordon Hongkong Bank Parr's Bank Yokohama Specie Bank (London) Société Générale (Paris)
1909	Matsui Muslin Spinning Co.	250	6½ [6.5]	100	debenture	Daihyaku Bank	A. Gysin (Paris)
1909	Keihin Electric Railway	200	5½ (to company)	92	debenture	–	Sale & Frazer Co. (London)
1910	Hokkaidō Colonial Bank	5,000	5 [5.1]	97⅞	debenture (8th)	Koike Gōshi	Sale & Frazer Co. (possibly London and Paris)
1911	South Manchurian Railway	58,578++	4½ [4.6]	98	government guaranteed debenture (4th)	Industrial Bank	Hongkong Bank Parr's Bank Yokohama Specie Bank (London)
1913	Oriental Colonial Corp.	19,350+*	5 [5.2]	96¾	government guaranteed debenture (1st)	Industrial Bank	Banque Franco-Japonaise (Paris)

Sources: *NKGGS*, 94–5; The Industrial Bank of Japan, *Nihon Gaisai Shōshi, (Short History of Japanese Foreign Loans)* (Tokyo, 1948); Finance Bureau of Japanese Ministry of Finance, *Kin-yū-Jikō Sankōsho (Annual Reference Bulletin on Financial Matters) for the year of 1920* (Tokyo, 1920), 27–8; Jitsugyo no Sekai [ed.], *Zaikai Sanjyūnenpu (Thirty-year Chronology of Japanese Business Circles)*, 1 (Tokyo, 1938); London Stock Exchange (Guildhall Library), Loan and Company Prospectuses.

Notes: – implies no information;
The issue amounts were based on Japanese records and not converted at the fixed rate of exchange (for instance, ¥1=2 s. ½d. and ¥1=Fr2 11/19);
* the original amount was £1,000,000;
** the original amount was £4,000,000;
\+ the original amount was £2,000,000;
++ the original amount was £6,000,000;
+* the original amount was Fr50,000,000.

Notes

INTRODUCTION

1 Platt paid attention to the availability of new capital on the Paris capital market for foreign investment after the turn of the century (D.C.M. Platt, *Britain's Investment Overseas on the Eve of the First World War* [1986], 131–4).

2 Landes depicted this as 'its [merchant banking's] very nature of a team activity' which included 'a nucleus of two or three correspondents in different major markets' (D.S. Landes, *Bankers and Pashas* [Cambridge [Mass.], 1958 reprinted 1979], 16).

3 W.J. Macpherson, *The Economic Development of Japan c.1868–1941* (1987), 34; E.P. Reubens, 'Foreign capital and domestic development in Japan' in S. Kuznets, W.E. Moore and J.J. Spengler (eds.), *Economic Growth* (Durham, N.C., 1955), 179.

4 G.C. Allen, *A Short Economic History of Modern Japan, 1867–1937* (1972), 50.

5 'Mr. Korekiyo Takahashi', *Bankers' Magazine*, 78 (1904), 355–6. He acted as the Japanese government special loan commissioner in 1904, 1905 and 1907.

6 H. Feis, *Europe the World's Banker, 1870–1914* (New Haven, 1930 reprinted 1964), 422–9.

7 M. Takahashi, *Meiji Zaiseishi Kenkyū (Study on the Financial History in the Meiji Era)* (Tokyo, 1964), 200.

8 G.C. Allen, *A Short Economic History of Modern Japan, 1867–1937* (1972), 50; M.S. Gordon, 'Japan's balance of international payments, 1904–1931' in E.B. Schumpeter (ed.), *The Industrialization of Japan and Manchukuo* (New York, 1940), appendix (863–925) and U. Kobayashi, *War and Armament Loans of Japan* (New York, 1922) did not refer to the loan issue process.

9 A.R. Hall, *The London Capital Market and Australia, 1870–1914* (Canberra, 1963).

10 R.S. Gilbert, 'London financial intermediaries and Australian over-

seas borrowing, 1900–29', *Australian Economic History Review*, 11 1 (1971), 39–47.

11 For the argument on the influence of foreign investment over the British economy, see A.K. Cairncross, *Home and Foreign Investment 1870–1913* (Cambridge, 1953); P.L. Cottrell, *British Overseas Investment in the Nineteenth Century* (1975); M. Edelstein, *Overseas Investment in the Age of High Imperialism* (1982) and S. Pollard, 'Capital exports, 1870–1914: harmful or beneficial?', *Economic History Review*, second series, xxxviii 4 (1985), 489–514.

12 P.L. Cottrell, *British Overseas Investment in the Nineteenth Century* (1975), 33.

13 Jacob Viner, 'International finance and balance of power diplomacy, 1880–1914', *Southwestern Political and Social Science Quarterly*, ix 4 (1929), 407–8.

14 No academic researcher has yet had access to the archives of the Yokohama Specie Bank and the Industrial Bank, however, the Yokohama Specie Bank's official histories: the Yokohama Specie Bank, (N. Skamoto [ed.]) *Yokohama Shōkin Ginkōshi, Shiryō, Furoku (History of the Yokohama Specie Bank with Appendices and Data)*, 1–11 (Yokohama, 1920 reprinted 1976); the Bank of Tokyo, *Yokohama Shōkin Ginkōzenshi (Complete History of the Yokohama Specie Bank)*, 1–6 (Tokyo, 1980–1984) and the Industrial Bank of Japan, *Nippon Kōgyō Ginkō Gojūnenshi (Fiftieth Anniversary History of the Industrial Bank of Japan)* (Tokyo, 1957) have, to a considerable degree, provided their business affairs.

15 I should like to express my sincere thanks to the favour granted to me by the Bank of Japan and the Mitsui Bank (now the Sakura Bank).

16 The Japanese Ministry of Finance, *Meiji Zaiseishi (History of Japanese Finance in the Meiji Era)*, 8 (Tokyo, 1904) has included the government foreign loan issues up to 1902; the Japanese Ministry of Finance, *Meiji Taishō Zaiseishi (History of Japanese Finance in the Meiji and Taishō Eras)*, 12 (Tokyo, 1937) has covered the government foreign loan issues fully from 1870 to 1913. In addition, *Komura Gaikōshi (History of the Diplomat Komura Jutarō)*, written by the Japanese Ministry of Foreign Affairs, has described the Japanese government foreign loan issues during the Russo-Japanese War (1904–1905) as one of his diplomatic activities.

CHAPTER 1: FOREIGN GOVERNMENT LOAN ISSUES IN LONDON 1870–1913

1 L.H. Jenks, *The Migration of British Capital to 1875* (1927, reprinted 1971), 36.

2 E.V. Morgan and W.A. Thomas, *The Stock Exchange* (1962), table v (280–1).

3 C.P. Kindleberger, *A Financial History of Western Europe* (1984), 265–7 and *The Formation of Financial Centers: A Study in Comparative Economic History* (New Jersey, 1974), 58–60.

4 *The Economist*, 27 December 1873, 1561.

5 L.H. Jenks, *The Migration of British Capital to 1875* (1927 reprinted 1971), 267–71; S. Chapman, *The Rise of Merchant Banking* (1984), 55; V.P. Carosso, *Investment Banking in America: A History* (Cambridge [Mass], 1970), 91–2.

6 Kennedy labelled the foreign government bonds of 1870 'moderate risk' but they came to be 'safest' in 1913 (W.P. Kennedy, *Industrial Structure, Capital Markets and the Origin of British Economic Decline* [Cambridge, 1987], 128–9).

7 M. Simon, 'The pattern of new British portfolio foreign investment, 1865–1914' in A.R. Hall (ed.), *The Export of Capital from Britain, 1870–1914* (1968), 38–9.

8 Chapman complained 'none of these published sources is complete' (*The Rise of Merchant Banking* (1984), 191 [note 23]).

9 M. Lévy-Leboyer, 'Presentation' in M. Lévy-Leboyer (ed.), *La position internationale de la France* (Paris, 1973), 25.

10 R.L. Nash, *A Short History into the Profitable Nature of Our Investments* (1881), 31–2; R.A. Lehfeldt, 'The rate of interest on British and foreign investments', *JRSS*, lxxvi (1913), 196–207 and 415–16; lxxvii (1914), 432–5; lxxviii (1915), 452–3; A.K. Cairncross, *Home and Foreign Investment 1870–1913* (Cambridge, 1953), ch. ix; M. Edelstein, *Overseas Investment in the Age of High Imperialism* (1982), ch. 5.

11 Viscount Goschen, *Essays and Addresses on Economic Questions, 1865–1893* (1905), 26.

12 P.G.M. Dickson, *The Financial Revolution in England* (1967), 301.

13 W.P. Kennedy, *Industrial Structure, Capital Markets and the Origin of British Economic Decline* (1987), ch. 5.

14 M. Edelstein, 'Realised rates of return UK home and overseas portfolio investment in the age of high imperialism', *Explorations in Economic History*, 13 3 (1976), 302–6; *Overseas Investment*, 130–40.

15 M. Edelstein, 'The rate of return on UK home and foreign investment, 1870–1913', unpublished Ph. D. thesis, University of Pennsylvania, 1970, 73–6. But note that in order to obtain a good statistical fit for his calculations of 'risk-adjusted' yields, Edelstein must introduce for preference and debenture issues a dummy variable that takes on a significant negative coefficient (M. Edelstein, *Overseas Investment in the Age of High Imperialism* [1982],

131–5). This means that British wealth-holders systematically paid too much for preference and debenture issues relative to their realized patterns of risk and return. Without this adjustment, the 'risk-adjusted returns' on foreign investment, shown in Edelstein's Table 5.7, would have been markedly lower, rather than only slightly lower (138–9), than the returns in domestic investment. However, the differential between 'risk- adjusted returns' on overseas and domestic equity remains.

16 J.D. Bailey, 'Australian company borrowings 1870–1913: a study in British overseas investment', unpublished D. Phil. thesis, Oxford University, 1958, 63.

17 C. Jones, 'Who invested in Argentina and Uruguay', *Business Archives*, 48 (1982), 2. It is possible to derive the subscribers' names, addresses, occupations and amounts of the colonial government loans from the Bank of England Archives. Bailey analysed the subscribers of the Queensland government loans of 1883, 1884, 1888 and 1891 (J.D. Bailey, 'Australian company borrowings 1870–1913: a study in British overseas investment', unpublished D.Phil. thesis, Oxford University, 1958, 55–63 and appendix ii [iii–xiii]).

18 S. Pollard, 'Capital exports, 1870–1914: harmful or beneficial?', *Economic History Review*, second series, xxxviii 4 (1985), 498.

19 Viscount Goschen, *Essays and Addresses on Economic Questions, 1865–1893* (1905), 133. In August 1897, Japanese government 5 per-cent bonds, based on silver standard, were quoted at 46½ per cent (yielding 10.75 per cent at market) on the London Stock Exchange, but 5 per-cent bonds, endorsed to pay the principal and interest in gold, at 101½ (yielding 4.93 per cent at market) (*IMM*, August 1897).

20 P.R. Gregory, 'The Russian balance of payments, the gold standard, and monetary policy', *Journal of Economic History*, 39 2 (1979), 393.

21 Usually colonial governments paid a 1–¼ per-cent loan issue bank commission and a ¼ per-cent broking commission (T. Schilling, *London als Anleihemarkt der englischen Kolonien* [Stuttgart, 1911], 52). The Bank of England charged a very low issue bank commission, ⅛ per cent (at a fixed price) and 1/16 per cent (at tender) (Committee of Enquiry into the Organization of the Crown Agents' Office, Minutes of Evidence and Appendices, BPP 1909, xvi, [Cd.4474], Q.4179 [E. Blake – Senior Crown Agent]). Hall's figures of the costs in New South Wales government loan issues were higher (A.R. Hall, *The London Capital Market and Australia, 1870–1914* [Canberra, 1963], 107). It seems likely that his calculation would include all the costs

for the loan issues, such as the British stamp duty, printing and others.

22 For the tender method, see chapter 2.

23 See chapter 2.

24 Report of the Select Committee on Loans to Foreign States, BPP 1875, xi, appendix, no.6.

25 Report of the Select Committee on Loans to Foreign States, BPP 1875, xi, no.28. Burk pointed out J.S. Morgan & Co.'s large commission in the Chilean government loan issues of 1867 (K. Burk, *Morgan Grenfell 1838–1988* [Oxford, 1989], 33).

26 See chapter 3.

27 O. Gasslander, *History of the Stockholms Enskilda Bank to 1914* (Stockholm, 1962), *passim*.

28 LJSBA, Q 70, Special German Correspondence and others, no date.

29 LJSBA, London Joint Stock Bank to the General Direction of the Seehandlung Society, 10 November 1879.

30 HA, Ms.19,119, Italian Government Loan Syndicate Account (1880–1882).

31 HA, Ms.19,168, Swedish Government 4 per-cent Loan of 1880.

32 For underwriting, see chapter 2.

33 RAL, XI/111/50, Chilean Government 5 per-cent Loan (1911).

34 R.G. Lévy, 'Les grands marchés financiers', *Revue économique internationale*, 1905, 479.

35 V.P. Carosso, *Investment Banking in America: A History* (1970), 79–82.

36 Ministère de l'Economie et des Finances, *Annuaire statistique de la France 1966* (Paris, 1967), 532. The figures included French colonial security issues.

37 M. de Cecco, *Money and Empire* (Oxford, 1974), 106; also see D.C.M. Platt, *Britain's Investment Overseas on the Eve of the First World War* (1986), 134.

38 P. Leroy-Beaulieu, 'Les emprunts des Etats étrangers et le gouvernement français', *L'Economiste Français*, 1 October 1910, 487.

39 As will be seen in chapter 7, this gap often frustrated simultaneous loan issues on the international capital markets when loan issue banks fixed loan issue prices.

40 Ministère de l'Economie et des Finances, *Annuaire statistique de la France 1966* (1967), 520; *Marché financier, 1907–8*, 345. D.K. Sheppard, *The Growth and Role of UK Financial Institutions, 1880–1962* (1971), 190–1.

41 MA, Bank 13-6, T. Toyama, 'Mitsui Ginkō Ō-Bei shucchōin

hōkokusho (Report of an officer dispatched by the Mitsui Bank to Europe and America)' (Tokyo, 1909), 29; MTZ, 12, 240–1.

42 M. Labordère, 'Mechanism of foreign investment in France', *Economic Journal*, xxiv (1914), 532.

43 H. Gans, 'L'intervention gouvernementale et l'accès du marché financier', *Revue politique et parlementaire*, lix (1909), 249.

44 H. Feis, *Europe the World's Banker, 1870–1914* (New Haven, 1930 [reprinted 1964]), 133; J.W. Long, 'The economics of the Franco-Russian alliance, 1904–1906', unpublished Ph.D thesis, University of Wisconsin, 1968, 18; R. Wakatsuki, *Kofūan Kaikoroku (My Recollection)* (Tokyo, 1950), 111–13.

45 E. Becqué, *L'internationalisation des capitaux* (Montpellier, 1912), 113–14.

46 For instance, the British government guaranteed the Turkish government 4 per cent loan issue in 1855 during the Crimean War (The London House of Rothschild [J. Ayer], *A Century of Finance, 1804 to 1904* [1905], 46). Feis, however, noticed the accord between the British government's diplomatic policy and Russian government's financial operations in London (*Europe the World's Banker, 1870–1914* [1930], 89).

47 For instance, in the 1890s the British Foreign Office was much concerned with Persia but the London Stock Exchange Committee did not readily admit the quotation of the 1892 loan (LSEA, Ms.14,600, 64, Stock Exchange General Purpose Committee Minutes, 22 June 1896, Application of the Persian Government 6 Per-cent Loan of 1892 – refused).

48 JNDL, K. Inoue Papers, 686-8, K. Takahashi to T. Katsura and A. Sone, 21 September 1905. In 1909 the officer dispatched by the Mitsui Bank noted the significant difference between the British stamp duty (½ per cent) and the French one (2 per cent) (MA, Bank 13-6, T. Toyama, 'Mitsui Ginkō Ō-Bei shucchōin hōkokusho (Report of an officer despatched by the Mitsui Bank to Europe and America)' [Tokyo, 1909], 25–6).

49 Lysis (pseudonym – E. Le Tailleur), *Contre l'oligarchie financière en France* (Paris, 1908), 26–8.

50 J. Thobie, 'Placements et investissements français dans l'empire ottoman, 1881–1914' in M. Lévy-Leboyer (ed.), *La position internationale de la France* (Paris, 1977), 293. He did not give the source for his calculations.

51 See chapter 6 and chapter 7.

52 E. Kaufmann (translated by A.S. Sacker), *La Banque en France* (Paris, 1914), 122.

53 See chapter 7.

CHAPTER 2: LOAN ISSUE MECHANISM OF THE LONDON CAPITAL MARKET

1 F. Lavington, *The English Capital Market*, 3rd ed. (1934), 190.
2 Once R.H. Coase strongly suggested the study of industrial organization (*The Firm the Market and the Law* [Chicago, 1988], 58–9).
3 J.K. Galbraith, *The Affluent Society*, fourth ed. (Boston, 1984), 84.
4 The latest explanation of this speculation is given by F.G. Dawson, *The First American Debt Crisis* (1990).
5 J.W. Gilbart [revised by S.E. Sykes], *The History, Principles and Practice of Banking*, 1 (1922), 65–6.
6 L.H. Jenks, *The Migration of British Capital to 1875* (1927 reprinted 1971), 47.
7 *The Times*, 24 October 1826.
8 *The Times*, 28 October 1826.
9 [Anon], *A Statement of Some Circumstances connected with the Mode of Contracting the Colombian Loan* (probably 1825), 8–15.
10 The following phrase typically illustrates their way of business : 'a family that works together is invincible' (Count Corti [translated from the German by Brian & Beatrix Lunn], *The Reign of the House of Rothschild*, [1928], 465). The London Rothschilds' official history (*The London House of Rothschild* [J. Ayer], *A Century of Finance, 1804 to 1904* [1905]) often details their co-operation in security issues (13–81).
11 *The Times*, 24 October 1826. Jacob and Samson were younger brothers of the famous David Ricardo (D. Weatherall, *David Ricardo* [Hague, 1976], 132).
12 F. Lavington, *The English Capital Market*, 3rd ed. (1934), 196–9.
13 A.R. Hall, *The London Capital Market and Australia, 1870–1914* (Canberra, 1963), 73–81 and 99–107.
14 A.R. Hall, *The London Capital Market and Australia, 1870–1914* (Canberra, 1963), 196 (note 59).
15 T. Schilling, *London als Anleihemarkt der englischen Kolonien* (Stuttgart, 1911), 52.
16 Hereafter used as underwriting.
17 D. Finnie, *Capital Underwriting* (1934), 6–7.
18 Report from the Select Committee on Loans to Foreign States; together with the Proceedings of the Committee, Minutes of Evidence, and Index, BPP 1875, xi (hereafter cited as Committee on Loans).
19 L.H. Jenks, *The Migration of British Capital to 1875* (1927 reprinted 1971), 400.

20 *Bondholder's Register*, 8 July 1873.
21 *Bankers' Magazine*, 33 (1873), 1000.
22 Evidence taken before Committee on Loans, Q.5014 (A. Grant, Grant Brothers & Co.).
23 MGA, Ms.21,760, HC 4.3.4, Memorandum of Agreement, 28 January 1870.
24 Huth, Frederick & Co. Archives, Ms. 10.700, box 1, no.1983.
25 *Bankers' Magazine*, 36 (1876), 518.
26 For academic research on the role of underwriting in loan issues, see D.C.M. Platt, *Britain's Investment Overseas on the Eve of the First World War* (1986), 141–5; S. Chapman, *The Rise of Merchant Banking* (1984), 88–9 and 100–1. Neither referred to the development of underwriting.
27 *Bankers' Magazine*, 36 (1876), 518; Evidence taken before Committee on Loans, Q. 3543 (R. Foster, Knowles & Foster Co.).
28 D. Finnie, *Capital Underwriting* (1934), 2–4.
29 H.O. O'Hagan, *Leaves from My Life*, 1 (1929), 150.
30 For this division of the functions, the American practice of 'Syndicate No.1' and 'Syndicate No.2' is of interest here. 'Syndicate No.1 [a loan issue bank syndicate] simply buys the securities and then proceeds to form another syndicate ['Syndicate No.2 – an underwriting syndicate] for the purpose of selling them, and when formed they sell the securities to the second syndicate at an advance in price' (L.B. Franklin, 'Syndicates', *[American] Bankers Magazine*, 87 [1913], 665).
31 H.O. O'Hagan, *Leaves from My Life*, 1 (1929), 150.
32 H.O. O'Hagan, *Leaves from My Life*, 1 (1929), 151–2. O'Hagan wrote that 'they [Baring Brothers] were too proud to ask the smaller people to share theirs [their risks in issue]'. Baring Brothers would not underwrite their loan issues before the crisis in 1890 (378–9).
33 *The Statist*, 2 January 1897, 17.
34 C.W. Munn, *Clydesdale Bank* (1988), 145–6.
35 BEA, G23/69, W. Lidderdale to J.F. Garrick, 6 October 1891.
36 On the announcement of loan issue terms, a borrower and loan issue bank received tenders for the loan. The loan issue bank simply lent its reputation and influence on the market, but did not undertake the loan issue at its own risk when the applications of the tenders did not reach the full issue amount. The applicants were required to offer at a certain price a certain number of the bonds which they would take. Borrowers came to set a minimum issue price on the basis of the current quotation prices of similar securities. The whole issue was usually allotted among the applicants at an average price above the minimum issue price (*Bondholders' Register*, 26 January

1875; A.K. Cairncross, *Home and Foreign Investment 1870–1913* [Cambridge, 1953], 91–2).

37 BEA, G23/69, Lidderdale to Garrick, 25 January 1892.

38 R.S. Gilbert, 'London financial intermediaries and Australian overseas borrowing, 1900–29', *Australian Economic History Review*, 11 (1971), 42; *The Statist*, 28 January 1893, 98.

39 H. Lowenfeld, *All About Investment*, 2nd ed. (1909), 172.

40 His obituary (*The Times*, 1 April 1915).

41 D. Finnie, *Capital Underwriting* (1934), 106–15.

42 *The Economist*, 6 December 1913, 1236.

43 J.W. Gilbart [revised by E. Sykes], *The History, Principles and Practice of Banking*, 1 (1922), 247.

44 Acceptance business was that banks 'would add their names to bills of exchange either for their own customers or for those of their correspondents. The effect was to guarantee payment of the bills and to ensure that they could be discounted at the best rates' (C.W. Munn, *Clydesdale Bank* [1988], 143–4).

45 A steady decline in domestic transactions in the 1880s induced the London & Westminster Bank to exploit such business as a new earning source (T.E. Gregory, *The Westminster Bank through a Century*, i [1936], 269–71).

46 US National Monetary Commission, *Interviews on the Banking and Currency Systems of England, Scotland, France, Germany, Switzerland, and Italy* (Senate, 61st Congress, 2nd Session, no.405) (Washington, 1910), 69.

47 LJSBA, Q70, London Joint Stock Bank to the General Direction of the Seehandlung Society, 10 November 1879.

48 Evidence taken before the Committee on Loans, Q.801 (W. McKewan, the Joint General Manager of the London & County Bank).

49 *The Statist*, 15 May 1897, 789.

50 C.A.E. Goodhart, *The Business of Banking 1891–1914* (1972), 136.

51 A.W. Abbott, *A Short History of the Crown Agents and their Office* (1959), 23–4; No.5, (Extract) Memorandum on the Origin and Functions of the Department of the Crown Agents for the Colonies, by Sir Penrose G. Julyan, September 1878 (Crown Agents for the Colonies, Papers Explanatory of the Functions of the Crown Agents for the Colonies [August 1881], BPP 1881, lxiv, [C.-3075]).

52 No.6, Colonial Office to Treasury, 26 November 1880.

53 In the 1860s and 1870s, the Bank of England co-operated with the Crown Agents in some of the New Zealand government loan issues; the Consolidated Bank issued several Tasmanian government loans; the London & Westminster Bank became one of the loan issuers

in many Victorian government loans (London Stock Exchange [Guildhall Library], Loan and Company Prospectuses).

54 From 1864 Glyn, Mills, Currie & Co.

55 H. Feis, *Europe the World's Banker 1870–1914* (New Haven, 1930, reprinted 1964), 8.

56 R. Fulford, *Glyn's, 1753–1953* (1953), ch. 8.

57 LJSBA, Q8, Board Minutes, 3 August 1876. The bank was an agent for the Merchant Bank of Canada.

58 London Stock Exchange (Guildhall Library), Loan and Company Prospectuses. The bank was an agent for the Colonial Bank of Australia.

59 LJSBA, Q11, 9 May, 19 September, 17 October and 5 December 1901.

60 The reason is not clear, but the Consolidated Bank experienced difficulties after the 1866 crisis and towards the end of the 1880s, the bank adopted a policy of branch expansion in the Manchester area rather than in London (T.E. Gregory, *The Westminster Bank through a Century*, i [1936], ii, 51–68).

61 UBLA, B11488, Board Minutes, 25 January 1893.

62 C.A.E. Goodhart, *The Business of Banking 1891–1914* (1972), 491–517 (appendix iv-i).

63 There was a marked difference between the London clearing banks and French banques de dépôts (public deposit banks) *vis-à-vis* loan issue business in general, as Bouvier has pointed out (J. Bouvier, *Le Crédit Lyonnais de 1863 à 1882*, ii [Paris, 1961], 779–80). G. Manchez also noted this difference (*Sociétés de dépôts[;] banques d'affaires* [Paris, 1918], 113–14). Banques de dépôts welcomed such business, making it their main line. If the issue amount was underwritten fully, the risks were limited, as mentioned. Besides, banques de dépôts could, to a certain extent, internalize the loan issue market to their own customers: the direct placement method made a good channel for selling the bonds to their customers. This method became popular among banques de dépôts (A. Théry, *Les grands établissements de crédit français avant, pendant et après la guerre* [Paris, 1921], 45–6) and ensured firm demand for the loans they issued, not through public subscriptions (J. Dagneau, *Les agences régionales du Crédit Lyonnais, années 1870–1914* [originally presented as Thèse de Doctorat en histoire [3e Cycle] to the Université de Paris VIII [1975] [New York, 1977], 248). Customers, on the other hand, generally put full trust in their banks as investment advisers (H.D. White, *The French International Accounts 1880–1913* [Cambridge [Mass.], 1933], 279). Direct placement, which was not an institution built into the British financial counterparts (R.

Michie, 'Different in name only?: the London stock exchange and foreign bourses, c.1850–1914', *Business History*, xxx no.1 [1988], 63), made a major channel between financiers and investors in France, and could effectively disperse loan issue banks' risks to customers (E. Kaufmann [translated by A.S. Sacker], *La banque en France* [Paris, 1914], 306). The reason for banques de dépôts entering into loan issue business on a large scale lay in this structure of the French loan issue market.

64 R. Fulford, *Glyn's, 1753–1953* (1953), ch. 8.

65 LJSBA, Board Minutes, Q8, 2 March 1871; W.F. Crick and J.E. Wadsworth, *A Hundred Years of Joint Stock Banking* (1958), 308.

66 CIBA, ACC293/1, Arrangement Book, 1, f.465.

67 CIBA, E8, Board Minutes, 8 September 1885.

68 CIBA, 14 December 1886.

69 A.R. Holmes and E. Green, *Midland: 150 Years of Banking Business* (1986), 135–6.

70 LSWBA, Board Minutes, 25 July 1889.

71 LSWBA, 27 June 1895.

72 PBA, B11416, Board Minutes, 24 June 1897.

73 F. Capie and A. Weber, 'Truth and fiction' in Institute of Commonwealth Studies (University of London), *Collected Seminar Papers*, 36 (The City and the Empire) (1987), 28.

74 Nishimura confirmed the decline of advances plus discounts/deposits ratios of banks in England and Wales in the late nineteenth century (S. Nishimura, *The Decline of Inland Bills of Exchange in the London Money Market 1855–1913* [Cambridge, 1971], table 26 [107–9]).

75 R.J. Truptil, *British Banks and the London Money Market* (1936), 166.

76 D. Joslin, *A Century of Banking in Latin America* (1963), 20; J.A. Henry (ed. by H.A. Siepmann), *The First Hundred Years of the Standard Bank* (1963), 44.

77 G. Jones, *British Multinational Banking 1830–1990* (Oxford, 1993), 119–30.

78 The direct causes of the Oriental Bank's suspension in 1884 were as follows: a failure of the Ceylon coffee crop; a loss in Mauritius through frauds and cyclones; failure of Chilean government loan flotations; a cumulative fall in the rupee. Most of the bank's assets were locked up in illiquid investments such as railway shares and advances to planters in Ceylon when the bank was in difficulties (A.S.J. Baster, *The Imperial Banks* [1929], 258–9; *Banker's Magazine*, 44 [1884], 664–70).

79 C. Mackenzie, *Realms of Silver* (1954), 206.

80 The Hongkong Bank's diplomatic role appeared especially in the Sino-Japanese War indemnity loan issue negotiations in the period from 1895 to 1898 (S.F. Wright, *Hart and the Chinese Customs*, [Belfast, 1950], ch. xx; D. McLean, 'The Foreign Office and the Chinese indemnity loan, 1895', *Historical Journal*, xvi no.2 [1973], 303–21).
81 FO17/1330, E. Cameron to F. Bertie, 23 December 1897.
82 FO17/1356, E.W. Hamilton to Bertie, 7 February 1898.
83 BEA, G23/70, G.F. Glennie to Hamilton, 21 March 1898. The same arrangement had been made in 1896 (G23/69, Glennie to Cameron, 26 March 1896).
84 F.H.H. King, *The Hongkong Bank in Late Imperial China, 1864–1902*, 1 (Cambridge, 1987), 545; B.H.D. MacDermot, *Panmure Gordon & Co., 1876–1976* (1976), 13–14, 42 and 53. The name of the company was Panmure Gordon, Hill & Co. from 1885 to 1902.
85 For these loan issues, see G. Jones, *Banking and Empire in Iran* (Cambridge, 1986), 51–4 and 120–4.
86 G. Jones, *Banking and Empire in Iran* (Cambridge, 1986), 87–9.
87 FO371/965, G.H. Barclay to Lord Grey, 27 October 1910.
88 BTLA, C2/1, London to Santiago, 75, 1 July 1898.
89 BTLA, C2/3, 178 and 180, London to Santiago, 5 and 19 September 1902. The name of the bank was now the Bank of Tarapacá & Argentina.
90 LBBA, G3/5, Supplement 39/53, 19 December 1901.
91 LBBA, G3/10, Head Office to Rio de Janeiro, 24 February 1910.
92 London Stock Exchange (Guildhall Library), Loan & Company Prospectuses.
93 HSBA, Board Minutes, 1 October 1896.
94 HSBA, Board Minutes, 12 November 1898.
95 *Bankers' Magazine*, 62 (1896), 536; 63 (1897), 617; 66 (1898), 507; 67 (1899), 774.
96 R.F. Holder, *Bank of New South Wales*, 1 (Sydney, 1970), 341. The role of the bank in this loan issue was one of the agents for receiving the tenders (London Stock Exchange [Guildhall Library], Loan and Company Prospectuses).
97 BTAA, C2/3, London to Santiago, 174 (11 July 1902) and 178 (5 September 1902).
98 W.F. Spalding, 'The establishment and growth of foreign branch banks in London, and the effect, immediate and ultimate, upon the banking and commercial development of this country', *JIB*, xxxii (1911), 438.
99 F. Schuster, 'Foreign trade and the money market', *JIB*, xxv (1904), 58–62. Low transaction costs and a low discount rate for

sterling bills on the London money market were attractive to foreign banks (P. Hertner, 'German banks abroad before 1914' in G. Jones [ed.], *Banks as Multinationals* [1990], 101).

100 W.F. Spalding, 'The establishment and growth of foreign branch banks in London, and the effect, immediate and ultimate, upon the banking and commercial development of this country', *JIB*, xxxii, 451.

101 HA, Ms.19,082, Hambros to C.F. Tietgen, 15 November 1894.

102 B.J. Truptil, *British Banks and the London Money Market* (1936), 179.

103 Banques d'affaires – public banks for investment business. The French 'banque d'affaires' meant 'investment bank' in English (D. Landes, 'The old banks and the new' in F. Crouzet, W.H. Chaloner and W.M. Stern [eds.], *Essays in European Economic History, 1789–1914* [Alva, 1969], 113 [note 2]).

104 M. Pohl, 'Deutsche Bank London agency founded 100 years ago' in Deutsche Bank (ed.), *Studies on Economic and Monetary Problems and on Banking History* (Mainz, 1988), 233.

105 M. Pohl, 'Deutsche Bank London agency founded 100 years ago' in Deutsche Bank (ed.), *Studies on Economic and Monetary Problems and on Banking History* (Mainz, 1988), 236.

106 M. Pohl, 'Deutsche Bank London agency founded 100 years ago' in Deutsche Bank (ed.), *Studies on Economic and Monetary Problems and on Banking History* (Mainz, 1988), 237.

107 A. Biliotti, *La Banque Impériale Ottomane* (Paris, 1909), 18–21; A. Autheman, *History of the Ottoman Bank* (Istanbul, 1988), 1–4.

108 A. Autheman, *History of the Ottoman Bank* (Istanbul, 1988), 4.

109 *Banker's Magazine*, lxxix (1905), 362.

110 YSGZS, 2, 38.

111 T. Balogh, *Studies in Financial Organization* (Cambridge, 1947), 233; A.R. Hall, *The London Capital Market and Australia, 1870–1914* (Canberra, 1963), 72.

112 'British capital abroad', *The Economist*, 20 November 1937, 362.

113 M. Simon, 'The pattern of new British portfolio foreign investment, 1865–1914' in A.R. Hall (ed.), *The Export of Capital from Britain* (1968), 15–44.

114 M. de Cecco, *Money and Empire* (Oxford, 1974), 95.

115 M. de Cecco, *Money and Empire* (Oxford, 1974), 96–7.

116 P. Einzig, *The Fight for Financial Supremacy* (1931), 29.

117 S. Chapman, *The Rise of Merchant Banking* (1984), 166–7.

118 S.J. Diaper, 'The history of Kleinwort, Sons & Co. in merchant banking, 1855–1961', unpublished Ph. D. thesis, University of Nottingham, 1983, 62–3.

119 S.J. Diaper, 'Merchant banking growth in the second half of the nineteenth century: the experience of Kleinwort, Son & Co.' in the Institute of Commonwealth Studies (University of London), *Collected Seminar Papers*, no.35 (The City & the Empire) (1985), 95.
120 S. Chapman, *The Rise of Merchant Banking* (1984), 62.
121 S.J. Diaper, 'The History of Kleinwort, Sons & Co. in merchant banking, 1855–1961', unpublished Ph. D. thesis, University of Nottingham, 1983, 264–5.
122 S. Chapman, *The Rise of Merchant Banking* (1984), 129.
123 K. Burk, *Morgan Grenfell, 1838–1988: The Biography of a Merchant Bank* (Oxford, 1989), appendix ii and iii (264–70). For Schröders' case, see Richard Roberts, *Schroders: Merchants & Bankers* (1992), appendix IV(ii) (532–4).
124 L.E. Davis and R.A. Huttenback covered the general activities of the crown agents but gave little discussion of loan issues (*Mammon and Pursuit of Empire* [Cambridge, 1986], 180–2).
125 T. Schilling, *London als Anleihemarkt der englischen Kolonien* (Stuttgart, 1911), 40; Evidence taken before the Committee of Enquiry into the Organization of the Crown Agents' Office (hereafter cited as Committee of Crown Agents' Office), BPP 1909, xvi, [Cd.4474], Q.3730 (J.A. Mullens, a partner of Mullens, Marshall & Co.); London Stock Exchange (Guildhall Library), Loans and Company Prospectuses.
126 J. Clapham, *The Bank of England*, ii (Cambridge, 1944), 301–2.
127 BEA, G4/97, Court of Directors Minutes, 24 February 1876.
128 BEA, G8/43, Treasury Committee Minutes, 29 May 1878; London Stock Exchange (Guildhall Library), Loan and Company Prospectuses.
129 Clapham, ii, 302.
130 Evidence taken before the Committee of Crown Agents' Office, Q.3732 (Mullens).
131 The facilities of inscribed stocks for investors will be mentioned in chapter 4.
132 J.& A. Scrimgeour & Co., a stockbroker, co-operated with Mullens, Marshall & Co. when the bank took up New Zealand government loan issues; R. Nivison & Co., a stockbroker, also worked with Mullens, Marshall & Co. for Indian government loan issues (London Stock Exchange [Guildhall Library], Loans and Company Prospectuses).
133 BEA, G23/69, W. Lidderdale to S. Samuel, 13 August 1891.
134 *SEOI*, for 1895, 160–1.
135 BEA, G23/69, Lidderdale to Garrick, 25 January 1892.

136 BEA, G23/69, H. Cubb to J.F. Garrick, 16 January 1892.
137 BEA, G8/51, Treasury Committee Minutes, 12 August 1908.
138 Charles Duguid, *The Stock Exchange*, fifth ed. (1926), 31–2. Lavington as well simply described 'the brokers who lend their names to the prospectuses, assign the underwriting on payment of an 'overriding' commission, carry through many of the technical formalities and open up a market among their clients' (F. Lavington, *The English Capital Market*, 3rd ed. (1934), 184).
139 N. Grieser, 'The British investor and his sources of information', unpublished M.Sc.(Econ.) thesis, University of London, 1940, 76–7.
140 W.J. Reader, *A House in the City* (1979), 93. This was Foster & Braithwaite's case.
141 H.O. O'Hagan, *Leaves from My Life*, 1, 150–1. J. Soyeda, the president of the Industrial Bank of Japan, emphasised this role of stockbrokers in Japanese loan issues (TKZ, 60–1504, 30 April 1910, 743–5).
142 Y. Cassis, 'British finance: success and controversy' in J.J. van Helten and Y. Cassis [eds.], *Capitalism in a Mature Economy* (1990), 8–9. Foxwell criticized the British financial system for 'excessive specialisation and almost complete lack of organisation' (H.S. Foxwell, 'The financing of industry and trade', *Economic Journal*, 27 [1917], 518).
143 T. Schilling, *London als Anleihemarkt der englischen Kolonien* (Stuttgart, 1911), 46.
144 Such a practice was also confirmed in Indian government guaranteed railway loan issues. Railway companies had their own stockbrokers (Evidence taken before the Committee of the Crown Agents' Office, Q.715 [H.W. Badock, Accountant General at the Indian Office]).
145 London Stock Exchange (Guildhall Library), Loans and Company Prospectuses.
146 Evidence taken before the Committee of the Crown Agents' Office, Q.3714 (Mullens).
147 Evidence taken before the Committee of the Crown Agents' Office, Q.3712 (Mullens).
148 Evidence taken before the Committee of the Crown Agents' Office, Q.3713 (Mullens).
149 Evidence taken before the Committee of the Crown Agents' Office, QQ.3705 and 3708 (Mullens).
150 R.S. Gilbert, London financial intermediaries and Australian overseas borrowing, 1900-29', *Australian Economic History Review*, 11 1 (1971), 43. 'All banks and governments, including the

Commonwealth, used the same broking firm – Nivison & Co.' (41) is misled.

151 Robert Nivison, the founder of the company, was employed by the British Linen Bank (1863–1868) and the London & Westminster Bank (1869–1881). At that time the London & Westminster Bank took an active interest in the financial affairs of colonial governments. Forming a partnership for stockbroking with another members (T.P. Baptie & Co.), he set up R. Nivison & Co. in 1887 (Obituary of Lord Glendyne [Robert Nivison], *The Times*, 16 June 1930).

152 'The successful manner in which they (loan or share issues) were carried through is largely attributed to the skill with which he, Nivison, built up his underwriting connexions' (Obituary of Lord Glendyne [Robert Nivison], *The Times*, 16 June 1930).

153 D. Wainwright, *Government Broker* (East Molesey, 1990), 55. Also see, N.G. Butlin, *Investment in Australian Economic Development 1861–1900* (Cambridge, 1964), 343–4.

154 The Japanese government regarded Panmure Gordon & Co. as its specialized stockbroker (R. Wakatsuki, *Kofūan Kaikoroku (My Recollection)* (Tokyo, 1950), 109.

155 B.H.D. MacDermot, *Panmure Gordon & Co., 1876–1976* (1976), 14.

CHAPTER 3: EARLY LOAN ISSUES

1 The total debts of the feudal clans (*Daimyō*) taken over by the Meiji government amounted to nearly Mexican $6 million (approximately £135,000) (*MTZ*, 12, 2). It is difficult to calculate accurately because of a silver currency (A.P. Andrew, 'The end of the Mexican dollar', *Quarterly Journal of Economics*, xviii-no.3 [1904], 321–56).

2 MBA, M153/44, Interview between T.R. Hughes and C. Whitburn, 3 June 1896. In comparison with the yield at issue in 1873 (7.6 per cent), the return shows that the price of this loan rose remarkably in 1896.

3 *Bankers' Magazine*, 30 (1870), 584.

4 *The Economist*, 25 June 1870, 786–7.

5 D.S. Landes, *Bankers and Pashas* (Cambridge [Mass.], 1958 reprinted 1979), 57.

6 T. Tanaka, *Meiji Ishin no Seikyoku to Tetsudō Kensetsu (Political Situations of the Meiji Restoration and Railway Construction in Japan)* (Tokyo, 1963), 69–70.

7 T. Tanaka, *Meiji Ishin no Seikyoku to Tetsudō Kensetsu* (Tokyo, 1963), 89–91.

8 T. Tanaka, *Meiji Ishin no Seikyoku to Tetsudō Kensetsu* (Tokyo, 1963), 102.
9 There are two studies on Lay: J. King, 'Oratio [Horatio is the right name – author] Nelson Lay, C.B. – a pioneer of British influence in the Far East', *Journal of the American Asiatic Association*, xiv-no.2 (1914), 49–54; J.J. Gerson, 'Horatio Nelson Lay: his role in British relations with China, 1849–65', unpublished Ph.D. thesis, University of London, 1967 (this thesis was published as *Horatio Nelson Lay and Sino-British Relations, 1854–1864* [Harvard East Asian Monographs 47] [Cambridge [Mass.]], 1972). Neither throws light on Lay's activities connected with Japan.
10 His father G. Tradescant Lay was in China from 1841 to 1845 as the HBM Consul in Amoy (J.J. Gerson, 'Horatio Nelson Lay: his role in British relations with China, 1849–65', unpublished Ph.D. thesis, University of London, 1967, 34).
11 S.F. Wright, *Hart and the Chinese Customs* (Belfast, 1950), ch. ix.
12 C16/676/5146, 1870. S. No.146, the Answer of Horatio Nelson Lay, 2.
13 C16/676/5146, 1870. S. No.146, the Answer of Horatio Nelson Lay, 2-3.
14 Lay to T. Fairbairn, 18 March 1869 (C.16/676/5146, 1870. S. No.146, the Answer of Horatio Nelson Lay, 3).
15 C16/676/5146, 1870. S. No.146, the Answer of Horatio Nelson Lay, 4.
16 C16/676/5146, 1870. S. No.146, the Answer of Horatio Nelson Lay, 6.
17 Lay to Fairbairn, 19 July 1869 (C16/676/5146, 1870. S. No.146, the Answer of Horatio Nelson Lay, 6-7).
18 C16/676/5146, 1870. S. No.146, Amended Bill of Complaint, 10, Fairbairn to Lay, 29 July 1869.
19 C16/676/5146, 1870. S. No.146, the Answer of Horatio Nelson Lay, 4.
20 Japanese Mint, *Zōheikyoku Hyakunenshi (One Hundredth Anniversary History of the Japanese Mint)* (Tokyo, 1976), 29–39; K. Tatewaki, *Zainichi Gaikoku Ginkōshi (History of Foreign Banks in Japan)* (Tokyo, 1987), ch. 6.
21 FO262/188, H.S. Parkes to Lord Clarendon, 31 July 1870; F.V. Dickins and S. Lane-Poole, *The Life of Sir Harry Parkes*, ii (1894), 157.
22 WUA, S. Ōkuma Papers, C.719, E. Satow to S. Ōkuma, no date.
23 C16/676/5146, the Answer, 7.
24 C16/676/5146, Complaint, 4.
25 T. Tanaka, *Meiji Ishin no Seikyoku to Tetsudō Kensetsu* (Tokyo,

1963), 127.
26 *MTZ*, 12, 13.
27 SA, Japanese Customs Loan File, the Contract dated 14 and 28 December 1869; there was also the Japanese edition including some additional contracts in *MZZKSS*, 10, 11–17.
28 FO 262/188, Parkes to Lord Clarendon, 21 July 1870.
29 FO391/15, Parkes to E. Hammond, 4 July 1870.
30 C16/676/5146, the Answer of Horatio Nelson Lay, 10–11.
31 C16/676/5146, the Answer of Horatio Nelson Lay, 12–13.
32 C16/676/5146, the Answer of Horatio Nelson Lay, 14–15.
33 C16/676/5146, the Answer of Horatio Nelson Lay, 16.
34 There was a prospectus in FO46/126, 21 July 1870.
35 SA, Japanese Customs Loan File, An Agreement between Lay, Erlanger and Baron Henry Schröder dated 23 April 1870; C.16/676/5146, 1870. S. No. 146, Affidavits Filed on the Part of the Defendant Horatio Nelson Lay (J.H.W. Schröder, 14 May 1872).
36 S. Chapman, *The Rise of Merchant Banking* (1984), 85.
37 Roberts depicted their relations as 'a key figure in the history of the firm [Schröder] from the 1860s and the 1880s' (Richard Roberts, *Schroders: Merchants & Bankers* [1992], 62).
38 *The Economist*, 30 April 1870, 530.
39 *Financier*, 6 May 1870.
40 C.E. De Long to the Japanese Ministry of Foreign Affairs, 22 June 1870 (*NGB*, 3, 490–4).
41 FO262/188, Parkes to Lord Clarendon, 21 July 1870.
42 FO46/126, Parkes to Hammond, 25 July 1870.
43 T. Tanaka, *Meiji Ishin no Seikyoku to Tetsudō Kensetsu* (Tokyo, 1963), 122–3.
44 FO391/15, Parkes to Hammond, 22 April 1870.
45 FO391/15, Parkes to Hammond, 22 July 1870.
46 N. Sekiyama, *Nihon Kahei Kin-yūshi Kenkyū (Study on Monetary History in Japan)* (Tokyo, 1943), 70–2.
47 T. Tanaka, *Meiji Ishin no Seikyoku to Tetsudō Kensetsu* (Tokyo, 1963), 196.
48 SA, Japanese Customs Loan File; there was also the Japanese edition in *MZZKSS*, 10, 23–4.
49 Japanese government to Oriental Bank, 22 June 1870 (*MZZKSS*, 10, 23).
50 Japanese government to Oriental Bank, 29 June 1870 (*MZZKSS*, 10, 24–5).
51 P. Campbell to Oriental Bank's Yokohama Branch, 26 August 1870 (*MZZKSS*, 10, 34–5).
52 WUA, Ōkuma Papers, C.684, J. Russel to H. Itō, 10 December

1870; Richard Roberts, *Schroders: Merchants & Bankers* (1992), 71–2.

53 WUA, Ōkuma Papers, C.687, Imperial Government of Japan Customs Loan signed by E. Erlanger and H.N. Lay dated 6 December 1870.

54 *MTZ*, 12, 13–14.

55 C16/676/E5146, 1870. S. No. 146, 14 May 1872, Affidavits (J.E. Turner), Filed on the Part of the Defendant Horatio Nelson Lay, 5.

56 *The Economist* 1 March 1873, 250.

57 FO262/188, Parkes to Lord Clarendon, 31 July 1870.

58 M. Takahashi, *Meiji Zaiseishi Kenkyū (Study on the Financial History in the Meiji Era)* (Tokyo, 1964), 34.

59 Council of the Corporation of Foreign Bondholders, *Annual Report*, first report, (1874), 21.

60 *SID*, 2, 170–1.

61 *MTZ*, 12, 24.

62 *MTZ*, 12, 24.

63 M. Senda, 'Meiji Roku-nen nanabu ritsuki gaisai no boshūkatei (Seven per-cent foreign loan issue in 1873)', *Shakai keizai shigaku (Japanese Socio-Economic Journal)*, 49-no.5 (1983), 18.

64 The bank's surviving record (PRO, J.90/1770–1774) on customers' securities for borrowings has no bearing on the Japanese government loan issue.

65 Letter from Scrimgeour, Kemp-Gee & Co. dated 21 August 1984.

66 FO46/154, Parkes to Lord Granville, 17 June 1872.

67 T. Sagami, 'Nanban ginkō toraiki (Introduction of western banks into Japan) 2', *[Japanese] Finance*, 10-4 (1974), 49–51. Sagami's article was based on the Bank of California Archives.

68 T. Sagami, 'Nanban ginkō toraiki (Introduction of western banks into Japan) 2', *[Japanese] Finance*, 3, 10-5 (1974), 47. Yoshida was displeased with the Oriental Bank because of this telegram.

69 Yoshida's Diary 1 (*MZZKSS*, 10, 57–8).

70 Schiff regretted Yoshida's death in 1891 (C. Adler, *Jacob H. Schiff: His Life and Letters*, 1 [New York, 1928], 212).

71 Yoshida's Diary 1 (*MZZKSS*, 10, 70–3).

72 Yoshida's Diary 2 (*MZZKSS*, 10, 81–3).

73 P. Thane, 'Financiers and the British state: the case of Sir Ernest Cassel', *Business History*, xxviii-1 (1986), 81.

74 Yoshida's Diary 2 (*MZZKSS*, 10, 85).

75 Yoshida's Diary 3 (*MZZKSS*, 10, 127–8).

76 V.P. Carosso, *Investment Banking in America* (Cambridge [Mass.], 1970), 22.

77 Yoshida's Diary 3 (*MZZKSS*, 10, 111).
78 Yoshida's Diary 3 (*MZZKSS*, 117–18).
79 Yoshida's Diary 2 (*MZZKSS*, 83–5).
80 Yoshida's Diary 4 (*MZZKSS*, 133–4).
81 BBA, HC.17,296, Wercher-Bonverg to Baring Brothers, 28 December 1872.
82 Yoshida's Diary 4 (*MZZKSS*, 10, 149).
83 Parkes, Ōkuma and Itō established very close relations with J. Robertson, the manager of the Oriental Bank's Yokohama branch (MA, Iko–W–3–37, Stenographic Note of Discussion [20 March 1912]).
84 F.V. Dickins and S. Lane-Poole, *The Life of Sir Harry Parkes*, ii (1894), 243.
85 D.J.S. King, 'China's first public loan: the Hongkong Bank and the Chinese imperial government "foochow" loan of 1874' in F.H.H. King (ed.), *Eastern Banking* (1983), 239.
86 *The Economist*, 10 May 1884, 567.
87 Yoshida's Diary 2 (*MZZKSS*, 10, 93–4). The Oriental Bank did not mention the borrowing period.
88 Yoshida's Diary 3 (*MZZKSS*, 10, 119). This letter was also signed by K. Ueno and E.Shibusawa.
89 Yoshida's Diary 3 (*MZZKSS*, 10, 120).
90 Yoshida's Diary 3 (*MZZKSS*, 10, 121–2).
91 *Bankers' Magazine*, 32 (1872), 630.
92 Yoshida's Diary 4 (*MZZKSS*, 10, 145).
93 Yoshida's Diary 4 (*MZZKSS*, 10, 145–6). The actual loan issue charges to the government including the interest on the deposit and communication charges amounted to £101,700, about 4⅕ per cent of the total loan issue amount (*MZ*, 8, 640–1).
94 Yoshida's Diary 4 (*MZZKSS*, 10, 149).
95 Yoshida's Diary 4 (*MZZKSS*, 10, 155–9); *MTZ*, 12, 24–5.
96 The average price of a *koku* of rice should be equivalent to 16s. 8d.
97 WUA, Ōkuma Papers, C.642, J. Robertson to Ōkuma, 13 February 1873; Yoshida's Diary 5 (*MZZKSS*, 10, 169).
98 UBLA, 1513, Investment Ledger.
99 *The Economist*, 18 January 1873, 60.
100 F.O.46/166, Parkes to Lord Granville, 23 May 1873.

CHAPTER 4: SINO-JAPANESE WAR LOAN ISSUES

1 *NGH*, 1, 120 and 217–18; G.C. Allen, *A Short Economic History of Modern Japan 1867–1937* (1972), 50–7; R.W. Goldsmith, *The Financial Development of Japan, 1868–1977* (New Haven, 1983), 24–7.

2 *YSGZ*, 2, 27–37; *Banker's Magazine*, 59 (1896), 69–70.
3 *MHSKT*, 128.
4 *MHSKT*, 278–9 and 298–9.
5 *MTZ*, 12, 414.
6 LSEA, Ms.14,600, General Purpose Committee Minutes, 65, 12 October 1896; also Ms.18,000, 43B/557, Quotation Application.
7 JMFA, S. Matsuo Papers, 44-13, no.3.
8 FO46/314, P. Le P. Trench to Foreign Office, 2 August 1884.
9 *The Economist*, 24 April 1897, 603. The whole text of the Japanese gold standard act appears in M. Matsukata, *Report on the Adoption of the Gold Standard in Japan* (Tokyo, 1899), 192–5.
10 G. Droppers, 'Monetary changes in Japan', *Quarterly Journal of Economics*, xii (1898), 176–7.
11 *MTZ*, 12, 418. In Japan, the role of this bureau was of extreme importance in circulating government domestic bonds in the embryonic capital market. The Deposit Money Bureau, established in 1885, invested the government's funds and postal saving money (*MTZ*, 13, 565–7).
12 In 1896 the Deposit Money Bureau held Japanese government bonds for ¥56,408,199 (*MTZ*, 13, 809).
13 Marcus Samuel was famous as a joint founder of the Shell Transport & Trading Co. (R. Henriques, *Marcus Samuel* [1960], 59–60).
14 JMFAA, 3–4–4–4, Minister of Finance to T. Katō, no date; secret (secretariat) no.99, M. Matsukata to Katō, 26 January 1897.
15 R. Henriques, *Marcus Samuel* (1960), 61.
16 JMFAA, 3–4–4–4, secret (secretariat) no.99 M. Matsukata to Katō, 26 January 1987. Marcus Samuel's mother was a cousin of Lionel Nathan Rothschild, the former head of the London Rothschilds (AGA, Ms.11,038B, Information Book).
17 JMFAA, 3–4–4–4, no.5, Katō to S. Ōkuma, 17 December 1896.
18 JMFA, M. Matsukata Papers, 40-36, I. Tajiri and S. Matsuo to Matsukata, 19 April 1897. Tajiri misleadingly wrote that the Chartered Bank was a French bank.
19 JMFAA, 3–4–4–4, no.71, Minister of Finance to Katō, 14 May 1897.
20 *CSS*, 13 May 1897.
21 JMFAA, 3–4–4–4, no.71, Minister of Finance to Katō, 14 May 1897.; Panmure Gordon & Co. to K. Sonoda, 12 May 1897.
22 JMFA, Matsuo Papers, 44–13, no.4.
23 The yield at issue was 4.9 per cent at the 101½ per-cent issue price.
24 C. Mackenzie, *Realms of Silver* (1954), 206. Gwyther was the chairman of the Bank from 1896 to 1904.

25 Unfortunately the forming of the syndicate could not be traced because of the lack of information.
26 R.S. Sayers, *Lloyds Bank in the History of English Banking* (Oxford, 1957), 18.
27 T. Skinner, *London Banks, and Kindred Companies & Firms* (1905); JMFAA, 3–4–4–4, Katō to Ōkuma, 14 May 1897. For the bank's contemporary activities, see [Capital & Counties Bank], *The Capital and Counties Bank, Limited* (1896).
28 In 1902 the Capital & Counties Bank also acted as loan issuers of the City of Yokohama 6 per-cent loan and the City of Osaka 6 per-cent one which S. Samuel & Co. undertook. It is regrettable that there are no surviving records on the Japanese government loans in 1897 and 1899 at the M. Samuel & Co. Archives (interview with D.G. Corble, the archivist of Hill Samuel & Co., on 10 July 1984).
29 *The Statist*, 39, 15 May 1897, 789.
30 *MTZ*, 12, 419–23.
31 CBA, Extract from Board Minutes, 10 May 1897.
32 JMFA, Matsukata Papers, no.40–37, K. Takahashi to K. Inoue, 31 May 1898.
33 FO46/484, Lowther to Marquis of Salisbury, 11 June 1897.
34 *TKZ*, 35–877, 22 May 1897, 901–2.
35 *TKZ*, 35–880, 20 June 1897, 1116.
36 JMFAA, 3–4–4–4, received no.502, Katō to Ōkuma, 24 May 1897.
37 *MTZ*, 1, 221.
38 *MHSKT*, 158.
39 *MTZ*, 12, 35–6.
40 *SID*, 4, 569–70.
41 *TKJ*, 2, 102.
42 *TKJ*, 2, 112–13.
43 PBA, U. Yoneyama, *Alexander A. Shand* (Tokyo, no date), 5–6; there were Shand's obituaries in *The Times*, 16 April 1930 and *Bankers' Magazine*, 129 (1930), 7. Also see O. Checkland, *Britain's Encounter with Meiji Japan, 1868–1912* (1989), 250 (note 79).
44 PBA, D1080, Connection of the Alliance Bank and Parr's Bank on the New Account Signature Books of the Alliance Bank, Bartholomew Lane; *YSGZ*, 1, 96 (note 10).
45 PBA, B11416, Board Minutes, 5 December 1895.
46 T. Tsuchiya, *Shand* (Tokyo, 1966), 120.
47 JMFA, 40-37, Takahashi to Inoue, 31 May 1898; *TKJ*, 2, 125.
48 Long discussed Russia's 'highly-efficient apparatus of faithful financial agents' (J.W. Long, 'The economics of the Franco-Russian alliance, 1904–1906', unpublished Ph.D thesis, University of Wisconsin, 1968, 13–14). The Japanese government learnt much

from the Russian government's financial activities in London and Paris. But it was only after the Russo-Japanese War (1904–1905) that the Japanese government created a standing post of loan commissioner.

49 JMFA, Matsukata Papers, 40–40, Takahashi to Matsukata, 14 February 1899.

50 JMFA, Matsuo Papers, 45-10, Inoue to Katō, 16 June 1898.

51 As mentioned previously, the commission was not exorbitant.

52 JMFAA, 3–4–4–6, secret no.76, Katō to T. Nishi, 24 June 1898.

53 JMFA, Matsuo Papers, 45–10, Katō to Inoue, 24 June 1898.

54 JMFA, Matsuo Papers, 45–11, M. Matsuda to Katō, no date.

55 JMFA, Matsuo Papers, Katō to Ōkuma, 3 September 1898.

56 *MZ*, 8, 171–5.

57 *MZ*, 8, 168.

58 BJA, Draft of Report to the Prime Minister on the Foreign Loan Issue of 1899 – Cabinet Decision on the Foreign Loan Issue (M. Matsukata to T. Yamamoto, 23 January 1899).

59 BJA, Order & Announcement of the Loan Issue of 1899 – secretariat no.278 (secret), Matsukata to the Bank of Japan, 23 March 1899.

60 For his business career, see his obituary in *Anglo-Japanese Gazette*, February 1903, 33.

61 BJA, the Bank of Japan to Y. Nakai, 23 March 1899.

62 BJA, Draft of Report to the Prime Minister on the Foreign Loan Issue of 1899 – no.5, S. Matsuo's Diary on the Loan Issue, 9 May 1899.

63 BJA, no.16, Apology to the Press on the Loan Issue.

64 MGA, Ms.21,760, HC 5.2.14, J.R. Morse to F.B. Jennings, 29 April 1898.

65 BJA, S. Matsuo's Diary, 6 May 1899.

66 JMFA, Z314–2, *Gikai Sankōsho (Reference Book for Diet [4th Session] – Questions & Answer of the Foreign Loan Issue)* (1899).

67 BJA, S. Matsuo's Diary, 30 April 1899.

68 BJA, S. Matsuo's Diary, 29 April and 8 May 1899.

69 JMFAA, 3–4–4–6, secret no.76, Katō to Nishi, 24 June 1898.

70 JMFAA, 3–4–4–6, secret no.33, K. Matsui to S. Aoki, 29 July 1899.

71 *GKS*, 1, 3–6.

72 The bank took them as portfolio investment (BJA, Order & Announcement of the Loan Issue of 1899 – Bank of Japan to Nakai, 23 March 1899).

73 JMFAA, 3–4–4–6, no.30, Matsui to Aoki, 20 May 1899.

74 The contract stated the loan issue commission for £400,000 (not 4

per cent) (PBA, D6800, Agreement, 1 June 1899). This amounts to 5 per cent if £8 million is the actual loan issue amount on the market.

75 *Investors' Review*, 13 May 1899, 671–2 and 3 June 1899, 775.

76 *IMM*, 30 June 1899.

77 BJA, Draft of Report to the Prime Minister on the Foreign Loan Issue of 1899 – Report of the Financial Minister to the Prime Minister, 21 October 1899.

78 *NGHS*, 2, 111–12. Of £2,500,000, £1,700,000 of the bonds were held by the Deposit Money Bureau at the Ministry of Finance. The Yokohama Specie Bank agreed with the other loan issue banks that the bank should make up 50 per cent of the deficiency if applications from the underwriters fell short of £8,000,000 (PBA, D6800, Agreement among Parr's Bank, the Chartered Bank, the Hongkong Bank and the Yokohama Specie Bank, 2 June 1899).

79 MGA, Ms.21,760, HC 5.2.17, Panmure Gordon, Hill & Co. to J. Pierpont Morgan, 4 September 1900; also see V.P. Carosso, *The Morgans: Private International Bankers 1854–1913* (Cambridge [Mass.], 1987), 424.

80 PBA, D1354, General Manager's Report.

81 In 1902 J.S. Morgan & Co. participated in the syndicate for the sale of the unsubscribed bonds for £65,000 (MGA, Ms.21,760, HC 5.2.17, Panmure Gordon, Hill & Co. to J.S. Morgan & Co., 20 January 1902; Ms.21,793, 2).

82 BJA, Draft of Report to the Prime Minister on the Foreign Loan Issue of 1899 – Report of the Financial Minister to the Prime Minister, 21 October 1899.

83 *GTR*, no.164 (15 July 1899), 976.

84 JMFAA, 3–4–4–6, secret no.33, Matsui to Aoki, 29 July 1899.

85 In 1901 the Deposit Money Bureau held 5 per-cent domestic bonds for ¥57,572,734 (*MTZ*, 12, 809). The objects of this loan were railway construction and improvement, the establishment of steelworks, the expansion of the telephone service, the tobacco monopoly, military outlay and the colonization of Fomosa.

86 *TKZ*, 44–1101, 5 October 1901, 696–7; *Japan Daily Mail*, 20 October 1901.

87 N. Takizawa, *Kōhon Nihon Kin-yūshiron (Manuscript of Japanese Financial History)* (Tokyo, 1912 reprinted 1968), 701.

88 JMFA, Z317–1, *Gikai Sankōsho (Reference Book for Diet [17th Session])* (1902); Japanese Public Record Office, Meiji 36nen Kōbun Zappen (Miscellaneous Official Documents for the Year of 1903), Ministry of Finance, 1–14–2A/13/Hen 696.

89 *YSGZS*, 2, 22-37; *NGHS*, 1, 382–3; Bank of Tokyo, *Shōkin Kawase*

Shikin no Shiteki Hatten (Historical Development of Foreign Exchange Funds at the Yokohama Specie Bank), 1 (Tokyo, no date), 20–3.

90 *NKGGS*, 22–37.

91 *TKJ*, 2, 158–61.

92 FO46/560, the London Rothschilds to F. Bertie, 17 September 1902.

93 BBA, PF302, Lord Lansdowne to Lord Revelstoke, 27 September 1902.

94 BBA, PF302, Copy of telegram from Yokohama, 27 and 29 September 1902.

95 JNDL, Y. Sakatani Papers, 497–10, Papers on the finance, 21 August 1902. Y. Sakatani, the vice-minister of finance, thought that the resale price should be more than 95 per cent and that in this operation the Industrial Bank should co-operate with the Bank of Japan and the Yokohama Specie Bank.

96 JNDL, A. Sone Papers, 1–28, contract of a resale of the 5 per-cent domestic bonds dated 30 September 1902.

97 The yield at issue was 5 per cent at the issue price of £102 1s. 8d. (100 per cent).

98 BBA, PF302, Telegram to Yokohama, 1 October 1902.

99 *YSGZS*, 2, 95–6.

100 BBA, PF302, Telegram from Yokohama, 3 October 1902.

101 PBA, D6801, Panmure Gordon, Hill & Co. to R.W. Whalley, 2 October 1902.

102 BBA, PF302, Cameron to Lord Revelstoke, 29 September 1902.

103 BBA, PF302, Baring Brothers to Banque de Paris, 26 September 1902.

104 BBA, PF302, Banque de Paris to Baring Brothers, 27 September 1902.

105 BBA, PF302, Banque de Paris to Baring Brothers, 1 October 1902.

106 BBA, PF302, Hottinguer to Baring Brothers, 2 October 1902.

107 BBA, PF302, Baring Brothers to Hope & Co., 30 September 1902.

108 BBA, PF302, Banque Federal to Baring Brothers, 3 October 1902.

109 For their intimate relations with Baring Brothers, see V.P. Carosso, *More than A Century of Investment Banking* (New York, 1979), 21–3.

110 BBA, PF302, Kidder Peabody & Co. to Baring Brothers, 1 October 1902.

111 J. Orbell, *Baring Brothers & Co., Ltd.* (1985), 65. The Company was formed in 1891 out of the old Kidder Peabody partnership.

112 BBA, PF302, Baring Brothers to Baring Magoun & Co., 30 September 1902.

113 BBA, PF302, Hambros to Baring Brothers, 29 September 1902.

114 BBA, PF302, the London Rothschilds to Baring Brothers, 29 September 1902.
115 *SEOI*, for 1903, 8. The Bank of England did not charge for inscriptions of bonds (the prospectus in BBA, PF302).
116 *SEOI*, for 1891, 120–1.
117 BBA, PF302, Cameron to Lord Revelstoke, 29 September 1902.
118 FO46/560, E.W. Hamilton to T.H. Sanderson, 30 September 1902.
119 BEA, G4/125, Court of Directors Minutes, 9 October 1903 and SJ/Jap/1, Stock Jacket.
120 *The Statist*, 11 October 1902, 626.
121 LSEA, Ms.18,000, 83B/464 and 89B/236, Quotation Application.
122 A Russian financier depicted a first-class merchant bank's (J.S. Morgan & Co.'s) financial power on the London capital market as 'we want a flag and a name in London and we think that the go and spirit that you have shown everywhere will insure a glorious success' (MGA, Ms.21,760, HC 12.3, Alexander Koch to J. Pierpont Morgan, 10/22 February 1898).

CHAPTER 5: RUSSO-JAPANESE WAR LOAN ISSUES (1)

1 For Russia's financial operations in Paris during the Russo–Japanese War, see B.A. Romanov [translated from the Russian by S.W. Jones], *Russia in Manchuria (1892–1906)* (Michigan, 1952), ch. vii; J.W. Long, 'The economics of Franco–Russian alliance, 1904–1906', unpublished Ph.D thesis, University of Wisconsin, 1968, 29–35.
2 K. Takahashi (T. Uetsuka [ed.]), *Takahashi Korekiyo Jiden (Autobiography of Takahashi Korekiyo)*, 2 (Tokyo, 1976).
3 Recently the Japanese National Diet Library obtained Takahashi's diary (from 22 February to 18 December 1904), written in English, which fully covered the period when he acted as the Japanese government special loan commissioner in 1904. Obviously this becomes a new source for the study of foreign loan issues during the Russo-Japanese War (JNDL, K. Takahashi Papers, 135, Diary). In 1992 the diary was translated into Japanese by K. Fujimura (S. Hatano [ed.]) *(Takahashi Korekiyo to Kokusai Kin-yū [Takahashi Korekiyo and the International Finance]*, 1 [Tokyo, 1992], 85–283), but his translation and explanations have included a considerable number of errors.
4 The following pioneering studies mentioned the Japanese government war loan issues: U. Kobayashi, *War and Armament Loans of Japan* (New York, 1922), 61–91; *MTZ*, 12, 50–86; M. Kajima,

Nippon Gaikōshi (Diplomatic History of Japan), 7 (Tokyo, 1970), 127–37. Nish argued the matter mainly from the diplomatic viewpoint on the basis of the British Foreign Office Papers, A.J. Balfour Papers and J. Austen Chamberlain Papers (I.H. Nish, *The Anglo-Japanese Alliance*, 2nd. ed. [1985], 287–9).

5 *TKJ*, 2, 205.

6 Japanese Ministry of Finance (S. Usami), *Shōwa Zaiseishi (History of Japanese Finance in the Shōwa Era)*, iv (Tokyo, 1955), 9 and 16–17; *MTZ*, 1, 245–6.

7 FO46/577, C.M. MacDonald to Lord Lansdowne, 18 February 1904.

8 FO46/578, MacDonald to Lord Lansdowne, received 31 May 1904.

9 I.H. Nish, *The Anglo-Japanese Alliance*, 2nd. ed. (1985), 216–17; A.M. Pooley (ed.), *The Secret Memoirs of Count Tadasu Hayashi* (London, 1915), ch. iii-v.

10 R. Henriques, *Marcus Samuel* (1960), 59–60.

11 JNDL, Y. Sakatani Papers, 498-13, no.91, T. Hayashi to J. Komura, 31 December 1903.

12 R. Henriques, *Marcus Samuel* (1960), 472. For Hayashi's career, see A.M. Pooley (ed.), *The Secret Memoirs of Count Tadasu Hayashi* (London, 1915), 1–23.

13 FO46/575, Lord Lansdowne's Memorandum, 29 December 1903.

14 FO46/564, Lord Lansdowne to MacDonald, 31 December 1903.

15 Add. Ms.49,728, A.J. Balfour to Lord Lansdowne, 22 December 1903.

16 Add. Ms.49,735, Extract from Letter to Lord Lansdowne in J.Austen Chamberlain to Balfour, 30 December 1903.

17 FO46/575, E. Cameron to Lord Lansdowne, 26 December 1903.

18 FO46/575, Cameron to F. Campbell, 28 December 1903.

19 Japanese Ministry of Foreign Affairs, *Komura Gaikōshi (History of the Diplomat Komura Jutarō)* (Tokyo, 1953 reprinted 1966), 407–8.

20 FO46/564, Lord Lansdowne to MacDonald, 29 December 1903.

21 Add. MS49,728, Lord Lansdowne to Balfour, 29 December 1903.

22 Add. MS49,728, Balfour to Lord Lansdowne, 31 December 1903.

23 Add. MS49,735, J.A. Chamberlain to Balfour, 2 January 1904.

24 FO46/576, Lord Lansdowne to MacDonald, 1 January 1904.

25 FO46/576, Lord Lansdowne to MacDonald, 1 January 1904.

26 BEA, G23/87, Secretary to C.B. Norman, 4 August 1896.

27 No.32, Komura to Hayashi, 15 January 1904 (*NGB*, 37–2, 125–6); JNDL, Sakatani Papers, 498-15, 7 January 1904.

28 No.31, Komura to Hayashi, 15 January 1904 (*NGB*, 37–2, 125).

29 Count Corti, (translated by Brian and Beatrix Lunn) *The Reign of*

the House of Rothschild (1928), 459–60.
30 JNDL, Takahashi Papers, 135, Diary, 3 May 1904.
31 No number, Hayashi to Komura, 15 January 1904 (*NGB*, 37–2, 126–7).
32 No.34, Hayashi to Komura, 6 January 1904 (*NGB*, 37–2, 127–8).
33 FO46/587, Cameron to F. Campbell, 8 January 1904.
34 FO46/587, Cameron to British Foreign Office, 9 January 1904.
35 BBA, PF303, Hongkong Bank Yokohama branch to London office, 17 February 1904.
36 BBA, PF303, Hongkong Bank London office to Yokohama branch, 18 February 1904.
37 BBA, PF303, 19 February 1904; Memorandum given to Cameron, 12 February 1904.
38 BBA, PF303, Count A. Benckendorff to Lord Revelstoke, Friday February 1904 [no date].
39 Add. MS49,728, Lord Lansdowne to Balfour, 21 February 1904.
40 BBA, PF303, Extract form Letter E. Noetzlin to Lord Revelstoke, 20 February 1904. For a history of the Banque de Paris, see H. Collas, *La Banque de Paris et des Pays-Bas et les émissions d'emprunts publics et privés* (Dijon, 1908) and E. Bussière, *Paribas 1872–1992: Europe & the World* (Antwerp, 1992).
41 RAL, XI/101/62, the Paris Rothschilds to the London Rothschilds, 29 February 1904.
42 BBA, PF303, Baring, Magoun & Co. to Baring Brothers, 3 March 1904.
43 BBA, PF303, Baring, Magoun & Co. to Baring Brothers, 3 March 1904. For the business relations between the National City Bank and Kuhn, Loeb & Co., see H. van B. Cleveland and T.F. Huertas, *Citibank, 1812–1970* (Cambridge [Mass.], 1985), 37-41.
44 BBA, PF303, Hugo Baring to Lord Revelstoke, 4 March 1904. For the history of the Kidder, Peabody Co., see V.P. Carosso, *More Than a Century of Investment Banking* (New York, 1979).
45 BBA, PF303, Baring, Magoun & Co. to Baring Brothers, 9 March 1904.
46 BBA, PF303, Baring Brothers to Baring, Magoun & Co., 9 March 1904.
47 BBA, PF303, Extract from letter Lord Revelstoke to Hugo Baring, 8 March 1904. Later Takahashi found that Baring Brothers 'have so much interest in Russia and at this moment they don't want to come out' (JNDL, Takahashi Papers, 135, Diary, 22 September 1904).
48 *TKJ*, 2, 195–6. There is no record of this proposal in Baring Brothers' Archives. It may have been made verbally.
49 FO800/134, R.W. Whalley to Takahashi, 1 November 1905.

50 RAL, XI/89/10A, W. Kokovtzoff to the London Rothschilds, 7 February 1904.
51 The London Rothschilds sent much money to the Jewish Committee in Russia (RAL XI/130A/0, the London Rothschilds to the Paris Rothschilds, 1 January 1906).
52 Add. MS49,747, Alfred Rothschild to Balfour, 4 April 1905.
53 BBA, PF303, Hongkong Bank in Tokyo to London office, 3 March 1904.
54 BBA, PF303, Cameron to Lord Revelstoke, 4 March 1904.
55 BBA, PF303, Hongkong Bank London office to Yokohama branch, 7 March 1904.
56 *TKJ*, 2, 186–89.
57 JMFA, K. Shōda Papers, 27–1, Cabinet Decision on the Foreign Loan Issue, 17 February 1904.
58 JMFA, Shōda Papers, 27-1, Order dated 22 February 1904.
59 JNDL, Takahashi Papers, 135, Diary, 12 April 1904.
60 JNDL, Takahashi Papers, 135, Diary, 7 and 13 April 1904.
61 JNDL, Takahashi Papers, 135, Diary, 12 April 1904. I.D. Cameron, of Panmure Gordon & Co., informed me in his letter of 18 July 1984 that no record of the Japanese government loan issues during this period survives at its archives.
62 JNDL, Takahashi Papers, 135, Diary, 13 April 1904.
63 There is no description of the Japanese government loan in court minutes of the Union of London & Smiths Bank from February to June in 1904 (ULSBA, B11498) nor in the letter book from Felix Schuster from July 1902 to March 1905 (ULSBA, D3610).
64 JNDL, Takahashi Papers, 135, Diary, 14 April 1904.
65 JNDL, Takahashi Papers, 135, Diary, 13 April 1904.
66 Beeton had close business connections with Cassel (E. Fukai, *Kaiko Shichijūnen [Retrospect for Seventy Years]* [Tokyo, 1941], 75).
67 JNDL, Takahashi Papers, 135, Diary, 22 April 1904. Beeton was asked to visit Takahashi by Malcolm D. McEacharn, McIlwraith, McEacharn & Co., an Australian merchant, shipowner and commission agent.
68 *TKJ*, 2, 194. For Cassel's business career, see P. Thane, 'Financiers and the British state: the case of Sir Ernest Cassel' (*Business History*, xxviii–1 [1986], 80–99); A. Allfrey, *Edward VII and his Jewish Court* (1991), ch. 6 and 7. There is a description of Cassel's transaction with de Zoete & Gorton, a stockbroker, in *de Zoete & Gorton: A History* (no place and date), 48–9.
69 *London Stock Exchange Daily Official List*, January and February 1904.
70 *TKJ*, 2, 199–201.

71 Japanese Ministry of Finance, *Report on the War Finance* (Tokyo, 1906), 24.
72 No.210, Komura to Hayashi, 8 April 1904 (*NGB*, 37–2, 134).
73 *TKJ*, 2, 194.
74 Parr's Bank's board of directors agreed to present Shand with £1,000 for his services in the Japanese government loan and in maintaining for the bank the Japanese connections (PBA, B11417, Board Minutes, 23 June 1904).
75 FO800/134, Hayashi to Lord Lansdowne, 2 November 1905.
76 JNDL, Takahashi Papers, 135, Diary, 18 and 20 April 1904.
77 JNDL, Takahashi Papers, 135, Diary, 17 April 1904; no.217, Komura to Hayashi, 189 April 1904 (*NGB*, 37–2, 136); Japanese Ministry of Finance, *Ōkurashō Hyakunenshi (One Hundredth Anniversary History of the Japanese Ministry of Finance)*, 1 (Tokyo, 1969), 192.
78 *London Stock Exchange Daily Official List*, April and May 1904.
79 JNDL, Takahashi Papers, 135, Diary, 24 April 1904.
80 JNDL, Takahashi Papers, 135, Diary, 27 April 1904; JMFA, Shōda Papers, 27–1, telegram from Takahashi, 27 April 1904.
81 No.230, S. Matsuo to Takahashi through Komura, 30 April 1904 (*NGB*, 37–2, 136).
82 JNDL, Takahashi Papers, 135, Diary, 2 May 1904; no.147, Hayashi to Komura, 1 May 1904 (*NGB*, 37–2, 137).
83 No.149, Hayashi to Komura, 2 May 1904 (*NGB*, 37–2, 139–40).
84 BBA, PF303, Lord Revelstoke to G. Farrer, 31 March 1904.
85 BBA, PF303, G. Farrer to Lord Revelstoke, 6 April 1904.
86 E. Fukai, *Kaiko Shichijūnen [Retrospect for Seventy Years]* (Tokyo, 1941), 70.
87 C. Adler, *Jacob H. Schiff: His Life and Letters*, 2 (New York, 1928), 337.
88 E. Fukai, *Jinbutsu to Shisō (Men and Thought)* (Tokyo, 1939), 60.
89 C. Adler, *Jacob H. Schiff: His Life and Letters*, 2 (New York, 1928), 1, 6 and 11. For the foundation of Kuhn, Loeb & Co., see [Kuhn, Loeb & Co.], *Investment Banking through Four Generations* (New York, 1955), 7–8. It is regrettable that the archives of Kuhn, Loeb & Co. at Shearson Lehman Brothers Co. are not accessible (letter from S.A. Gates, a vice-president of Shearson Lehman Brothers Co., dated 1 October 1992).
90 AJAA, Schiff Papers, Box 442, Schiff to Cassel, 13 May 1915.
91 Adler, *Jacob H. Schiff: His Life and Letters*, 2 (New York, 1928), 1, 10.
92 Southampton University Library, Sir Ernest Cassel Papers, X17, Lord Revelstoke to Cassel, 28 April 1904. Schiff depicted Lord

Revelstoke's negotiations as 'your masterly and straight-forward conduct of affairs' (C. Adler, *Jacob H. Schiff: His Life and Letters*, 2 (New York, 1928), 1, 230).

93 BBA, PF303, Lord Revelstoke to Farrer, 3 May 1904.

94 JNDL, Takahashi Papers, 135, Diary, 3 May 1904.

95 No.153, Hayashi to Komura, 4 May 1904 (*NGB*, 37–2, 140–1).

96 No.240, Komura to Hayashi, 5 May 1904 (*NGB*, 37–2, 143–4).

97 No.249, Governor of the Bank of Japan [Matsuo] to Deputy-Governor [Takahashi], 7 May 1904 (*NGB*, 37–2, 144).

98 BBA, PF303, Lord Revelstoke to J. Stillman, 4 May 1904.

99 BBA, PF303, Memorandum of conversation held at 8 Bishopsgate on 5 May 1904.

100 FO800/134, R.W. Whalley to Takahashi, 1 November 1905.

101 E. Fukai, *Jinbutsu to Shisō (Men and Thought)* (Tokyo, 1939), 60.

102 C. Adler, *Jacob H. Schiff: His Life and Letters*, 2 (New York, 1928), 1, 218. *The Economist* paid much attention to this point by saying that 'it is also noted that the Jewish factor in the floating of the loan here [in New York] is pronounced, and the popular inference is that something of sentiment is behind it all, in view of what has been so heartily resented – Russia's treatment of Jews' (21 May 1904, 872).

103 [Kuhn, Loeb & Co.] *Investment Banking through Four Generations*, (New York, 1955), 18.

104 K. Burk, *Morgan Grenfell 1838–1988* (1989), 112.

105 BBA, PF303, Cassel to Lord Revelstoke, 9 May 1904.

106 Takahashi anticipated the great rise of the New York capital market in the post the First World War (AAJA, Schiff Papers, Box 446, Takahashi to Schiff, 11 February 1915).

107 V.P. Carosso, *Investment Banking in America* (Cambridge [Mass.], 1970), 81.

108 Lord Lansdowne wrote on the back of the correspondence that 'we must be very careful to steer clear of any official connection into the loan issue' (F.O.46/581, MacDonald to Lord Lansdowne, 9 May 1904).

109 J. Schiff, 'Japan after the war' in *North American Review*, 183–no.dxcvii (1906), 162.

110 PBA, D.6802, Agreement, 7 May 1904.

111 FO46/578, MacDonald to Lord Lansdowne, 7 June 1904.

112 The Agreement Clause 5 and 6 (BBA, PF303, 54–8).

113 *Financial Times*, 9 May 1904.

114 BBA, PF303, 54–8.

115 Schiff was also a director of these two banks at that time (J.N. Ingham, *Biographical Dictionary of America Business Leaders* [Connecticut, 1983]).

116 *The Statist*, 7 May 1904, 894.
117 *Financial Times*, 13 May 1904.
118 LBBA, G3/7, Head office to Rio de Janeiro, 12 May 1904.
119 HSBA, G8. I, Extract from enclosure to letter from Hongkong Bank's New York branch dated 1 July 1949.
120 *MTZ*, 12, 75.
121 RAL, XI/148/390, the London Rothschilds to Iavasche Bank (Amsterdam), 12 May 1904.
122 *Financial Times*, 13 May 1904.
123 *The Times*, 14 May 1904.
124 Secret no.3, M. Arakawa to Komura (Report on the Japanese Government Bond Subscriptions addressed to Minister of Finance, dated 19 May 1904), 19 May 1904 (*NGB*, 37–2, 155).
125 'When subscriptions to a foreign issue are invited by means of a public prospectus, it is almost certain that that issue will be vouched for by one of these issuing houses [merchant banks] whose name will be evidence that it has been thoroughly examined and the interests of the investors protected as far as possible' (Committee on Finance and Industry, Report, 1931 [Cmd. 3897], BPP 1930–31, xiii, para 387).
126 *Financial Times*, 19 May 1904.
127 PBA, D6802, Agreement, 7 May 1904.

CHAPTER 6: RUSSO-JAPANESE WAR LOAN ISSUES (2)

1 D.S. Landes, *Bankers and Pashas* (Cambridge [Mass.], 1958 reprinted 1979), 16.
2 *Anglo-Japanese Gazette*, November 1905, 107.
3 *MTZ*, 12, 87.
4 *MTZ*, 12, 88.
5 *MTZ*, 12, 88.
6 *MTZ*, 12, 88. He admitted that 'in order to float [a] 5% [loan] some change or turn is necessary' (JNDL, K. Takahashi Papers, 135, Diary, 10 September 1904).
7 Secret no.6, M. Arakawa to J. Komura, 16 September 1904 (*NGB*, 37–2, 175).
8 BBA, PF304, Parr's Bank to Kuhn, Loeb & Co., 11 October 1904; JNDL, Takahashi Papers, 135, Diary, 11 October 1904.
9 BBA, PF304, Kuhn, Loeb & Co. to Parr's Bank, 14 October 1904.
10 *London Stock Exchange Daily Official List* and *Commercial & Financial Chronicle*, from August to November 1904.
11 BBA, PF304, Kuhn, Loeb & Co. to Lord Revelstoke, 14 October 1904.

12 BBA, PF304, Kuhn, Loeb & Co. to Parr's Bank, 17 and 18 October 1904.
13 BBA, PE304, Parr's Bank to Kuhn, Loeb & Co., 14 and 17 October 1904.
14 No.61, S. Matsuo to K. Takahashi, 17 October 1904 (*NGB*, 37–2, 186).
15 No number, Matsuo to Takahashi, 19 October 1904 (*NGB*, 37–2, 186). After the continued victories in Manchuria the public in Japan would not be satisfied with the 87½ per cent (JNDL, Takahashi Papers, 135, Diary, 19 October 1904).
16 No number, Matsuo to Takahashi, 21 October 1904 (*NGB*, 37–2, 187–8); JNDL, Takahashi Papers, 135, Diary, 21 October 1904.
17 S. Nishimura, *The Decline of Inland Bills of Exchange in the London Money Market 1855–1913* (Cambridge, 1971), table 30.
18 Secret (secretariat) no. 1965, A. Sone to J. Komura, 25 October 1904 (*NGB*, 37–2, 188–9); JNDL, Takahashi Papers, 135, Diary, 25 and 26 October 1904.
19 BBA, PF304, Lord Revelstoke to R.H. Whalley, 21 October 1904.
20 No.83, M. Arakawa to Komura, 7 October 1904 (*NGB*, 37–2, 181); *Commercial & Financial Chronicle*, lxxix, 2053, 5 November 1904.
21 *The Times*, 26 October 1904; *The Economist*, 29 October 1904, 1725.
22 BBA, PF304, Kuhn, Loeb & Co. to Parr's Bank, 28 October 1904.
23 BBA, PF304, Kuhn, Loeb & Co. to Parr's Bank, 29 October 1904. Takahashi even proposed to cancel Kuhn, Loeb & Co.'s participation (JNDL, Takahashi Papers, 135, Diary, 30 October 1904).
24 J. Riesser, *The German Great Banks and their Concentration in Connection with the Economic Development of Germany* (Washington, 1911), 353.
25 BBA, PF304, Parr's Bank to Kuhn, Loeb & Co., 2 November 1904; PBA, D6802, Agreement, 8 November 1904.
26 BBA, PF304, Lord Revelstoke to Kuhn, Loeb & Co., 17 October 1904.
27 For Speyer Brothers' history, see T.C. Barker and M. Robbins, *A History of London Transport*, ii (1974), 70–1 and 372 (note 44); A.M. Mandeville, *The House of Speyer* (1915).
28 Similarly Burk placed much emphasis on the advantageous position of J.S. Morgan & Co. as an Anglo–American house in loan issues (K. Burk, *Morgan Grenfell 1838–1988* [1989], 123).
29 S. Chapman, *The Rise of Merchant Banking* (1984), 158. On this point Landes mentioned that 'it was easier to absorb rivals [in the syndicate] than to fight them' (D.S. Landes, *Bankers and Pashas* (Cambridge [Mass.], 1958 reprinted 1979), 30).

30 BBA, PF304, Lord Revelstoke to Kuhn, Loeb & Co., 18 October 1904.
31 BBA, PF304, Kuhn, Loeb & Co. to Speyer Brothers, 10 November 1904.
32 BBA, PF304, Speyer Brothers to Kuhn, Loeb & Co., 11 November 1904. But Speyer Brothers joined the underwriting in London for £500,000.
33 BBA, PF304, f.130; WBA, D2469.
34 BBA, PF304, Parr's Bank to Kuhn, Loeb & Co., 11 November 1904.
35 *MTZ*, 12, 109.
36 BBA, PF304, Kuhn, Loeb & Co. to Parr's Bank, 22 November 1904. *MTZ* mentioned fourfold oversubscribed (12, 109).
37 HSBA, LOHI/57, Hamburg branch to London office, 15 November 1904.
38 FO46/579, C.M. MacDonald to Lord Lansdowne, 21 November 1904.
39 Secretariat secret 1983, Sone to I. Motono, 28 October 1904 (*NGB*, 189–90).
40 J. Komura to T. Uchida, 10 December 1904 (*NGB*, 37–2, 198).
41 Secret no.1, Motono to Komura, 5 January 1905 (*NGB*, 38–2, 46–8).
42 H. Lemke, *Finanztransaktionen und Aussenpolitik* (Berlin, 1985), 14; V.N. Kokovtsov (ed. by H.H. Fisher and translated by L. Matveev), *Out of My Past* (Stanford University [California], 1935), ch. iv.
43 *The Times*, 18 March 1905.
44 No.86, K. Inoue to Komura, 3 March 1905 (*NGB*, 38–2, 55–6).
45 *TKJ*, 2, 223.
46 Secret no.4, Komura to Hayashi, 16 February 1905 (*NGB*, 38–2, 50–2).
47 BBA, PF305, Kuhn, Loeb & Co. to Lord Revelstoke, 3 February; Lord Revelstoke to Kuhn, Loeb & Co., 15 February 1905.
48 BBA, PF305, Kuhn, Loeb & Co. to Lord Revelstoke, 9 March 1905.
49 BBA, PF305, Baring Brothers to Kuhn, Loeb & Co., 20 March 1905.
50 BBA, PF305, Parr's Bank to Kuhn, Loeb & Co., 20 March 1905; PBA, B11417, Board Minutes, 23 and 30 March 1905.
51 *GKS*, 1, 137–41.
52 BBA, PF305, Baring Brothers to Kuhn, Loeb & Co., 20 March 1905.
53 BBA, PF305, Kuhn, Loeb & Co. to Lord Revelstoke, 9 March 1905.

54 They had filial relations (E. Rosenbaum and A.J. Sherman, *M.M. Warburg & Co., 1798–1938* [1979], 94).
55 BBA, PF305, Kuhn, Loeb & Co. to Lord Revelstoke, 10 March 1905; PBA, D6804, Max Warburg to Parr's Bank, 25 March 1905.
56 BBA, PF305, Lord Lansdowne to Lord Revelstoke, 15 March 1905.
57 BBA, PF305, Baring Brothers to Kuhn, Loeb & Co., 21 March 1905; F.O.46/602, the Hongkong Bank to F.A. Campbell, 27 March 1905. For the relations between the Hongkong Bank and the Deutsch-Asiatische Bank, see M. Müller-Jabusch, *Fünfzig Jahre Deutsch-Asiatische Bank, 1890–1939* (Berlin, 1940), 206–8.
58 PAAA, Abteilung I A, Japan 3, Finanzen, Bd., 5, A.4893, the Deutsche Bank to G.L. Klehmet, 23 March 1905; A.4816, 22 March 1905.
59 BBA, PF305, Lord Revelstoke to Kuhn, Loeb & Co., 21 March 1905; no.99, Komura to Hayashi, 25 March 1905 (*NGB*, 38–2, 59); PAAA, Abteilung I A, Japan 3, Finanzen, Bd. 5, A.4816, dated 22 March 1905.
60 BBA, PF305, Parr's Bank to Kuhn, Loeb & Co., 23 March 1905; *The Economist*, 23 March 1905, 486.
61 *The Standard*, 22 March 1905.
62 M.M. Warburg, *Aus Meinen Aufzeichnungen* (New York, 1952), 19; E. Rosenbaum and A.J. Sherman, *M.M. Warburg & Co., 1798–1938* (1979), 101.
63 SOASA, PP MS 14/23, Addis Diary, 23 March 1905.
64 *MTZ*, 12, 133.
65 BBA, PF305, Warburg to Lord Revelstoke, 30 March 1905.
66 National Provident Institution Archives, Ms.20,274, Investment Ledger, 1.
67 BBA, PF305, Kuhn, Loeb & Co. to Baring Brothers, 30 March 1905.
68 I.H. Nish, *The Anglo-Japanese Alliance*, 2nd ed. (1985), 293–7; Japanese Ministry of Foreign Affairs, *Komura Gaikōshi (History of the Diplomat Komura Jutarō)* (Tokyo, 1966), 459–620.
69 *TKJ*, 2, 244–5.
70 *TKJ*, 2, 247–8.
71 BBA, PF305, Kuhn, Loeb & Co. to Parr's Bank, 19 June 1905.
72 BBA, PF305, Lord Revelstoke to Kuhn, Loeb & Co., 19 June 1905; T. Davidson to Lord Revelstoke, 20 June 1905.
73 BBA, PF305, Parr's Bank to Takahashi, 19 June 1905.
74 BBA, PF305, Takahashi to Parr's Bank, received 21 June 1905.
75 BBA, PF305, Kuhn, Loeb & Co. to Lord Revelstoke, 21 June 1905.
76 Secret no.11, Inoue to Komura, 31 March 1905 (*NGB*, 38–2,

64–9).
77 *TKJ*, 2, 250.
78 BBA, PF305, Parr's Bank to Takahashi, no date.
79 BBA, PF305, Parr's Bank to Takahashi, 23 June 1905.
80 BBA, PF305, Warburg to Lord Revelstoke, 27 June 1905; PAAA, Abteilung I A, Japan 3, Finanzen, Bd., 6, A.11080 (26 June 1905) and A.11128 (27 June 1905).
81 M. Müller-Jabusch, *Fünfzig Jahre Deutsch-Asiatische Bank, 1890–1939* (Berlin, 1940), 31–2; J. Riesser, *The German Great Banks and their Concentration in Connection with the Economic Development of Germany* (Washington, 1911), 455–6.
82 *The Economist*, 8 July 1905, 1124.
83 JMFA, K. Mizumachi Papers, 5–8, no.12, K. Takahashi to K. Saionji and Y. Sakatani, 25 December 1906.
84 M. Müller-Jabusch, *Fünfzig Jahre Deutsch-Asiatische Bank, 1890–1939* (Berlin, 1940), 208–9.
85 BBA, PF305, Baring Brothers to Kuhn, Loeb & Co., 4 July 1905.
86 *The Economist*, 15 July 1905, 1162.
87 WBA, D2469; *GKS*, 1, 171–5.
88 *MTZ*, 12, 174–5; *The Economist*, 22 July 1905, 1199; BBA, PF305, Kuhn, Loeb & Co. to Baring Brothers, 11 July 1905 and Warburg to Baring Brothers, 12 July 1905.
89 *The Statist*, 15 July 1905, 105.
90 G.P. Gooch and H. Temperley (eds.), *British Documents on the Origins of the War 1898–1914*, iv (1929), 107–11.
91 *MHSKT*, 158.
92 JNDL, Kaoru Inoue Papers, 686–8, Takahashi to T. Katsura and Sone, 21 September 1905. According to Takahashi's autobiography, the amount of the domestic bonds was ¥200 million (*TKJ*, 2, 281).
93 JMFAA, 3–4–4–25, Secret no.5, I. Motono to Komura, 24 March 1903.
94 Secret no.6, Arakawa to Komura, 16 September 1904 (*NGB*, 37–2, 176).
95 Secret no.1, Motono to Komura, 5 January 1905 (*NGB*, 38–2, 46–8).
96 *TKJ*, 2, 272–3.
97 JNDL, Inoue Papers, 686-8, Takahashi to Katsura and Sone, 21 September 1905.
98 No.74, Takahashi to Sone, 15 July 1905 (*NGB*, 38–2, 89).
99 *TKJ*, 2, 285–7.
100 No.183, Motono to Katsura, 20 September 1905 (*NGB*, 38–2, 94); RAL, XI/101/68, the Paris Rothschilds to the London Rothschilds, 20 September 1905.

101 JNDL, Inoue Papers, 686–9, Takahashi to Kaoru Inoue, 27 September 1905. F. Stern, *Gold and Iron: Bismarck, Bleichröder, and the Building of the German Empire* (1977 reprinted 1987), 73.
102 *TKJ*, 2, 288–9.
103 K. Burk, *Morgan Grenfell, 1838–1988* (1989), 31.
104 RAL, XI/101/68, the Paris Rothschilds to the London Rothschilds, 13 September 1905.
105 RAL, XI/101/68, 15 September 1905.
106 BBA, PF305, Whalley to Kuhn, Loeb & Co., 25 October 1905; JNDL, Inoue Papers, 686–9, Takahashi to Inoue, 27 September 1905.
107 RAL, XI/101/69, the Paris Rothschilds to the London Rothschilds, 3 October 1905.
108 *The Economist*, 30 September 1905, 1552.
109 BBA, PF305, Memorandum between Whalley and Baring Brothers, 1 November 1905; Whalley to Kuhn, Loeb & Co., 25 October 1905.
110 BBA, PF305, Lord Revelstoke to J. Schiff, 29 September 1905.
111 BBA, PF305, Baring Brothers to Kuhn, Loeb & Co., 3 November 1905.
112 BBA, PF305, Kuhn, Loeb & Co. to Parr's Bank, 4 November 1905.
113 BBA, PF305, Kuhn, Loeb & Co. to Baring Brothers, 14 November 1905.
114 BBA, PF305, Parr's Bank to Kuhn, Loeb & Co., 15 November 1905.
115 BBA, PF305, Baring Brothers to Kuhn, Loeb & Co., 14 November 1905.
116 BBA, PF305, Baring Brothers to Kuhn, Loeb & Co., 20 November 1905.
117 BBA, PF305, Whalley to Kuhn, Loeb & Co., 11 November 1905.
118 All the Japanese government loans issued during 1904 and 1904 were sterling loans. Their interest and principal were paid at the fixed rates of exchange.
119 *Anglo-Japanese Gazette*, November 1905, 108.
120 No.14, M. Rouvier to Boutiron, 12 January 1906 (*DDF*, 2e série, viii, 517).
121 *TKJ*, 2, 294–5; no.228, Katsura to Motono, 4 November 1905 (*NGB*, 38–2, 94–5).
122 No.203, Motono to Katsura, 13 November 1905 (*NGB*, 38–2, 95).
123 AMAE, N.S.53, M.A. Nelidoff to President, 17 November 1905.
124 RAL, XI/101/69, the Paris Rothschilds to the London Rothschilds, 9 November 1905.

125 RAL, XI/176/47, the London Rothschilds to the Paris Rothschilds, 13 November 1905.
126 Obituary of Baron Alphonse de Rothschild (*The Economist*, 3 June 1905, 918).
127 BBA, PF305, Extract from Lord Revelstoke's Letter to E. Noetzlin, 15 November 1905.
128 RAL, XI/101/69, the Paris Rothschilds to the London Rothschilds, 16 November 1905; *TKJ*, 2, 295.
129 RAL XI/101/69, the Paris Rothschilds to the London Rothschilds, 2 November 1905.
130 BBA, PF305, Extract from Noetzlin's letter, 14 November 1905.
131 JNDL, Inoue Papers, 686–9, Takahashi to Inoue, 27 September 1905; AMF, F30-376, Ministère des Finances to M. de Verneuil, 1 October 1905; RAL, XI/101/69, the Paris Rothschilds to the London Rothschilds, 6 October 1905.
132 RAL, XI/101/69, the Paris Rothschilds to the London Rothschilds, 25 November 1905.
133 Takahashi clearly understood this point (*JNDL* Inoue Papers, 686-8, Takahashi to Inoue, 27 September 1905).
134 SOASA, PP MS 14/23, C.S. Addis Diary, 15 November 1905.
135 BBA, PF305, Parr's Bank to Kuhn, Loeb & Co., 15 November 1905.
136 *TKJ*, 2, 296–7.
137 BBA, PF305, 83–8, Agreement between the London Issuing Syndicate and Kuhn, Loeb & Co.
138 £250,000, out of £3,250,000 in Germany, was ceded to the loan issue in New York (*MTZ*, 12, 187).
139 The London Rothschilds were not always anxious to rely upon underwriting, complaining that 'it is astonishing how this form of speculation [underwriting] invariably appeals to our Public' (RAL, XI/130A/1, the London Rothschilds to the Paris Rothschilds, 7 March 1907).
140 RAL, XI/111/33, Underwriting List.
141 BBA, PF305, 68–9.
142 SOASA, PP MS 14/23, Addis Diary, 28 November 1905.
143 BBA, PF305, Kuhn, Loeb & Co. to Parr's Bank, 28 November 1905; *MTZ*, 12, 218.
144 WBA, D2469.
145 The direct placement through a 'guichet (counter)' was the placement of bonds which loan issuers took directly to other banks or their customers. In France this method became the preferred channel to place bonds (E. Baldy, *Les banques d'affaires en France depuis 1900* [Paris, 1922], 83).

146 *Syndicat de prise ferme et de placement* took the loan issue amount fully or partly at a fixed price from the borrower at their own risk, that is to say, it directly purchased a full or a certain part of the issue amount and subsequently carried out the placement. The profit of the syndicate came from a difference between the purchase and the placement prices. (E. Baldy, *Les banques d'affaires en France depuis 1900* [Paris, 1922], 64–7).
147 AN, 132/AQ/69, B–13–1/8.
148 PBA, D6804, Agreement, 24 November 1905.
149 *Commercial and Financial Chronicle*, lxxix (1904), 2174.

CHAPTER 7: LOAN ISSUES AFTER THE RUSSO-JAPANESE WAR

1 *MTZ*, 1, 259–72; T. Nakamura, *Meiji-Taishōki no Keizai (Japanese Economy 1867–1925)* (Tokyo, 1985), 89–91. In comparison with Britain the response of taxpayers towards increased taxation is not strong in Japan, especially the pre-1945 Japan.
2 *MHSKT*, 131.
3 FO371/271, H. Lowther to Lord Grey, 22 January 1907.
4 *SEOI*, for 1912, xciii.
5 Secret (secretariat) no.2344, Y. Sakatani to T. Hayashi, 22 August 1906 (*NGB*, 39–1, 387–8); *MTZ*, 12, 240.
6 *The Statist*, 3 February 1906, 193–4.
7 *The Economist*, 16 February 1907, 6–7 ('Commercial history and review').
8 JMFA, K. Mizumachi Papers, 5-8, 7th Report, K. Takahashi to K. Saionji and Sakatani, 20 November 1906.
9 *The Economist*, 16 February 1907, 5. According to Simon, £128,900, 000 (calls total) of Colonial and foreign loan issues in 1905 decreased to £85 million in 1906 (M. Simon, 'The pattern of new British portfolio foreign investment, 1865–1914' in A.R. Hall [ed.], *The Export of Capital from Britain 1870–1914* [1968], 39).
10 RAL, XI/130A/0, the London Rothschilds to the Paris Rothschilds, 8 May 1906.
11 *MTZ*, 12, 241.
12 JMFA, Mizumachi Papers, 5-8, 10th Report, 27 November 1906.
13 RAL, XI/130A/0, the London Rothschilds to the Paris Rothschilds, 9 October 1906.
14 A. Gérard, *Ma mission au Japon, 1907–1914* (Paris, 1919), 13.
15 Secret no.35, S. Kurino to T. Hayashi, 5 December 1906 (*NGB*, 39-1, 515–21).
16 S. Pichon to P. Cambon, 16 and 22 November 1906 (*DDF*, 2e série, x, 435–37, 471–72).

17 No.94, Kurino to Hayashi, 16 November 1906 (*NGB*, 39–1, 511).
18 JMFA, Mizumachi Papers, 5-8, 7th Report, 20 November 1906.
19 Cambon to Pichon, 24 November 1906 (*DDF*, x, 486–90).
20 Pichon to M. Bompard, 17 November 1906 (*DDF*, x, 446–47).
21 Bompard to Pichon, 10 December 1906 (*DDF*, x, 546).
22 *The Times*, 28 December 1906.
23 AMAE, N.S.53, Note Verbale, 23 January 1907; no.3, Kurino to Hayashi, 10 January 1907 (*NGB*, 40–2, 46–7).
24 Bompard to Pichon, 17 January 1907 (*DDF*, x, 620–3).
25 JMFA, Mizumachi Papers, 5–8, 13th Report, 15 January 1907.
26 See chapter 1.
27 Secret no.25, Kurino to Hayashi, 10 August 1906 (*NGB*, 39-1, 385–6).
28 JMFA, Mizumachi Papers, 5–8, 14th Report, 7 February 1907.
29 No.42, Hayashi to Kurino, 21 June 1906 (*NGB*, 39–1, 379).
30 RAL, XI/130A/0, the London Rothschilds to the Paris Rothschilds, 20 June 1906.
31 JMFA, Mizumachi Papers, 5–8, 13th Report, 15 January 1907.
32 JMFA, Mizumachi Papers, 5–8, 13th Report, 15 January 1907.
33 No.16, Hayashi to I. Motono, 9 February 1907 (*NGB*, 40–2, 56–7).
34 No.28, Motono to Hayashi, 13 February 1907 (*NGB*, 40–2, 59–60).
35 No.16, Kurino to Hayashi, 15 February 1907 (*NGB*, 40–2, 61).
36 No.17, Kurino to Hayashi, 15 February 1907 (*NGB*, 40–2, 61–2).
37 No.18, Kurino to Hayashi, 18 February 1907 (*NGB*, 40–2, 63–4).
38 No.18, Kurino to Hayashi, 18 February 1907 (*NGB*, 40–2, 63–4).
39 AMAE, N.S.53, Note verbale, 19 February 1907.
40 RAL, XI/130A/1, the London Rothschilds to the Paris Rothschilds, 20 February 1907. On 7 February 1907 Takahashi considered that he would issue a 5 per-cent loan in Britain, the United States and Germany unless the French government admitted the quotation within two weeks (JMFA, Mizumachi Papers, 5–8, 14th Report, 7 February 1907).
41 No.17, Takahashi to Japanese Government, 3 February 1907 (JMFA, Mizumachi Papers, 5–8, 14th Report).
42 *IMM*, December 1906.
43 The price was on 2 January 1907 (*Commercial and Financial Chronicle [Bank & quotation section]*, lxxxiv, no.2189 [8 June 1907]).
44 RAL, XI/130A/1, the London Rothschilds to the Paris Rothschilds, 8 January 1907.
45 RAL, XI/130A/1, the London Rothschilds to the Paris Rothschilds, 5 February 1907.
46 RAL, XI/130A/1, the London Rothschilds to the Paris Rothschilds, 6 February 1907.

47 RAL, XI/130A/1, the London Rothschilds to the Paris Rothschilds, 19 February 1907.
48 RAL, XI/101/74, the Paris Rothschilds to the London Rothschilds, 15 February 1907; JMFA, Mizumachi Papers, 5–8, 15th Report, 3 March 1907.
49 JMFA, Mizumachi Papers, 5–8, 15th Report, 3 March 1907. The Paris Rothschilds were 'afraid of artificial markets' (RAL, XI/130A/1, 18 February 1907).
50 There was a legal debate on a 5 per-cent loan issue between the Japanese government and the Paris Rothschilds, because the Paris Rothschilds regarded this issue as the remaining part of the 4 percent loan of 1905 (RAL, XI/101/74, the Paris Rothschilds to the London Rothschilds, 20 February 1907).
51 JMFA, Mizumachi Papers, 5–8, 16th Report, 7 March 1907.
52 JMFA, Mizumachi Papers, 5–8, 16th Report, 7 March 1907.
53 RAL, XI/130A/1, the London Rothschilds to the Paris Rothschilds, 20 February 1907.
54 RAL, XI/130A/1, the London Rothschilds to the Paris Rothschilds, 22 February 1907.
55 RAL, XI/101/74, the Paris Rothschilds to the London Rothschilds, 26 February 1907; JMFA, Mizumachi Papers, 5-8, 16th Report.
56 RAL, XI/130A/1, the London Rothschilds to the Paris Rothschilds, 27 February 1907.
57 RAL, XI/130A/1, the London Rothschilds to the Paris Rothschilds, 28 February 1907.
58 RAL, XI/101/74, the Paris Rothschilds to the London Rothschilds, 1 March 1907.
59 RAL, XI/101/74, the Paris Rothschilds to the London Rothschilds, 4 March 1907; AN, 132/AQ/69, B–13–2/3, Provisional Contract dated 4 March 1907.
60 This quotation would finally be realized in 1910 (AMF, F30-377, A. Gérard to Pichon, 27 February 1910).
61 BBA, COF–05–2–9, Kuhn, Loeb & Co. to Parr's Bank, 22 February 1907.
62 BBA, COF–05–2–9, Kuhn, Loeb & Co. to Baring Brothers, 27 February 1907; Parr's Bank to Kuhn, Loeb & Co., 27 February 1907.
63 BBA, COF–05–2–9, Kuhn, Loeb & Co. to Baring Brothers, 1 March 1907.
64 FO371/271, A.M. Townsend to F. Campbell, 4 March 1907.
65 PBA, D6805, Agreement, 6 March 1907.
66 RAL, XI/111/36, Japanese government 4 per-cent loan of 1907.
67 RAL, XI/111/36, Japanese government 4 per-cent loan of 1907.

68 SOASA, PP MS 14/25, C.S. Addis Diary, 9 March 1907.
69 RAL, XI/101/74, the Paris Rothschilds to the London Rothschilds, 12 March 1907.
70 AN, 132/AQ/69, B–13–2/1.
71 Other costs were not revealed.
72 *MTZ*, 12, 226.
73 *MTZ*, 11, 881–2.
74 *MHSKT*, 130 and 158.
75 *MTZ*, 12, 270–1.
76 *MTZ*, 11, 885–6 and 12, 270–1.
77 *The Economist*, 12 February 1910, 313.
78 *The Times*, 14 January 1910.
79 RAL, XI/130A/4, the London Rothschilds to the Paris Rothschilds, 7 March 1910.
80 *MTZ*, 12, 271–2.
81 RAL, XI/130A/4, the London Rothschilds to the Paris Rothschilds, 15 April 1910.
82 *MTZ*, 12, 272–4.
83 AMAE, N.S.56, Note, 23 April 1910; JMFAA, 3–4–4–45, no.30, Kurino to J. Komura, 22 April 1910.
84 JMFAA, 3–4–4–47, Secret no.24, Kurino to Komura, 25 July 1910.
85 AMF, F30-^{377}, G. Cochery to Ministère des Affaires Etrangères, 24 February 1910; AMAE, NS.56, Ministère des Affaires Etrangères to Ministre des Finances, 12 February 1910.
86 *GKS*, 1, 165–9.
87 AN, 132/AQ/70, B–14–1/4.
88 AN, 132/AQ/70, B–14–1/2, Prospectus.
89 AN, 132/AQ/70, B–14–1/4.
90 RAL, XI/130A/4, the London Rothschilds to the Paris Rothschilds, 28 April 1910.
91 RAL, XI/130A/4, the London Rothschilds to the Paris Rothschilds, 2 May 1910.
92 RAL, XI/130A/4, the London Rothschilds to the Paris Rothschilds, 11 June 1906.
93 PBA, D6806, Agreement, 5 May 1910.
94 SOASA, PP MS 14/28, Addis Diary, 18 May 1910.
95 HSBA, LOHI/2.
96 *The Economist*, 26 February 1910, 425; *The Times*, 24 February 1910.
97 *YSGZ*, 2, 144.
98 The quotation price of the Japanese government 4 per-cent loan of 1905 at the end of May 1910 was about 95 3/4 (*IMM*).

99 In the 1910s the method of short-term bill issues became popular in the London capital market (*The Economist*, 14 December 1912, 1205–6). In 1913 the Japanese government placed one year Treasury bills and note for £1.5 million respectively.

CHAPTER 8: MUNICIPAL AND COMPANY LOAN ISSUES

1 Annual Series Diplomatic and Consular Reports (Japan) for 1901, no.2789 (1902), 22.
2 Annual Series Diplomatic and Consular Reports (Japan) for 1902, no.3009 (1903), 35.
3 BBA PF297, C.V. Sale to Lord Revelstoke, 15 January 1904.
4 *SID*, 5, 109–13.
5 J.H. Schiff, 'Japan after the war', *North American Review*, 183–no.dxcvii (August, 1906), 166; C. Adler, *Jacob H. Schiff: His Life and Letters*, 1 (New York, 1928), 236.
6 H. Dyer, 'Japanese industries and foreign investments', *Financial Review of Reviews*, no.4 (February 1906); 'Commercial morality of Japan', *Financial Review of Reviews*, no.7 (May 1906); 'Legal aspects of foreign investments in Japan', *Financial Review of Reviews*, no.10 (August 1906).
7 Annual Series Diplomatic and Consular Reports (Japan) for 1905, no.3377 (1906), 3.
8 Y. Horie, Gaishi Yunyū no Kaiko to Tenbō (Recollection and Prospect of the Import of Foreign Capital to Japan) (Tokyo, 1950), 60–2.
9 R. Wakatsuki, *Kofūan Kaikoroku (My Retrospect)* (Tokyo, 1950), 146–7.
10 'The Japanese loan conversion: interview with Mr. K. Takahashi, the government commissioner', *Financial Review of Reviews*, no.13 (1906), 333.
11 Reubens dealt largely with the Japanese government foreign loans and only limited consideration was given to the investment in private sectors (E.P. Reubens, 'Foreign capital and domestic development in Japan' in S. Kuznets, W.E. Moore and J.J. Spengler [eds.], *Economic Growth* [Durham [N.C.], 1955], ch. 6).
12 F. List, *Schriften, Reden, Briefe*, vi (Das nationale System der politischen Ökonomie) (Berlin, 1930), 42.
13 *MTZ*, 12, 237. This idea stemmed from T. Megata's proposal in 1902 (JMFAA, T. Megata Papers, 9–5, 9 May 1902).
14 Mark Mason, 'With reservations: prewar Japan as host to Western Electric and ITT' in T. Yuzawa and M. Udagawa (eds.), *Foreign Business in Japan before World War II* (Tokyo, 1990), 175.

15 *NKGGS*, 22–8. No bank record covering this period survives at the bank's archives (letter from M. Nunome, former chief of the research department of the Industrial Bank, dated 20 August 1986).
16 *NKGGS*, 30–1.
17 BBA, PF295, Nippon Kogyoginko (a pamphlet). In 1903 the Industrial Bank applied to the Bank of England for making advances to the Industrial Bank, but the Bank of England refused this (BEA, G23/88, S.H. Morley to J. Soyeda, 30 November 1903).
18 *SID*, 5, 96–7.
19 Secret (Secretariat), no.295, A. Sone to K. Takahashi, 9 February 1905 (*NKGGS*, 57).
20 BBA, PF298, Sale to Baring Brothers, 11 February 1905.
21 J. Tsushima, *Hōtō Zuisō (My Essay)*, 12 (on K. Mori) (Tokyo, 1964), 251–4. Sale & Frazer Co.'s business was to import steam-locomotives, rail and other manufactured goods into Japan and to export Japanese government and municipal bonds to London (*TKZ*, 53–1339, 2 June 1906, 920).
22 BBA, PF297, C.W. MacDonald to Lord Revelstoke, 9 October 1903.
23 BBA, PF298, Memorandum from K. Takahashi, 6 April 1905.
24 BBA, PF298, Sale to Baring Brothers, 11 February 1905; Farrer to Sale, 11 April 1905.
25 JNDL, K. Inoue Papers, 686–5, Takahashi to Inoue, 16 May 1905.
26 *TKJ*, 2, 269–70.
27 JNDL, Inoue Papers, 687–15, no.119, 3 October 1905. In December 1905 ¥2,500,000 (£255,208) capital was paid up and the bank's paid-up capital increased to ¥5 million (£510,416).
28 S. Matsuo to Takahashi, 25 August 1905 in *TKJ*, 2, 270–1.
29 *NKGGS*, 59 and 98.
30 Industrial Bank of Japan, *Honkoku ni okeru Gaishi Dōnyū Shōshi (Short History of Capital Imports in Japan)* (Tokyo, 1948), 5.
31 MA, Ikō–W–4–689, Stenographic Notes of J. Soyeda's Speech (20 April 1929). The agent of a British merchant bank as well confirmed the Japanese government's 'plan of avoiding all profits to [foreign] intermediaries'(BBA, PF301, Sale & Frazer Co. to Baring Brothers, 18 May 1906).
32 FO371/86, MacDonald to Lord Grey (Memorandum of the Industrial Bank of Japan), 29 May 1906.
33 FO371/86, MacDonald to Lord Grey, 26 September 1906. *TKZ* also criticized the government's intervention on loan issue negotiations (54–1350, 18 August 1906, 283–4 and 310–11; 60–1500, 24 July 1909, 158–9).

34 *NKGG*, 60 and 83. The Japanese government increased the Industrial Bank's capital by ¥7,500,000 (£765,625) only, in spite of the Panmure Gordon & Co.'s previous proposal.
35 J. Clapham, *The Bank of England*, ii (Cambridge, 1944), appendix b (431–2; *NGHS*, vol. Shiryō, 426.
36 City of Kobe, *Kobe-shishi (History of Kobe)*, Honpen kakusetsu ge (Kobe, 1924), 258; *TKZ*, 40–988, 22 July 1899, 202.
37 *MTZ*, 12, 714.
38 BBA, PF295, W. Bisset to Lord Revelstoke, 26 July 1902.
39 Ministry of Home Affairs Circular, dated 4 July 1902 (*MTZ*, 12, 715).
40 City of Nagoya, *Taishō Shōwa Nagoyashishi (History of the City of Nagoya from 1917)*, 7 (Nagoya, 1955), 236.
41 Contract dated 11 October 1902 in *GKS*, 2, 308–16.
42 JMFAA, 3–4–4–5, 1, Daisan Bank to J. Komura, 22 October 1902; *SEOI*, for 1906.
43 *TKZ*, 45–1134, 31 May 1902, 1010; *SEOI*, for 1909.
44 *MTZ*, 12, 717–18. This was in accordance with the decision of the cabinet meeting on 21 August 1906 which has been mentioned previously.
45 *MTZ*, 12, 718. However, in the City of Yokohama harbour work loan of 1907 S. Samuel & Co. received only a 2½ per-cent commission including the British stamp duty. This low level of the commission was favourable to the municipality (Contract dated 14 September 1906 in *GKS*, 2, 351–4; *TKZ*, 54–1350, 18 August 1906, 284). This reason may have lain in the condition that the payment of the proceeds be made in yen.
46 For Antony Gibbs's history, see [Antony Gibbs & Sons], *Merchants and Bankers: Antony Gibbs & Sons and its Associated Houses' Business during 150 Years 1808–1958* (1958); M.J. Daunton, 'Inheritance and succession in the City of London in the nineteenth century', *Business History*, xxx–no.3 (1988), 276–82.
47 AGA, Ms.11,040, Brien Cokayne to Herbert Gibbs, 28 July 1905.
48 AGA, Ms.11,040, Brien Cokayne to Herbert Gibbs, 29 July 1905.
49 AGA, Ms.11,040, Vicary Gibbs to Herbert Gibbs, 31 July 1905 and Henry Gibbs to Herbert Gibbs, 1 August 1905.
50 AGA, Ms.11,040, Brien Cokayne to Herbert Gibbs, 25 September 1905.
51 Provisional Contract between the City of Tokyo and the Industrial Bank dated 30 June 1906 in *GKS*, 2, 7–8.
52 BBA, PF301, Sale & Frazer to Baring Brothers, 20 July 1906.
53 BBA, PF301, Sale & Frazer to Baring Brothers, 20 July 1906.
54 HSBA, Board Minutes, 17 July 1906.

55 HSBA, LOHI/2.
56 LBA, W.94/5, Memorandum of Provisional Contract, 8 May 1909.
57 PBA, B11418, Board Minutes, 29 April 1909; HSBC, LOHI/2.
58 HSBA, LOHI/2; Contract between the City of Osaka and the Industrial Bank dated 22 May 1909 in *GKS*, 2, 319–22.
59 HSBA, LOHI/2 and 51; London Stock Exchange (Guildhall Library), Loan and Company Prospectuses.
60 Contract between the City of Tokyo and the Industrial Bank dated 6 February 1912 in *GKS*, 2, 40–3; *NKGGS*, 94–5.
61 Contract (B) between K. Mori and Panmure Gordon & Co. dated 16 February 1912 in *GKS*, 2, 51–3; AMEA, NS57, French Chargé d'Affaires in Tokyo to R. Poincaré, 3 February 1912.
62 JMFA, K. Shōda Papers, 28-7, K. Mori to K. Shōda, 5 December 1911.
63 *GKS*, 2, 41–53.
64 HSBA, LOHI/48.
65 AMEA, NS54, French ambassador in Tokyo to S. Pichon, 3 September 1907.
66 AMEA, NS59, French ambassador in Tokyo to Pichon, 3 April 1907.
67 MA, Ikō–182, T. Masuda's Interview in France, no date.
68 AMEA, NS55, French ambassador in Tokyo to Pichon, 20 January 1909.
69 MTBA, 4–2, Shitenchōkai ssokiroku (Stenographic notes of branch managers' meeting) held on 21 September 1907, 7.
70 Mitsui Bank, *Mitsui Ginkō Hachijūnenshi (Eightieth Year Anniversary History of the Mitsui Bank)* (Tokyo, 1958), 184–5.
71 MTBA, 12–10, Telegram, Manager at Kyoto branch to S. Hayakawa (Managing Director of the Mitsui Zaibatsu), 21 March 1909.
72 At that time Watanabe was in charge of the bank's affairs in Europe (MTBA, 2–1, Board Minutes, 1, 2 November 1909).
73 AMF, F30-377, S. Watanabe to A. Kahn (Copy), 3 August 1909.
74 MA, Ginkō 13–6, T. Toyama, Mitsui Ginkō Ō-Bei shucchoin hōkokusho (Report of an officer dispatched by the Mitsui Bank to Europe and America) (1909), 106-18.
75 MA, Ginkō 13–6, T. Toyama, Mitsui Ginkō Ō-Bei shucchoin hōkokusho (Report of an officer dispatched by the Mitsui Bank to Europe and America) 122–3.
76 Mitsui Ginkō Ō-Bei shucchoin hōkokusho (Report of an officer dispatched by the Mitsui Bank to Europe and America), 118-21.
77 MTBA, 5–7, Hōchi (Announcement), dated 6 July 1909.
78 AMF, F30-377, Order 38, Ministère des Finances to Syndic, 8 July 1909.

79 JMFAA,3–4–4–42, secret no.24, S. Kurino to Komura, 26 August 1909.
80 MTBA, 2–1, Board Minutes, 12 and 26 August 1909.
81 AMF, F30-377, no.643, Ministère des Affaires Etrangères to Ministère des Finances, 18 June 1909.
82 MTBA, 4–2, Shitenchōkai ssokiroku (Stenographic notes of branch managers' meeting) held on 13 September 1909, 5.
83 Osaka Merchant Shipping Co., *Osaka Shōsen Kabushiki Kaisha Gojyūnenshi (Fiftieth Anniversary History of the Osaka Merchant Shipping Co.)* (Osaka, 1934), 507.
84 BBA, PF295, Bisset to M. Sengoku, 12 November 1902.
85 BBA, PF298, G. Farrer to C.V. Sale, 11 April 1905.
86 BBA, PF295, Bisset to R.J. Kirby, 7 August 1902; Shibusawa's Diary 5 September 1902 in *Shibusawa Eiichi Denki Shiryō (Shibusawa Eiichi's Biographical Records)*, appendix 1 (Diary 1) (Tokyo, 1966).
87 *Shūgi-in Giji Ssokkiroku (Stenographic Journal of the Japanese Lower House)*, 20 (Tokyo, 1905 [reprinted 1980]), 345.
88 For Baring Brothers' Japanese railway investment, see T. Suzuki, 'Foreign government loan issues on the London capital market, 1870–1913, with special reference to Japan', unpublished Ph.D thesis, University of London, 1991, 315–20.
89 JMFA, S. Matsuo Papers, 74–48.
90 FO 371/87, MacDonald to Lord Grey, 9 June 1906.
91 BBA, 296, R.J. Kirby to Baring Brothers, 25 October 1903.
92 FO 371/475, MacDonald to Lord Grey, 9 April 1908.
93 Hokkaidō Colonial Bank, *Hokkaidō Takushoku Ginkōshi (History of the Hokkaidō Colonial Bank)* (Sapporo, 1971), 62–3.
94 Hokkaidō Collier & Coal Railway Co., *Nanajūnenshi (Seventieth Anniversary History)* (Tokyo, 1958), 76–7; *Gojyūnenshi Kōhon (Manuscript of Fiftieth Anniversary History)*, 156–60.
95 AMF, F30-377, Charpentier to Pichon, 13 February 1909.
96 AMF, F30-377, Charpentier to Pichon, 14 May 1909.
97 AMEA, NS57, French ambassador in Tokyo to Ministère des Affaires Etrangères, 8 March 1913.
98 For the South Manchurian Railway Co. loan issues in 1907, 1908 and 1911, see T. Suzuki, 'Foreign government loan issues on the London capital market, 1870–1913, with special reference to Japan', unpublished Ph.D thesis, University of London, 1991, 321–4.
99 JMFO, 3–4–4–23, secret no.3, M. Arakawa to T. Katsura, 13 October 1905.
100 BBA, 297, Sale to Lord Revelstoke, 15 January 1904.
101 *Anglo-Japanese Gazette*, October 1905, 82. The Corporation had no assets to secure the debenture stock.

102 *Anglo-Japanese Gazette*, July 1908, 100–2.
103 AMF, F30-377, Note pour Ministre, 4 April 1912.
104 *Kin-yū-Jikō Sankōsho (Annual Reference Bulletin on Financial Matters for 1920)* (Tokyo, 1917), 57.
105 Special Research Section of the Japanese Ministry of Foreign Affairs, *Nippon niokeru Gaikoku Shihon (Foreign Capital in Japan)* (Tokyo, 1948), 61. It is also difficult to trace private borrowings abroad, although the Japanese Ministry of Finance temporarily compiled them (*MTZ*, 17, 379–80).
106 M. Udagawa made a table of 'Major foreign-affiliated manufacturing companies in prewar' (T. Yuzawa and M. Udagawa [eds.], *Foreign Business in Japan before World War II* [Tokyo, 1990], 6–13). T. Kuwahara improved the table ('Dainiji-taisen zen-no gaikoku-kigyō no tai-Nichi tōshi [Foreign multinationals' investment in Japan in the pre W W II days: Survey of the proceeding works]', (Kyoto Sangyo University) *Keizai keiei ronshū [Economic and Business Administration Review]*, 26–2 [1991], 46–51). As for the bibliography of direct investment in Japan, see M. Wilkins, 'The contributions of foreign enterprises to Japanese economic development' (T. Yuzawa and M. Udagawa [eds.], *Foreign Business in Japan before World War II* [Tokyo, 1990], 50–1); M. Mason, *American Multinationals and Japan: The Political Economy of Japanese Capital Controls 1899–1980* (Cambridge [Mass.], 1992), 341–62.
107 *Anglo-Japanese Gazette*, January 1907, 112.
108 BBA, PF301, C.V. Sale to Baring Brothers, 18 May 1906.
109 *Anglo-Japanese Gazette*, March 1903, 57.
110 M. Mason 'With reservations: prewar Japan as host to Western Electric and ITT' in T. Yuzawa & M. Udagawa (eds.), *Foreign Business in Japan before World War II* (Tokyo, 1990), 188.
111 Quoted from H. Dyer, 'Japanese industries and foreign investment', *Financial Review of Reviews*, no.4 (February, 1906), 92.
112 JMFAA, 3–4–2–1, Official no.112, K. Takahira to T. Kato, 20 December 1900.
113 JMFAA, 3–4–4–23, secret no.3, Arakawa to Katsura, 13 October 1905.
114 FO371/475, MacDonald to Lord Grey, 14 March 1908.
115 FO371/689, MacDonald to Lord Grey, 2 April 1909.
116 FO371/689, MacDonald to Lord Grey, 2 April 1909.
117 BBA, PF290, Birch Kirby & Co. to Juno Birch & Co., 20 January 1903.
118 *TKZ*, 52–1305, 30 September 1905, 652.
119 FO371/477, Notes on Japanese-Foreign Joint Undertakings in Osaka, 16 December 1909.

120 *Anglo-Japanese Gazette*, March 1903, 58 and February 1906, 181.
121 For instance, foreigners could still not own land as individuals and engage in mining as individuals (J.E. De Becker, *De Becker's Japanese Law of Trading Partnerships and Companies* [Yokohama, 1906], 132–3).
122 S. Nicholas, 'British business interests in Japan before 1941: origins, evolutions, and operations' in T. Yuzawa and M. Udagawa (eds.), *Foreign Business in Japan before World War II* (Tokyo, 1990), 78.
123 JMFAA, 3–4–4–23, secret no.3, M. Arakawa to T. Katsura, 13 October 1905.
124 A.J. Brown, 'Britain in the world economy 1870–1914', *Yorkshire Bulletin of Economic and Social Research*, 17–1 (1965), 56.

CHAPTER 9: EFFECTS OF JAPANESE GOVERNMENT LOAN ISSUES

1 There are several Japanese studies on specie holdings abroad: S. Kitsukawa, *Meiji Zaisei Keizaishi Kenkyū (Study on the Financial and Economic Histories in the Meiji Era)* (Tokyo, 1969), ch. 4; H. Kojima, *Nippon no Kinhon-isei Jidai 1897–1917 (The Gold Standard Era in Japan)* (Tokyo, 1981), ch. 2; H. Saitō, *Kinhon-iseika no Zaigai Seika (Specie Holdings abroad under the Gold Standard)* (Tokyo, 1981); K. Noji, 'Ni-Sshin Nichi-Ro-sengo keiei to taigai zaisei 1896–1913 (The political and economic policies after the Sino– and Russo-Japanese War, and the foreign public finance in Japan in the period 1896–1913)', *Tochiseido shigaku ([Japanese] Journal of Agrarian History)*, 92, (1981), 19–40; M. Itō, 'Nichi-Ro-sengo no Nihon kinhon-isei to chūōginkō seisaku (The Japanese gold standard and central bank policy after Russo-Japanese War)' in K. Fujise and A. Yoshioka [eds.], *Kokusai Kinhon-isei to Chūōginkō Seisaku (The International Gold Standard and Central Bank Policies)* (Nagoya, 1987), ch. 9; M. Yokouchi, 'Nijusseiki-shotō ni okeru zaigai seika to London kin-yū shijyō (Specie holdings abroad and the London money market at the beginning of the twentieth century)', (Ni-igata University Junior College of Commerce) *Ni-igata daigaku shōgaku ronshū (Journal of Commerce)*, no.19 (1987), 121–86; T. Kamiyama, 'Nichi-Ro-sengo no seika seisaku to zaisei (Japanese government's specie policy and public finances after the Russo-Japanese War)', *Shigaku zasshi ([Japanese] Historical Journal)*, 98–no.1 (1989), 48–80. These studies, however, do not give sufficient explanations, from the viewpoint of the London money market, of the relationships between foreign loans and trade balance under the gold standard.
2 M. Matsukata, *Report on the Post-Bellum Financial Administration in*

Japan 1896–1900 (Tokyo, 1900), 218–21.

3 R.S. Sayers, *The Bank of England 1891–1944*, 1 (Cambridge, 1976), 31 (note 2).

4 *Bankers' Magazine*, 32 (1872), 630. Also see, A.E. Monroe, 'The French indemnity of 1871 and its effects', *Review of Economic Statistics and Supplements*, preliminary volume 1 (1919), 269–81.

5 BEA, Museum 903, B.B. Greene to M.W. Collet, 20 October 1896.

6 BEA, Museum 903, B.B. Green to M.W. Collet, 18 November 1895.

7 J. Viner, *Canada's Balance of International Indebtedness 1900–1913* (Cambridge [Mass.], 1924), 182–3; J.D. Bailey, 'Australian company borrowing, 1870–1893: a study in British overseas investment', unpublished D.Phil. thesis, Oxford University, 1958, 212 and appendix iii (xiv xxiv); K.S. Isle, 'Australian monetary policy', *Economic Record*, vii (1931), 1–5.

8 P.B. Whale, 'The working of the pre-war gold standard' in T.S. Ashton and R.S. Sayers (eds.), *Papers in English Monetary History* (Oxford, 1953), 161–2.

9 P.H. Lindert, 'Key currencies and the gold exchange standard, 1900–1913', unpublished Ph.D. thesis, Cornell University, 1967, ch. 2.

10 A.Z. Arnold, *Banks, Credit and Money in Soviet Russia* (New York, 1937), 16; R.G. Hawtrey, *The Gold Standard in Theory and Practice* (1939), 72–3.

11 Chilean Government Central Statistics Bureau, *Statistical Abstract of the Republic of Chile* (Santiago, 1917), 65.

12 P.H. Lindert, *Key Currencies and Gold, 1900–1913* (New Jersey, 1969), 10–11, 16.

13 C.J. Smit, 'The pre-war gold standard', *Proceedings of Academy of Political Science*, xvi–1 (1934), 53. This paragraph is based on the following standard works on the pre-1914 gold standard: R. Triffin, *The Evolution of the International Monetary System: Historical Reappraisal and Future Perspective* (New Jersey, 1964), 6–7; W.M. Scammell, 'The working of the gold standard', *Yorkshire Bulletin of Economic and Social Research*, 17–1 (1965), 32–3; M.D. Bordo, 'The classical gold standard: some lessons for today', *Federal Reserve Bank of St. Louis Review*, no.63 (1981), 6; I.M. Drummond, *The Gold Standard and the International Monetary System 1900–1939* (1987), 16–20.

14 For the actual forms of bills on London, see Gillett Brothers Discount Co. Ltd., *The Bills on London* (1952).

15 Britain's overseas investment of that period was 'quite exceptional'

(R. Nurkse, 'International investment to-day in the light of nineteenth-century experience', *Economic Journal*, lxiv [1954], 744).

16 W.E. Beach, *British International Gold Movements and Banking Policy, 1881–1913* (Cambridge [Mass.], 1935), ch. ix; A.I. Bloomfield, *Monetary Policy under the International Gold Standard: 1880–1914* (New York, 1959), 42.

17 Allen regarded Japan's currency system before 1914 as having 'a considerable resemblance to the gold exchange standard' (G.C. Allen, 'The recent currency and exchange policy of Japan', *Economic Journal*, xxxv [1925], 69; K. Matsuoka, *Kinkawase Hon-isei no Kenkyū (Study on the Gold Exchange Standard)* (Tokyo, 1936), 537). Yet, even internally, the gold standard act still provided the metallic basis (conversion of gold), although there was no circulation of gold coin.

18 E. Fukai, *Shintei Tsūka Chōsetsuron (On Regulation of Currency*, newly revised) (Tokyo, 1938), 281.

19 A.I. Bloomfield, *Monetary Policy under the International Gold Standard: 1880–1914* (New York, 1959), 55.

20 *The Collected Writings of John Maynard Keynes*, 1 (Indian Currency and Finance) (1971), 19–20.

21 A.I. Bloomfield, *Monetary Policy under the International Gold Standard: 1880–1914* (New York, 1959), 14.

22 A.I. Bloomfield, *Monetary Policy under the International Gold Standard: 1880–1914* (New York, 1959), 52.

23 G. Cassel, *The Downfall of the Gold Standard* (Oxford, 1936), 2–3; M.D. Bordo, 'The classical gold standard: some lessons for today', *Federal Reserve Bank of St. Louis Review*, no.63 (1981), 4–7.

24 M.D. Bordo, 'The classical gold standard: some lessons for today', *Federal Reserve Bank of St. Louis Review*, no.63 (1981), 4.

25 League of Nations [R. Nurkse and W.A. Brown, Jr.], *International Currency Experience* (Geneva, 1944 reprinted 1979), 28–30.

26 League of Nations [R. Nurkse and W.A. Brown, Jr.], *International Currency Experience* (Geneva, 1944 reprinted 1979), 105–6.

27 L. von Mises, 'The foreign exchange policy of the Austro-Hungarian Bank', *Economic Journal*, xix (1909), 203.

28 O. Crisp, *Studies in the Russian Economy before 1914* (1976), 103 and 105; T.H. Von Laue, *Sergei Witte and the Industrialization of Russia* (Columbia, 1963), 112–14; G. v. Schulze-Gävernitz, *Volkswirtschafliche Studien aus Russland* (Leipzig, 1899), 502–36. It is an interesting fact that Adolph Rothstein, who had introduced the gold standard into Austria-Hungary, became S. Witte's adviser when Witte, the Minister of Finance, established the gold standard in Russia (Von Laue, 140). Obviously Russia based

itself on Austria-Hungary's experience in managing the gold standard.

29 L. Jonung, 'Swedish experience under the classical gold standard, 1873–1914' in M.D. Bordo and A.J. Schwartz (eds.), *A Retrospective on the Classical Gold Standard, 1821–1931* (Chicago, 1984), 380–2 and 384.

30 The Japanese Government [probably], *Seika Kyūshū Saku toshiteno Gaikoku Kawase Seisaku (Foreign Exchange Policy for absorbing Specie)* (mimeo) (no place and date).

31 E. Fukai, the governor of the Bank of Japan (1935–1937), admitted that he learnt the management of foreign exchange operations from Keynes's book on the gold exchange standard (E. Fukai, *Kaiko Shichijūnen (Retrospect for Seventy Years)* [Tokyo, 1941], 84–5).

32 *Investors' Guardian*, 27 January 1894, 57; *The Collected Writings of John Maynard Keynes*, 1, ch. 5–6; B.R. Tomlinson, *The Political Economy of the Raj, 1914–1947* (1979), 17–18; Y.S. Pandit, *India's Balance of Indebtedness* (1937, reprinted 1979), 138–9 and 144–50); E.W. Kemmerer, *Gold and the Gold Standard* (New York, 1944 reprinted 1979), 152–63.

33 For instance, F. Schuster, 'Our gold reserves' in *JIB*, xxviii (1907), 1–22.

34 A.G. Ford, 'Notes on the working of the gold standard before 1914', *Oxford Economic Papers*, new series, 12–no.1 (1960), 60–1; *Gold Standard 1880–1914* (Oxford, 1962), 19–20.

35 E. Despres, C.P. Kindleberger and W.S. Salant, 'The dollar and world liquidity', *The Economist*, 5 February 1966, 526–9; W.S. Salant, 'The balance of payments of a financial center' in W. Fellner, F. Machlup and R. Triffin and others, *Maintaining and Restoring Balance in International Payments* (Princeton, 1966), 179–80; P.H. Lindert, *Key Currencies and Gold, 1900–1913* (New Jersey, 1969), 61; K.W. Dam, *The Rules of the Game* (Chicago, 1982), 69–70.

36 C.P. Kindleberger, *International Capital Movements* (Cambridge, 1987), 53–4.

37 J. Viner, 'Clapham on the Bank of England', *Economica*, new series, xii (1945), 63.

38 R.S. Sayers, *The Bank of England 1891–1944*, 1, 39–40; *The Collected Writings of John Maynard Keynes*, 1, 88–91. *The Economist* depicted this operation as 'it is stated that the India Council has been co-operating in this [taking money off the market] by calling in loans and lending the money to the Bank' (14 June 1890, 749).

39 R.S. Sayers, *The Bank of England 1891–1944*, 1, 40–1.

40 The term 'specie' included gold and gold standard foreign currencies (E. Fukai, *Shintei Tsūka Chōsetsuron (On Regulation of Currency,* newly revised) (Tokyo, 1938), 263–64).

41 *MZ*, 2, 570–1.

42 E. Fukai, *Shintei Tsūka Chōsetsuron (On Regulation of Currency,* newly revised) (Tokyo, 1938), 313–14. In 1904 W.M. Koch, Panmure Gordon & Co., suggested to K. Takahashi, the Japanese Government Loan Commissioner, that he [Takahashi] should agree to put in the prospectuses the phrase that the loans are to be kept in London to replenish the gold reserves of the Bank of Japan (NDL, K. Takahashi Papers, 135, Diary, 30 April 1904).

43 For the figures of specie received and paid by the Japanese government and the Bank of Japan from 1903 to 1913, see JMFA, K. Shōda Papers, 49–1, 14, 16 and 23; for Japan's specie holding at the end of the years from 1900 to 1913, see *NGKHS*, Shiryō, 332–3.

44 E. Fukai, *Shintei Tsūka Chōsetsuron (On Regulation of Currency,* newly revised) (Tokyo, 1938), 287–8.

45 JMFA, K. Mizumachi Papers, 5–26.

46 E. Fukai, *Kaiko Shichijūnen (Retrospect for Seventy Years)* (Tokyo, 1941), 83.

47 For the figures of 31 January 1908, see JMFA, Mizumachi Papers, 5–26.

48 *NGHS*, 2, 168–71. Some of specie holdings abroad were used for bank-note-issue-reserves in Japan. Apart from the temporary permission of 1896 (*Azukeai Kanjyo* [the mutual deposit account]), from 1903 the Bank of Japan was empowered to issue notes on specie holdings abroad (*MTZ*, 13, 352–3).

49 E. Fukai, *Shintei Tsūka Chōsetsuron (On Regulation of Currency,* newly revised) (Tokyo, 1938), 289–93.

50 G.C. Allen, 'The recent currency and exchange policy of Japan', *Economic Journal*, xxxv (1925), 70–1.

51 E. Fukai, *Kaiko Shichijūnen (Retrospect for Seventy Years)* (Tokyo, 1941), 85–6.

52 The Japanese Ministry of Finance [probably], *Seika Kyūshū Nijyūgo Saku (Twenty-five Policies for absorbing Specie)* (mimeo) (no place and date), Otsu–13, 14, 27 and 28.

53 The Russian Treasury as well kept large gold and foreign exchange in its own account (I.M. Drummond, 'The Russian gold standard 1897–1914', *Journal of Economic History*, xxxvi–3 [1976], 682; O. Crisp, 'Russia 1860–1914' in R. Cameron (ed.), *Banking in the Early Stage of Industrialization* [New York, 1967], 231).

54 *TKZ*, 66–1667, 5 October 1912, 616–17.

55 E. Fukai, *Shintei Tsūka Chōsetsuron (On Regulation of Currency,* newly revised) (Tokyo, 1938), 280–1.
56 T.H. Milner, *Some Remarks on the Bank of England* (1849), 36; also see L. von Mises, 'The foreign exchange policy of the Austro-Hungarian Bank', *Economic Journal*, xix (1909), 203.
57 The Japanese Ministry of Finance [probably], *Seika Kyūshū Nijyūgo Saku (Twenty-five Policies for absorbing Specie)*, Otsu–11.
58 Canadian banks' 'secondary reserve' or 'outside reserve' also produced income. Most of this reserve was invested in call money in New York but could immediately return to Canada when the proportion of cash reserve to total liability at Canadian banks lowered (J. Viner, *Canada's Balance of International Indebtedness 1900–1913* (Cambridge [Mass.], 1924), 170–90; T.J.O. Dick and J.E. Floyd, *Canada and the Gold Standard: Balance-of-Payments Adjustment, 1871–1913* [Cambridge, 1992], ch. 8; R.A. Shearer, 'The foreign currency business of Canadian chartered banks', *Canadian Journal of Economics and Political Science*, xxxi–3 [1965], 331).
59 The role of Canadian banks' 'secondary reserve' or 'outside reserve' was similar to that of Japan's specie holdings abroad. Eckardt pointed out 'the sudden injection of so much new capital would have created disturbance in the Canadian financial system. So the funds were placed abroad at first and brought into use in the Dominion gradually and carefully' (H.M.P. Eckardt, 'The immediately available reserve', *Journal of the Canadian Bankers' Association*, xx [1913], 253).
60 F.W. Taussig, *International Trade* (New York, 1927, reprinted 1966), 239–40; R. Triffin, *The Evolution of the International Monetary System: Historical Reappraisal and Future Perspective* (New Jersey, 1964), 2–3.
61 *The Collected Writings of John Maynard Keynes*, 5 (A Treatise on Money) (1971), 320.
62 BBA, COF–05–2–8, Sale & Frazer Co. to Farrer, 26 March 1907.
63 FO 371/1667, Currie to Law, 25 March 1913; W.C. Greene to Foreign Office, 12 April 1913.
64 RAL, XI/130A/3, the London Rothschilds to the Paris Rothschilds, 13 May 1908.
65 FO 371/1387, D.C. dated 28 February 1912.
66 BLPESA, R(S.R.) 1016, R. Giffen Correspondence, ii, 101, Edgar Crammond to R. Giffen, 12 June 1907. [Crammond] was the author of an article entitled 'British investments abroad' (*Quarterly Review*, ccvii–no.412 [1907], 245–72) and suggested a statistical estimate of British foreign investment to examine Britain's balance of payments.

67 W.P. Kennedy, 'Foreign investment, trade, and growth in the United Kingdom, 1870–1913', *Explorations in Economic History*, 11–no.4 (1974), 415–44, especially 436–9; S. Pollard, 'Capital exports, 1870–1914: harmful or beneficial?', *Economic History Review*, second series, xxxviii 4 (1985), 489–514; M. Wilkins, *The History of Foreign Investment in the United States to 1914* (Cambridge [Mass.], 1989), 612–15.

68 S.B. Saul, *Studies in British Overseas Trade, 1870–1914* (Liverpool, 1960), 69.

69 'The multilateral settlement of world trade: i.e. payments involving a third party or even more, had been for centuries a major feature of world economic relations' (S.B. Saul, *Studies in British Overseas Trade, 1870–1914* [Liverpool, 1960], 43).

70 Also there was a time lag between the time of loan issues and the increase of imports.

71 S.B. Saul, *Studies in British Overseas Trade, 1870–1914* (Liverpool, 1960), 87.

72 *MHSKT*, 278–9 and 298–9.

73 Short-term capital movements were a residual item, the net balance is calculated from other items and includes errors and omissions (I. Yamazawa and Y. Yamamoto, *Chōki Keizai Tōkei 14, Bōeki to Kokusai Shūshi [Estimates of Long-term Economic Statistics of Japan]*, 14 [Foreign Trade and Balance of Payments] [Tokyo, 1979], 223–4).

74 *MHSKT*, 290–5.

75 Report on the Trade of Japan for the Year 1905, no.3675 (1906), 8–9.

76 Japanese Bureau of Statistics, *Nippon Teikoku 26 Tōkei Nenkan (Statistics of the Imperial Japan, No.26)* (Tokyo, 1907), 460–72.

77 J. Saville, 'Some retarding factors in the British economy before 1914', *Yorkshire Bulletin of Economic and Social Research*, 13–1 (1961), 59; W.P. Kennedy, 'Foreign investment, trade, and growth in the United Kingdom, 1870–1913', *Explorations in Economic History*, 11–no.4 (1974), 437 and *Industrial Structure, Capital Markets and the Origins of British Economic Decline* (Cambridge, 1987), 154.

78 The Japanese data did not reveal movements of gold and silver by country (I. Yamazawa and Y. Yamamoto, *Chōki Keizai Tōkei 14, Bōeki to Kokusai Shūshi [Estimates of Long-term Economic Statistics of Japan]*, 14). Japan's capital movements in this period are still uncertain.

79 Armstrongs and Vickers supplied warships and guns to the Imperial Japanese Navy. The agent of Armstrong in Japan was Takada & Co. and of Vickers the Mitsui Bussan Corporation.

80 In 1913 an Imperial Japanese naval general staff calculated the shipbuilding costs in Britain as the lowest (JNDL, M. Saitō Papers, 301, Shipbuilding Costs [per ton] in the World).
81 Kenneth Warren, *Armstrongs of Elswick: Growth in Engineering and Armaments to the Merger with Vickers* (1989), appendix c (263).
82 C. Trebilcock, *The Vickers Brothers: Armaments and Enterprise 1854–1914* (1977), 121–5 and appendix b (161).
83 *The Economist*, 15 July 1905, 1162.

CONCLUSION

1 'The success of Japanese financial undertakings is owing to intermediaries who initiated the world into the value of Japanese bonds' (RAL, IX/130A/1, the London Rothschilds to the Paris Rothschilds, 25 February 1907).
2 C. Marichal, *A Century of Debt Crises in Latin America* (Princeton [N.J.], 1989), 4 and 95. For the historical perspective of international lending waves and boom loans, see C.P. Kindleberger, 'Debt situation of the developing countries in historical perspective' in S.H. Goodman (ed.), *Financing and Risk in Developing Countries* (New York, 1977), 3–11; C. Suter, *Debt Cycles in the World-Economy: Foreign Loans, Financial Crises, and Debt Settlements, 1820–1990* (Boulder, 1992).
3 'Theory would say that the gold standard, relative to flexible exchange rates, should have partly cushioned the domestic money stock and national product against domestic shocks and partly exacerbated their vulnerability to foreign-trade shocks' (P.H. Lindert, 'Comment' in M.D. Bordo and A.J. Schwartz [eds.], *A Retrospective on the Classical Gold Standard, 1821–1931* [Chicago, 1984], 402).
4 A. Gerschenkron, *Economic Backwardness in Historical Perspective* (Cambridge [Mass.], 1962), 17.
5 *NGHS*, 2, 295–6.
6 For solving debt problems there is only a conventional way that borrowing countries would develop their internal resources and secure trade surpluses.
7 Sweden also experienced 'the luck' to repay its foreign debts when the First World War occurred (E.E. Fleetwood, *Sweden's Capital Imports and Exports* [Stockholm, 1947], 40).

APPENDIX A

1 Originally the City of Buenos Aires loan.
2 *IMM*.

3 Consolidation of public debt; no London issue amount; the unredeemable amount was £175 million (*IMM* [Quotations]).
4 Consolidation of public debt; no London issue amount; the unredeemable amount was £348 million (*IMM* [Quotations]).
5 £1,220,000 (*IMM*).
6 *IMM*; LCP.
7 *IMM*; LCP; the paid-up amount in London was £4 million (*Ec*, 11 March 1871, 35).
8 *IMM*.
9 *IMM*.
10 LJSBA, Q70.
11 *IMM*.
12 The issue price was at 82½ per cent (*SEY* [80]).
13 *IMM*.
14 *IMM*.
15 Conversion; *IMM*; no *SEOI*.
16 Consolidation; *IMM*.
17 *IMM*; LCP.
18 Conversion; no London issue amount.
19 *IMM*; the issue amount was £22,222,220 (*SEOI*).
20 Confederation; *IMM*.
21 £3,370,000 (*IMM*); the issue amount was £3 million (LA).
22 *IMM*.
23 *IMM*.
24 £100 million (*IMM*); the issue amount was £97.5 million (*RH*); the paid-up amount in London was £26,960,000 (*Ec*, 16 March 1872, 48).
25 No *SEOI*.
26 *IMM*.
27 *IMM*.
28 LJSBA, Q70.
29 *IMM*.
30 *IMM*.
31 Consolidation; *IMM*.
32 *IMM*; the issue amount was £2,622,781 (LA and LCP).
33 *IMM*; LCP; the issue amount was £20,907,000 (*Fn* [89]).
34 *IMM*.
35 Funded loan; no London issue amount; £41 million (in exchange) (*IMM*); the issue amount was £41 million at 92% (*RH*); £45 million and £16,875,000 at 91% (*Ec*).
36 *IMM*.
37 Confederation; *IMM*.
38 *IMM*.

39 £2,400,000 (*IMM*); the issue amount was £2,400,000 (*SEY* [80] and *Fn* [89]).
40 No London issue amount; £120,000,000 (*IMM*); the issue amount was £141,500,000 (*RH*); the paid-up amount in London £45,600,000 (*Ec*).
41 £2 million (*IMM*); the issue amount was £2 million (*SEY* [80], *Fn* [89] and LA).
42 Consolidation; *IMM*.
43 Consolidation; *IMM*.
44 £10,625,000 (*IMM* and CLP); the issue amount was £10,625,000 (*Ec*); £35,029,000 (*Fn* [89]).
45 Originally the City of Buenos Aires loan.
46 *IMM*.
47 *IMM*.
48 Conversion; *IMM*.
49 Conversion; no London issue amount; *IMM*; LCP.
50 *IMM*; the issue amount was £3 million (*Fn* [80]); £5,400,000 (LA).
51 *IMM*.
52 Consolidation; *IMM*; the issue amount was £8 million (*Fn* [89]).
53 Conversion; no London issue amount.
54 *IMM*; the issue amount was £27,777,780 (*SEY* [80]); £27,197,000 (*Fn* [89]).
55 Funded loan; no London issue amount; the issue amount was £61,682,500 at £102 16s. 2d. per $500 (about 99 7/10%) (RH).
56 Confederation; *IMM*.
57 *IMM*.
58 *IMM*.
59 £5,250,000 (*IMM*); the issue amount was £5 million (*Fn* [89] and LA).
60 £1 million (*IMM*); the issue amount was £1,143,000 (*SEY* [80]); £1,900,000 (*Fn* [80] and LA).
61 No *FBH*; the issue amount was £627,675 at 98 8s. 11d. (about 98 9/20%) (*SEY* [80]).
62 *IMM*; no *SEOI*.
63 Consolidation; £8 million (*IMM*); the issue amount was £8 million (*Fn* [89]).
64 No London issue amount.
65 £1 million (*IMM*); the issue amount was DM20,250,000 (£995,625) (*SEY* [80]).
66 *IMM*; no *SEOI*.
67 *IMM*.
68 *IMM*; the issue amount was £2 million (*SEY* [80], *Fn* [89]

and LA).
69 Funded loan; no London issue amount; the issue amount was £62,100,000 at £$103\frac{1}{2}$ per $500 (about $100\frac{9}{25}$ %) (*RH*).
70 *IMM*.
71 Conversion.
72 Unification; LCP.
73 Redemption; £3,500,000 (*IMM*); the issue amount was £8 million (*RH* and LCP); £40 million (*SEOI*).
74 Consolidation; £6,500,000 (*IMM*); LCP.
75 No London issue amount; the issue amount was £13,397,700 (*SEY* [80]).
76 *IMM*.
77 Funded loan; no London issue amount; the issue amount was £143,850,000 at £$102\frac{3}{4}$ per $500 (about $99\frac{16}{25}$%) (*RH*).
78 Redemption; *IMM*; LCP.
79 *IMM*; LCP.
80 *IMM*; the figure includes the issue amount in Germany (HA, Ms.19,131).
81 *IMM*; LCP.
82 *IMM*; the issue amount was £1 million including Paris (HA, Ms.19,167).
83 *IMM*.
84 Conversion; the issue amount was £1,200,000 (*SEY* [90]); £724,000 (*Fn* [89]).
85 Part of conversion; £1,156,000 (*IMM*); the issue amount was £881,000 (HA, Ms.19,132/1).
86 Conversion; £2,610,000 (*IMM*).
87 Consolidation; LJSBA, Q70.
88 *IMM*.
89 See 1881 and 1883.
90 Redemption; HA, Ms.19,168/3.
91 *IMM*.
92 £3,800,000 (*IMM*); the issue amount was £1,250,000 (*Fn* [98] and LA).
93 Conversion; *RH*; the issue amount was £68,400,000 (1881–1888) (*SEOI*); £16 million (LA).
94 *IMM*.
95 *IMM*; HA, Ms.19,168/3.
96 Conversion; the issue amount was £2,750,000 (*Fn* [98]).
97 *IMM*.
98 *IMM*; HA, Ms.19,119.
99 *IMM*; the issue amount included the Paris issue (HA, Ms.19,160).
100 Conversion (LCP).

101 *IMM*.
102 £4,500,000 (*IMM*).
103 Conversion; LCP.
104 HA, Ms.19,168/2.
105 Unification; the issue amount was £11,113,000 (*Fn* [89]).
106 *IMM*; the issue amount was £1,714,200 (*Fn* [98] and *FBH* [81]); £1,683,100 (LA).
107 *IMM*.
108 £3,014,000 (*IMM* net); the issue amount was £6,800,000 (LA); £4,238,600 (*SEOI*).
109 Conversion.
110 Conversion; the issue amount was £12,473,960 at 77⅜ (in cash) (LCP).
111 *IMM*.
112 *IMM*; the issue amount was £2,095,000 (LA).
113 Conversion; LCP; no *SEOI*.
114 £719,921 (*IMM* net).
115 *IMM*.
116 *IMM*.
117 *IMM*.
118 £9 million (*IMM* net).
119 Guaranteed by Britain, France, Germany, Russia, Italy and Austria-Hungary.
120 See 1887.
121 £3,200,000 (*IMM* net).
122 £5,700,000 (*IMM*).
123 Conversion; £315,000 (in cash) (*IMM*); the issue amount was £6,050,000 (LA).
124 Consolidation; the issue amount was £525,000; £1,475,000 (*SEOI* and LA).
125 Conversion; the issue amount was £35 million (*SEOI*).
126 Consolidation.
127 £263,625 (*IMM* net).
128 Conversion; £1,666,000 (*IMM* net).
129 Conversion; the issue amount was £843,500 and £160,100 (*SEOI*).
130 £3,668,035 (*IMM* net); the issue amount was £4,333,000 (*SEY* [12]); £4,290,000 (LA); £8,333,000 in total in 1886 and 1887 (*FBH* [91]).
131 See 1888 and 1889.
132 £1,188,500 (*IMM*).
133 £1,085,937 (*IMM*).
134 £4,239,000 (*IMM*); the issue amount was £5,400,000 (*SEY* [12]); £1,900,000 (*SEOI*, *Fn* [98] and LA).

135 £3,422,217 (*IMM*); the issue amount was £1,900,000 (*Fn* [98]); £3,973,700 (*FBH* [91]); £3,933,580 (LA).
136 £1,410,000 (*IMM* net).
137 £5,820,000 (*IMM*).
138 £2,225,100 (*IMM* net).
139 See 1889; no *IMM*.
140 Conversion; the issue amount was £815,000 (*Fn* [89]); £922,700 (LA).
141 Part of conversion; £2,904,500 (*IMM* net); the issue amount was £3,700,000 (LA); £10,500,000 in total (*SEY* [90]).
142 Conversion.
143 Conversion; the issue amount was £85,532,634 (*SEOI*).
144 Conversion.
145 Conversion.
146 Conversion.
147 Conversion; no *RH*.
148 The issue amount was £1,500,000 (*SEOI*).
149 £3,610,423 (*IMM*).
150 £1,133,154 (*IMM*).
151 Conversion; the issue amount was £5,290,000 (*SEY* [12] and *FBH* [91]); £5,263,560 (LA).
152 Conversion.
153 Conversion; the issue amount was £19,837,000 (*SEOI* and *RH*); £20 million (LA).
154 Conversion; the issue amount was £1,871,100 (LA); £1,847,580 (*SEOI*); £1,816,326 (*SEY* [90]).
155 £1,573,452 (*IMM* net).
156 Conversion.
157 Conversion.
158 Conversion.
159 *IMM*.
160 Conversion; the issue amount was £7,761,000 (*SEOI*); £8,358,199 (*SEY* [90]).
161 Conversion; *IMM*.
162 Conversion.
163 Conversion.
164 Part of conversion and redemption; £26,754,000 (*IMM* net).
165 Conversion; *IMM*.
166 £3,343,350 (*IMM* and *SEY* [12]).
167 *IMM*; the issue amount was $2,500,000 (£515,625) (LA).
168 £5,610,000 (*IMM* net).
169 Conversion; £13,244,000 (*IMM*).
170 Conversion; *IMM* did not include this amount in the creation

amount.

171 Conversion; *IMM* did not include this amount in the creation amount.

172 The loan was issued in Amsterdam.

173 Redemption; no *RH*.

174 Part of conversion; £1,077,412 (*IMM* net); the issue amount was £4,545,000 (*SEOI*).

175 Conversion; *IMM*.

176 Funding; the issue amount was £7,630,680 (*SEY* [01]); £2 million (LA); £14,880,000 in total (*SEOI*).

177 *IMM*.

178 Conversion; *IMM*.

179 Conversion and redemption.

180 The issue amount was £2 million (*SEOI*, *SEY* [01] and LA).

181 £1,710,000 (*IMM* net); the issue amount was £149,000 and the balance was withdrawn (*SEOI*); £1,800,000 (LA).

182 *IMM*.

183 £475,000 (*IMM* net).

184 Consolidation; the issue amount was £19,300,000 (LA).

185 Conversion.

186 Funding; the issue amount was £4 million (*SEOI*); £365,507 (LA).

187 Conversion.

188 *IMM*.

189 £760,290 (*IMM*); the figure includes the issue amount in Paris (HA, Ms.19,082).

190 £1,764,410 (*IMM* net); the issue amount was £2,594,720 (*FBH* [95]); £2,335,200 (LA).

191 Part of conversion; £2,166,120 (*IMM* net).

192 The issue price was 94$\frac{4}{6}$ per cent per £98 17s. 6d. (95¾ %) (*RH*).

193 £15,100,000 (*IMM*).

194 Conversion; £1,265,890 (*IMM*); the issue amount was £990,000 (LA).

195 Redemption; *IMM*.

196 £5,100,000 (*IMM*).

197 £1,870,000 (*IMM* net).

198 £2,895,000 (*IMM* net).

199 £1,060,000 (*IMM* net).

200 Part of conversion; the issue amount was £1,534,090 (*SEOI*); £1,494,700 (LA).

201 £1,633,594 (*IMM* net).

202 The issue amount was $62,317,500 (£12,852,984) at £227 per $1,000 (about 109$\frac{19}{20}$%) (*RH*); $31,157,700 (£6,426,275) was offered in London (*Fn* [98]).

203 £3,982,000 (*IMM*).
204 £9,875,000 and £5,940,000 (*IMM*); the figure includes the issue amount in Berlin.
205 The loan was in Paris.
206 The loan was issued in Paris.
207 The loan was issued in 1895.
208 The issue amount was £11,607,100 (*FBH* [00–1]); £11,514,500 (*SEOI*); £404,000 (LA).
209 Conversion; £3,889,905 (*IMM*).
210 £4,455,426 (*IMM*).
211 Unification; the issue amount was £1,500,000 (*SEOI*); £1,017,200 (LA).
212 Unification; £680,000 (*IMM* net); the issue amount was £14,211,680 (*SEOI*); £1 million (LA).
213 Conversion.
214 Conversion.
215 Conversion.
216 *RH*; funded; the issue amount was £8,613,392 (LA).
217 £14,400,000 (*IMM* net); the figure includes the issue amount in Berlin.
218 £5,029,925 (*IMM*).
219 £4,673,363 (*IMM*).
220 £2,231,000 (*IMM* net).
221 *IMM*; no S.E.I.O..
222 £9 million (*IMM* net).
223 Consolidation; the issue amount was £22,700,000 (*SEOI*); £3,787, 960 (LA).
224 Conversion.
225 Conversion.
226 No *RH*.
227 From 1910 the interest was 3½ per cent.
228 £1,960,000 (*IMM*); the issue amount was £2 million (*SEOI*); £947,000 (LA).
229 *RH*; the issue amount was £8,800,920 (LA). The purpose of this loan was the purchase of railway companies.
230 £3,796,820 (*IMM*).
231 See 1904 and 1906.
232 £734,800 (*IMM* net); the total issue amount was £2,250,000; £880,000 (LA).
233 *IMM*.
234 Conversion; £2,046,692 (*IMM*).
235 £1,273,323 (*IMM* net); the issue amount was £2 million (*SEOI*); £1,430,700 (LA).

236 £2,410,526 (*IMM* net); the issue amount was £2,976,000 and the issuer was J.S. Morgan & Co. (*SEOI*); £2,770,000 (LA).
237 See 1905.
238 £4,950,000 (*IMM* net).
239 Unification (*SEY* [12]).
240 See 1907.
241 £2,193,750 (*IMM* net).
242 The amount of the English scrip was $7,624,000 (£1,576,162) (LA).
243 The issue amount was £77,990 (LA).
244 £730,800 (*IMM* net).
245 £4,675,000 (*IMM* net).
246 £5,430,000 (*IMM* net).
247 Conversion.
248 £2,910,000 (*IMM*).
249 £1,239,250 (*IMM*).
250 £970,000 (*IMM* net).
251 £13,500,000 (*IMM* net).
252 £9 million (*IMM* net).
253 £5,850,000 (*IMM* net).
254 £500,000 was issued in Paris (*SEY* [12]).
255 Conversion.
256 £3,496,500 (*IMM*).
257 The issue amount was £270,000 (LA).
258 £11,659,890 (*IMM* net); the issue amount was £13,101,000 (LA).
259 £2,178,000 (*IMM* net); the issue amount was Fr50 million (£1,979,166) (LA).
260 Conversion; the issue amount was £2,911,169 (*SEY* [12]); £170,003 (LA).
261 £2,515,500 (*IMM* net); the issue amount was £2,580,000 (*SEOI* and LA).
262 Conversion; £11,442,500 (*IMM* net).
263 £2,940,000 (*IMM*).
264 The issue amount was Fr50 million (£1,979,166) (LA); total issue amount from 1899 to 1902 was Fr500 million (£19,791,665) (*SEOI*).
265 The issue amount was £517,760 (*SEY* [12]).
266 See 1909.
267 £1,096,125 (*IMM* net); the issue amount was £1,110,000 (LA).
268 £1,485,000 (*IMM* net).
269 Redemption.
270 £194,000 (*IMM* net); the issue amount was £400,000 (LA).
271 Conversion.

272 £2,940,000 (*IMM* net).
273 £2,900,800 (*IMM* net); the issue amount was £10 million (LA).
274 Conversion; £2,895,500 (*IMM* net).
275 *IMM*.
276 See 1910 and 1911.
277 Conversion or redemption.
278 £5,285,061 (*IMM* net); the London issue amount was £5,955,000 (LA).
279 £979,398 (*IMM* net).
280 £1,780,000 (*IMM* net).
281 Conversion.
282 £2,574,000 (*IMM* net).
283 £1,115,550 (*IMM* net); the issue amount was £3 million (*SEOI*); £1,100,000 (LA).
284 £1,572,120 (*IMM* net).
285 Conversion.
286 £4,925,000 (*IMM* net); the total issue amount of the two loans was £9,905,000 (*SEY* [16]); £5 million (LA).
287 The issue amount was £1,500,000 (LA).
288 Conversion.
289 Conversion; the London issue amount was £573,764 (LA).
290 £1,206,250 (*IMM* net).
291 £1,154,814 (*IMM* net); the issue amount was £1,172,000 (LA).
292 The issue amount was £1,099,000 (LA).
293 £4,750,000 (*IMM* net).
294 £2,425,000 (*IMM* net); the issue amount was £2,500,000 (LA).
295 £990,000 (*IMM* net); the issue amount was £1,425,200 (*SEOI*); £1 million (LA).
296 £341,300 (LA).
297 Conversion.
298 £1,074,144 (*IMM* net).
299 Reorganisation; £6,674,940 (*IMM* net); the issue amount was £7,416,680 (LA).
300 Conversion; the London issue amount was £1,980,000 (LA).

Select Bibliography

The bibliography is largely confined to sources referred to in the book. The place of publication is London unless otherwise stated.

MANUSCRIPT SOURCES

Britain

British Library
Additional Manuscripts
49,683–49,962 A.J. Balfour Papers
Guildhall Library
Antony Gibbs Archives
Ms.11,038B, private information book (firm).
Ms.11,040, private letters to partners.
C.J. Hambro & Son Archives.
Ms.19,033, annual balance accounts.
Ms.19,036, annual statements of balances of stocks and shares.
Ms.19,082, Danish government 3 per-cent loan of 1894.
Ms.19,119, Italian government loans (1880–1882).
Ms.19,168, Swedish government 4 per-cent loan of 1880.
Huth, Frederick & Co. Archives
Ms.10,700, Box 1–2.
Kleinwort & Sons Co. Archives
Ms.22,105, stocks account ledgers (1890–1918).
Ms.22,025, Cape, East Indies, China Japan and Australia information books (1875–1909).
London Stock Exchange Archives
Ms.14,600, general purpose committee minutes.
Ms.18,000, quotation applications.
Ms.18,001, index of quotation applications.
Loan and Company Prospectuses.
Morgan Grenfell Archives (J.S. Morgan & Co. Archives to 1910)
Ms.21,760, house correspondence.

Ms.21,795, private copy out-letter book (1867–1910).
Ms.21,793, loans and options (1880–1910).
National Provident Institution Archives.
Ms.20,274, investment ledgers.
Public Record Office
Chancery
C.16/676/5146, 1870. S. No.146, Chancery Proceedings W. Smith and A.H. Novelli – H.N. Lay, S. Osborn and T. Fairbairn.
Foreign Office
FO17, general correspondence (China) (before 1906).
FO46, general correspondence (Japan) (before 1906).
FO262, Embassy and Consular (Japan, correspondence) (1859–1930).
FO371, political class (after 1906).
FO391, E. Hammond papers.
FO800/68, E. Grey's private papers (Japan).
FO800/134, Lord Lansdowne papers (Japan).
FO800/163, F. Bertie's private papers (Japan).
Treasury
T.168, E.W. Hamilton papers.
DMS Watson Library, University College (University of London)
Bank of Tarapacá and London Archives (Bank of Tarapacá and Argentine Archives from 1900) (Anglo-South American Bank Archives from 1907)
C2, letter book from London to Santiago and Valparaiso.
London and Brazilian Bank Archives
G3, letters from London to Rio de Janeiro.
British Library of Political and Economic Science Archives (University of London)
R(S.R.) 1016, R. Giffen correspondence, i-ii (1861–1910).
School of Oriental and African Studies Archives (University of London)
C.S. Addis Papers
PP MS14, Box 2 and 3, 15-23, Addis Diary (1897-1905).
Box 38, 354, business papers (1904 and 1905).
Southampton University Library
Sir Ernest Cassel Papers
X17, miscellaneous letters to Cassel.
Banks and Other Archives
Baring Brothers & Co. Archives
HC17,296, Wercher-Bonverg to Baring Brothers, 28 December 1872.
PF295–301, Japanese railway loan papers (1901–6).
PF302–305, Japanese government loan papers (1902, and 1904–1905).

COF–05–2–8/9, Japanese government loan papers (1907–8).
Kleinwort, Benson Co. Archives
Benson & Co. Archives
balance sheet.
Bank of England Archives
G4, court of directors minutes.
G8, committee of Treasury minutes.
G23/69–71, secretary's letter book (white) (1891–1920).
G23/87–88, secretary's letter book (red) (1894–1911).
SJ/Jap/1, stock jacket.
Museum 903, E.E. Greene to M.W. Collet.
Barclays Bank Archives
London & South Western Bank Archives
board of directors minutes.
British Bank of Middle East Archives
Imperial Bank of Persia Archives
S24, board of directors minutes.
W2/1–2, investment ledger.
X6, semi-official letter book to Persia.
Lazard Brothers & Co. Archives
W.94/5, papers on the City of Nagoya loan.
Lloyds Bank Archives
Capital and Counties Bank Archives
A53b/1, chairman's private book of signed minutes of board meetings.
A53/3, annual report.
A53b/76, letters, papers and forms re application for Imperial Japanese government 5 per-cent bonds (1897).
Midland Bank Archives
City Bank Archives
E5–10, board of directors minutes.
ACC293/1, arrangement book.
London Joint Stock Bank Archives.
Q7–13, board of directors minutes.
Q70, special German correspondence and others.
Midland Bank Archives (London & Midland Bank from 1891) (London City & Midland Bank from 1898)
ACC/26, Holden's diary.
ACC/26, Murray's diary.
ACC/35/231, France and England and the future Russian loan (1909).
ACC/150/2, Mr. Holden's report on his visit to America, 10 September to 5 November 1904.

M153/44, interview between T.R. Hughes and C. Whitburn, 3 June 1896.

National Westminster Bank Archives

Parr's Bank Archives

D1080, connection of Alliance Bank and Parr's Bank on the new account signature books of Alliance Bank, Bartholomew Lane.

D1354, general manager's report (John Dun).

D6800–6806, papers on the Imperial Japanese government loans.

B110201, general meeting minutes.

B11416–22, board of directors minutes (1865–1917).

U. Yoneyama, A. Shand: a friend of Nippon (Tokyo, no date).

Union of London & Smiths Bank Archives (Union Bank of London Archives to 1902)

B11468–99, court of directors minutes (1873–1904).

B11513–14, investment ledger.

D3610, letter book of Sir F. Schuster and others (1902–1905).

B11508–9, profit and loss account.

Westminster Bank Archives

D2469, Imperial Japanese government 6 per-cent sterling loan of 1924 – minutes etc.

N.M. Rothschild & Sons Archives

VIII/13/191, cash book with the Union of London and Smiths Bank.

XI/89, letters from Russian government.

XI/101, private letters received from de Rothschild Frères.

XI/111, loan issue papers.

XI/130A, letters from Nathaniel Mayer to Rothschild cousin (French banks).

XI/148, letter copy book (general).

XI/176, telegram copy book.

Standard Chartered Bank Archives

Chartered Bank of India, Australia and China Archives

Extract from the board of directors minutes.

Extract letter from Yokohama.

Wagg, Schroder & Co. Archives

J.H. Schröder & Co. Archives

Japanese customs loan file.

United States

American Jewish Association Archives (Cincinnati)

Schiff Papers

Box 446, Takahashi (1915).

" 454, Takahashi (1916).

" 461, Takahashi (1917).
" 469, Takahashi (1918).
" 470, Takahashi (1920).

France

Archives du Ministère des Affaires Etrangères (Paris)
Correspondance politique, Japon, Nouvelle Série
N.S. 50–7, finances publiques – emprunts (1895–1913).
" 59, etablissements financiers – banques (1898 and 1903–1912).
" 60, etablissements financiers – banques (1912–1917).
Archives du Ministère des Finances (Paris)
(Archives Economiques et Financières)
Mouvement général des fonds
F30-376, Japon (1907–1945).
F30-377, Japon (1907–1945).
Archives Nationales (Paris)
M.M. Rothschild Frères Archives
132/AQ/69-72, emprunts japonais.
132/AQ/5400-5620, lettres reçues (maison de Londres).

Germany

Politische Archiv des Auswärtigen Amts (Bonn)
Abteilung IA
Japan 3, Finanzen, Bd. 4,5 and 6 (1903–1906).

Hongkong

Hongkong & Shanghai Banking Corporation Archives
Board of directors minutes.
G8.I, correspondence on Japanese loans.
K1.1, King letters.
LOHI/2, Loans issued.
LOHI/34, 46–49, 51, 54 and 57, Loan Issue Papers.

Japan

Japanese Ministry of Finance Archives (Tokyo)
M. Matsukata Papers
40, foreign loans.
S. Matsuo Papers
44-45, national debts and foreign loans.
T. Megata Papers
9, foreign loans.

K. Mizumachi Papers
5, foreign loans and specie.
K. Shōda Papers
27–28, foreign loans.
49, specie.
A. Sone Papers
1, national debts.
Gikai Sankōsho (reference book for Diet)
Z314–1/2, 14th session (1899).
Z317–1, 17th session (1902).
Japanese Ministry of Foreign Affairs Archives (Tokyo)
3–4–2, finance (1868–1925).
3–4–3, banks (1868–1925).
3–4–4, loans (1868–1925).
Japanese National Diet Library (Tokyo)
K. Inoue Papers
685–686, finance.
M. Saitō Papers
301, shipbuilding costs [per ton] in the world.
Y. Sakatani Papers
497, papers on financial matters (1900–1910).
498, papers related to war finance during 1904–1905.
K. Takahashi Papers
135, diary (from 22 February to 18 December 1904).
Japanese Public Record Office (Tokyo)
Meiji 36nen Kōbun Zappen (miscellaneous official documents for the year of 1903), Ministry of Finance, 1–14.
Waseda University Archives (Tokyo)
S. Ōkuma Papers, letters, reports and memoranda from foreigners.
Bank of Japan Archives (Tokyo)
Order and announcement of loan issue of 1899.
Draft of report to Prime Minister on loan issue of 1899.
Mitsui Archives (Tokyo)
Ginkō–13–6, report of an officer dispatched by the Mitsui Bank to Europe and America (T. Toyama) (1909).
Ikō–W–3–37, stenographic notes of discussion, 20 March 1912.
Ikō–W–4–689, stenographic notes of speech by J. Soyeda, 20 April 1929.
Ikō–W–4–710, stenographic notes of speeches by K. Takahashi, Y. Mori and C. Watanabe, 3 December 1931 and 14 January 1932.
Sakura Bank Archives (Tokyo)
Mitsui Bank Archives
2–1, board of directors minutes, 1–6.

4–2, stenographic notes of the managers' meeting.
5–7, announcements.
12–10, papers on the city and company loans (Kyoto Branch).
12–27, history of the Kyoto branch (1940).

Unpublished Theses

Bailey, J.D., 'Australian company borrowing, 1870–1893: a study in British overseas investment', D. Phil. thesis, Oxford University, 1958.

Diaper, S.J., 'The history of Kleinwort, Sons & Co. in merchant banking, 1855–1961', Ph.D. thesis, University of Nottingham, 1983.

Edelstein. M., 'The rate of return on UK home and foreign investment, 1870–1913', Ph.D. dissertation, University of Pennsylvania, 1970.

Gerson, J.J., 'Horatio Nelson Lay: his role in British relations with China, 1849–65', Ph.D. thesis, University of London, 1967.

Grieser, N., 'The British investor and his sources of information', M.Sc.(Econ.), University of London, 1940.

Lindert, P.H., 'Key currencies and the gold exchange standard, 1900–1913', Ph.D. thesis, Cornell University, 1967.

Long, J.W., 'The economics of Franco-Russian alliance, 1904–1906', unpublished Ph.D thesis, University of Wisconsin, 1968.

Suzuki, T., 'Foreign government loan issues on the London capital market 1870–1913, with special reference to Japan', unpublished Ph.D thesis, University of London, 1991.

PRINTED SOURCES

British Parliamentary Papers

Report and Evidence taken before the Committee on Loans to Foreign States (1875, xi).

Papers Explanatory of the Functions of the Crown Agents for the Colonies (1881, lxiv) [c.–3075].

Evidence taken before the Committee of Enquiry into the Organization of the Crown Agents' Office (1909, xvi) [Cd.4474].

Report and Evidence of the Committee on Finance and Industry [Cm.3897] (1930–31, xiii).

Annual Series Diplomatic and Consular Reports (Japan) for 1901, no.2789 (1902).

Annual Series Diplomatic and Consular Reports (Japan) for 1902, no.3009 (1903).

Annual Series Diplomatic and Consular Reports (Japan) for 1905, no.3377 (1906).

Report on the Trade of Japan for the Year 1905, no.3675 (1906).

English Language Periodicals

Anglo-Japanese Gazette, 1902–1909
Bankers' Magazine
Banking Almanac
Bondholder's Register
Burdett's Official Intelligence, 1882–1898
Commercial and Financial Chronicle
Economic Journal
The Economist
Financial Review of Reviews
Financial Times
Council of the Corporation of Foreign Bondholders, *Annual Report*
Investor's Monthly Manual
Investors' Review
Journal of the Institute of Bankers
Journal of the Royal Statistical Society
London Banks, and Kindred Companies and Firms (by T. Skinner)
London Post Office Directory
London Stock Exchange Daily Official List
The Statist
Stock Exchange Official Intelligence, 1899–1913
Stock Exchange Year-Book
The Times

French Language Periodicals

L'Economiste français (Paris)
Marché financier (by A. Raffalovich), 1887–1913 (Paris)

Japanese Language Periodicals

Chugai Shōgyō Shinpō (Domestic and Foreign Commercial News) (Tokyo)
Ginkō Tsūshin Roku (Japanese Bankers' Magazine) (Tokyo)
Tokyo Keizai Zasshi (Tokyo Economic Journal) (Tokyo)
Tōyō Keizai Shinpō (Oriental Economist) (Tokyo)

English Language Books

Anon., *A Statement of Some Circumstances connected with the Mode of Contracting the Colombian Loan* (1825).
Abbott, A.W., *A Short History of the Crown Agents and their Office* (1959).

Adler, C., *Jacob H. Schiff: His Life and Letters, 1-2* (New York, 1928).
Allen, G.C., *A Short Economic History of Modern Japan*, 1867–1937 3rd. ed. (1972).
Allfrey, A., *Edward VII and his Jewish Court* (1991).
Amphlett, G.T., *History of the Standard Bank of South Africa Ltd. 1862–1913* (Glasgow, 1914).
Arnold, A.Z., *Banks, Credit, and Money in Soviet Russia* (New York, 1937).
Autheman, A., *History of the Ottoman Bank* (Istanbul, 1988).
Ayer, J., [N.M. Rothschild & Sons Co.] *A Century of Finance, 1804 to 1904* (1905).

Balogh, T., *Studies in Financial Organization* (Cambridge, 1947).
Barker, T.C. and Robbins, M., *A History of London Transport: Passenger Travel and the Development of the Metropolis*, ii (1974).
Baster, A.S.J., *The Imperial Banks* (1929).
Beach, W.E., *British International Gold Movements and Banking Policy, 1881–1913* (Cambridge [Mass.], 1935).
Bloomfield, A.I., *Monetary Policy under the International Gold Standard: 1880–1914* (New York, 1959).
Borchard, E., *State Insolvency and Foreign Bondholders*, i (New Haven, 1951).
Bordo, M.D. and Schwartz, A.J. (eds.), *A Retrospective on the Classical Gold Standard, 1821–1931* (Chicago, 1984).
Broadberry, S.N. and Crafts, N.F.R. (eds.), *Britain in the International Economy 1870–1939* (Cambridge, 1992).
Burk, K., *Morgan Grenfell 1838–1988: The Bibliography of a Merchant Bank* (Oxford, 1989).
Bussière, E., *Paribas 1872–1992: Europe and the World* (Antwerp, 1992).

Cairncross, A.K., *Home and Foreign Investment 1870–1913: Studies in Capital Accumulation* (Cambridge, 1953).
Carosso, V.P., *Investment Banking in America: A History* (Cambridge [Mass.], 1970).
——, *More than a Century of Investment Banking: The Kidder, Peabody & Co. Story* (New York, 1979).
——, *The Morgans: Private International Bankers 1854–1913* (Cambridge [Mass.], 1987).
Cassel, G., *The Downfall of the Gold Standard* (Oxford, 1936).
Chapman, S., *The Rise of Merchant Banking* (1984).
Checkland, O., *Britain's Encounter with Meiji Japan, 1868–1912* (1989).

Chilean Government Central Statistic Bureau, *Statistical Abstract of the Republic of Chile* (Santiago, 1917).
Clapham, J., *The Bank of England: A History*, ii (Cambridge, 1944).
Cleveland, H. van B. and Huertas, T.F., *Citibank, 1812–1970* (Cambridge [Mass.], 1985).
Coase, R.H., *The Firm, the Market and the Law* (Chicago, 1988).
Collins, M., *Banks and Industrial Finance in Britain 1800–1939* (1990).
Corti, Count, (translated from the German by Brian and Beatrix Lunn) *The Rise of the House of Rothschild* (1928).
——, *The Reign of the House of Rothschild* (1928).
Cottrell, P.L., *British Overseas Investment in the Nineteenth Century* (1975).
Crick, W.F. and Wadsworth, J.E., *A Hundred Years of Joint Stock Banking* (1958).
Crisp, O., *Studies in the Russian Economy before 1914* (1976).

Dam, K.W., *The Rules of the Game* (Chicago, 1982).
Davis, L.E. and Huttenback, R.A., *Mammon and the Pursuit of Empire: The Political Economy of British Imperialism, 1860–1912* (1986).
Dawson, F.G., *The First Latin American Debt Crisis: The City of London and the 1822–1825 Loan Bubble* (1990).
Dayer, R.A., *Finance and Empire: Sir Charles Addis, 1861–1945* (1988).
De Cecco, M., *Money and Empire: The International Gold Standard, 1890–1914* (Oxford, 1974).
[de Zoete and Gorton], *de Zoete & Gorton: A History* (no issue place or date).
Dick, T.J.O. and Floyd, J.E., *Canada and the Gold Standard: Balance-of-Payments, Adjustment, 1871–1913* (Cambridge, 1992).
Dickins, F.V. and Lane-Poole, S., *The Life of Sir Harry Parkes*, i-ii (1894).
Dickson, P.G.M., *The Financial Revolution in England: A Study in the Development of Public Credit 1688–1756* (1967).
Drummond, I.M., *The Gold Standard and the International Monetary System 1900–1939* (1987).
Drummond-Wolff, H., *Rambling Recollections*, ii (1908).
Duguid, C., *The Stock Exchange*, fifth ed. (1926).

Edelstein, M., *Overseas Investment in the Age of High Imperialism: The United Kingdom 1850–1914* (1982).
Edwards, E.W., *British Diplomacy and Finance in China, 1895–1914* (Oxford, 1987).

Einzig, P., *The Fight for Financial Supremacy* (1931).

Feinstein, C.H., *National Income, Expenditure and Output of the United Kingdom 1855–1965* (Cambridge, 1972).
Feinstein, C.H. and Pollard, S. (eds.), *Studies in Capital Formation in the United Kingdom, 1750–1920* (Oxford, 1988).
Feis, H., *Europe the World's Banker, 1870–1914* (New Haven, 1930 reprinted 1964).
Fenn, C., *Compendium of the English and Foreign Funds, Debts and Revenues of all Nations*, 14th ed. (by R.L. Nash)(1889); 16th ed. (by S.F. van Oss) (1898).
Finnie, D., *Capital Underwriting* (1934).
Fleetwood, E.E., *Sweden's Capital Imports and Exports* (Stockholm, 1947).
Ford, A.G., *The Gold Standard 1880–1914: Britain and Argentina* (Oxford, 1962).
Fulford, R., *Glyn's 1753–1953: Six Generations in Lombard Street* (1953).

Galbraith, J.K., *The Affluent Society*, fourth ed. (Boston, 1984).
Gasslander, O., *History of Stockholms Enskilda Bank to 1914* (Stockholm, 1962).
Gerschenkron, A., *Economic Backwardness in Historical Perspective: A Book of Essays* (Cambridge [Mass.], 1962).
Gilbart, J.W., *The History, Principles and Practice of Banking*, 1 (1922).
Gillett Brothers Discount Co. Ltd., *The Bills on London* (1952).
Gooch, G.P. and Temperley, H. (eds.), *British Documents on the Origin of the War 1898–1914*, iv (1929).
Goodhart, C.A.E., *The Business of Banking 1891–1911* (1972).
Viscount Goschen, *Essays and Addresses on Economic Questions, 1865–1893* (1905).
Gregory, T.E., *The Westminster Bank through a Century*, 1-2 (1936).

Hall, A.R., *The London Capital Market and Australia, 1870–1914* (Canberra, 1963).
——(ed.), *The Export of Capital from Britain, 1870–1914* (1968).
Hawtrey, R.G., *The Gold Standard in Theory and Practice*, fourth ed. (1939).
Henriques, R., *Marcus Samuel: First Bearsted and Founder of the 'Shell' Transport and Trading Company, 1853–1927* (1960).
Henry, J.A., (edited by H.A. Siepmann) *The First Hundred Years of the Standard Bank* (1963).

Hertner, P. and Jones, G. (eds.), *Multinationals: Theory and History* (Aldershot, 1986).
Hobson, C.K., *The Export of Capital* (1914).
Holder, R.F., *Bank of New South Wales: A History*, 1-2 (Sydney, 1970).
Holmes, A.R. and Green, E., *Midland: 150 Years of Banking Business* (1986).
Homer, S., *A History of Interest Rates* (New Brunswick, 1963).

Imlah, A.H., *Economic Elements in the Pax Britannica* (New York, 1969).
Ingham, J.N., *Biographical Dictionary of American Business Leaders*, 1-4 (Connecticut, 1983).
Inoue, J., *Problems of the Japanese Exchange 1914–1926* (Glasgow, 1931).

Japanese Ministry of Finance, *Report on the War Finance* (Tokyo, 1906).
Jenks, L.H., *The Migration of British Capital to 1875* (1927 reprinted 1971).
Jeremy, D.J. (ed.), *Dictionary of Business Biography*, 1-5 (1984-1986).
Jones, G., *Banking and Empire in Iran* (Cambridge, 1986) .
——, *British Multinational Banking 1830–1990* (Oxford, 1993).
——(ed.), *Banks as Multinationals* (1990).
Jones, S., *Two Centuries of Overseas Trading: The Origins and Growth of the Inchcape Group* (1986).
Joslin, D., *A Century of Banking in Latin America* (Oxford, 1963).

Kemmerer, E.W., *Gold and the Gold Standard* (New York, 1944 reprinted 1979).
Kennan, G. E.H., *Harriman's Far Eastern Plan* (New York, 1917).
Kennedy, W.P., *Industrial Structure, Capital Markets and the Origins of British Economic Decline* (Cambridge, 1987).
Keynes, J.M., *The Collected Writings of John Maynard Keynes*, 1 (Indian Currency and Finance) (1971); 5 (A Treatise on Money) (1971).
Kindleberger, C.P., *A Financial History of Western Europe* (1984).
——, *International Capital Movements* (Cambridge, 1987).
King, F.H.H., *The Hongkong Bank in Late Imperial China, 1864–1902: On an Even Keel*, 1 (Cambridge, 1987).
——, *The Hongkong Bank in the Period of Imperialism and War, 1895–1918: Wayfoong, the Focus of Wealth*, 2 (Cambridge, 1988).
——(ed.), *Eastern Banking: Essays in the History of the Hongkong and Shanghai Banking Corporation* (1983).

Kirby, M.W., *The Decline of British Economic Power since 1870* (1981).
Kokovtsov, V.N., (edited by H.H. Fisher and translated by L. Matveev], *Out of My Past: The Memoirs of Count Kokovtsov* (Stanford University [California], 1935).
[Kuhn, Loeb & Co.], *Investment Banking through Four Generations* (New York, 1955).

Landes, D.S., *Bankers and Pashas: International Finance and Economic Imperialism in Egypt* (New York, 1958 reprinted 1979).
Lavington, F., *The English Capital Market*, third ed. (1934).
League of Nations (R. Nurkse and W.A. Brown, Jr.), *International Currency Experience* (Geneva, 1944, reprinted 1979).
Lindert, P.H., *Key Currencies and Gold, 1900–1913* (Princeton [N.J.], 1969).
Lowenfeld, H., *All About Investment*, second ed. (1909).

McCloskey D.N. (ed.), *Essays on a Mature Economy: Britain after 1840* (1971).
MacDermot, B.H.D., *Panmure Gordon & Co., 1876–1976: A Century of Stock Broker* (1976).
Mackenzie, C., *Realms of Silver* (1954).
McLean, D., *Britain and her Buffer States: The Collapse of the Persian Empire, 1890–1914* (1979).
Macpherson, W.J., *The Economic Development of Japan c.1868–1941* (1987).
Mandeville, A.M., *The House of Speyer: A Candid Criticism of Speyer Flotations* (1915).
Marichal, C., *A Century of Debt Crises in Latin America: From Independence to the Great Depression, 1920–1930* (Princeton [N.J.], 1989).
Masson, M., *American Multinationals and Japan: The Political Economy of Japanese Capital Controls 1899–1980* (Cambridge [Mass.], 1992).
Matsukata, M., *Report on the Adoption of the Gold Standard in Japan* (Tokyo, 1899).
——, *Report on the Post-bellum Financial Administration in Japan 1896–1900* (Tokyo, 1900).
Milner, T.H., *Some Remarks on the Bank of England* (1849).
Mitchell, B.R., *British Historical Statistics* (Cambridge, 1988).
Morgan, E.V. and Thomas, W.A., *The Stock Exchange: Its History and Functions* (1962).
Moulton, H.G., *Japan: An Economic and Financial Appraisal* (1932).
Munn, C.W., *Clydesdale Bank: The First One Hundred and Fifty Years* (1988).

Nash, R.L., *A Short Inquiry into the Profitable Nature of our Investments* (1880).
Nish, I.H., *The Anglo-Japanese Alliance*, second ed. (1985).
Nishimura, S., *The Decline of Inland Bills of Exchange in the London Money Market 1855–1913* (Cambridge, 1971).

O'Hagan, H.O., *Leaves from my Life*, 1-2 (1929).
Orbell, J., *Baring Brothers & Co., Ltd.: A History to 1939* (1985).

Pandit, Y.S., *India's Balance of Indebtedness* (1937 reprinted 1979).
Platt, D.C.M., *Finance, Trade, and Politics in British Foreign Policy 1815–1914* (Oxford, 1968)..
——, *Britain's Investment Overseas on the Eve of the First World War: The Use and Abuse of Numbers* (1986).
Pooley, A.M. (ed.), *The Secret Memoirs of Count Tadasu Hayashi* (1915).
Pressnell, L.S. and Orbell, J., *A Guide to the Historical Records of British Banking* (1985).

Reader, W.J., *A House in the City: A Study of the City and of the Stock Exchange based on the Records of Foster & Braithwaite, 1825–1975* (1979).
Riesser, J., *The German Great Banks and their Concentration in Connection with the Economic Development of Germany* (US Senate Document, 61st Congress, 2nd Session, no.593) (Washington, 1911).
Roberts, R., *Schroders: Merchants & Bankers* (1992).
Romanov, B.A., (translated by S.W. Jones) *Russia in Manchuria 1892–1906* (Michigan, 1952).
Rosenbaum, E. and Sherman, A.J., *M.M. Warburg & Co., 1798–1938: Merchant Bankers of Hamburg* (1979).

Saul, S.B., *Studies in British Overseas Trade, 1870–1914* (Liverpool, 1960).
Sayers, R.S., *Lloyds Bank in the History of English Banking* (Oxford, 1957).
——, *Bank of England 1891–1944*, 1-2 and appendices (Cambridge, 1976).
Schumpeter, E.B. (ed.), *The Industrialization of Japan and Manchukuo: Population, Raw Materials and Industry* (New York, 1940).
Stern, F., *Gold and Iron: Bismarck, Bleichröder, and the Building of the German Empire* (1977 reprinted 1987).
Suter, C., *Debt Cycles in the World-Economy: Foreign Loans, Financial Crises, and Debt Settlement, 1820–1990* (Boulder, 1992).

Taussig, F.W., *International Trade* (1927 reprinted 1966).
Tomlinson, B.R., *The Political Economy of the Raj, 1914–1947* (1979).
Trebilcock, C., *The Vickers Brothers: Armaments and Enterprise 1854–1914* (1977).
Triffin, R., *The Evolution of the International Monetary System: Historical Reappraisal and Future Perspective* (New Jersey, 1964).
Truptil, R.J., *British Banks and the London Money Market* (1936).

US National Monetary Commission, *Interviews on the Banking and Currency Systems of England, Scotland, France, Germany, Switzerland, and Italy* (US Senate Document, 61st Congress, 2nd Session, no.405) (Washington, 1910).

Van Helten, J.J. and Cassis, Y. (eds.), *Capitalism in a Mature Economy: Financial Institutions, Capital Exports and British Industry, 1870–1939* (Aldershot, 1990).
Viner, J., *Canada's Balance of International Indebtedness 1900–1913* (Cambridge [Mass.], 1924).
Von Laue, T.H., *Sergei Witte and the Industrialization of Russia* (Columbia, 1963).

Wainwright, D., *Government Broker: The Story of an Office and of Mullens & Co.* (East Molesey, 1990).
Warner, F., *Anglo-Japanese Financial Relations: A Golden Tide* (1991).
Warren, K., *Armstrongs of Elswick: Growth in Engineering and Armaments to the Merger with Vickers* (1989).
Whale, P.B., *Joint Stock Banking in Germany: A Study of the German Credit Banks before and after the War* (1930).
White, H.D., *French International Accounts, 1880-1913* (Cambridge [Mass.], 1933).
Wilkins, M., *The History of Foreign Investment in the United States to 1914* (Cambridge [Mass.], 1989).
Wright, S.F., *Hart and the Chinese Customs* (Belfast, 1950).
Wynne, W.H., *State Insolvency and Foreign Bondholders*, ii (New Haven, 1951).

Yuzawa, T. and Udagawa, M. (eds.), *Foreign Business in Japan before World War II (The International Conference on Business History 16 Proceedings of the Fuji Conference)* (Tokyo, 1990).

Ziegler, P., *The Sixth Great Power: Barings 1762–1929* (1988).

French Language Books

Baldy, E., *Les banques d'affaires en France depuis 1900* (Paris, 1922).
Becqu, E., *L'internationalisation des capitaux: étude économique financière et politique* (Montpellier, 1912).
Biliotti, A., *La Banque Impériale Ottomane* (Paris, 1909).
Bouvier, J., *Le Crédit Lyonnais de 1863 à 1882: les années de formation d'une banque de dépôts*, 1-2 (Paris, 1961).

Collas, H., *La Banque de Paris et des Pays-Bas, et les émissions d'emprunts publics et privés* (Dijon, 1908).
Compagnie des Agents de Change, *Annuaire des valeurs admises à la cote officielle, années 1915–1917*, 1-2 (Paris, 1917).

Dagneau, J., *Les agences régionales du Crédit Lyonnais: années 1870–1914* (originally presented as Thèse de Doctorat en histoire [3e Cycle] to the Université de Paris VIII [1975]) (New York, 1977).
Druon, M., *Les messieurs de Rothschild* (Paris, 1968).

Gérard, A., *Ma mission au Japon, 1907–1914, avec un épilogue de 1914 à 1919 et quatre portraits* (Paris, 1919).

Icard, I., *Le gold exchange standard* (Montpellier, 1912).

Kaufmann, E., (translated by A.S. Sacker) *La banque en France* (Paris, 1914).

Lévy-Leboyer, M. (ed.), *La position internationale de la France: aspects économiques et financiers xixe-xxe siècles* (Paris, 1977).
Lysis (pseud. E. Le Tailleur), *Contre l'oligarchie financière en France* (Paris, 1908).

Manchez, G.M., *Sociétés de dépôts [:] banques d'affaires* (1918).
Ministère des Affaires Etrangères, *Documents diplomatiques français (1871–1914)* (Paris); 2e série, tome 8 (1938); tome 10 (1948).
Ministère de l'Economie et des Finances, *Annuaire statistique de la France 1966* (Paris, 1967).

Sayous, A., *Les banques de dépôt[s]: les banques de crédit et les sociétés financières* (Paris, 1901).

Théry, A., *Les grands établissements de crédit français avant, pendant et après la guerre* (Paris, 1921).

German Language Books

Bosenick, A., *Neudeutsche gemischte Bankwirtschaft* (Munich and Berlin, 1912).
Lemke, H., *Finanztransaktionen und Aussenpolitik* (Berlin, 1985).
List, F., *Schriften, Reden, Briefe*, 6 (Das nationale System der politischen Ökonomie) (Berlin, 1930).
Müller-Jabusch, M., *Fünfzig Jahre Deutsch-Asiatische Bank, 1890–1939* (Berlin, 1940).
Schilling, T., *London als Anleihemarkt der englischen Kolonien* (Stuttgart, 1911).
Schulze-Gävernitz, G. v., *Volkswirtschafliche Studien aus Russland* (Leipzig, 1899).
Spiethoff, A.C., *Die wirtschaftlichen Wechsellagen*, ii (Tübingen, 1955).
Warburg, M.M., (Warburg, E.M.[ed.]) *Aus meinen Aufzeichnungen* (New York, 1952).

Japanese Language Books

Bank of Japan, *Meijiikō Honpō Shuyō Keizai Tōkei (Hundred-year Statistics of the Japanese Economy)* (Tokyo, 1966).
——, *Nippon Ginkō Hyakunenshi (One Hundredth Anniversary History of the Bank of Japan)* (Tokyo); 1 (1983); 2 (1983); *Shiryō* (1986).
Bank of Tokyo, *Yokohama Shōkin Ginkōzenshi (Complete History of the Yokohama Specie Bank)*, 2 (Tokyo, 1981).
——, *Shōkin Kawase Shikin no Shiteki Hatten (Historical Development of Foreign Exchange Funds at the Yokohama Specie Bank)* (1) (2), (Tokyo, no date).
Bureau of Statistics, *Nippon Teikoku 26 Tokei Nenkan (Statistics of the Imperial Japan, No.26)* (Tokyo, 1907).

Emi, K. and Shionoya Y., *Chōki Keizai Tōkei 7, Zaisei Shishitsu (Estimates of Long-term Economics of Japan)*, 7 (Financial Expenditure) (Tokyo, 1966).

Fujimura, K., *Takahashi Korekiyo to Kokusai Kinyū (Takahashi Korekiyo and International Finance)*, 1-2 (Tokyo, 1992).
Fukai, E., *Shintei Tsūka Chōsetsuron (On Regulation of Currency,* newly revised*)* (Tokyo, 1938).
——, *Jinbutsu to Shisō (Men and Thought)* (Tokyo, 1939).
——, *Kaiko Shichijūnen (Retrospect for Seventy Years)* (Tokyo, 1941).

Hokkaidō Colonial Bank, *Hokkaidō Takushoku Ginkōshi (History of the Hokkaidō Colonial Bank)* (Sapporo, 1971).
Hokkaido Collier and Coal Railway Co., *Nanajūnenshi (Seventieth Anniversary History)* (Tokyo, 1958).
Horie, Y., *Gaishi Yunyū no Kaiko to Tenbō (Recollection and Prospect of Capital Imports to Japan)* (Tokyo, 1950).

Industrial Bank of Japan, *Nihon Gaisai Shōshi (Short History of Japanese Foreign Loans)* (Tokyo, 1948).
——, *Honkoku ni okeru Gaishi Dōnyū Shōshi (Short History of Capital Imports in Japan)* (Tokyo, 1948).
——, *Nippon Kōgyō Ginkō Gojūnenshi (Fiftieth Anniversary History of the Industrial Bank of Japan)* (Tokyo, 1957).
[Inoue, K.], *Segai Inoue-kō Den (Biography of Inoue Kaoru)* (Tokyo, 1934), 2, 4, 5.
Ishii, K., *Kindai Nippon to Igirisu Shihon: Jardine, Matheson & Co. o chūshinni (Modern Japan and British Capital: Mainly on Jardine, Matheson & Co.)* (Tokyo, 1984).

Japanese Ministry of Communications, *Tetsudōkyoku Nenpō (Annual Report of the Railway Department for 1907)* (Tokyo, 1909 reprinted 1981).
Japanese Ministry of Finance, *Meiji Zaiseishi (History of Japanese Finance in the Meiji Era)* (Tokyo), 2 (1904), 8 (1904).
——, *Kin-yū-Jikō Sankōsho (Annual Reference Bulletin on Financial Matters for 1912, 1915 and 1920)* (Tokyo, 1912, 1915 and 1920).
——, *Gaisai Kankei Shiryō (Papers related to Foreign Loans), 1-2 (Tokyo, probably 1937).*
——, *Meiji Taishō Zaiseishi (History of Japanese Finance in the Meiji and Taishō Eras)* (Tokyo), 1 (1940), 11 (1936), 12 (1937), 13 (1939), 16 (1938), 17 (1940).
[Usami, M.], *Shōwa Zaiseishi (History of Japanese Finance in the Showa Era)*, iv (Tokyo, 1955).
Japanese Ministry of Finance, *Ōkurashō Hyakunenshi (One Hundredth Anniversary History of the Japanese Ministry of Finance)*, 1 (Tokyo, 1969).
——, *Seika Kyūshū Nijyūgo Saku (Twenty-five Policies for absorbing Specie)* (mimeo) (no place and date).
——, *Seika Kyūshū Saku toshiteno Gaikoku Kawase Seisaku (Foreign Exchange Policy for absorbing Specie)* (mimeo) (no place and date).
Japanese Ministry of Foreign Affairs, *Komura Gaikōshi (History of the Diplomat Komura Jutarō)* (Tokyo, 1966).
——, *Nichi-Ei Gaikōshi (Anglo-Japanese Diplomatic History)*, 1 (Tokyo, 1936).

——, *Nippon Gaikō Bunsho (Japanese Diplomatic Records)* (Tokyo), 3 (1938), 31–1 (1954), 37–2 (1958), 38–2 (1959), 39–1 (1959), 40–2 (1961).

——, *Nippon niokeru Gaikoku Shihon (Foreign Capital in Japan)* (Tokyo, 1948).

Japanese Mint, *Zōheikyoku Hyakunenshi (One Hundredth Anniversary History of the Japanese Mint)* (Tokyo, 1976).

Jitsugyō no Sekai, *Zaikai Sanjyūnenpu (Thirty-year Chronology of Japanese Business Circles*, 1 (Tokyo, 1938).

Kajima, M., *Nippon Gaikōshi (History of Japanese Diplomacy)*, 7 (Tokyo, 1970).

Kitsukawa, S., *Meiji Zaisei Keizaishi Kenkyū (Study on Financial and Economic Histories in the Meiji Era)* (Tokyo, 1969).

Kizokuin, *Kizokuin Giji Sokkiroku (Stenographic Journal of the Japanese Upper House)*, 22 (Tokyo, 1906 reprinted 1980).

Kobe, City of, *Kobe-Shishi (History of Kobe City)*, honpen kakusetsu ge (Kobe, 1924).

Kojima, H., *Nippon no Kinhon-isei Jidai, 1897–1917 (The Gold Standard Era in Japan)* (Tokyo, 1981).

Matsuoka, K., *Kinkawase Hon-isei no Kenkyū (Study on the Gold Exchange Standard)* (Tokyo, 1936).

Mitsui Bank, *Mitsui Ginkō Hachijūnenshi (Eightieth Anniversary History of the Mitsui Bank)* (Tokyo, 1958).

Nagoya, City of, *Taishō Shōwa Nagoyashishi (History of the City of Nagoya from 1917)*, 7 (Nagoya, 1955).

Nakamura, T., *Meiji-Taishōki no Keizai (Japanese Economy, 1867–1925)* (Tokyo, 1985).

Nakanishi, K., *Nihon Shiyū Tetsudōshi Kenkyū (Study on the History of Japanese Private Railways)* (Kyoto, 1979).

Nishikawa, S. and Yamamoto, Y. (eds.), *Sangyōka no Jidai (Age of Industrialisation in Japan)*, 2 (Tokyo, 1990).

Oriental Colonial Corp., *Tōtaku Jūnenshi (Tenth Anniversary History of the Oriental Colonial Corp.)* (Tokyo, 1918).

Osaka Merchant Shipping Co., *Osaka Shōsen Kabushiki Kaisha Gojyūnenshi (Fiftieth Anniversary History of the Osaka Merchant Shipping Co.)* (Osaka, 1934).

Saitō, H., *Kinhon-iseika no Zaigai Seika (Specie Holdings abroad under the Gold Standard)* (Tokyo, 1981).

Sekiyama, N., *Nihon Kahei Kin-yūshi Kenkyū (Study on the Monetary History in Japan)* (Tokyo, 1943).

[Shibusawa, E.], *Shibusawa Eiichi Denki Shiryō (Shibusawa Eiichi's Bibliographical Records)*, appendix 1 (Tokyo, 1966).

Shūgiin, *Shūgi-in Giji Ssokiroku (Stenographic Journal of the Japanese Lower House*, 20 (Tokyo, 1905 reprinted 1980).

Takahashi, K., (Uetsuka, T. ed.) *Takahashi Korekiyo Jiden (Autobiography of Takahashi Korekiyo)*, 2 (Tokyo, 1976).

Takahashi, M., *Meiji Zaiseishi Kenkyū (Study on the Financial History in the Meiji Era)* (Tokyo, 1964).

Takizawa, N., *Kōhon Nihon Kin-yūshiron (Manuscript of Japanese Financial History)* (Tokyo, 1912 reprinted 1968).

Tanaka, T., *Meiji Ishin no Seikyoku to Tetsudō Kensetsu (Political Situations of the Meiji Restoration and Railway Construction)* (Tokyo, 1963).

Tatewaki, K., *Zainichi Gaikoku Ginkōshi (History of Foreign Banks in Japan)* (Tokyo, 1987).

Tōyō Keizai, *Kinyū Rokujyūnenshi (Sixtieth Anniversary Monetary History)* (Tokyo, 1924).

——, *Nihon Bōeki Seiran (Foreign Trade: A Statistical Survey)* (Tokyo, 1935).

Tsuchiya, T., *Shand* (Tokyo, 1966).

——, *Oyatoi Gaijin (Honourable Foreign Advisers)*, 8 (Money and Finance) (Tokyo, 1969).

Tsuchiya, T. and Ōuchi, H. (eds.), *Meiji Zenki Zaisei Keizai Shiryō Shūsei (Collected Papers on the Financial and Economic Histories in the Early Period of the Meiji Era)*, 10 (Tokyo, 1935).

Tsushima, J., *Hōtō Zuisō (My Recollection)*, 11–12 (on K. Mori (Tokyo, 1963–1964).

Wakatsuki, R., *Kofūan Kaikoroku (My Recollection)* (Tokyo, 1950).

Yamazawa, I. and Yamamoto, Y., *Chōki Keizai Tōkei 14, Bōeki to Kokusai Shūshi (Estimate of Long-term Economic Statistics of Japan)*, 14 (Foreign Trade and Balance of Payments) (Tokyo, 1979).

Yokohama Specie Bank, (N. Skamoto [ed.]) *Yokohama Shōkin Ginkōshi, Shiryō, Furoku (History of the Yokohama Specie Bank with Appendices and Data)*, 1–11 (Yokohama, 1920 reprinted 1976).

English Language Articles

Allen, G.C., 'The recent currency and exchange policy of Japan', *Economic Journal*, xxxv (March, 1925).

Andrew, A.P., 'The end of the Mexican dollar', *Quarterly Journal of Economics*, xviii no.3 (1904).

Best, M.H. and Humphries, J., 'The City and industrial decline' in B. Elbaum & W. Lazonick (eds.), *The Decline of the British Economy* (Oxford, 1986).
Bordo, M.D., 'The classical gold standard: some lessons for today', *Federal Reserve Bank of St. Louis Review*, no.63 (1981).
Brown, A.J., 'Britain in the world economy 1870–1914', *Yorkshire Bulletin of Economic and Social Research*, 17–1 (1965).

Cain, P.J. and Hopkins, A.G. 'The political economy of British expansion overseas, 1750–1914', *Economic History Review*, second series, xxxiii, no.4 (1980).
——, 'Gentlemanly capitalism and British expansion overseas, I. the old colonial system, 1688–1850', *Economic History Review*, second series, xxxix, no.4 (1986).
——, 'Gentlemanly capitalism and British expansion overseas, II. new imperialism, 1850–1945', *Economic History Review*, second series, xl, no.1 (1987), 1–26.
Capie, F. and Weber, A., 'Truth and fiction: actual and published profits in British banking' in Institute of Commonwealth Studies (University of London) *Collected Seminar Papers*, no.36 (the City and the Empire) (1987).
[Crammond, A.], 'British investments abroad', *Quarterly Review*, ccvii, no.412 (July 1907).
Crisp, O., 'Russia 1860–1914' in R. Cameron (ed.), *Banking in the Early Stage of Industrialization* (New York, 1967).

Daunton, M.J., 'Inheritance and Succession in the City of London in the Nineteenth Century', *Business History*, xxx, no.3 (1988).
——, '"Gentlemanly capitalism" and British industry 1820–1914', *Past and Present*, no.122 (1989).
Despres, E., Kindleberger, C.P. and Salant, W.S, 'The dollar and world liquidity', *The Economist*, 5 February 1966.
Diaper, S.J., 'Merchant banking growth in the second half of the nineteenth century: the experience of Kleinwort, Son & Co.' in Institute of Commonwealth Studies (University of London), *Collected Seminar Papers*, no.35 (the City and the Empire) (1985).
Drummond, I.M., 'The Russian gold standard 1897–1914', *Journal of Economic History*, xxxvi, 3 (1976).
Dunning, J.H., 'Changes in the level and structure of international production: the last one hundred years' in M. Casson (ed.), *The Growth of International Business* (1983).
Dyer, H., 'Japanese industries and foreign investments', *Financial Review of Reviews*, no.4 (February, 1906).

——, 'The commercial morality of Japan', *Financial Review of Reviews*, no.7 (May, 1906).
——, 'Legal aspects of foreign investments in Japan', *Financial Review of Reviews*, no.10 (August, 1906).

Eckardt, H.M.P., 'The immediately available reserve', *Journal of the Canadian Bankers' Association*, xx (1913).
Edelstein, M., 'Rigidity and bias in the British capital market, 1870–1913' in D.N. McCloskey (ed.), *Essays on a Mature Economy* (1971).
——, 'Realized rates of return on UK home and overseas portfolio investment in the age of high imperialism', *Explorations in Economic History*, 13, no.3 (1976).

Feinstein, C.H., 'Britain's overseas investments in 1913', *Economic History Review*, second series, xliii, no.2 (1990).
Fishlow, A., 'Lessons from the past: capital markets during the 19th century and the interwar period', *International Organization*, 39–3 (1985).
Ford, A.G., 'Notes on the working of the gold standard before 1914', *Oxford Economic Papers*, new series, 12, no.1 (1960).
Foxwell, H.S., 'The financing of industry and trade', *Economic Journal*, 27 (December, 1917), 518.
Fuller, F.J. and Rowan, H.D., 'Foreign competition in its relation to banking', *JIB*, xxi (1900).

Gilbert, R.S., 'London financial intermediaries and Australian overseas borrowing, 1900–29', *Australian Economic History Review*, 11, no.1 (1971).
Gordon, M.S., 'Japan's balance of international payments, 1904–1931' in Schumpeter (ed.), *The Industrialization of Japan and Manchukuo: Population, Raw Materials and Industry* (New York, 1940), appendix.
Gregory, P.R., 'The Russian balance of payments, the gold standard, and monetary policy: a historical example of foreign capital movements', *Journal of Economic History*, 39, no.2 (1979).

Hertner, P., 'German banks abroad before 1914' in G. Jones (ed.), *Banks as Multinationals* (1990).

Jonung, L., 'Swedish experience under the classical gold standard, 1873–1914' in M.D. Bordo and A.J. Schwartz (eds.), *A Retrospective on the Classical Gold Standard 1821–1931* (Chicago, 1984).

Kennedy, W.P., 'Foreign investment, trade, and growth in the United Kingdom, 1870–1913', *Explorations in Economic History*, 11, no.4 (1974).

——, 'Institutional response to economic growth: capital markets in Britain to 1914' in L. Hannah (ed.), *Management Strategy and Business Development: An Historical and Comparative Study* (1976).

Kindleberger, C.P., 'Debt situation of the developing countries in historical perspective' in S.H. Goodman (ed.), *Financing and Risk in Developing Countries* (New York, 1978).

King, D.J.S., 'China's first public loan: the Hongkong Bank and the Chinese Imperial government "Foochow" loan of 1874', in F.H.H. King (ed.) *Eastern Banking* (1983).

King, J., 'Oratio [Horatio is the right name – author] Nelson Lay, C.B. – a pioneer of British influence in the Far East', *Journal of the American Asiatic Association*, xiv, no.2 (1914).

Labordère, M., 'The mechanism of foreign investment in France and its outcome, 1890–1914', *Economic Journal*, xxiv (December, 1914).

Landes, D., 'The old bank and the new: the financial revolution of the nineteenth century' in F. Crouzet, W.H. Chaloner and W.M. Stern (eds.), *Essays in European Economic History, 1789–1914* (1969).

Lehfeldt, R.A., 'The rate of interest on British and foreign investments', *JRSS*, lxxvi–lxxviii (1913–15).

McLean, D., 'The Foreign Office and the Chinese indemnity loan, 1895', *Historical Journal*, xvi, no.2 (1973).

Mason, M., 'With reservations: prewar Japan as host to Western Electric and ITT' in T. Yuzawa and M. Udagawa (eds.), *Foreign Business in Japan before World War II (The International Conference on Business History 16 Proceedings of the Fuji Conference)* Tokyo, 1990).

Michie, R., 'Different in name only? the London Stock Exchange and foreign bourses, c.1850–1914', *Business History*, xxx, no.1 (1988).

Mises, L. von, 'The foreign exchange policy of the Austro-Hungarian Bank', *Economic Journal*, xix (1909).

Monroe, A.E., 'The French indemnity of 1871 and its effects', *Review of Economic Statistics and Supplements*, preliminary volume 1 (1919).

Nicholas, S., 'British business interests in Japan before 1941: origins, evolutions, and operations' in T. Yuzawa and M. Udagawa (eds.), *Foreign Business in Japan before World War II (The International*

Conference on Business History 16 Proceedings of the Fuji Conference) Tokyo, 1990).
Nurkse, R., 'International investment to-day in the light of nineteenth-century experience', *Economic Journal*, lxiv (1954).

Paish, G., 'Great Britain's capital investments in other lands', *JRSS*, lxxii (1909).
——, 'Great Britain's capital investments in individual colonial and foreign countries', *JRSS*, lxxiv (1911).
——, 'The export capital and the cost of living', *The Statist*, 14 February 1914 (supplement).
Penson, L.M., 'The origin of the Crown Agency Office', *English Historical Review*, xl (1925).
Pohl, M., 'Deutsche Bank London Agency founded 100 years ago' in the Deutsche Bank (ed.), *Studies on Economic and Monetary Problems and on Banking History* (Mainz, 1988).
Pollard, S., 'Capital exports, 1870–1914: harmful or beneficial?', *Economic History Review*, second series, xxxviii, no.4 (1985).

Reubens, E.P., 'Foreign capital and domestic development in Japan' in S. Kuznets, W.E. Moore and J.J. Spengler (eds.), *Economic Growth: Brazil, India, Japan* (Durham [N.C.], 1955).
Rozenraad, C., 'The international money market', *JIB*, xxiii (1902).

Salant, W.S., 'The balance of payments of a financial center' in W. Fellner, F. Machlup and R. Triffin and others, *Maintaining and Restoring Balance in International Payments* (Princeton, 1966).
Saville, J., 'Some retarding factors in the British economy before 1914', *Yorkshire Bulletin of Economic and Social Research*, 13–1 (1961).
Scammell, W.M., 'The working of the gold standard', *Yorkshire Bulletin of Economic & Social Research*, 17–1 (1965).
Schiff, J., 'Japan after the war', *North American Review*, 183, no.dxcvii (August, 1906).
Schuster, F., 'Foreign trade and the money market', *JIB*, xxv (1904).
——, 'Our gold reserves', *JIB*, xxviii (1907).
Segal, H.H. and Simon, M., 'British foreign capital issues, 1865–1894', *Journal of Economic History*, xxi, no.4 (1961).
Shearer, R.A., 'The foreign currency business of Canadian chartered banks', *Canadian Journal of Economics & Political Science*, xxxi, 3 (1965).
Simon, M., 'The pattern of new British portfolio foreign investment, 1865–1914' in A.R. Hall (ed.), *The Export of Capital from Britain 1870–1914* (1968).

Smit, C.J., 'The pre-war gold standard', *Proceedings of Academy of Political Science*, xvi–1 (1934).

Spalding, W.F., 'The establishment and growth of foreign branch banks in London, and the effect, immediate and ultimate, upon the banking and commercial development of this country', *JIB*, xxxii (1911).

Svedberg, P., 'The portfolio-direct composition of private foreign investment in 1914 revisited', *Economic Journal*, 88 (December 1978).

Tamaki, N., 'The Yokohama Specie Bank: a multinational in the Japanese interest 1879–1931' in G. Jones (ed.), *Banks as Multinationals* (1990).

Thane, P., 'Financiers and the British state: the case of Sir Ernest Cassel', *Business History*, xxviii, no.1 (1986).

Trebilcock, C., 'British multinationals in Japan, 1900–1941: Vickers, Armstrong, Nobel, and the Defense Sector' in T. Yuzawa and M. Udagawa (eds.), *Foreign Business in Japan before World War II (The International Conference on Business History 16 Proceedings of the Fuji Conference)* (Tokyo, 1990).

Tsunoyama, S., 'Japanese consular reports', *Business History*, xxiii, no.3 (1981).

Udagawa, M. 'Business Management and Foreign-Affiliated Companies in Japan before World War II' in T. Yuzawa and M. Udagawa [eds.], *Foreign Business in Japan before World War II (The International Conference on Business History 16 Proceedings of the Fuji Conference)* (Tokyo, 1990).

Viner, J., 'International finance and balance of power diplomacy, 1880–1914', *Southwestern Political and Social Science Quarterly*, ix, no.4 (1929).

——, 'Clapham on the Bank of England', *Economica*, new series, xii (1945).

Whale, P.B., 'The working of the pre-war gold standard' in T.S. Ashton and R.S. Sayers (eds), *Papers in English Monetary History* (Oxford, 1953).

French Language Articles

Gans, H., 'L'intervention gouvernementale et l'accès du marché financier', *Revue politique et parlementaire*, lix (1909).

Leroy-Beaulieu, P., 'Les emprunts des Etats étrangers et le gouvernement français', *L'Economiste français* (October 1910).
Lévy, R.G., 'Les grands marchés financiers', *Revue économique internationale* (September 1905).
Thobie, J., 'Placements et investissements français dans l'empire ottoman, 1881–1914' in M. Lévy-Leboyer (ed.), *La position internationale de la France: aspects économiques et financiers xixe–xxe siècles* (Paris, 1977).

Japanese Language Articles

Fujimura, T., 'Nanabu ritsuki gaikoku kōsairon (Seven per-cent foreign loan issue in 1873', *Kinyū Keizai ([Japanese] Journal of Monetary Economics)*, no.142 (1973).
Itō, M., 'Nichi-Ro-sengo no Nihon kinhon-isei to chūō-ginkō seisaku (The Japanese gold standard and central bank policy after Russo-Japanese War)' in K. Fujise and A. Yoshioka [eds.], *Kokusai Kinhon-isei to Chūōginkō Seisaku (The International Gold Standard and Central Bank Policies)* (Nagoya, 1987).
Kamaike, T., 'Nichi-Ro sensō o meguru gaisai mondai (Problem of foreign loans related to the Russo-Japanese War)' in S. Shinobu (ed.), *Nichi-Ro Sensōshi no Kenkyū (Study of the history of the Russo-Japanese War)* (Tokyo, 1959).
Kamiyama, T., 'Nichi-Ro-sengo no seika seisaku to zaisei (Japanese government's specie policy and finances after the Russo-Japanese War)', *Shigaku zasshi ([Japanese] Historical Journal)*, 98, no.1 (Tokyo, 1989).
Kuwahara, T., 'Dainiji-taisen zen-no gaikoku-kigyō no tai-Nichi tōshi (Foreign multinationals' investment in Japan in the pre WW II days: survey of the proceeding works)', (Kyoto Sangyo University) *Keizai keiei ronshū [Economic & Business Administration Review]*, 26–2 (1991).
Noji, K., 'Nis-Shin Nichi-Ro-sengo keiei to taigai zaisei, 1896–1913 (The political and economic policies after the Sino- and the Russo-Japanese War, and the foreign public finance in Japan in the period 1896–1913)', *Tochiseido shigaku ([Japanese] Journal of Agrarian History)*, no.92 (Tokyo, 1981).
Sagami, T., 'Nanban ginkō toraiki (Introduction of western banks into Japan, 2–3', *[Japanese] Finance*, 10, no.4 and no.5 (Tokyo, 1974).
Senda, M., 'Meiji Roku-nen nanabu ritsuki gaisai no boshū katei (Seven per-cent foreign loan issue in 1873)', *Shakai Keizai Shigaku ([Japanese] Socio-Economic Journal)*, 49, no.5 (Tokyo, 1984).
——, 'Meiji Roku-nen nanabu ritsuki gaisai no boshū katei (Seven per-cent foreign loan issue in 1873)' (Faculty of Economics,

Nippon University, *Keizai shūshi (Journal of Economics)*, 54, no.1 (1984).

Shimizu, M., 'Zaidan teitōhō (Japanese foundation mortgage law)' in N. Ukai, M. Fukushima, T. Kawashima and K. Tsuji (eds.), *Nihon Kindaihō Hattatsushi [History of the Progress of Japanese Modern Law]*, 4 (Tokyo, 1958) .

Soyeda, J., 'Gaishi yunyū gairon (Outline of Capital Imports)', *Ginkō tsūshin roku ([Japanese] Bankers' Magazine)*, 41, no.248 (Tokyo, 15 June 1906).

Yokouchi, M., 'Nijusseiki-shotō ni okeru zaigai seika to London kin-yū shijyo (Specie holdings abroad and the London money market at the beginning of the twentieth century)', [Ni-igata University, Junior College of Commerce] *Ni-igata daigaku shōgaku ronshū (Journal of Commerce)*, no.19 (Ni-igata, 1987).

Index of Names

Index of Subjects and Places